John Stuart Mill on Economic Theory and Method

T0347370

This book, the third in a series of Samuel Hollander's essays, covers thirteen studies on the economic theory and method of John Stuart Mill. This volume provides an accessible sourcebook on Mill's relationship with David Ricardo, and the Classical School, as well as confirming his relevance for modern economics, and for the place of economics within the social sciences.
The collection includes:

- a standard view, since abandoned by Hollander, of Mill as inconsistently adhering to two incompatible systems: the Ricardian and the neo-classical
- a diagrammatic addendum (by Paul Samuelson) to the essay on Mill's exposition of the canonical growth model
- an essay on Mill's defence of a key Ricardian theorem which reveals links with Mountifort Longfield, who is often represented as a dissenter
- an investigation of the comparative positions of Mill and the Cambridge natural scientist William Whewell on the methodology of political economy
- two essays which contain responses to critical evaluations of Hollander's views on Mill's methodological stance

Samuel Hollander is internationally recognised as one of the most important and controversial historians of economic thought. He is University Professor Emeritus, University of Toronto; and *Chercheur Associé au Centre National de la Recherche Scientifique*, LATAPSES University of Nice. He is Fellow of the Royal Society of Canada and was recently appointed Officer of the Order of Canada. He is affiliated with Ben Gurion University of the Negev, Israel. His other publications with Routledge include: *Ricardo, the New View: Collected Essays I*, and *The Literature of Political Economy: Collected Essays II*. In November 1999, he was awarded an honorary doctorate of law by McMaster University, Ontario, Canada.

John Stuart Mill on Economic Theory and Method

Collected essays III

Samuel Hollander

Routledge
Taylor & Francis Group

LONDON AND NEW YORK

First published 2000
by Routledge
2 Park Square, Milton Park, Abingdon, Oxfordshire OX14 4RN

Simultaneously published in the USA and Canada
by Routledge
711 Third Avenue, New York, NY 10017

First issued in paperback 2014

Routledge is an imprint of the Taylor & Francis Group, an informa business

© 2000 Samuel Hollander

Typeset in Garamond by Taylor & Francis

British Library Cataloguing in Publication Data
A catalogue record for this book is available from the British Library

Library of Congress Cataloging in Publication Data
John Stuart Mill on economic theory and method/Samuel Hollander.
   Includes bibliographical references and index. I. Mill, John Stuart,
   1806–1873. 2. Economics. I. Title.
   HB103.M7 A5 2000
   330.15'3 12–dc21
   99–045097

ISBN 978-0-415-14236-6 (hbk)
ISBN 978-0-415-75690-7 (pbk)

In memory of my aunt,
Friedel Bornstein
c. 1875 (Crackow) – 1960 (London)

Contents

Illustrations

Figures

Preface

I have said all that I want to say by way of general introduction at the appropriate places in the first two volumes in this series, so there is no need for a further prologue. I shall proceed to the papers included in the present volume.

The two earliest essays still appear in anthologies and are frequently referred to in the journals so I have chosen to include them. Though I believe they remain valid, they do require amendment. As for the first, it is doubtful that I was right to put such emphasis on Mill's 'first proposition on capital' as a *deliberate* formulation of fixed proportions between labour and capital. Yet the terms 'cooperation' (p. 2) and 'assisted by' (p. 3) used to describe the relation between real capital and labour do point to a complementary relationship; and the supporting evidence to this effect given in the paper stands, as does the demonstration that the need for technological capital pertains only in productive sectors, so that excess labour can under some circumstances be absorbed into the service sector. I would also emphasise the caution that the complementary character of technological relations could at best only have contributed to an underrating of the significance of aggregate demand in the (Marshallian) short run, since 'when it is possible to vary all inputs, we have to rely on Say's Law alone to account for the classical position' (p. 7). Similarly, my comment that Mill's fourth proposition on capital entails an implicit assumption of homogeneous capital (Chapter 1, note 12) is otiose, since the proposition applies to the long run when 'capital' can change its form.

The second chapter relates Mill's recantation of the wages fund doctrine to preclusion of (short-run) variation in the intensity of capital usage; a rise (fall) in the wage leaves employment unchanged and simply raises (reduces) the aggregate wage bill. I admit that '[t]here is no explicit statement by Mill... to the effect that he was deliberately assuming fixed technical coefficients', but rely on the *doctrine of evidence* – shades of Physiocracy! – to make my case: 'it is evident that if he had been aware of the possibility of input substitution... he could not have avoided recognizing that... a wage-rate reduction would in fact lower costs and make profitable expanded production and employment, even in the short run' (pp. 26–7). But I had neglected to take proper account of the rationalisation that Mill did explicitly specify – that 'a fall of wages does not necessarily make [the employer] expect a larger sale of his commodity, nor, therefore, does it necessarily increase his demand for labour' (cited p. 25). Mill's case thus turns on the derived-demand principle presuming zero elasticity of demand (in the 'short-run') for the final product. This correction is first made in Chapter 7, pp. 151–4, and absorbed into *The Economics of John Stuart Mill* (1985). Yet as the evidence provided in Chapter 2 again suggests, it does seem to be the case that Mill precluded a variable substitution relationship between labour and capital in the Marshallian short run, and to that extent much of the general argument of the paper stands. I do think, though, that the final section of the paper is stated too forcefully; inter-industry substitution plays a larger part in the classical literature than I there assert.

Chapter 3, dated 1976, was prepared for a conference held three years earlier (see Acknowledgements). It discerns a severe internal conflict in Mill's theoretical writings between 'Ricardian' and 'neo-classical' elements, a position implying the 'dual' development of nineteenth-century doctrine typical of Cambridge and most orthodox historians, which I had also adopted in my *Economics of Adam Smith* (1973). But by the time of publication of the essay I had already moved away from that notion on grounds of the *essential compatibility* of Ricardian and 'neo-classical' doctrine. I am happy to reprint the contribution for easy comparison with the position taken in *The Economics of John Stuart Mill*. The 'new view', whereby imaginary problems of inconsistency fall away, is argued in Chapters 4, 7 and 10, and also in Chapter 13, which appears for the first time, and reinforces the representation of Mill as Ricardian from the perspective of price-theoretic allocation economics.

Chapter 5 – which because of its length was omitted from *The Economics of John Stuart Mill* – is rarely referred to in the literature on doctrinal history, possibly because of its location in a journal on the history and philosophy of science. It received, for me, unprecedented attention from a wide range of working natural scientists, measuring enthusiasm by requests for offprints. I am particularly proud of this contribution for that reason.

Mill's version of the 'prudential' wage path analysed in Chapter 6 has appended to it a diagrammatic representation of the argument by Paul Samuelson. The diagrams which place the analysis formally into the context provided by Samuelson's 'canonical classical growth model' (*Journal of Economic Literature*, 1978) were originally prepared by Professor Samuelson to accompany the textual formulation of 1984.

Chapter 8, 'Exogenous factors and classical economics', is frequently reproduced in anthologies. The interested reader might consult the volume *Interfaces in Economic and Social Analysis*, edited by Ulf Himmelstrand (Routledge 1992), for the background to the interdisciplinary project for which the paper was designed.

The two papers that follow contain brief, and therefore I hope convenient, statements of the essentials of Mill's economics viewed from different perspectives.

Chapter 11 is my invited response to an analysis of *The Economics of John Stuart Mill* by Professor Neil de Marchi. I was, and still am, happy with his serious treatment of my book and the opportunity it provided me to restate the so-called 'continuity thesis'. The penultimate paper on 'John Stuart Mill's method in principle and practice' – which I have written together with Professor Sandra Peart – can be viewed in part as a further response to reactions to *The Economics of John Stuart Mill*, in particular to criticisms of the view there taken of Mill's position on the role of 'verification'. It also considers some of the literature on this and related methodological issues published in the past decade or so.

Samuel Hollander
Sophia Antipolis, Valborne, France
November 1999

Acknowledgements

The essays in this collection first appeared in the following outlets: Chapter 1: *Canadian Journal of Economics and Political Science*, 30 May 1964, 175–84. Chapter 2: *Oxford Economic Papers*, 29, 1968, 320–41. Chapter 3: in J. M. Robson and M. Laine (eds) *James and J. S. Mill: Papers of the Centenary Conference*, Toronto: University of Toronto Press, 1976, 67–85. Chapter 4: *Revue d'Economie Politique*, 93 (6) 1983, 894–9. Chapter 5: *Studies in the History and Philosophy of Science*, 14 (2) 1983, 127–68. Chapter 6: *Kyklos*, 37 (2) 1984, 247–65. Chapter 7: *Eastern Economic Journal*, 10, January–March 1984, 87–98. Chapter 8: *Social Science Information*, 24 (3) 1985, 423–56. Chapter 9: in R. D. C. Black (ed.) *Ideas in Economics* (Proceedings of the British Association for the Advancement of Science, Strathclyde, 1985), Basingstoke: Macmillan, 1986, 129–59. Chapter 10: in John Eatwell, Murray Milgate and Peter Newman (eds) *The New Palgrave: A Dictionary of Economics*, New York: Macmillan, 1987, vol. III, 471–6. Chapter 11: in W. Thweatt (ed.) *Classical Political Economy: A Survey of Recent Literature*, Boston: Kluwer Academic Publishers, 1988, 163–77. Chapter 12: *Journal of the History of Economic Thought*, 21(4) 1999, 369–98. Chapter 13: hitherto unpublished.

I gratefully acknowledge permission to reproduce the essays by The Canadian Economics Association (Chapter 1); Oxford University Press (Chapter 2); The University of Toronto Press (Chapter 3); the *Revue d'Economie Politique* (Chapter 4); Pergamon Press (Chapter 5); Helbing and Lichtenhahn Verlag AG and the American Economic Association (Chapter 6); the Eastern Economic Association (Chapter 7); Sage Books (Chapter 8); Macmillan (Chapters 9 and 10); Kluwer Academic Publishers (Chapter 11); and the History of Economics Society (Chapter 12).

I much appreciate the funding provided by the Social Sciences and Humanities Research Council of Canada relating to the Preface and last two chapters of this collection, and the excellent facilities at Sophia Antipolis, France, made available to me in carrrying the work through its final stages, by LATAPSES (Université de Nice/CNRS). In this regard I am particularly indebted to Professor Richard Arena.

Chapter 1

Technology and aggregate demand in J. S. Mill's economic system[1]

The literature on the relationship between Keynesian and classical economics lays almost exclusive emphasis on monetary phenomena; relatively little attention is paid to technological relationships,[2] although an understanding of the precise nature of the production function assumed in each system is clearly of relevance. In particular, the assumption of variable proportions between inputs is crucial to Keynes' approach, and it is usually taken to be an assumption of classical writers too. At times, it is recognised that the classics denied the possibility of obtaining additional output by increasing the quantity of labour used with other (given) inputs, but rarely is this seen as important.[3] The customary interpretation possibly derives, in part, from the fact that the classics made use of the wages fund whereby full employment of labour is assured; attention is diverted, by this theory, from technological capital to wage-goods capital, and it becomes easy to jump to the conclusion that output in the classical system can be regarded as a simple function of the quantity of labour employed.

In this paper I shall argue first that in fact considerable attention was given to the assumption of fixed coefficients of production in classical economic literature. Second, it will be necessary to show how this assumption could reasonably be maintained by writers who, at the same time, advocated the wages fund theory. In concluding the paper, I shall suggest a possible implication of the classical authors' approach to technology for their macroeconomic policy, in particular for their tendency to minimise the significance of aggregate demand as a determinant of aggregate output.

Although my main interest is to examine a problem in the classical system of economics, no attempt will be made to cover the literature as a whole. The discussion will be confined to the work of J. S. Mill,[4] partly because Mill can be regarded as a representative author,[5] and partly in order to keep the discussion within manageable limits. Much of the argument will be concerned with Mill's celebrated propositions on capital.

My discussion of the production function in J. S. Mill's system takes as its starting point the troublesome proposition, 'industry is limited by capital' (*Principles*, Book I: 63). Edwin Cannan regarded the proposition as no more than a 'useful catchword with which to attack the protectionist fallacy of giving employment or "creating an industry"' (Cannan 1924: 119). Mill had argued that:

> industry is limited by capital. . . . The following are common expressions implying its truth. The act of directing industry to a particular employment is described by the phrase 'applying capital' to the employment. . . . Again, we often speak of the 'productive powers of capital'. This expression is not literally correct. The only productive powers are those of labour and natural agents; or if any portion of capital can by a stretch of language be said to have a productive power of its own, it is only tools and machinery, which, like wind and water, may be said to co-operate with labour. The food of labourers and the materials of production have no productive power; but labour cannot exert its productive power unless provided with them. There can be no more industry than is supplied with materials to work up and food to eat . . . it is often forgotten that the people of a country are maintained and have their wants supplied, not by the produce of present labour, but of past. They consume what has been produced, not what is about to be produced. Now, of what has been produced, a part only is allotted to the support of productive labour, and there will not and cannot be more of that labour than the portion so allotted (which is the capital of the country) can feed and provide with the materials and instruments of production.
>
> (Mill, *Principles*, I: 63–4)

Cannan reacted strongly to this statement:

> It is perfectly obvious that industry or labour can never be brought to a stand by the inaccessibility of materials or the instruments of production as long as food, drink, and, in some situations, clothing and fuel are obtainable. The inaccessibility of materials and the absence of instruments of production will make production a more laborious task, but it will not stop labour. So Mill's argument really depends entirely on the necessity of food for labourers, though he has perfunctorily introduced the materials and instruments of production.
>
> (Cannan 1924: 118)

Cannan is obviously correct in pointing out that as long as the means of feeding and clothing labourers are available men can be set to work producing *something*. However, the important question is whether, given the pattern of expenditure by consumers and others, it is possible to produce each of the various goods desired by alternative methods, and in particular, whether it is possible to substitute 'a more laborious' method for that hitherto in operation. By the time Cannan wrote, fixed coefficients had long been assumed in the literature as a device to simplify analysis of the General Equilibrium problem; but fixed coefficients can also be considered a frequent fact of industrial life. It is suggested, then, that Mill by his first proposition meant to introduce into his analysis the assumption of fixed technical coefficients of production.

In point of fact the first proposition is taken, almost verbatim, from an earlier essay, and the interpretation suggested above can again be applied:

> Capital, strictly speaking, has no productive power. The only productive power is that of labour; assisted, no doubt, by tools and acting upon materials. The portion of capital which consists of tools and machinery, may be said, perhaps, without any great impropriety, to have a productive power, because they contribute, along with labour, to the accomplishment of production....
>
> The proper view of capital is that anything whatever, which a person possesses, constitutes his capital, provided he is able, and intends, to employ it, not in consumption for the purpose of enjoyment, but in possessing himself of the means of production, in the intention of employing those means productively. Now the means of production are labour, implements, and materials. The only productive power which anywhere exists, is the productive power of labour, implements, and materials.
>
> We need not, on this account, altogether proscribe the expression 'productive power of capital'; but we should carefully note, that it can only mean the quantity of real productive power which the capitalist, by means of his capital, can command.
>
> (Mill 1948 [1844]: 90–1)

I have interpreted Mill's comments on equipment and materials as referring not merely to the notion that production requires the presence of inputs in addition to labour, but more specifically to the assumption that factors must be used in fixed proportions. This interpretation can be supported by the following observations. In the first place, we can infer that the assumption of fixed coefficients was quite commonly posited from the fact that Mill, in common with other members of the classical school, framed the law of diminishing returns only in terms of the application of composite units of capital and labour to land. It might be argued that this procedure is to be expected, since land was considered the fixed factor *par excellence*. On the other hand, Mill stated explicitly that capital too, even in the long run, was not in perfectly elastic supply; thus the fact that the law was never applied to the case where varying amounts of labour are used in conjunction with a fixed amount of capital, lends support to the likelihood that fixed technical coefficients were generally assumed to hold.

Second, it will be recalled that Ricardo, in his chapter 'On machinery', had suggested the possibility of substitution between capital equipment and labour with respect to the production of a given commodity as a reaction to a relative rise in the price of labour (Ricardo 1951: I, ch. XXXI).[6] The bulk of his discussion in the chapter, however, is taken up with the case of a technical change representing the commercial implementation of some technological invention. The new technique involves, by assumption, a higher ratio of equipment to labour for the production of a given level of output, but its introduction does not depend on relative input-prices; under any price structure, the new method would be preferable. The 'Ricardo effect', which assumes variable factor proportions then, is given but scant attention in this chapter and is not incorporated into the general body of Ricardo's work. When Mill takes up the problems of 'machinery'[7] he does not carry Ricardo's analysis any further and pays no attention to the 'Ricardo effect'. For example, in his account of the expenditure-pattern of entrepreneurs at the close of a production-period, relative input-prices are ignored:

> With the proceeds of his finished goods, a manufacturer will partly pay his work-people, partly replenish his stock of the materials of his manufacture, and partly provide new buildings and machinery, or repair the old; how much will be devoted to one purpose, and how much to another, depends on the nature of the manufacture, and the requirements of the particular moment.
>
> (Mill, *Principles*, I: 99)

Finally, nowhere does Mill refer explicitly to the relevance of relative input-prices in the choice between alternative processes. For example, a tax imposed upon a process of production may encourage the utilisation of 'the untaxed process, though the inferior of the two', but the 'inferiority' of the untaxed process is not regarded explicitly as a function of current input-prices, implying that under any price configuration the alternative method would be preferable:

> Suppose that a commodity is capable of being made by two different processes; as a manufactured commodity may be produced either by hand or by steam-power; sugar may be made either from the sugar-cane or from beet-root, cattle fattened either on hay and green crops, or on oil-cake and the refuse of breweries. It is the interest of the community that, of the two methods, producers should adopt that which produces the best article at the lowest price. . . . Suppose, however, that a tax is laid on one of the processes, and no tax at all, or one of smaller amount, on the other. . . . [If] the tax falls, as it is of course intended to do, upon the one which they [the producers] would have adopted, it creates an artificial motive for preferring the untaxed process, though the inferior of the two.
>
> (Mill, *Principles*, V: 847)

Although I have interpreted Mill's proposition that 'industry is limited by capital' as a deliberate reference to input-complementarity in production, there is a sense in which Cannan's interpretation is valid. Consider in particular the 'corollary' to the proposition:

> While on the one hand, industry is limited by capital, so on the other, every increase in capital gives, or is capable of giving, additional employment to industry; and this without assignable limit. I do not mean to deny that the capital, or part of it, may be so employed as not to support labourers, being fixed in machinery, buildings, improvements of land, and the like.... What I do intend to assert is, that the portion which is destined to their maintenance, may... be indefinitely increased without creating an impossibility of finding them employment; in other words that if there are human beings capable of work, and food to feed them, they may always be employed in producing something.
>
> (Mill, *Principles*, I: 66)

But what is the evidence presented by Mill to support this corollary? He draws an analogy with a 'benevolent government': a benevolent government with food at its disposal

> could be in no danger of wanting a field for the employment of this productive labour, since as long as there was a single want unsaturated... the labour of the community could be turned to the production of something capable of satisfying that want.
>
> (*Principles*, I: 67)[8]

Another analogy is with the entrepreneur who cuts his unproductive expenditure and puts aside 'from conscientous motives, the surplus of his profits', and the entrepreneur whose 'abstinence [is] not spontaneous, but imposed by law or opinion'. In all these cases production is organised by the government or by entrepreneurs activated by 'conscientous motives' or by some external pressure, rather than by profit-seeking entrepreneurs. It is doubtless true that in these circumstances industry would not be constrained by a possible deficiency of aggregate demand; as long as the means of maintaining labour are available, workers 'may always be employed in producing something', and industry is indeed only brought to a halt by a want of food and clothing. But Mill is not concerned at this point with a world of profit-maximising entrepreneurs facing a particular pattern of expenditure by consumers and others. In such a world the precise nature of technology (as well as the level of pecuniary demand) becomes relevant to the employment of labour.

In the classical tradition, generally, flexible wage rates ensure full employment of labour. Wages are paid from the wages fund. If there is an excess supply in the labour market, wages will be driven down by competition until equilibrium is reached. But we have argued above that Mill postulated fixed coefficients of production; if the production function and demand conditions make it profitable to employ 1,000 men and if the labour market bids down the wage rate, then there is no obvious reason why the entrepreneur should employ more men at the lower wage rate; rather he might be expected to pay the original 1,000 employees the lower rate. In brief, it is quite probable that there will be a conflict between the volume of employment offered by entrepreneurs and the full employment volume implied by the wages fund. What, then, motivates employers to add more men to the labour force in a situation of excess labour supply?

The simplest answer, but one which attributes the crudest version of the wages fund theory to Mill, would be that employers are indifferent to the number of men on the wage roll; a certain fund exists for the payment of labour and the employer is indifferent as to the number of men who will share it. The determination of the number of man-hours which will actually be made use of in production is another matter, and will depend upon technical conditions, in particular upon the availability of the complementary inputs. This argument depends on an extreme version of the wages fund theory in which wages are not only a fixed cost in aggregate, but also a fixed cost for each individual employer. However, it is not necessary to go to such lengths to reconcile the assumption of fixed technical coefficients and the wages fund theory. A more convincing argument can be based on the distinction between productive and unproductive labour.

The wages fund theory attempted to explain how the wage rate was determined for *both productive and unproductive labour*. By the supply of labour in the theory, Mill referred to those 'who work for hire', and by the demand, to that part of circulating capital 'which is expended in the direct purchase of labour' together with 'all funds which, without forming a part of capital, are paid in exchange for labour, such as the wages of soldiers, domestic servants, and all other unproductive labourers' (*Principles*, II: 343–4).[9] It is true that Mill goes on to point out that 'as the wages of productive labour form nearly the whole of that fund, it is usual to overlook the smaller and less important part, and to say that wages depend on population and capital'. For the purpose of the particular chapter in which this passage occurs, the precise nature of the elements entering into the demand and supply sides of the labour market was not a vital question, but for our understanding of Mill's general approach to the determination of wages, it is essential to bear in mind the fact that he did not limit the wages fund theory to productive labour alone.

The assumption of fixed coefficients, on the other hand, was applied to productive labour only, for the first proposition on capital, which I have argued relates to input-complementarity, refers solely to productive labour. Thus output produced in the productive sector would only be forthcoming if the constraints imposed by the nature of the technology used in each industry are satisfied. Unproductive labour is not made dependent upon perfectly complementary equipment and materials.

It follows that technical restraints would, at any time, limit the level of employment in the productive sector, and the wages fund would determine the wage rate and ensure full employment of the entire working population. There need be no conflict between the assumption of fixed coefficients and the wages fund theory.

The view has developed, especially since the publication of Keynes' *General Theory*, that the tendency in the classical literature to minimise the significance of aggregate demand as a determinant of aggregate output is a direct result of Say's Law. According to that principle, it is claimed, there is no hoarding in the economy; either by dint of the notion that 'savings are consumed', or as a result of a flexible interest rate, savings pass into investment so that there can be no deficiency of aggregate demand, and hence only other influences can restrain aggregate output.[10]

However, it is possible that the lack of significance accorded to aggregate demand by Mill and others can also be explained by the inflexible nature of technology in the classical system: output in the productive sector could not respond to changes in aggregate demand simply as a result of varying the amount of productive labour applied to a fixed complex of other inputs. The close relation between demand, and employment, which plays such an important role in Keynes' system, disappears under these circumstances.[11] But the nature of technology can only help explain the tendency to underrate the significance of aggregate demand in the short run; in the long run, when it is possible to vary all inputs, we have to rely on Say's Law alone to account for the classical position.

Mill does allow, however, that in certain circumstances a change in aggregate demand may lead to a change in the volume of employment and output in the productive sector. For in fact the stock of equipment in use is not necessarily a *datum*. One activity — domestic manufacturing — has the characteristic that equipment, and complementary labour, are brought into activity and withdrawn as the result of changes in the relative attractiveness of leisure compared with income. To this extent, if a fall in aggregate demand should increase the relative attractiveness of leisure, then some equipment and its labour complement may be withdrawn. Conversely, a rise in aggregate demand may lead to an increase in domestic manufacturing, if it should reduce the attractiveness of leisure. Mill's position can be inferred from his treatment of the fourth proposition on capital, that 'demand for commodities is not demand for labour' (*Principles*, I: 79).

This hypnotic phrase has been interpreted convincingly by a number of commentators as a statement to the effect that a switch by consumers from one product to another (within a given aggregate demand) would not affect the total demand for labour: 'The configuration of demand was irrelevant to the distribution of the product between profit and wages' (Dobb 1940: 45).[12] Mill then turns to what apparently is an exception to this rule:

> The general principle, now stated, is that demand for commodities determines merely the direction of labour... but not ... the aggregate of wealth. But to this there are two exceptions. First, when labour is supported, but not fully occupied, a new demand for something which it can produce may stimulate the labour thus supported to increased exertions, of which the result may be an increase of wealth.... Work which can be done in the spare hours of persons subsisted from some other source, can (as before remarked) be undertaken without withdrawing capital from other occupations, beyond the amount (often very small) required to cover the expense of tools and materials, and even these will often be provided by savings made expressly for the purpose.
>
> (Mill, *Principles*, I: 87)

By the parenthetical note 'as before remarked' Mill is recalling a qualification, made earlier in the chapter, to the *first* proposition. In the discussion of the proposition 'industry is limited by capital', Mill concluded that it was impossible for governments to 'create industry' without 'creating capital' (*Principles*, I: 64). There were, however, qualifications:

> An exception must be admitted when the industry created or upheld by the restrictive law belongs to the class of what are called domestic manufactures. These being carried on by persons already fed – by labouring families, in the intervals of other employment – no transfer of capital to the occupation is necessary to its being undertaken, beyond the value of the materials and tools, which is often inconsiderable.
>
> (64–5n)

Thus the so-called exception to the fourth proposition is misnamed, for it refers back to the first proposition. It is clear, however, that the two propositions were almost indistinguishable in Mill's mind, for otherwise there would be no reason for recalling the qualification. The relationship between the propositions revolves on the inability of 'changes in demand' to influence the total demand for labour and aggregate output under certain conditions: aggregate demand for labour and aggregate output will not be influenced either by an expansion of aggregate demand, on the assumption of full employment of at least one input (the implication of the first proposition), or by a change in demand by consumers between products, on the implicit assumption of identical technical coefficients from industry to industry (the fourth proposition).

When the qualification is understood as relevant to the first proposition, 'industry is limited by capital', it is clear that Mill is allowing for the fact that an expansion of total demand may lead to increased aggregate production if it is possible to break the 'bottlenecks' responsible for the physical inability to expand. In the case at hand, that of domestic manufactures, idle equipment and its complement of productive labour may be brought into use upon an increase in aggregate demand.[13] The labourers in this occupation are also 'entrepreneurs', so that in effect Mill is arguing that 'entrepreneurship' may increase upon an expansion in demand. The decision to put equipment to work, made by the 'labourer-entrepreneurs', depends, Mill explains, not upon the 'necessity of living by their trade but that of earning enough by the work to make that social employment of their leisure hours not disagreeable' (*Principles*, III: 684); the decision hinges upon the price of income in terms of leisure. The increase in demand will raise the price of domestically produced goods and may thereby render leisure relatively less attractive. The converse may be true for the case of a reduction in demand.

Mill, therefore, allows for fluctuations in the volume of productive employment and output following changes in aggregate demand, but apparently considers these fluctuations as of relatively small importance; they are 'exceptions' rather than the rule.

Conclusion

There is a general tendency in economics of the Keynesian type to assume a one-to-one relationship between output and employment of labour; output is increased by the application of labour services to other (given) inputs. Whether or not entrepreneurs will be prepared to offer additional employment depends, in these circumstances, upon their judgement respecting the possibility of selling the resultant output at profitable prices. The commodity market is considered to be the reflection of the labour market and *vice versa*, and attention is concentrated on the single input: labour.

For Mill, however, according to the above interpretation, what must be considered is the complex of inputs in the productive process, and not labour alone. Output can only be increased by increases in the rate of employment, or the rate of utilisation, of all necessary inputs at one and the same time. Thus changes in demand cannot be followed by changes in the employment of labour by itself, and to that extent, aggregate demand as the sole determinant of the employment of labour loses its significance. All this, however, applies only to labour in the productive sector. Unproductive labour can yield its services without complementary inputs; thus full employment of labour is always possible, provided that wage rates are flexible, since not all labour need be employed in the productive sector.[14]

I do not intend to deny that Say's Law is sufficient, in equilibrium, to eliminate the possibility of an inadequate final demand. My point is that even if Say's Law is rejected, there remains an additional explanation for the classical approach to aggregate demand, namely the form of the classical production function.

Appendix

Generally, the classical writers assumed flexible wage rates. However, as an example of the influence of rigidity of technology on employment, let us consider the case of a reduction in aggregate demand from an initial situation of full employment of labour, where, by assumption, the money wage rate is inflexible. In this case, the real wage rate will rise as the price level falls and the given wages fund will support fewer workers. If, however, all firms in each industry in the productive sector are similar, a decline in the price level would not result in firms leaving any industry unless prices fall below average variable costs; in this case *all* firms will close down. Thus the given stock of equipment in each industry will either be used in its entirety *with its fixed labour complement*, or it will not be used at all. If it is assumed that activity in any industry does not come to a complete standstill, then the initial reduction in aggregate demand will not, in the short run at least, alter the volume of output and employment. Little attention is paid in classical literature to a cost-ladder of firms in the industrial sector or to an 'extensive margin', so that the assumption of similar firms is, in fact, strongly implied.

The aggregate wages fund, however, supports fewer men so that unemployment is created; but it will be unemployment of unproductive workers only, for activity in the productive sector is unchanged. Idle menials would be considered by classical writers as of relatively little import.

A modification of this result may be made to allow for the case of 'domestic manufacturing' referred to in the third section of the text. The initial fall in aggregate demand is accompanied by a rise in the real wage rate; if the income effect of this rise in real wages is positive and relatively powerful, productive labourers engaged in part-time domestic manufacturing may be induced to reduce such activities and enjoy more leisure. To this extent output and employment in the productive sector will decline.

The argument of the Appendix can be stated symbolically. Let us define the relevant variables as follows:

L quantity demanded of unproductive labour

N quantity demanded of unproductive and productive labour

M_1 stock of equipment in the productive sector apart from that in 'domestic' manufacturing

a_1 labour/equipment ratio in the productive sector, other than in 'domestic' manufacturing

M_2 stock of equipment in use in 'domestic' manufacturing

a_2 labour/equipment ratio in 'domestic' manufacturing

K the wages fund in real terms
w the real wage rate
E 'entrepreneurship' of 'labourer-entrepreneurs' in 'domestic' manufacturing

The principal relationships can now be expressed as

$$N = a_1 M_1 + a_2 M_2 + L,$$ [1]

but M_2 is related proportionally to 'entrepreneurship' (which itself is a function of the real wage rate) in the form

$$M_2 = bE(w),$$ [2]

where b is a positive constant and E a decreasing function of w. Substituting expression [2] into [1] we obtain

$$N = a_1 M_1 + a_2 bE(w) + L.$$ [3]

By the wages fund theory,

$$K = w(a_1 M_1 + L);$$ [4]

it will be recalled that earnings of 'domestic' manufacturers are not advanced out of the wages fund, so that $a_2 M_2$ does not appear in expression [4].

Expression [4] can be rewritten as

$$L = K/w - a_1 M_1$$ [5]

and expression [3] can be rewritten as

$$N - L = a_1 M_1 + a_2 bE(w).$$ [6]

Expression [5] describes the quantity of unproductive labour which will be demanded, and expression [6] the quantity of productive labour demanded.

Let us assume an initial situation of full employment of labour. If money wages are *rigid*, then a fall in aggregate demand will increase the real wage rate, w, and it is clear from [5] that there will be a fall in the quantity of unproductive labour demanded, creating unemployment in the unproductive sector. The demand for productive labour, described by expression [6], will decline only to the extent that the rise in real wages reduces the volume of 'entrepreneurship' offered in 'domestic' manufacturing, thereby reducing $M_2 (= bE(w))$.

Notes

1   I am indebted to Professor W. J. Baumol, Professor D. F. Gordon, and Dr R. L.
    Meek for helpful criticism of an earlier draft. I would like to thank Professor
    Hugh Rose, in particular, for constructive comments.
2   See for example the seminal papers by Hicks (1937) and Modigliani (1944). By
    'classical economics' we shall mean in this paper the body of 'orthodox'
    economic thought in Britain from Smith to the 1870s.
3   An exception is to be found in Sraffa 1960. See in particular v–vi.
4   J. S. Mill, *Principles of Political Economy*, 7th edn (1871), ed. W. J. Ashley
    (London, 1920); cited hereafter as *Principles*.
5   This was the view both of Keynes and Schumpeter. See Keynes (1957: 18) and
    Schumpeter (1954: 383).
6   Mark Blaug (1958: ch. IV) has recognised that the Ricardo effect plays a minor
    role in Ricardo's thinking. He also implies the generality of the assumption of
    fixed coefficients: 'the machinery chapter opens up a whole series of
    unanswered questions about Ricardo's system. Firstly, the chapter abandons
    the assumption of fixed technical coefficients of production' (Blaug 1958: 70).
7   The relevant section in Mill's *Principles* is Book I, ch. VI, 'On circulating and
    fixed capital'.
8   In fact Mill also allows the government to have 'implements and materials' at
    its disposal.
9   A clear statement of the all-inclusive nature of the wages fund theory is also to
    be found in Mill's own summary in the celebrated 'recantation':

    > It will be said that ... supply and demand do entirely govern the price
    > obtained for labour. The demand for labour consists of the whole circulating
    > capital of the country, including what is paid in wages for unproductive
    > labour. The supply is the whole labouring population.
    > (quoted in *Ashley's Bibliographical Appendix*, O, 992, from *Dissertations and
    > Discussions*, IV: 42)

10 Say's Law is postulated by Mill as an equilibrium proposition; he allows that
    there may be 'temporary' crises due to hoarding. In brief, Say's Law is not an
    identity, but an equality. Cf. Becker and Baumol 1952. Yet it is difficult to
    understand why so little emphasis was placed upon the admission that an
    excess of aggregate output was a possibility, and why the full implications of
    the admission were not explored.
11 It can be shown, for example, that as a result of rigidity of technology, a fall in
    aggregate demand may not lead to reduced activity and unemployment in the
    productive sector even if money wages are inflexible. Inflexible money wages
    may at worst create unemployment in the unproductive sector only, an event of
    relatively little import to the classical writers. This particular case is discussed
    in the Appendix to this chapter.
12 Mr Dobb points out that the proposition depends upon the assumption 'like so
    much of Ricardian reasoning ... that the proportions between capital and
    labour were equal in all industries'. It may be added that it depends on a
    further implicit assumption that fixed capital is homogeneous and can be used
    in any industry. Mr Dobb's interpretation is essentially accepted by H. G.
    Johnson (1949: 535), although Professor Johnson goes on to draw the full
    implications of the proposition.

13 That the need for available fixed capital is in fact taken seriously can be seen from further comments on 'domestic' or 'family' manufacture:

> In winter... the whole family employ themselves in it: but as soon as spring appears, those on whom the early field labours devolve abandon the in-door work; many a shuttle stands still;... till at last, at the harvest... all hands seize the implements of husbandry; but in unfavourable weather and in all otherwise vacant hours, the work in the cottage is resumed ....
>
> (*Principles*, III: 683)

At the same time, it is clear that Mill often contravenes the implicit assumption that technical coefficients are identical everywhere, for in the case of domestic manufacture the capital/labour ratio is apparently lower than in other industries. However, the assumption is really most relevant for the case of changes in demand between products rather than for the case of a general increase in demand with which he is here concerned.

14 In the extreme case of similar firms, if *rigid* money wage rates are postulated, a reduction in aggregate demand will create unemployment, but, with minor exceptions, this would affect the unproductive sector only. See Appendix to this chapter.

References

Becker, G. S. and Baumol, W. J. (1952) 'The classical monetary theory: the outcome of the discussion', *Economica*, 19 (November): 355–76.

Blaug, Mark (1958) *Ricardian Economics: A Historical Study*, New Haven CT: Yale University Press, ch. IV.

Cannan, Edwin (1924) *A History of the Theories of Production and Distribution in English Political Economy from 1776 to 1848*, 3rd edn, London: P. S. King.

Dobb, M. H. (1940) *Political Economy and Capitalism*, revised edn, London: Routledge and Kegan Paul.

Hicks, J. R. (1937) 'Mr Keynes and the classics, a suggested interpretation', *Econometrica*, 5 (January): 147–59.

Johnson, H. G. (1949) 'Demand for commodities is not demand for labour', *Economic Journal*, 59 (December): 535.

Keynes, J. M. (1957) *The General Theory of Employment, Interest, and Money*, London: Macmillan.

Mill, J. S. (1920) [1871] *Principles of Political Economy*, 7th edn, ed. W. J. Ashley, London: Longmans, Green.

——(1948) [1844] 'On profits and interest', in *Essays on Some Unsettled Questions of Political Economy*, reprint of 1st edn, London: London School of Economics and Political Science.

Modigliani, Franco (1944) 'Liquidity preference and the theory of interest and money', *Econometrica*, 12 (January): 45–88.

Ricardo, David (1951–73) *The Works and Correspondence of David Ricardo*, ed. P. Sraffa, I: *Principles of Political Economy*, Cambridge: Cambridge University Press.

Schumpeter, J. A. (1954) *History of Economic Analysis*, New York: Oxford University Press.

Sraffa, Piero (1960) *Production of Commodities by Means of Commodities*, Cambridge: Cambridge University Press.

Chapter 2

The role of fixed technical coefficients in the evolution of the wages-fund controversy[1]

It is frequently stated in the classical literature that a specific annual real wages bill is 'destined' to be paid out to labour, so that annual wage income should be treated as a constant. From this assumption follows the celebrated labour demand curve of unitary elasticity. The most explicit statement of this doctrine is by J. S. Mill at the time of his retraction of belief in the existence of a 'wages fund'. Here he laid out what he considered to be received doctrine:

> The demand for labour consists of the whole circulating capital of the country, including what is paid *in wages for unproductive labour*. The supply is the whole labouring population. If the supply is in excess of what the capital can at present employ, wages must fall. If the labourers are all employed, and there is a surplus of capital still unused, wages will rise. This series of deductions is generally received as incontrovertible. They are found, I presume, in every systematic treatise on political economy, my own certainly included. . . .
>
> The theory rests on what may be called the doctrine of the wages fund. There is supposed to be, at any given instant, a sum of wealth, which is unconditionally devoted to the payment of wages of labour. This sum is not regarded as unalterable, for it is augmented by saving, and increases with the progress of wealth; but it is reasoned upon as at any given moment a predetermined amount. More than that amount it is assumed that the wages-receiving class cannot possibly divide among them; that amount, and no less, they cannot but obtain. So that, the sum to be divided being fixed, the wages of each depend solely on the divisor, the number of participants. In this doctrine it is by implication affirmed, that the demand for labour not only increases with the cheapness, but increases in exact proportion to it, the same aggregate sum being paid for labour whatever its price may be.
>
> (Mill 1869: 515, emphasis added)[2]

The data in the analysis of the wage rate – when we consider a period of time during which the population is unchanged – are the aggregate wages bill constituting labour demand, and the given work force, constituting labour supply. We shall refer to this treatment as the *ex ante* wages-fund theory to reflect the characteristic role of the wages bill as a predetermined quantity.

There is in the classical literature an 'alternative' treatment of the labour market wherein the wages bill is not predetermined, but is the *dependent variable* of the analysis. This treatment is to be found in its most explicit form in the work of Robert Torrens in 1834, and in that of J. E. Cairnes in 1874.[3] To assure the employment of any given work force, it is presumed that a specific quantum of non-labour inputs must be provided, that is, fixed technical coefficients between labour and 'fixed capital' are assumed. An increase in the capital stock, for example, will take the form of wage payments entirely *if the labour force is unchanged*; a *rise* in the work force, on the other hand, requires the support of more fixed capital so that less remains as the counterpart for wage payments. The wages bill appears in a sense as the 'residual' portion of the capital stock, but it is to be emphasised that it is the *competitive process* which assures that what remains of aggregate capital is devoted to wage payments. The wages bill is thus the equilibrium outcome in a competitive model, the data of which are aggregate capital and the technical coefficients of production – which together generate the labour demand curve – and the working population – which, as usual, constitutes labour supply. We shall refer to the Torrens–Cairnes version as the *ex post* wages-fund theory to reflect the fact that the wages bill is derived as the solution in an equilibrating market process.

We may formalise the Torrens–Cairnes version of the wages-fund theory by means of simple equations. In their treatment the quantity demanded of labour in aggregate, (P) is dependent upon the aggregate capital stock (C), the technically determined constant ratio (λ) between labour and non-labour inputs or 'fixed capital', and the wage rate (w), and may be written as

$$P = \frac{C}{1/\lambda + w}.$$ [1]

This is derived directly from the constraint that total capital is made up of fixed capital (M) and wages capital (wP), that is $C = M + wP$. Replacing M by P/λ we may immediately obtain expression [1].

The supply of labour (S) is given. Equilibrium will be assured by the full employment condition

$$P = S$$ [2]

and the wage rate may be immediately obtained by inserting expression [1] into [2] since w is the only unknown to be determined. Thus

$$\frac{C}{1/\lambda + w} = S$$

and

$$w = C/S - 1/\lambda. \tag{3}$$

Expression [3] may be compared with the *ex ante* wages-fund theory wherein

$$w = C'/S$$

C' referring to *circulating* capital (or wage capital) only, rather than aggregate capital.

According to the present version of the theory, the amount of wage payments is not given independently of the size of the working population. An exogenous increase in the work force will actually lead to a smaller equilibrium wages fund since a larger fraction of total capital is required to take the form of fixed capital. The percentage decline in the wage rate thus exceeds the percentage increase in population. In brief, the demand curve for labour is relatively inelastic, in contrast to the unitary elasticity of the *ex ante* case.[4]

Even a casual survey of neo-classical and modern commentaries on the wages-fund theory shows that it is the *ex ante* version which is attributed to the classical school. All discussions of the manner in which the classics envisaged the 'pre-allocation' of the total capital stock between fixed and wage-goods capital are only relevant to the *ex ante* version, where the size of the wages fund is a datum of the analysis. It will be noted that the pre-allocation attributed to the classics is usually regarded as a technological matter: 'Like all "classical" leaders, he [J. S. Mill] took the relationship between technological [fixed] and wage capital as a datum, so that in the final result saving would increase both of them in proportion' (Schumpeter 1954: 642).[5] Moreover, very little attention is paid to the insistence by Mill that the *ex ante* version of the theory applies not only to productive but also to service labour. The relevance of this characteristic will become clear presently.

By contrast, Torrens's contribution is for the most part neglected, whereas that of Cairnes is usually regarded as peculiar to him alone and atypical of classical doctrine. Marshall, for example, described Cairnes's contribution in such terms:

> After a while Cairnes, in his *Leading Principles*, endeavoured to resuscitate the Wages-fund theory by expounding it in a form which he thought would evade the attacks that had been made on it. But, though in the greater part of his exposition, he succeeded in avoiding the old pitfalls,

he did so only by explaining away so much which is characteristic of the doctrine, that there is very little left in it to justify its title.

(Marshall 1947 [1920]: 825)[6]

Similarly, Schumpeter comments that Cairnes 'interpreted the wages fund in a way that left little to defend' (1954: 670n). It is doubtless Mill's account of received doctrine which did more than anything to establish the content of the 'classical' wages fund theory.

The first object of the present paper is to reconsider the role played by the wages fund in Mill's *Principles*. We will attempt to determine whether the analysis in the *Principles* implies a belief in the existence of a predetermined fund destined for wage payment, or whether the wages fund constituted – as Cairnes believed – the equilibrium outcome of a market-clearing process.[7] Our conclusion is that the Cairnes-type approach played a key role in Mill's analysis and that the version of the wages-fund theory rejected by Mill represented an incomplete account of his original position.

Second, it will be made clear that the Torrens–Cairnes–Mill version of the wages-fund theory was applied only to the productive sector. In this context the service sector of the economy was neglected, and accordingly their treatment was incomplete. The reason for the restriction of their model is that the key assumption of constant technical coefficients between fixed capital and labour was regarded by all three economists to be inapplicable in the service sector where, it was believed, labour is employed independently of the support of other inputs. Certain well-known 'formal' accounts of the wages-fund theory which appear in Mill's *Principles*, and which apparently refer to the notion of a predetermined wages fund, are shown, by contrast, to allow for a service sector.

The logical demand curve in the case where the wages fund is a predetermined amount is of *unitary elasticity*. If the possibility of input substitutability is neglected, however, it should follow that the marginal product of labour – when a given fixed capital stock is assumed – will be of *zero elasticity*. The third objective of this paper is to suggest that it was precisely this conflict which led Mill to reject the notion of a predetermined wages fund; the problem of fixed capital was responsible for Mill's recantation.

We shall show that Mill's argument in 1869 in favour of a completely inelastic labour demand curve was applied only to the productive sector. Had Mill allowed for the existence of service labour in his critique he might have avoided the conclusion that a competitive solution could not be applied in the labour market in the face of zero demand elasticity for productive labour.

The rejection of a predetermined wages fund had wider implications than Mill apparently realised. The historical significance of the recantation lies in the conclusion that the wage rate may not be amenable to competitive demand-supply analysis so that some form of 'bargaining' theory is required.

Although there is no evidence that Mill was aware of it, the logic of his case is applicable, it will be shown, to the version of the wages-fund theory developed by Torrens and Cairnes, which appears also in Mill's *Principles*, and not merely to the *ex ante* version which yields a labour demand curve of unitary elasticity. For the Torrens–Cairnes–Mill version also fails to provide an adequate account of competitive wage-rate determination in the short run when the fixed capital stock is given.

In the final section we consider whether, within the context of classical theory, inter-industry differences in technical coefficients might have contributed to a competitive solution for the labour market. The general conclusion is that such differences did not play a significant role in the classical analysis of the labour market.

According to the *ex ante* wages-fund theory, the wages bill – and the allocation of a given capital stock between fixed and wages-goods (or circulating) capital – is given independently of the labour supply, and an increase in the capital stock will involve a proportionate increase in both sub-categories. By contrast, according to the *ex post* version the wages bill is the outcome of the equilibrium process and is thus dependent upon the labour supply. An increase in the capital stock will not generally involve a proportionate increase in fixed and circulating capital. The allocation will be entirely dependent upon the assumptions made regarding the labour force. In this section we shall consider two 'case studies' from Mill's *Principles*, relating to the effects on wage income of increased investment on the one hand and disinvestment on the other, in order to isolate the implicit assumptions employed by Mill.

Analysis of the effects of increased investment

The implicit assumptions utilised by Mill may be examined first by reference to his analysis of the effects on labour income of an increased rate of investment. Mill admitted that an excess supply of commodities due to a temporary excess demand for money was to be recognised. This proposition, however, was strictly separated from the argument put forward by Malthus and others that it was possible for investment to be carried on at an excessive rate. When investment occurs, Mill argued, purchasing power remains intact: when capitalists 'turn their income into capital, they do not thereby annihilate their power of consumption; they do but transfer it from themselves to the labourers to whom they give employment' (Mill 1965: 68). In the eventuality that population is increasing there is no problem since 'the production of necessaries for the new population, takes the place of the production of luxuries for a portion of the old, and supplies exactly the amount of employment which has been lost'. There is thus a reduction in the output of luxury goods consumed by capitalists and an increase in the production of 'necessaries' consumed by the larger work force. But even if population is presumed to be *constant* there will be no problem. The attempt by capitalists to expand the aggregate capital stock will be thwarted by the lack of a sufficient labour supply, and competition for the given labour force will cause the wage rate to rise until the additional investment outlays simply take the form of increased labour income. The income distribution will turn in favour of labour, but at no point will there occur a deficiency of purchasing power:

> But suppose that there is no increase of population. The whole of what was previously expended in luxuries, by capitalists and landlords, is distributed among the existing labourers, in the form of additional wages. We will assume them to be already sufficiently supplied with necessaries. What follows? That the labourers become consumers of luxuries; and the capital previously employed in the production of luxuries, is still able to employ itself in the same manner: the difference being, that the luxuries are shared among the community generally, instead of being confined to a few.
>
> (Mill 1965: 68)

An increased investment programme, financed by a reduction in consumption by capitalists, will thus result in an alteration in the income distribution in favour of wages in the case that the working force is constant, but at no stage will there occur a deficiency of purchasing power. This analysis is consistent with the Torrens–Cairnes theory of wage-rate determination according to which aggregate labour income is determined as the competitive outcome of a demand-supply equation, and hence *will depend upon the actual size of the working population*. For when the labour supply is constant the entire increase in capital, as we have seen, 'becomes' higher wage income. Yet Mill stated also:

> I do not mean to deny that capital, or part of it, may be so employed as not to support labourers, being fixed in machinery, buildings, improvements of land, and the like. In any large increase of capital, a considerable portion will be thus employed.
>
> (66)

This latter qualification can only refer to the case where population is rising. Thus it is evident that the division of total capital, and accordingly the size of the wages bill, depends upon the work force itself, and is not given independently.[8]

Analysis of the effects of disinvestment: the case of war loans

Mill considered the case of a war loan raised by the government, where the funds are assumed to be derived from reductions in investment outlays. In essence he treats a case of disinvestment:

> we will suppose the most unfavourable case possible: that the whole amount borrowed and destroyed by the government, was abstracted by the lender from a productive employment in which it had actually been invested. The capital, therefore, of the country, is this year diminished by so much. But unless the amount abstracted is something enormous, there is no reason ... why next year the national capital should not be as great as ever. The loan cannot have been taken from that portion of the capital of the country which consists of tools, machinery, and buildings. It must have been wholly drawn from the portion employed in paying labourers: and the labourers will suffer accordingly. But if none of them are starved; if their wages can bear such an amount of reduction, or if charity interposes between them and absolute destitution, there is no reason that their labour should produce less in the next year than in the year before. If they produce as much as usual, having been paid less by so many millions sterling, these millions are gained by their employers. The breach made in the capital of the country is thus instantly repaired, but repaired by the privations and often the real misery of the labouring class.
>
> (Mill 1965: 76)

It is apparent, in the present instance, that employment is dependent upon fixed capital; it is only *because the community's fixed capital stock remains unchanged* that it is possible to maintain the same level of employment as in previous periods. The 'wages fund' is reduced by the disinvestment, but there occurs no reduction in the fixed capital stock.

This is the sequence of events which must follow from the analysis of Cairnes and Torrens. Full employment requires the support of a specific fixed-capital complex, and any given capital outlays must – in equilibrium – allow for such necessary expenditures, so that only the remainder is available for wage payment. Hence a reduction in capital outlays for any reason will simply reduce the 'residual' available for wage payments.[9]

In the case studies relating to the effects on wage income of increased investment and of disinvestment, Mill did not apply the *ex ante* wages-fund theory. We conclude that Cairnes's account of the theory developed in the *Leading Principles* was by no means atypical of received doctrine as it appeared in Mill's *Principles*.[10]

We do not wish to imply, however, that the notion of a predetermined wages bill is entirely absent from the *Principles*. On the contrary, the 'formal' – and perhaps best-known – accounts of the doctrine, although ambiguous, seem on balance to imply the notion of a predetermined fund.[11] But it is essential to note that in these formal statements – as distinct from the particular cases we have considered – allowance is made for a service sector. This distinction between the theory implied by the formal accounts (where a service sector is recognised) and that implied in Mill's consideration of specific issues relating to the effects of investment which deal only with a 'productive' sector, is not accidental. The Torrens–Mill–Cairnes version of the wages-fund theory – where the wages fund appears as the outcome of a competitive supply-demand equation – is applicable to the productive sector only because the assumption of fixed technical coefficients, which is the *sine qua non* of the argument, was regarded by all three economists as irrelevant to the service sector.

In the case of Torrens, the observation supporting fixed technical coefficients – 'a given number of hands can use only a given quantity of seed, materials, and machinery' (see Appendix to this chapter) – is to be understood as relevant to the productive sector only since service labour, Torrens holds, does not require the support of other inputs:

> The effectual demand for labour...consists merely in the offer of an adequate quantity of subsistence. Productive labour, indeed, cannot be put into operation unless the labourers, in addition to their subsistence, are furnished with tools and material. But an increased supply of the necessaries of life is of itself sufficient to enable us to engage an increased number of menial servants and unproductive retainers.
>
> (Torrens 1965 [1821]: 355)

Similarly, Cairnes limits the discussion to productive labour, the characteristic of which is the requirement of strictly complementary inputs:

> It will be remembered that in the enunciation which I quoted from Mr Mill of the wages question, the Wages-fund is stated to consist of two distinct parts – one, the largest and by much the most important, constituting a portion of the general capital of the country; while the other is derived from that part of the nation's wealth which goes to support unproductive labor, of which Mr Mill gives as an example the wages of soldiers and domestic servants. In proceeding to deal with the wages question, it will be convenient to omit for a time all consideration of the latter part: it will be more easily dealt with when we have ascertained the causes which govern the main phenomenon.
>
> Restricting our view then for the present to that portion of the general Wages-fund which goes to support productive labor, we have, in the first place, to observe that the hiring of labor for productive purposes is an incident of the investment of capital. A capitalist engages and pays a workman from precisely the same motives which lead him to purchase raw material, a factory, or a machine.
>
> (Cairnes 1874: 168)

Although Cairnes promises to take up the problem of service labour, he does not return to examine the issue.

Reference to our case studies from the *Principles* of J. S. Mill, which imply the use of a 'Torrens–Cairnes' model, will show that Mill's concern too was with the productive sector only. By contrast, Mill in the *Fortnightly Review* opens his attack with a formal statement of 'received doctrine' which includes a service sector – 'The demand for labour consists of the whole circulating capital of the country, including what is paid in wages *for unproductive labour*' (quoted above, p. 15).

The notion of a predetermined fund for wage payments thus comes to the fore in those instances where the Torrens–Cairnes–Mill version of the wages-fund theory cannot be applied, namely where a service sector is introduced. The formal generalisations which appear in Mill's *Principles*, and in his account of 'received doctrine' at the time of his recantation, which refer to a predetermined fund are, unfortunately, vague in the extreme, in the sense that there are no specific references to the production function envisaged, and accordingly, to the manner in which the demand for labour is derived. The statements are open to all the criticisms that have been directed against the notion of a predetermined fund. At best they sufficed to suggest that the artificial imposition of a minimum wage rate might restrain the level of activity, and to indicate the need for population control on the part of the working class, and for these purposes, it may be argued, exemplary precision in the construction of the demand curve for labour is not essential.

In this section, we consider Thornton's attack on the 'wages fund' doctrine and Mill's recantation. Mill's formal rejection of the notion of a predetermined wages fund occurs in his review of the first edition of Thornton's *On Labour* (1869). Much of the relevant material in this work was repeated from Thornton's 'What determines the price of labour or rate of wages?' which had appeared two years earlier. Here was presented a general criticism of simple supply–demand equilibrium analysis resulting from the presence of completely inelastic schedules, severe discontinuities, and the like.[12] The argument was applied to the labour market, as well as to commodity markets, on the grounds principally that both the labour demand and supply schedules were, at least over wide ranges, completely inelastic. Since employers' combinations were easily formed and workers were badly organised, it followed that in practice the wage rate was determined by the employers' *dictat*: '[employers] both can and do force them [the labourers] to take as little more than the bare means of subsistence as it pleases them to offer' (Thornton 1867: 564). Such an arbitrary process was not necessarily to the workers' detriment, since in cases of excess labour supply the wage rate might be set at a higher level than would have resulted were employers to remain passive and workers to compete for scarce jobs (561, 563). In the absence of the employers' intervention, the wage rate would be driven down to the lowest conceivable level, the excess supply remaining apparently uncorrected.

Although employers' combinations in the case of excess supply might operate in practice in labour's interest, such combinations in the case of excess demand function to prevent competition between the employers and upward pressure on the wage rate. Employers realise that it is 'better for them to go without part of the labour they desire, rather than for the sake of obtaining that portion, to incur the obligation of paying a greatly increased price for all the labour they employ' (560–1). Again, the divergence between demand and supply would not have been corrected, apparently, by changing wage rates.

Some reference is made to coincidental schedules. In such instances the wage rate will in practice also be determined arbitrarily by the employers.

The crucial practical outcome of Thornton's treatment is that workers' unions have a significant role to play: 'counter combinations may be potent enough to unsettle and resettle' the wage rate determined otherwise by one-sided 'artificial' and 'capricious' rulings (565). The 'new view' led Thornton to reject the notion of a predetermined wages fund. But very little attention was in fact paid to the issue in the first edition of *On Labour*; no more than a lengthy footnote was devoted to the wages-fund theory.[13] The wages bill, Thornton argued, cannot be regarded as a fixed cost to each individual employer; his demand is for a certain specific quantity of labour, and there is no reason for him to spend the maximum sum which he may have available for wage payments:

> But has any individual any such fund? Is there any specific portion of any single individual's capital which the owner must necessarily expend upon labour? Of course, there is a certain amount which every effectual employer can afford to spend upon labour, as also there is in every instance a certain limit to that amount which cannot possibly be exceeded. But must the amount, so limited, which is thus applicable to the purchase of labour, be necessarily so applied? Does any farmer or manufacturer or contractor ever say to himself, I can afford to pay so much for labour: therefore, for the labour I hire, whatever the quantity be, I will pay so much? Does he not rather say, '*So much labour I require,* so much is the utmost I can afford to pay for it, but I will see for how much less than the utmost I can afford to pay, I can get all the labour I require'?
>
> (Thornton 1869: 84–5n)[14]

Since wages are not a fixed cost to the individual employer, Thornton concluded too hastily that there can be no aggregate wages fund.

These arguments were accepted by Mill, who pleaded guilty to having maintained the notion of a predetermined wages fund. But it was Mill, not

Thornton, who stated clearly that logically according to received doctrine the demand curve for labour is of unitary elasticity (see above, p. 15); Thornton had merely implied it. Second, Mill emphasised the special case of completely inelastic and *coincidental* schedules of supply and demand 'where neither sellers nor buyers are under the action of any motives derived from supply and demand to give way to one another' (Mill 1869: 514); Thornton considered instances of excess supply and demand too. Third, the rationale for a labour demand curve of zero elasticity is given more attention by Mill than by Thornton in the first edition of *On Labour*.[15] We turn now to consider Mill's argument in support of a labour demand curve of zero elasticity.

In an extraordinary passage, we read the following distinction between the demand for commodities and the demand for labour:

> Does the employer require more labour, or do fresh employers of labour make their appearance, merely because it can be bought cheaper? Assuredly, no. Consumers desire more of an article, or fresh consumers are called forth, when the price has fallen: but the employer does not buy labour for the pleasure of consuming it; he buys it that he may profit from its productive powers, and he buys as much labour and no more as suffices to produce the quantity of his goods which he thinks he can sell to advantage. A fall of wages does not necessarily make him expect a larger sale for his commodity, nor, therefore, does it necessarily increase his demand for labour.
>
> (Mill 1869: 516)

The outcome of the argument thus far is that the demand for labour by the *individual* employer in a particular occupation is of zero elasticity. But Mill turns immediately to counter the possible objection that although this may be so, a wage reduction releases capital and permits its investment in wage payments elsewhere, so that 'the whole of the wages-fund will be paying wages as before'. The objection is rejected. The wages bill cannot exceed the aggregate means of the employers (after allowance for their personal maintenance), it is true, but 'short of this limit, it is not, in any sense of the word, a fixed amount'. Mill's argument is not, therefore, limited to the micro-economic level of analysis but is intended to apply with equal force at the aggregate level.

We have seen that Mill considered the demand for final products to be responsive to price changes – 'consumers desire more of an article, or fresh consumers are called forth, when the price has fallen'.[16] Thornton may have believed that commodity markets are characterised by zero demand elasticity, but Mill did not. The inelasticity of demand for labour, therefore, cannot be ascribed to inelasticity of demand for final product.

It is impossible to be certain as to the precise rationale for Mill's position. Yet it may be significant that Mill for the most part had in mind, it would appear, the short-run case where the fixed capital stock is given. This seems clear from the sequel to the above passage:

> In the common theory, the order of ideas is this. The capitalist's pecuniary means consist of two parts – his capital, and his profits or income. His capital is what he starts with at the beginning of the year, or when he commences some round of business operations: his income he does not receive until the end of the year, or until the round of operations is completed. His capital, *except such part as is fixed in buildings and machinery, or laid out in materials*, is what he has got to pay wages with. He cannot pay them out of his income, for that he has not yet received. When he does receive it, he may lay by a portion to add to his capital, and as such it will become part of next year's wages-fund, but has nothing to do with this year's.
>
> This distinction, however, between the relation of the capitalist to his capital, and the relation to his income, is wholly imaginary. He starts at the commencement with the whole of his accumulated means, all of which is potentially capital: and out of this he advances his personal and family expenses. . . . If we choose to call the whole of what he possesses applicable to the payment of wages, the wages fund, that fund is co-extensive with the whole proceeds of his business, *after keeping up his machinery, buildings and materials*, and feeding his family; and it is expended jointly upon himself and his labourers. The less he expends on the one, the more may be expended on the other, and *vice versa*. The price of labour, instead of being determined by the division of the proceeds between the employer and the labourers, determine[s] it. If he gets his labour cheaper, he can afford to spend more upon himself. If he has to pay more for labour, the additional payment comes out of his own income. . . . There is no law of nature making it inherently impossible for wages to rise to the point of absorbing not only the funds which he had intended to devote to carrying on his business, but the whole of what he allows for his private expenses, beyond the necessaries of life. The real limit to the rise is the practical consideration, how much would ruin him, or drive him to abandon his business: not the inexorable limits of the wages-fund.
>
> (Mill 1869: 516–17, emphasis added)

In this critique Mill states clearly that allowance must be made for certain specific expenditures upon 'machinery, buildings, and materials'. The new point is that the quantity demanded of labour services is now said to be unresponsive to wage-rate reductions. It would thus appear that Mill's critique was based upon a short-run view of the theory of employment where it is *taken for granted* that a given fixed capital stock cannot be utilised with more or less intensity by the 'variable' input labour.

There is no explicit statement by Mill in these passages to the effect that he was deliberately assuming fixed technical coefficients of production. But it is evident that if he had been aware of the possibility of input substitution – in the present context, the more intensive utilisation of a given fixed-capital complex by labour – he could not have avoided recognising the fact that in such instances a wage-rate reduction would in fact lower costs and make profitable expanded production and employment, even in the short run. The recantation may thus be interpreted as a simple and correct argument to the effect that the notion of a 'predetermined' wages fund cannot be maintained in the absence of input substitutability. Two further considerations in support of this interpretation may be noted.

It is particularly relevant to recall that although Mill, as we have seen at the outset of this paper, included a service sector in his account of received doctrine – 'the demand for labour consists of the whole circulating capital of the country, including what is paid in wages for unproductive labour' when he turned to reject the doctrine, on the grounds that the demand for labour is unresponsive to wage-rate changes – he limited his analysis solely to the productive sector.[17] But it is precisely in this sector that Mill – and also Torrens and Cairnes – assumed fixed technical coefficients, as we have seen earlier (see above, second section).

Second, we must refer at this point to Mill's clear recognition of the 'substitution effects' generated by relative price changes in the case of the consumer. In response to a letter from Cairnes, Mill wrote:

> Of the two or three points which we differ about, I will only touch upon one – the influence of price on demand. You say, if a tax is taken off beer and laid on tobacco in such a manner that the consumer can still, at the same total cost as before, purchase his usual quantity of both, his tastes being supposed unaltered, he will do so. Does not this assume that his taste for each is a fixed quantity? or at all events that his comparative desire for the two is not affected by their comparative prices? But I apprehend the case to be otherwise. Very often the consumer cannot afford to have as much as he would like of either: and if so, the ratio in which he will share his demand between the two may depend very much on their price. If beer grows cheaper and tobacco dearer, he will be able to increase his beer more, by a smaller sacrifice of his tobacco, than he could have done at the previous prices: and in such circumstances it is surely probable that some will do so. His apportionment of self-denial between his two tastes is likely to be modified, when the obstacle that confined them is in the one case brought nearer, in the other thrown farther off.
> (letter of 5 January 1865; in O'Brien 1943: 281)[18]

It is difficult believe that Mill could have written the review of 1869 if he had been aware of the counterpart in the theory of production of the substitution effect of relative price changes so brilliantly expressed in the theory of consumption.[19]

The formal rejection of the notion of a predetermined wages fund thus came when Mill was made aware of the strong likelihood that the labour demand curve will – given his basic assumptions regarding technology – be of zero, rather than of unitary, elasticity. But of greater importance than the rejection of the wages-fund theory was the rejection of a competitive solution, of any sort, to the wage rate. The reason for the failure to reach this conclusion earlier seems, in part at least, to be explicable by the tendency to include, in the formal discussions of the predetermined wages-fund which appear in the *Principles*, a service sector. Had Mill consistently recognised the service sector throughout his critique of 'received doctrine' in 1869, he might have continued to maintain a competitive solution to equilibrium in the labour market – even in the short run when the fixed capital stock is given – since the demand for labour as a whole would be responsive to wage-rate changes, although the demand for productive labour alone would be unresponsive.[20]

Although the essential result of the debate was the conclusion that workers' unions have a significant role to play, since the competitive solution is inoperative and the wage rate becomes the outcome of a 'contest of endurance' between opposing groups (1869: 515), Mill was not sufficiently careful in his review and failed to draw the full implications of the new view. Logically, the appearance of an excess labour supply could not be corrected by wage-rate reductions, since there is no wage rate at which demand and supply become equalised. Accordingly, wages should fall to zero, or at least to that level below which the entire labour supply is withdrawn from the market, unless workers' unions, or – as Thornton suggested – benevolent employers' combinations, imposed a higher rate. Yet in summarising the new position, Mill wrote as if the competitive equilibrium was somehow still meaningful:

> In short, there is abstractly available for the payment of wages, before an absolute limit is reached, not only the employer's capital, but the whole of what can possibly be retrenched from his personal expenditure; and the law of wages, on the side of demand, amounts only to the obvious proposition, that the employers cannot pay away in wages what they have not got. On the side of supply, the law as laid down by economists remains intact. The more numerous the competitors for employment, the lower, *caeteris paribus*, will wages be.
>
> (Mill 1869: 517)

Mill's attention was on the case of coincidental schedules and the problem of indeterminacy in this special instance. He failed to pay adequate attention to cases of excess demand or supply.

Mill in the recantation directed his critique specifically against the notion of a unitary elastic demand curve for labour. It should be noted, however, that in principle, the logic of his case could be applied effectively against the

Torrens–Cairnes–Mill version of the wages-fund theory. In this version, the role of fixed technical coefficients is to determine the amount of fixed capital required to assure full employment. What remains of the aggregate capital stock is devoted to wage payments as a result of the operation of the competitive process. But at this point a vital implicit assumption must be emphasised. In order to be assured of the competitive solution a labour demand curve of negative slope is required. To obtain such a demand curve when constant proportions between labour and fixed capital is the rule, it is necessary to allow for *hypothetical* variations in the quantity of fixed capital. For if an excess demand for labour should appear – as in the case immediately after an increase in investment – fixed coefficients between inputs presume that employers are prepared and able to allocate to the support of the additional labour required the necessary capital equipment. In point of fact, the wage rate is forced upwards towards a new equilibrium position by the scarcity of labour services, so that additional fixed capital is not actually constructed. The logic of the process, however, implies that firms are able to make additions to their fixed capital stocks. Thus the analysis is applicable only to the Marshallian long run. Once the *fixed capital* is in being, employers will not in the short run respond to wage-rate changes; the demand for labour will be completely inelastic, and there is no mechanism to assure that the residual portion of the capital stock will be devoted to wage payments. This problem was not recognised by Cairnes in 1874 – despite Mill's paper of 1869 – or by Torrens.

Even assuming a given fixed capital stock, wage-rate changes will lead to a response in the quantity of labour services demanded in the economy as a whole if the technical coefficients of production – constant in each industry – should differ between industries. Partial substitution via inter-industry differences in input ratios would perhaps have permitted a competitive solution.[21]

The classical literature provides quite a few instances of inter-industry differences in technical coefficients. Doubtless, the references thereto in Ricardo's first chapter 'On value' are best known. Yet this recognition played no great role in Ricardo's general system. On the contrary, the Ricardian model of distribution based upon the so-called measure of value requires the assumption that input ratios do *not* differ from sector to sector (cf. Dobb 1940: 45; Pasinetti 1960: 91).

Moreover, both the *ex post* and the *ex ante* versions of the wages-fund theory logically require that factor proportions should be identical throughout the economy. In the Torrens–Cairnes version of the theory, the capital/labour ratio is one of the data of the system and, accordingly, must remain unaffected by wage-rate changes and changes in the distribution of activity between sectors. Cairnes was well aware of this. He analysed changes in the pattern of final expenditure, and concluded that the 'effects would be limited to a mere transference of wealth' (1874: 192) between different groups of workers, there being no net increase in the wages fund. In a qualifying note he recognised and made explicit the key assumption implied in the argument, namely that technical coefficients were everywhere identical:

> In theoretical strictness, this position needs qualification. It would only be strictly true, if the Wages-fund bore always the same proportion to the capital employed in production, which is not the fact. Supposing, e.g., expenditure were largely directed from clothing to food, and that in consequence capital were transferred from manufactures to agriculture, inasmuch as a given amount of capital employed in agriculture will in general contain a larger element of Wages-fund than the same amount of capital employed in manufactures (owing to the larger use of fixed capital in the latter case), it follows that a substitution of a demand for food for a demand for clothes would in this case issue in an increase of the aggregate Wages fund.
>
> (Cairnes 1874: 192–3n)

The conclusion reached in his text was forced on him by the nature of the model, which was incapable of dealing with the case where factor ratios differ between industries so that the 'average' fixed capital/labour ratio becomes an unknown rather than a datum.[22]

Similarly the *ex ante* version of the theory, in which aggregate wages appear as a predetermined fund, does not permit the wage rate to affect the distribution of the total capital stock, thereby rendering the aggregate wages bill an unknown. This, of course, is the basic argument directed against the theory in the neo-classical period, as we have remarked earlier.

Thus, in developing the proposition that 'the demand for commodities is not the demand for labour', J. S. Mill quite explicitly and correctly ruled out the possibility that a change in the pattern of consumer demand between products will influence the demand for labour:

> The demand for commodities determines in what particular branch of production the labour and capital shall be employed; it determines the *direction* of the labour; but not the more or less of the labour itself, or of the maintenance or payment of the labour. These depend on the amount of the capital, or other funds directly devoted to the sustenance and remuneration of labour.
>
> (1965: 78)[23]

The technical ratios could not logically, *within the context of the wages-fund theory*, differ between industries.[24]

Yet the condemnation by Mill of the notion of a predetermined wages fund on the grounds of zero demand elasticity for labour at the level of the firm and the economy, is disappointing. For, once Mill had freed himself from the wages-fund theory, the possibility of inter-industry differences in technical coefficients could have been allowed for, and the role of input substitution – by way of alterations in the pattern of activity between industries – recognised. (Indeed, the condemnation of the concept of a predetermined wages fund might have been based upon the argument that technical coefficients, fixed in each industry, are not identical between industries.) The fact that Mill did not take this line shows how deeply encrusted had become the habit of assuming not merely fixed input coefficients, but identical coefficients throughout the economy.

Appendix

Extract from Robert Torrens, On Wages and Combination (London, 1834) 16–18

For when the farmer, in order to extend his cultivation, makes an addition to his capital, he will require a greater number of hands, and will seek to tempt them into his employ by the offer of higher wages. But as the increase of capital is supposed to be general, all other capitalists will require additional hands as well as our farmer, and will be offering higher wages also. All the capitalists will be unwilling to let their additional capital lie idle for want of hands, and, with the two-fold object of retaining their own labourers, and of obtaining those of their neighbours, will go on advancing wages, until the whole of their additional capital is absorbed.

Assuming that all the labourers are already employed, and that no addition is made to their numbers, it is morally certain, that the whole of every new accumulation of capital will assume the form of increased wages, until the reward of the labourer has reached its maximum. New accumulations of capital are made for the sake of obtaining advantage therefrom. But it is impossible that new accumulations of capital should be advantageously employed, unless labourers can be procured. The new capital, accumulated for the purpose of gaining an advantage by the employment of labourers, comes into the market and bids for hands; the old capital, in order to retain its hands, is compelled to bid against the new, and this process goes on until the whole existing capital is invested in wages, seed, materials, and machinery. But as a given number of hands can use only a given quantity of seed, materials, and machinery, these ingredients or component parts of capital cannot be increased, while the quantity of labour remains the same; and therefore it is only in the form of increased wages that the new accumulations of capital can appear.

When the number of labourers remains the same, nothing can prevent new accumulations of capital from appearing in the form of increased wages, except such an intimate understanding and concert among capitalists, as would induce each individual of the class, instead of seeking for additional hands, to allow his new accumulations of capital to remain idle and unproductive.... If such new accumulations are made, it is in order that they may be employed; and if they are employed the quantity of labour, and the state of applying mechanical power remaining the same, there is no form in which they can appear, except in that of increased wages.

Extract from J. E. Cairnes, Some Leading Principles of Political Economy (London, 1874) 186–7

Assuming a certain field for investment, and the prospect of profit in this such as to attract a certain aggregate capital, and assuming the national industries to be of a certain kind, the proportion of this aggregate capital which shall be invested in wages is not a matter within the discretion of the capitalists, always supposing they desire to obtain the largest practical return upon their outlay. To accomplish this, the instruments of production, labor, fixed capital and raw material, must be brought together in certain proportions – a condition which requires ... – the supply of labor being given – a distribution of the aggregate capital in certain proportions among those instruments. Supposing, now, capitalists to succeed in forcing down the rate of wages below the point at which, having regard to the number of the laboring population, the amount, which the fulfilment of this condition would assign to the payment of wages, was absorbed – either the capital thus withdrawn from the Wages-fund must remain uninvested and therefore unproductive, or if invested, and not invested in wages, it would take the form of fixed capital or raw material. But by hypothesis the fixed capital and raw material were already in due proportion to the labor force, and they would consequently now be in excess of it. A competition among capitalists for labor would consequently ensue; and what could this end in but a restoration to the Wages-fund of the amount withdrawn from it?

Notes

1   For constructive suggestions at various stages during the preparation of this paper, I would like to thank warmly my colleagues at Toronto: Professors V. W. Bladen, J. C. McManus, J. M. Robson, and Mrs Gwen Whittaker; and also Lord Robbins, Professors H. G. Johnson and G. J. Stigler, and Mrs Adelaide Weinberg.

2   If we designate C' as the predetermined wages fund, and w as the average wage, then the quantity of labour demanded, P, can be written in the form $P = C'/w$.

3   The relevant extracts are given in an appendix. A somewhat less explicit

statement of complementarity appears in Torrens 1835: 23–4. An excellent account of these contributions – and in fact of the entire classical wages-fund literature – is given by Stuart Wood (1890: 426–61). For a discussion of Wood's account see Stigler 1947: 640–9. The analysis in the present paper differs in several respects from that of Wood.

4    $$\frac{dP}{dW} \cdot \frac{w}{P} = \frac{1}{1/\lambda w + 1}.$$

This characteristic is emphasised by Cairnes only (1874: 173–4) and is not noticed by Torrens.

5   One of the basic criticisms directed against their predecessors by late-nineteenth-century economists relates precisely to the pre-allocation of the total capital stock between the two major subcategories, and Schumpeter's approach seems to be the one followed by these writers (see e.g. Sidgwick 1883: 315–16; Stephen 1900: 215ff; see also Stigler 1941: 283–5, and the comments on Knut Wicksell's critique).

6   This view is also maintained by T. W. Hutchison (1953: 260).

7   Cairnes in 1874 expressed surprise at Mill's recantation, because in his view Mill was mistaken in ascribing to himself the notion of a predetermined wages bill:

> The law of the supply of labor is no longer called in question; but several able writers have within a few years, in dissertations directed against what is known as the 'Wages-fund' doctrine, challenged the view hitherto received as to the law of its demand. Foremost among these have been Mr Thornton; ... nor is it possible to deny the ability and skill with which the assault has been conducted, when we find that he can boast, as among the first-fruits of his argument, no less a result than the conversion of Mr Mill. . . .
>
> I must own myself unconvinced by Mr Thornton's reasonings, strengthened and reinforced though these have been by the powerful comments of Mr Mill. Not indeed that I am prepared to defend all that has been written on what, for convenience, I may call the orthodox side of this question, but I believe the view maintained by those who have written on that side, and preeminently the view maintained by Mr Mill himself – taking it as set forth in his original work, not as explained in his retraction – to be substantially sound, though needing, as it seems to me, at once fuller development and more accurate determination than it has yet received.
>
> (Cairnes 1874: 157–8)

Yet in a letter to Mill (dated 23 May 1869) Cairnes had praised the review article: 'All that you have said on the subject of the wages-fund seems to me excellent. The conception, as now delineated, is, so far as I can see, invulnerable; while it retains all that is required to serve as a basis for a theory of wages' (quoted in O'Brien 1943: 283). Needless to say, Mill was delighted: 'You may imagine how gratifying it is to me that you give so complete an adhesion to the view I take of the wages fund' (23 June 1869, in O'Brien 1943: 284).

At some point in time after May 1869, Cairnes clearly had second thoughts. If these doubts were expressed to Mill we might better appreciate Mill's unwillingness to incorporate his new position on the wages-fund theory into the seventh edition of 1871; he too might have been having second thoughts:

there has been some instructive discussion [since the sixth edition] on the theory of Demand and Supply, and on the influence of Strikes and Trades Unions on wages, by which additional light has been thrown on these subjects; but the results, in the author's opinion, are not yet ripe for incorporation in a general treatise on Political Economy.

(Mill 1965: xciv)

A reading of the manuscript of Mill letters for forthcoming issues of the *Collected Works* does not bring to light any correspondence between Mill and Cairnes on the wages-fund issue (at least from Mill's side) after the letter of 23 June 1869, although it seems from the correspondence that the two probably met in London in July 1870.

8 Mill's analysis of increased investment accompanied by a rising population is incomplete. Resources hitherto producing luxury goods will now produce wages-goods for a larger population, but the state of affairs which exists when the increased labour force is in fact in operation is scarcely discussed beyond the statement that *aggregate* output will increase and real wages per head remain unchanged. That the additional labour force requires the support of more fixed capital is not *explicitly* repeated. In particular, Mill failed to note that, on the assumption of fixed coefficients, in order for the real wage rate to remain constant it is necessary for the supply of capital to rise *more* rapidly than the working population, since part of the net capital outlays takes the form of inputs other than labour.

9 Precisely the same analysis is followed in a discussion of the *speed of recovery from war damage*. A given working population requires the support of a certain fixed capital complex. If the necessary prerequisites are undamaged then employment will be unaffected; even though aggregate wages may be reduced, the economy is capable of the same industrial performance (Mill 1965: 75).

Discussions of *cyclical fluctuations* are rare in the classical literature. In one passage, however, Mill referred to the possibility that fluctuations in final demand may affect the volume of employment:

when there is what is called a stagnation . . . then workpeople are dismissed, and those who are retained must submit to a reduction of wages: though in these cases there is neither more nor less capital than before. . . . If we suppose, what in strictness is not absolutely impossible, that one of these fits of briskness or of stagnation should affect all occupations at the same time, wages altogether might undergo a rise or a fall. These, however, are but temporary fluctuations: the capital now lying idle will next year be in active employment.

(338–9)

What is particularly significant is the admission that during a depression, when capital has been temporarily withdrawn from the production process, not only will wages be low but unemployment will be created. It is not certain that the 'dismissal' of workpeople (as well as the reduction in wages) was recognised at the aggregate level of analysis. It is possible that only the wage reduction was admitted to be possible when the economy as a whole is considered. If unemployment is indeed recognised at the macroeconomic level then much light is thrown on the present investigation. For according to the simple wages-fund theory, flexible wages ensure full employment. It is true that the re-establishment of equilibrium, following a downward shift in the demand curve for labour, may take time, and during the interval some unemployment must persist. But in the present passage, Mill does not appear to have in mind the period of readjustment. Full employment apparently is only restored upon the recovery of final demand and the consequent full utilisation of the available capital stock. Such recognition of cyclical unemployment would be more consistent with an approach which takes account of non-labour inputs. For if fixed capital should be withdrawn from activity during the crisis, it may be true, assuming input complementarity, that wage flexibility cannot assure full employment.

The discussion of *technical change* by Mill (93ff) is *consistent* with the 'Cairnes-type' analysis (cf. Cairnes 1874: 180), but it is not certain that Mill here had in mind this version of the wages-fund theory, rather than the *ex ante* version.

10   Consideration of the section on wages in James Mill (1965 [1844]: 40ff) will show that it is by no means certain that the *ex ante* wages-fund theory – involving a predetermined wages fund – was invariably in mind. There is much to suggest that James Mill too was groping towards a Torrens–Cairnes-type version of the theory, where the wage rate is not obtained simply by dividing a given wages bill by the working population.

11   See in particular Mill 1965: 337–8, 356. That Mill's concern, in stating that the average wage rate is determined by the ratio of 'capital' to 'population', extended beyond the issue of employment in the industrial sector, was in fact stated clearly in a revealing footnote attached to the 1848 edition of the *Principles*:

> Although, in this place, where the subject under discussion is the causes and remedies of low wages, the question of population is treated chiefly as a labourer's question, the principle contended for includes not only the labouring classes, but all persons, except the few who being able to give to their offspring the means of independent support during the whole of life, do not leave them to swell the competition for employment.
>
> (372n; see also 419n)

Professor J. M. Robson has pointed out to the present writer that this is the one passage of the manuscript which *may* be in Harriet Taylor's hand.

12   It may be noted that as a result of criticism by Thornton on similar grounds many years earlier, Mill had altered, in his third edition (1852), the analysis of the determination of equilibrium in international exchange to meet the objection 'that several different rates of international value may all equally fulfil the conditions of this law' (Mill 1965: 608).

13   The particular formulation under attack was that by H. Fawcett (1865: 120), quoted in Thornton 1869: 84n: 'The circulating capital of a country is its wages fund. Hence, if we desire to calculate the average money wages received by each labourer, we have simply to divide the amount of capital by the number of the labouring population.'

14   Also 1867: 564. Thornton does not invariably assume a completely inelastic demand curve. Some examples he considers imply some response to wage-rate changes. It will be noted that in this passage it is implied that a determinate maximum exists to the wages bill.

15   But see note 19 below. Thornton was obsessed with the view that demand and supply schedules of all kinds – in commodity markets, in international trade, in the labour market – are of zero elasticity or portray sharp discontinuities. This was almost a matter of principle with him, and there was inadequate attention paid to the logic for such characteristics in *specific* cases.

16   Earlier, Mill had stated even more carefully: 'it is the next thing to impossible that more of the commodity should not be asked for at every reduction of price'

(1869: 509). This conclusion was applied specifically to cases of large markets where large numbers of buyers are involved.

17   This is evident from Mill's observation, just referred to, that 'consumers desire more of an article, or fresh consumers are called forth, when the price has fallen: but the employer does not buy labour for the pleasure of consuming it; he buys it that he may profit from its productive powers'. The fact is that the employer of service labour is indeed involved in purchases for final consumption.

18   Cairnes replied by repeating an earlier comment: 'a man's comparative desire for two commodities is not affected by their comparative prices', and he added: 'The animal propensity towards beer and tobacco in certain proportions to each other depends on physical conditions' (in O'Brien 1943: 281). See also Mill 1965: Appendix H, 1089–90. Cairnes clearly takes the same position in the theory of consumption (with regard to the absence of substitutability) as in the theory of production.

The debate arose out of Cairnes's critique of Mill's section on 'the effects produced on international exchange by duties on exports and on imports' (Mill 1965: 850ff). See Cairnes, *Notes on the Principles of Political Economy*, in Mill 1965: Appendix H, 1052–5.

The formulation of the issue between Cairnes and Mill – in modern terms – is such that the 'income effect' of a price change has been removed, leaving for investigation *solely* the effects on the pattern of choice between two commodities generated by a 'twist' of the budget line. Mill's understanding of the 'substitution effect' in consumption may be added to Stigler's list of original contributions by Mill to value theory: cf. Stigler 1955 (reprinted in Stigler 1965: 1–15).

In the preface to the sixth edition of the *Principles*, Mill refers to the introduction of new matter and minor improvements due to suggestions and criticisms by Cairnes (xciv), but he does not mention the discussion regarding the effects on demand of relative price changes in the preface, or in the text upon which Cairnes had commented.

19   There are, however, some difficulties presented by the interpretation of Mill's position offered here. For example, there is a reference to the possibility that even in the long run a wage reduction may be ineffective in raising the demand for labour: 'Does the employer require more labour, or do *fresh employers of labour* make their appearance, merely because it can be bought cheaper?' (quoted above, p. 25). Second, the rationale for Mill's position may represent no more than the naive view expressed by Thornton in his second edition that where there are certain essential, once-and-for-all jobs to be done immediately, an employer will pay whatever is asked of him – within limits – but will not respond to wage reductions. We shall outline in this note the amplification by Thornton of the main objections to the wages-fund theory which followed Mill's review of 1869. All references are to *On Labour*, second edition (London, 1870).

Thornton first denied the relevance of a firm's budget constraint: 'But is there any law fixing the amount of his [the employer's] domestic expenditure, and thereby fixing likewise the balance available for his industrial operations?' (84). Second, assuming the budget for industrial operations is given, it is impossible to forecast how much of it is 'available' for wage payments:

does he or can he determine beforehand how much shall be laid out on buildings, how much on materials, how much on labour? May not his outlay on repairs be unexpectedly increased by fire or by other accident? will not his outlay on materials vary with their dearness or cheapness, or with the varying demand for the finished article? and must not the amount available for wages vary accordingly?

(84)

Third, even if the amount available for wage payments is known, this sum constitutes the maximum that the employer can spend; as the wage rate declines he would spend a declining fraction of this available sum, since *his concern is to acquire the services of a certain quantity of labour*:

And even ... if he did know to a farthing how much he would be able to spend on labour, would he be bound to spend the utmost he could afford to spend? If he could get as much labour as he wanted at a cheap rate, would he voluntarily pay as much for it as he would be compelled to pay if it were dearer?

(84)

We admit that if an employer were to confine his domestic expenditure within the very narrowest bounds, were to spend on his plant only just so much as was necessary to keep it in working order, and were to purchase only just so much raw material as it was necessary for him to work up in order to go on working remuneratively, the remainder of his capital would represent both the utmost amount at his disposal for the payment of wages, and also an amount which he both could afford to spend, and would actually spend on wages, rather than not get the quantity of labour he required. What we deny is simply that, though an employer would spend this utmost amount on wages if he could not help himself, he would not if he could. We venture to think that, though he would pay the very highest price he could afford for labour if he could not get it cheaper, he would get it cheaper if he could. The believers in the wages-fund, on the other hand, insist that whether labour be cheap or dear the whole body of employers always spend upon labour the utmost amount they can afford to spend.

(86)

Finally, Thornton concluded that in all cases where both the demand and the supply curves are completely inelastic, traditional competitive equilibrium analysis must break down:

The quantity of labour which an employer needs, depends upon the work he wants to have done. If there are certain jobs which it is essential to him to get finished within a certain time, he will, if labour be dear, consent to pay pretty high for the quantity needed to complete the jobs within the time. But *he will not, merely because labour happens to be cheap instead of dear, hire more than that quantity. ... Whenever, as in the case of labour, demand does not increase with cheapness, demand, as Mr Mill has further pointed out, may be perfectly equalized with supply at many different prices.* If all the employers get all the labour they require, and if all the seekers for employment succeed in getting hired, there is a complete equation of supply and demand, whether the rate of hire be 6d. or 6s. *But when an employer's demand for labour is fully supplied, he can have no demand left requiring to be supplied ... he will not, merely because that rate happens to be a low one, either hire additional labour for which he has no employment, or voluntarily raise the rate,* instead of retaining the difference for himself. ... But if no one employer will do this, how can the whole body of employers do it? and if they do not, how can the same amount be spent upon labour, whether labour be cheap or dear? and how, again, unless this be done, can there be a sum unconditionally devoted to the payment of wages?

(Thornton 1870: 87–8, emphasis added)

Thornton implies in the last passage that the conclusion was first pointed out by Mill. As we have pointed out in the text, however, it was Mill who had derived it from Thornton's first edition. Doubtless Thornton desired to use the authority of Mill's name to strengthen his case.

20   One important analytical topic has been neglected in this paper, namely technological relationships in agriculture. To the extent that the ratio of labour to land was considered to be variable even in the short run, the equilibrium might again be saved. But labour and capital were usually assumed to be used in combined doses on land so that the problems introduced by any fixity of capital stocks would still remain. A full treatment of the classical approach to technology requires complete investigation of the issue.

21   This possibility assumes either that fixed capital is homogeneous and can be used in any industry, or alternatively, that fixed capital can be moved between industries by being worn out and rebuilt. But in the latter and more realistic case, there is little justification for also assuming that its aggregate quantity is constant. However, the objective in the present section is to isolate, for analytical purposes, the issue of inter-industry differences in technical coefficients. Recognition of such differences would in effect contribute to the development of any full (long-run) equilibrium solution in the labour market.

22   We find Cairnes struggling to avoid the issue at one point where he attempts to play down the negative effect on aggregate wage income of increases in the working population which follow from his model (see above, p. 17n4):

This occurs, I say, where labor is of a kind to be employed in conjunction with fixed capital and raw material; and, it may be added, that the effect would only assume sensible dimensions where those agencies constituted a substantial proportion of the whole capital invested. Indeed it would be a mistake to regard this particular condition – the supply of labor considered as a cause affecting, not the rate of wages, but the aggregate Wages-fund – as under any circumstances more than a subordinate and modifying influence in the case. The point is one of theoretic rather than of practical importance, and, in considering the variations of the Wages-fund, it will rarely be necessary to take account of more than the two main determining conditions of that phenomenon – the growth or decline of capital, and the nature of the prevailing industries.

(Cairnes 1874: 174)

It would appear from this passage that at times Cairnes did not fully appreciate his own argument. The wages fund in Cairnes's model is not a datum of the system; it is derived as the equilibrium solution of a demand-supply analysis. Without the 'supply' schedule (namely the working population) the wages fund cannot be determined. It thus seems to be the case that Cairnes remained – perhaps unconsciously – under the influence of the 'unsophisticated' version of the wages-fund theory, wherein the 'wages fund' constitutes a 'demand' for labour given independently of labour supply.

23   See Mill 1965: Appendix H, 1044–5 for Cairnes's influence on Mill.

24   For one to maintain either version of the wages-fund theory and at the same time to insist that factor proportions differ between industries, means that conflicting sets of assumptions are being made at one and the same time. This

is precisely the charge which may be directed against James Mill, and, to a lesser extent, McCulloch.

In McCulloch's discussion of the proposition that 'the demand for commodities is not the demand for labour' (1965 [1864]: 355–9), or to use his own terminology, that there exists a 'difference in their influence over wages between a demand for labour and for its products', we find an explicit statement of the significance for labour demand of differing input ratios between industries:

> But the influence of an increased demand for commodities, or for the produce of labour, is by no means identical with an increased demand for labour, and would depend partly on whether the commodity was wholly or in part the produce of labour or of machinery, and partly on its being suited or unsuited to the employment and subsistence of work people.
>
> (356)

But the first issue of differing coefficients between products is immediately dismissed as being 'of little importance; for, capital being itself the result of antecedent labour, whatever is expended upon it really goes to replace labour, and in the end is identical in its effects with a direct expenditure upon the latter' (356).

James Mill similarly argued that

> an increase of demand for labour can arise from two causes only; either from an increase of capital, the fund destined for the employment of labour; or a difference in the proportions between the demand for the produce of fixed capital and that of immediate labour.
>
> (1965 [1844]: 259–60)

'The first of these causes', he went on, 'needs no illustration'; but much attention was devoted to changes in the demand for labour resulting from taxation which diverts purchasing power to the government. If the government's expenditure by chance should involve commodities with a higher labour content than the commodities otherwise purchased, 'there would so far be an increase of demand for labour' (265). But whether or not there will be an effect on labour demand is, as Mill puts it, an 'extraneous circumstance', since anything is possible depending upon the patterns of expenditures actually involved. Yet the fact is that Mill recognised that *given* aggregate capital, the distribution of demand between products will be one determinant of the demand for labour. It is extraordinary that Mill failed to raise this issue in the section of his chapter on distribution devoted to wages, and more specifically that he failed to realise that the assumption rendered the wages-fund theory untenable.

References

Cairnes, J. E. (1874) *Some Leading Principles of Political Economy*, London and New York: Macmillan.

Dobb, M. H. (1940) *Political Economy and Capitalism*, revised edn, London: Routledge and Kegan Paul.

Fawcett, Henry (1865) *The Economic Position of the British Labourer*, London: Macmillan.

Hutchison, T. W. (1953) *A Review of Economic Doctrine, 1870–1929*, Oxford: Clarendon Press.

McCulloch, J. R. (1965) [1864] *Principles of Political Economy*, 5th edn, Edinburgh, 1864; New York: Augustus M. Kelley.

Marshall, Alfred (1920) *Principles of Economics*, 8th edn, London: Macmillan.

Mill, James (1965) [1844] *Elements of Political Economy*, 3rd edn, London, 1844; New York: Augustus M. Kelley.

Mill, J. S. (1869) 'Thornton on labour and its claims', Part I, *Fortnightly Review*, May: 505–18.

——(1965) [1848–71] *Collected Works of John Stuart Mill*, II and III, *Principles of Political Economy*, Toronto: University of Toronto Press.

O'Brien, George (1943) 'J. S. Mill and J. E. Cairnes', *Economica*, 10, November: 273–85.

Pasinetti, L. (1960) 'A mathematical formulation of the Ricardian system', *Review of Economic Studies*, 27, February.

Schumpeter, Joseph A. (1954) *History of Economic Analysis*, New York: Oxford University Press.

Sidgwick, Henry (1883) *The Principles of Political Economy*, London: Macmillan.

Stephen, Leslie (1900) *The English Utilitarians*, vol. III, London: Duckworth.

Stigler, George J. (1941) *Production and Distribution Theories*, New York: Macmillan.

——(1947) 'Stuart Wood and the marginal productivity theory', *Quarterly Journal of Economics*, 61, August: 640–9, reprinted in Stigler 1965: 287ff.

——(1955) 'The nature and role of originality in scientific progress', *Economica*, 22 (November), reprinted in Stigler 1965: 1–15.

——(1965) *Essays on the History of Economics*, Chicago: University of Chicago Press.

Thornton, W. T. (1867) 'What determines the price of labour, or the rate of wages?', *Fortnightly Review*, May: 551–66.

——(1869) *On Labour*, 1st edn, London: Macmillan.

——(1870) *On Labour*, 2nd edn, London: Macmillan.

Torrens, Robert (1965) [1821] *An Essay on the Production of Wealth*, London, 1821; New York: Augustus M. Kelley.

——(1834) *On Wages and Combination*, London: Longman, Rees, Orme, Brown, Green & Longman.

——(1835) *Colonisation of South Australia*, London: Longman, Rees, Orme, Brown, Green & Longman.

Wood, Stuart (1890) 'A critique of wages theories', *Annals of the American Academy of Political and Social Science*, I, 426–61.

Chapter 3

Ricardianism, J. S. Mill and the neo-classical challenge

It was J. A. Schumpeter's firm conviction that J. S. Mill was not really a Ricardian economist and must be excluded from that group which constitutes Ricardo's 'school', namely James Mill, McCulloch and De Quincey (Schumpeter 1954: 476). 'From Marshall's *Principles*', he wrote, 'Ricardianism can be removed without being missed at all. From Mill's *Principles*, it could be dropped without being missed very greatly' (529). This evaluation, although expressed with particular insistence by Schumpeter, is considerably more widespread than is commonly believed, and is characteristic of Marxist interpreters. It is my intention to subject the argument to a detailed analysis. Clearly, much depends upon what is meant by 'Ricardianism', and I shall pay particular attention to this matter to avoid a mere terminological debate. I shall try to show that, in fact, Ricardo's economics, in the strict sense adopted by Schumpeter, was accepted by Mill and indeed was formulated vigorously not only in the *Essays on Some Unsettled Questions* and the *Principles*, but also in the celebrated *Fortnightly Review* article (1869) in which Mill (apparently) abandoned the wages-fund theory.

The new political economy

Let me say at the outset that I do not take issue with Schumpeter's account of the content of Ricardo's economics insofar as he emphasises the key role played by the so-called absolute standard of value – a commodity produced by a constant quantity of labour – in the derivation of the proposition that profits depend upon wages, both conceived as proportionate shares in an output of constant value (see in particular Schumpeter 1954: 473, 490, 558f, 569, 590f, 653). But to clear the ground I should like to formulate more explicitly my own conception of the core of Ricardian economics.

Ricardo, I believe, was concerned basically with the *rate of return on capital* as distinct from the aggregate shares strictly speaking, although the rate of return was envisaged as a function of the share of profits in net output minus rent. He identified an increase in wages in terms of his 'gold' measure of value – which reduces to a labour-embodied unit – with an increase in the proportionate share of wages in the output to be divided between labourers and capitalists. But Schumpeter, who based himself upon Cannan's authority, is I believe wrong in stating that the identification lacks generality since all depends upon a presumed constancy of *aggregate* value, that is, of the total labour force (Schumpeter 1954: 592). Ricardo's attention in the first instance was not, in fact, upon the labour value of aggregate wages and output, but rather upon that of *per capita* wages and output; an increase in per capita 'gold' wages necessarily implies an increase in the share of wages in per capita output, which is of constant 'value' whatever may happen to total value.[1] The entire Ricardian scheme is thus designed to relate the rate of return on capital to changes in the value of wages per capita.

Profits appear as a 'residual' income in the Ricardian scheme – the 'leavings of wages' as one contemporary put it – and this is reflected in Ricardo's standard turn of phrase to the effect that 'profits depend on wages' rather than the reverse. Yet at the same time Ricardo recognised that the profit rate acts upon the rate of savings not only by way of the income effect ('the ability to accumulate') but also by way of the substitution effect ('the motive to accumulate'). Accordingly, labour demand and the wage rate and in turn the growth rate of population are affected by alterations in the rate of profit. Viewed from this perspective, profits appear to be a residual in nothing more than a formal sense – in the sense that the sole contractual payment in the system is that made to labour, and not in the substantive sense of a 'rent' or 'surplus value'. That Ricardo utilised a labour-embodied accounting unit and did not provide a label for the relationship between savings decisions and the rate of interest (such as that of 'abstinence') should not be allowed to detract from his recognition of such a relationship.

It was Ricardo's position that assuming an unchanged cost of production of the monetary metal, wage-rate increases are non-inflationary (at most generating an alteration in relative prices) and must reduce the rate of return. (The issue, it will be recalled, was formulated initially by Ricardo as a direct challenge to received doctrine based upon Adam Smith's analysis whereby wage-rate increases are passed on by capitalists in the form of higher prices and lower rents.) But his conclusion that wage-rate increases are non-inflationary is maintained quite generally – that is to say, it is applied to the 'real world' where the conditions required of the theoretical medium are not fulfilled.[2] (For example, it is applied to a world where a paper currency circulates in which a cost of production theory is inapplicable.) Ricardo's model (or engine of analysis) was designed to throw light on the underlying processes, which are not always apparent to the naked eye, whereby the rate of return is governed by the proportion of the workday devoted to the production of wage goods.

It is this doctrine which represents the 'New Political Economy', a term coined by contemporaries to describe Ricardo's particular contribution and his divergence from Smith. I exclude both Say's Law and the Comparative-

Cost doctrine quite deliberately as secondary to Ricardo's primary concern, which was to demonstrate that nothing but an alteration in the real cost of producing wage goods can affect the rate of return.[3] (In any event both were acceptable to neo-classical writers so that they scarcely represent doctrines which are peculiarly Ricardian.) I will have something to say, subsequently, about the Ricardian theory of employment capacity, or his version of the wages-fund theory. But this analysis is not so much of a breakaway from the Smithian position; it is rather an important extension. This is also perhaps an opportune moment to remark that the 'four fundamental propositions on capital' usually attributed to Mill are in fact part and parcel of the Ricardian analysis.[4]

There exists considerable accord amongst Marxist and non-Marxist historians regarding the fate of 'Ricardianism', despite apparent differences.[5] For it is generally agreed that Ricardian economics in the narrow and specific sense of the term which I outlined above – the use of a special theory of value (involving an absolute standard) in the derivation of the inverse relation between proportionate wages and proportionate profits – came to a very early end, while Ricardian economics in a broad sense had a pervasive influence.[6] It is this consensus that I wish to challenge. I shall try to justify the contention, with particular reference to J. S. Mill,[7] that Ricardianism in the strict and narrow sense lived on to a ripe old age.

Mill on value and distribution

Much of Schumpeter's case for the early demise of Ricardianism is based upon the appearance and supposed influence of Samuel Bailey's *Critical Dissertation* on value (1825): 'Bailey', we read,

> attacked the Ricardo–[James] Mill–McCulloch analysis on a broad front and with complete success. His *Dissertation*, which said, as far as fundamentals are concerned, practically all that can be said, must rank among the masterpieces of criticism in our field, and it should suffice to secure to its author a place in or near the front rank in the history of scientific economics.
>
> (Schumpeter 1954: 486)

And it is precisely because J. S. Mill, in Schumpeter's view, rejected on Bailey's grounds the conception of a measure of absolute value that he must be excluded from Ricardo's school. The value that really mattered to him, runs the contention, was *relative price*, and since value was a ratio, all values could not vary simultaneously. Similarly, there was no such thing as 'the total value of all the services of wealth (or of all wealth) taken as a whole', in contrast to the position adopted by Ricardo – and Marx (589). Indeed, 'the energy with which Mill insisted on the relative character of [exchange value] completely annihilated Ricardo's Real Value and reduced other Ricardianism to insipid innocuousness' (603). Precisely the same view of Mill's position is adopted by Professor Blaug:

> Mill does not derive the theorem about profits and wages, as Ricardo has done, from the concept of an invariable measure of value. Even the standard Ricardian thesis that 'general wages, whether high or low, do not affect values' is entirely divorced from the notion that value is to be measured by an invariant standard.... There is no mention in Mill's discussion ... of the important role assigned to the invariable measure of value in Ricardo's system.
>
> (Blaug 1958: 172–3)[8]

The issue can best be evaluated by consideration of the evolution of Mill's position from the youthful review of Malthus' objections to the so-called 'New School' (1825) and the paper 'On profits and interest' (1829), to the *Principles*, and finally to the famous *Fortnightly Review* article of 1869.

If Mill's position as stated in his first major paper were his final word, there would be little doubt of the justice of the view according to which Mill rejected the fundamental Ricardian position. For Mill neglected the analysis of deviations of price from labour value which served as a preliminary step in the derivation of the inverse profit-wage relationship (Mill [1825], *CW*, IV: 30ff). However, in the essay 'On profits and interest' the perspective is entirely altered, and Mill presents favourably the Ricardian position, accepting it with the 'slight modification' that the rate of profit is related not to the value of per capita wages – the direct and indirect labour embodied in the wage bill – but to the 'cost of wages' which includes the profit of the wage-goods producer (*CW*, IV: 293ff). But even this modification is withdrawn in Book II of the *Principles*, where Mill adopts the proposition that the profit rate varies inversely with the fraction of a person's labour time devoted to the production of their wages.[9]

We may take the matter a step further. The analysis of profits as presented in his Book II was, Mill observed, correct but nevertheless provisional, for a complete treatment required a discussion of value:

> It will come out in greater fulness and force when, having taken into consideration the theory of Value and Price, we shall be enabled to exhibit the law of profits in the concrete – in the complex entanglement of circumstances in which it actually works.
>
> (*CW*, II: 415)

A preliminary word is in order regarding Mill's position on the conception of absolute value.

Throughout the *Principles*, indeed in his first major article of 1825 mentioned above, Mill insisted upon the *relativity* of exchange value, and, like Bailey, rejected the notion of a general alteration in exchange values as logically incomprehensible. But he did of course allow for a general change in *prices*, which he pointed out 'is merely tantamount to an alteration in the value of money' (*CW*, III: 459; cf. 479). Mill, in the Ricardian manner, decided to use as *numeraire* a commodity money 'with the proviso that money itself do not vary in its general purchasing power, but that the prices of all things, other than that which we happen to be considering, remain unaltered' (458). The constancy of purchasing power is the consequence of a presumed constant cost of producing the monetary metal.

In the light of this procedure, we may perhaps better appreciate Mill's formal discussion in the chapter 'Of a measure of value' (III: xv). Here he rejects on Bailey's grounds the notion of a measure of exchange value as a conceptual impossibility, but *accepts* that of a measure of cost of production. The conditions for the measure are stated as follows:

> [Economists] have imagined a commodity invariably produced by the same quantity of labour; to which supposition it is necessary to add, that the fixed capital employed in the production must bear always the same proportion to the wages of the immediate labour, and must be always of the same durability: in short, the same capital must be advanced for the same length of time, so that the element of value which consists of profits, as well as that which consists of wages, may be unchangeable.
> (Mill, *CW*, III: 579)[10]

Now such a measure of cost, Mill insists, 'though perfectly conceivable, can no more exist in fact, than a measure of exchangeable value' because of the likelihood of changes in production cost for any commodity chosen. Nevertheless, gold and silver 'are the least variable' and, if used, the results obtained must simply be 'corrected by the best allowance we can make for the intermediate changes in the cost of the production itself'. This is far from an out-of-hand rejection of the measure of absolute value, and in fact represents precisely the position adopted by Ricardo.

The full analysis of the effects of wage-rate changes is undertaken in the important chapter 'Distribution, as affected by exchange' (III: xxvi). Now, much is made by commentators of Mill's treatment of production, distribution and exchange in three consecutive books, as indicative of a failure, characteristic of classicism, to envisage any relation between value theory and distribution. This is clearly a misunderstanding. The early discussion of distribution was provisional only; in the chapter at hand the order is reversed, and the problem of distribution is analysed in light of the theory of exchange value.

When the distribution of national income occurs via the mechanism of exchange and money, Mill argues, the 'law of wages' remains unchanged insofar as the determination of commodity wages is concerned, for this depends upon 'the ratio of population and capital' (695). As Mill has already explained, from the perspective of the employer it is not merely *commodity* wages that are relevant, but the 'cost of labour'; the new point is that under certain circumstances this cost will be reflected accurately by the *money* wages paid. This situation will obtain when money represents 'an invariable standard':

> Wages in the second sense, we may be permitted to call, for the present, money wages; assuming, as it is allowable to do, that money remains for the time an invariable standard, no alteration taking place in the conditions under which the circulating medium itself is produced or obtained. If money itself undergoes no variation in cost, the money price of labour is an exact measure of the Cost of Labour, and may be made use of as a convenient symbol to express it.
>
> (Mill, *CW*, III: 696)

Assuming money to be such an invariable measure, the rate of money wages will depend upon the commodity wage and the production costs, and accordingly the money prices of wage goods, particularly agricultural produce, which in turn is dependent upon 'the productiveness of the least fertile land, or least productive agricultural capital' (697). It is upon the 'cost of labour' that the rate of profit depends, as he had concluded earlier in Book II of the *Principles*, but the cost of labour is now identified with 'money' wages.[11]

In the present context Mill thus defines an inverse relation between the profit rate and the cost of labour, the latter identified with the money wage rate. He does not bother to equate the cost of labour, in contrast to his practice in Book II of the *Principles*, with the proportionate share of the labourer in per capita output. But there is no reason to believe that he no longer maintained this relation.[12] In effect, Mill has adopted the Ricardian 'proportions-measuring' money in terms of which a rise of wages implies an increased share of the labourer in the 'value' of his output and a reduced profit share and rate of return.[13]

The full analysis of the effects of 'money' wage increases upon profits – money presumed to be 'invariable' – involves a demonstration that such increases cannot be passed on in the form of higher commodity prices (479–80, 692, 698–9). The entire argument is beautifully summarised by Mill in a passage which emphasises that the wage increase which reduces profits is one involving a greater labour embodiment in wage goods, or a rise in labour's *proportionate* share:

> If the labourers really get more, that is, get the produce of more labour, a smaller percentage must remain for profit. From this Law of Distribution, resting as it does on a law of arithmetic, there is no escape. The mechanism of Exchange and Price may hide it from us, but is quite powerless to alter it.
>
> (Mill, *CW*, III: 479–80)

In his chapter on 'Distribution, as affected by exchange' Mill simply makes it clear that a measure of proportionate wages is provided by money wages, but only if money satisfies the conditions required of a stable absolute measure.

Mill on wages and prices

The theme which we have isolated – the effect of a wage-rate change upon the rate of return – is obviously not one introduced by Mill as a casual aside. It reappears throughout the *Principles*, and clearly the analysis of the issue was of the first importance to him in light of the common opinion that wage-rate increases can be passed on to consumers. The sharp distinction between Ricardo's position and that of Smith is kept to the fore as, for example, in Mill's criticism of Smith's analysis of the 'tendency of profits to a minimum' in terms of the competition of capital (733).[14] Moreover, in dealing with the contention that an increase in wages generates higher commodity prices, Mill, for the edition of 1871, replaced the introductory phrase 'it used formerly to be said' by 'it is not infrequently said', implying that the analysis remained of immediate relevance. But the clearest indication of the critical nature of the matter at hand appears in a letter to Cairnes some six months before Mill's death, wherein he expressed the inverse relation between wages and profits in terms more forceful than ever before:

> You must have been struck as I have been, by the thoroughly confused and erroneous ideas respecting the relation of wages to price, which have shewn themselves to be almost universal in the discussions about the recent strikes. The notion that a general rise of wages must produce a general rise of prices, is preached universally not only by the newspapers but by political economists, as a certain and admitted economical truth; and political economy has to bear the responsibility of a self-contradicting absurdity which it is one of the achievements of political economy to have exploded. It provokes one to see such ignorance of political economy in the whole body of its self-selected teachers. The Times joins in the chorus.... Certainly no one who knows, even imperfectly, what the Ricardo political economy is, whether he agrees with it or not, can suppose this to be it. I hope you will come down upon it with all the weight of your clear scientific intellect, your remarkable power of exposition, and the authority of your name as a political economist.
>
> (letter of 4 October 1872, in Mill, *CW*, XVII: 1909–10)[15]

The importance of the issue cannot be exaggerated, particularly in light of the contemporary buoyancy of trade-union activity.[16]

I shall now show that for Mill, as for Ricardo, the substantive prediction – that an increase of 'real' wages (i.e. of labour embodied in wages) is necessarily accompanied by an inverse movement in the rate of return – holds good quite generally, irrespective, that is to say, of the satisfaction by the medium of exchange of the necessary properties required to guarantee its theoretical suitability as invariable standard.

In the first place, Mill makes it clear that even if prices were to rise following an increase of wages, producers would not benefit therefrom, since all their expenses rise:

> It must be remembered too that general high prices, even supposing them to exist, can be of no use to a producer or dealer, considered as such; for if they increase his money returns, they increase in the same degree all his expenses.
>
> (Mill, *CW*, III: 479)

Ricardo's identical rendition will be recalled:

> If the prices of commodities were permanently raised by high wages, the proposition would not be less true, which asserts that high wages invariably affect the employers of labour, by depriving them of a portion of their real profits. . . . [The employer] would be in no better situation if his money profits had been really diminished in amount, and everything had remained at its former price.
>
> (Ricardo 1951, I: 126–7)

Second, Mill relies on the gold-standard mechanism involving the quantity theory to assure the result that wage increases are non-inflationary. Ricardo's rendition may first be noted:

> All commodities cannot rise at the same time without an addition to the quantity of money. This addition could not be obtained at home . . . nor could it be imported from abroad. To purchase any additional quantity of gold from abroad, commodities at home must be cheap, not dear. The importation of gold, and a rise in the price of all home-made commodities with which gold is purchased or paid for, are effects absolutely incompatible.
>
> (Ricardo 1951, I: 105)

I would like to demonstrate Mill's position regarding the latter mechanism by reference to his discussion of the inverse relation between wages and profits as it appears in his famous review article [1869] of W. T. Thornton's work, *On Labour* (*CW*, V: 631ff). While Mill here refuted the wages-fund theory, for which of course the review is so well known, he in no way abandoned the basic Ricardian theorem on distribution. Consider, then, the following comment upon Thornton's analysis of the potential efficacy of trade-union activity, an analysis that Mill in general adopted:

> [There] is a view of the question, not overlooked by the author, but

hardly, perhaps, made sufficiently prominent by him. From the necessity of the case, the only fund out of which an increase of wages can possibly be obtained by the labouring classes considered as a whole, is profits. This is contrary to the common opinion, both of the general public and of the workmen themselves, who think that there is a second source from which it is possible for the augmentation to come, namely, prices. The employer, they think, can, if foreign or other competition will let him, indemnify himself for the additional wages demanded of him, by charging an increased price to the consumer. And this may certainly happen in single trades. . . . But though a rise of wages in a given trade may be compensated to the masters by a rise of the price of their commodity, a rise of general wages cannot be compensated to employers by a general rise of prices. This distinction is never understood by those who have not considered the subject, but there are few truths more obvious to all who have.

(Mill, CW, V: 660–1)[17]

The reasons given by Mill for the inability of employers to pass on wage increases include the necessity for an increase in the money supply,[18] which would not, under the circumstances supposed, be forthcoming:

There cannot be a general rise of prices unless there is more money expended. But the rise of wages does not cause more money to be expended. It takes from the incomes of the masters and adds to those of the workmen; the former have less to spend, the latter have more; but the general sum of the money incomes of the community remains what it was, and it is upon that sum that money prices depend. There cannot be more money expended on everything, when there is not more money to be expended altogether. In the second place, even if there did happen a rise of all prices, the only effect would be that money, having become of less value in the particular country, while it remained of its former value everywhere else, would be exported until prices were brought down to nearly or quite their former level. But thirdly: even on the impossible supposition that the rise of prices could be kept up, yet, being general, it would not compensate the employer; for though his money returns would be greater, his outgoings (except the fixed payments to those to whom he is in debt) would be increased in the same proportion. Finally, if when wages rose all prices rose in the same ratio, the labourers would be no better off with high wages than with low; their wages would not command more of any article of consumption; a real rise of wages, therefore, would be an impossibility.

(Mill, CW, V: 661)

Precisely the same position was reiterated by Mill in correspondence after the appearance of the review. In June 1870 he wrote to George Adcroft:

I differ from you when you say that a general rise of wages would be of no use to the working classes because it would produce a general rise of prices. A general rise of prices, of anything like a permanent character, can only take place through a general increase of the money incomes of the purchasing community. Now a general rise of wages would not increase the aggregate money incomes, nor consequently the aggregate purchasing power of the community; it would only transfer part of that purchasing power from the employers to the labourers. Consequently a general rise of wages would not raise prices but would be taken out of the profits of the employers; always supposing that those profits were sufficient to bear the reduction.

The case is different with a rise of wages confined to a single, or a small number of employments. . . . The supply of these particular articles would fall short, their prices would rise so as to indemnify the employers for the rise of wages. But this would not happen in case of a rise of all wages, for as all capitalists would be affected nearly alike they could not as a body relieve themselves by turning their capital into another employment.

(Mill, CW, XVII: 1734–5)

The evidence presented thus far suggests a firm conviction on Mill's part of the justness of strict Ricardianism − that is to say a body of doctrine including, first, the relation between the rate of return on capital and the wage rate, identified with the often-called 'peculiar' principle of proportionate wages and profits; second, the formal derivation of the relation in terms of a money of invariable value, despite an emphasis upon the relativity of exchange value; and third, the view that the inverse relation holds good independently of the measure in that wage-rate increases can be shown to be non-inflationary.

It is this latter characteristic of Mill's work, in conjunction with a too hasty reading of the chapter formally devoted to the measure, which may be responsible for the view expressed by Blaug and Schumpeter, that, unlike Ricardo, Mill discusses the inverse relation without making use of an invariable measure. This view is misleading in two regards. First, the measure is in fact used as a conceptual device as we have seen; and second, Ricardo too maintained that the inverse relation holds in the real world independently of the measure. There is a complete identity of opinion between Mill and Ricardo on these fundamental issues. To refer to Mill's maintenance of an 'emasculated' version of Ricardo's system is surely unjustified.[19]

Mill's consistency: Ricardianism and neo-classicism

My argument thus far has been that Mill's economics retained the truly characteristic Ricardian elements. I also believe, although space limitations preclude any development of this contention, that the attack against Mill and orthodoxy in the 1860s and 1870s, including that implicit in Mill's recantation, was to a large extent misdirected and thus failed to reach the fundamental core of Ricardianism. There is a further matter, however, which remains for consideration here – that of Mill's consistency.[20]

The issue can fruitfully be envisaged from the perspective of the so-called marginal revolution. Jevons, unlike Walras, failed to develop in the *Theory of Political Economy* (1871) an alternative structure to the one he was criticising.[21] His work, he frankly informs us, without understatement, 'was never put forward as containing a systematic view of Economics' (Jevons 1924: xliii–xliv). Nevertheless, he did suggest, in the celebrated Preface to his second edition (1879), what the features of a 'true system of Economics' must be. Distribution must be envisaged as a matter of service pricing 'entirely subject to the principles of value and the laws of supply and demand' in which all prices are subject to the same rule; costs of production would reflect alternative opportunities foregone; and input prices would be 'the effect and not the cause of the value of the produce' (xlvi f).[22] Now what is quite fascinating in this account is the fact that Jevons found so much to admire in the work of the arch-villain himself. Thus he referred to J. S. Mill's own recognition of alternative cost in the case of land: 'When land capable of yielding rent in agriculture is applied to some other purpose, the rent which it would have yielded is an element in the cost of production of the commodity which it is employed to produce' (xlviii, regarding Mill's *Principles*, *CW*, III: 498). He pointed to the 'remarkable section' in which Mill 'explains that all inequalities, artificial or natural, give rise to extra gains of the nature of Rent' (li, regarding Mill, 494–6). He was equally impressed by Mill's analysis of pricing in the case of joint-production wherein, as he put it, Mill reverted 'to a law of value anterior to cost of production, and more fundamental, namely, the law of supply and demand' (197, regarding Mill, 583). Jevons might have gone further, as Professor Stigler's study of scientific originality makes clear (Stigler 1965: 6–11). I myself would add to the list Mill's recognition, in correspondence with Cairnes, of the substitution effects generated by relative price changes in consumption (see Hollander 1968: 334), and the recognition both in the *Principles* and the *Fortnightly Review* of a version of the derived-demand principle (*CW*, III: 747; V: 644).

In this context, Mill's objections to Smith's analysis of the wage structure deserves mention. Both financial and social obstacles, Mill insisted, prevented the attainment of skills by sufficiently large numbers to assure the eradication of monopoly returns in skilled trades, even in the absence of institutional constraints. The recognition that *within* the working class there were non-competing groups is the essence of the change (*CW*, II: 386–7). But Mill's objections went further. According to Smith it was to be expected that the least pleasant occupations would, *ceteris paribus*, be the highest paid. It was pointed out by Mill that, quite apart from impediments to mobility, the result envisaged presumed the (aggregate) labour market to be in equilibrium. Should unemployment exist in the labour market as a whole, it is likely that the least agreeable (and unskilled) trades would be the worst paid, since the excess supplies therein would be relatively great:

> Partly from this cause, and partly from the natural and artificial monopolies... the inequalities of wages are generally in an opposite direction to the equitable principle of compensation erroneously represented by Adam Smith as the general law of the remuneration of labour.
>
> (Mill, *CW*, II: 383)

The problem then which I wish to raise, relates to the relative status in Mill's work of the Ricardian and non-Ricardian elements. For it seems clear enough that some, at least, of the propositions I have referred to are incompatible with pure Ricardianism.[23] For example, the wage-structure analysis casts into doubt the entire conception of a *general* movement in wage rates. (It will be recalled that Ricardo commenced his value analysis with the assumption that 'the estimation in which different qualities of labour are held, comes soon to be adjusted in the market with sufficient precision for all practical purposes, and depends much on the comparative skills of the labourer, and intensity of the labour performed. *The scale when once formed, is liable to little variation*' [Ricardo 1951, I: 20].[24]) The introduction of derived demand has no place in the Ricardian scheme of things. The recognition of substitution-in-consumption, and of rent as a cost of production when land has alternative uses, are further instances. Jevons himself pointed out that Mill's generalisation of the rent conception 'when properly followed, will overthrow many of the principal doctrines of the Ricardo–Mill economics'. Jevons, however, was quite satisfied to leave the matter there, with the remark that

> those who have studied Mill's philosophic character as long and minutely as I have done, will not for a moment suppose that the occurrence of this section of Mill's book tends to establish its consistency with other positions of the same treatise.
>
> (Jevons 1924: li)[25]

Now it is not uncommon to suggest in Mill's defence that 'a textbook', such as the *Principles*, 'was not the place to rehearse technical anomalies' (Winch 1970: 29). There doubtless is something to this,[26] but I do not think it provides the whole solution. In the first place it is not clear to what extent Mill was in fact aware that certain of his propositions were problematic. And second, even if we assume that he was fully aware, it is not apparent how the inconsistencies could have been dealt with even for a technical audience. Whatever the reason, it is clear enough that Mill was much concerned to avoid even the impression that he was at any significant point diverging from Ricardo's authority.[27] His allowance that variations in the wage or profit structure will affect relative prices provides an interesting example: 'It thus appears', he wrote, 'that the maxim laid down by some of the best political economists, that wages do not enter into value, is expressed with greater latitude than the truth warrants, or than accords with their own meaning' (CW, III: 480). Now, in light of Mill's great emphasis elsewhere upon the phenomenon of non-competing groups, we might have expected that the weaknesses inherent in the concept of a general change in the level of wages would have been considered ruinous to any view that emphasises relative labour embodied as the main variable acting upon values.[28] Yet in fact Mill concludes that while 'in strictness . . . wages of labour have as much to do with value as quantity of labour' – a fact, he insists, that 'neither Ricardo nor any one else' had ever denied –

> in considering, however, the causes of *variations* in value, quantity of labour is the thing of chief importance; for when that varies, it is generally in one or a few commodities at a time, but the variations of wages (except passing fluctuations) are usually general, and have no considerable effect on value.
>
> (CW, III: 481)

Mill refused to allow his own innovation to damage the main structure.

It is frequently suggested that Mill's fidelity to Ricardo may lie in his conception of scientific development, whereby

> once humanity was purged of its prejudices, science could grow steadily through accumulation, each scientist adding a storey to the edifice initiated by his predecessors. . . . The idea that the theories of gifted economists like Ricardo could need a fundamental revision was alien to his idea of the cumulative growth of science.
>
> (Schwartz 1972: 236–7)[29]

The problem, however, is that Mill's 'innovations' were scarcely *consistent* with Ricardianism, and the suggestion fails to account for this significant characteristic of the *Principles*.

The failure to face squarely the problems created for the Ricardian scheme by various incompatible elements must remain something of a problem. Nonetheless, we know enough now of the innovatory process to realise that the presence of 'anomalies', even when they are recognised as such, may be quite inconsequential and fail to generate an alternative to the established structure – irrespective of any peculiarly powerful ingredient labelled 'filial respect'. It is worthwhile staying a moment with this issue, for it was consideration of the non-Ricardian features which led Schumpeter to his position that Mill's system was 'free from the objections which could be directed against that of Ricardo' and 'offered all the elements of the complete model that Marshall was to build'.[30] It is Schumpeter's reference to *Mill's system* which may be misleading. The choice as ultimate standard of reference of the microeconomic general-equilibrium model led Schumpeter, of course, to make the celebrated charge that the entire Ricardian episode was a mere 'detour' in the development of economic theory involving the construction of a 'faulty engine of analysis' (Schumpeter 1954: 474, 568). It also led him to read far more into those writings which appeared to recognise the 'true' economic problem and deal with it appropriately. Thus it is that the scattered presence in Mill's work of properties which Schumpeter considered desirable reassured him that Mill's heart was in the right place. If it appeared otherwise it was an illusion created by Mill's 'filial respect' (529). Faulty methodology, so it seems to me, led to an unjustified discounting of Mill's Ricardianism and to an undue premium upon the rest.[31] In the last resort, it is essential to remember, on the one hand, that the *only* full-fledged system in Mill's *Principles* is that of Ricardo, in light of which fact we should avoid referring to Mill's Ricardianism as a 'relic'; and on the other, that the recognition of theoretical elements which fit better into a neo-classical model must not be identified, even by inference, with the actual construction of such a model. Schumpeter, and in this regard Knight too (1956: 37ff), were prone to minimise the horrendous conceptual difficulties which stood in the way. The significance of neo-classical elements in the *Principles* must not be overstated.

It is in fact legitimate, I think, to regard the central Ricardian model as a genuine paradigm basically concerned with the treatment of macroeconomic issues. To envisage a transfer from this to the neo-classical system with its emphasis upon allocation by a process of shedding the weak elements and replacing them by superior ones – a view for which Marshall himself is partly responsible[32] – may be misleading, for there is an important sense in which the two schemes are incommensurable.[33] It is for this reason that I would avoid the designation 'halfway house' sometimes attached to Mill's *Principles* (Blaug 1958: 165).

The force of the contemporary challenge to orthodoxy must also not be exaggerated. Much is frequently made of the so-called French tradition of regarding commodities and factor services as subject to the same rules.[34] But Ricardo himself was fully aware of Say's criticisms of his approach along these lines, yet deliberately stayed with his chosen path.[35] In other words, the challenge in this key respect was not a new one. Accordingly, much of the case against Ricardianism should be temporally discounted, as it were, when considering Mill's position; he was aware of the case for the prosecution from the very outset. In this regard I would like to refer to a recent demonstration by Professor de Marchi, that on methodological grounds Mill saw little cause for rejoicing in Jevons' attempt to render consumption theory in mathematical terms (de Marchi 1972: 349).[36] There is a difference of 'principle' involved and not merely a question of wearing Ricardian blinkers, or of 'filial respect'.

Finally, we must keep in mind the crucial fact that Mill found the basic Ricardian approach genuinely useful. 'Filial respect' may have played some part in the Mill concoction, but it should not be given pride of place. For you will recall that Mill referred to the problem which the Ricardian model was designed to treat as one of topical and immediate concern, and not one of mere antiquarian interest. Its attempt to distinguish conceptually in the analysis of the rate of return on capital between nominal and real wage-rate changes (reflecting an altered share of wages in *per capita* income), it may be added, had by no means been undermined by direct challenge.

Notes

1   An increase in labour's per capita share implies, of course, an increase of the total wage share in the aggregate output to be divided between labour and capital.

2   Professor George Stigler has made the point as follows:

> Ricardo argues, almost parenthetically, that under certain conditions the inverse relationship between wages and profits holds also when they are expressed in terms of ordinary money rather than in an ideal standard. If a country is on the gold standard, its price level cannot vary (much) because of changes in domestic factor prices; gold flows will soon restore its former level. If, further, the productivity of capital and labour do not change, a rise in money wages would lead to a fall of money profits – in no other way can international monetary equilibrium be restored.
>
> (Stigler 1965: 191)

In our view, this characteristic is not 'parenthetical' but quite crucial to Ricardo's position. And, as we shall show, it is a feature of the positions of McCulloch and J. S. Mill.

3   See the evidence presented by Meek 1951: 51ff, regarding the status of Say's Law as hallmark of Ricardian economics. Compare also Fetter 1969: 68–9, 70–2.

4   'Industry is limited by capital'; 'capital is the result of saving'; 'all capital is consumed'; 'demand for commodities is not the demand for labour' (Mill, *CW*, II: 63ff).

5   See Marx 1965 [1873]: 14–15; Meek 1967: 62, 67, 68–73; 1972: 500–1; Schwartz 1972: 16.

6   By Ricardian economics 'in a broad sense' I have in mind, for example, an emphasis upon economic progress and the laws of distribution in a progressive economy subject to diminishing agricultural returns; an approach to the problem of value from the cost side; and an acceptance of Say's Law. On this see Meek 1967: 73; and Blaug 1958: 226 – 'The Ricardian emphasis on economic growth and the changes in the distributive shares so permeated economic thinking in the period that even those who revolted against Ricardo's authority

in fact accepted its essential outlook'. The distinction is implied in Lord Robbins' well-known review of Schumpeter's *History* (1970: 58–9).

7   Supporting evidence might also be drawn for our proposition from the works of J. R. McCulloch, Robert Torrens and Samuel Bailey.

8   Compare Stigler 1965: 190–1: 'Ricardo's basic theory on distribution – "a rise of wages . . . would invariably lower profits" – is thus strictly dependent on his measure of value' (this view is slightly modified subsequently; see above, note 2).

9   The 'cost of labour' is thus finally identified with labour embodied in per capita wages and with labour's share in per capita output (Mill, *CW*, II: 411ff).

10 All that is missing is the condition that the metal is produced by a process representing the mean proportions of those in the economy as a whole. But Mill may have been assuming identical proportions in all commodities, and for this reason neglected to be explicit about the matter.

11 An application of the principle appears in correspondence with Cairnes:

> Have you formed any opinion, or can you refer me to any good authority, respecting the ordinary rate of mercantile and manufacturing profit in the United States? I have hitherto been under the impression that it is much higher than in England, because the rate of interest is so. But I have lately been led to doubt the truth of this impression, because it seems inconsistent with known facts respecting wages in America. High profits are compatible with a high reward of the labourer through low prices of necessaries, but they are not compatible with a high cost of labour; and it seems to me that the very high *money* wages of labour in America, the precious metals not being of lower value there than in Europe, indicates a high *cost* as well as a high remuneration of labour.
>
> (Letter to Cairnes, 1 December 1864, in Mill, *CW*, XV: 967)

(Compare *CW*, XVI: 1002, 1009.)

12 In fact Mill refers back in the present context (*CW*, III: 698) to the earlier analysis of Book II.

13 An index of the extent of Mill's Ricardianism is provided by his treatment of capital-saving technical change. Mill raises the question whether the relationship between profits and wages – whereby 'the rate of profit and the cost of labour vary inversely as one another, and are joint effects of the same agencies or causes' – must not be modified in light of the fact that a reduction in the *time* for which capital is invested in all commodities (including the monetary metal) appears to raise the rate of return. His answer is revealing, for it indicates the strictest adherence to the Ricardo position. In the case at hand,

> since values and prices would not be affected, profits would probably be raised; but if we look more closely into the case we shall find, that it is because the cost of labour would be lowered. In this as in any other case of increase in the general productiveness of labour, if the labourer obtained only the same real wages, profits would be raised: but the same real wages would imply a smaller Cost of Labour; the cost of production of all things having been, by the supposition, diminished. If, on the other hand, the real wages of labour rose proportionally, and the Cost of Labour to the employer remained the same, the advances of the capitalist would bear the same ratio to his returns as before, and the rate of profit would be unaltered.
>
> (Mill, *CW*, III: 700–1)

The essence of the matter clearly lies in the assumption that the technical change in question, because it affects all goods, also affects wage goods and for *this* reason the rate of profit rises (for a similar emphasis upon technical change which affects wages-goods as distinct from those which do not, see 724, 742–5, 751).

In this context Mill refers his readers to the analysis in the essay 'On profits and interest', in which he had discussed the question of a capital-saving technical change. It is by no means clear that Mill is justified to do so. For it will be recalled that in the essay Mill had introduced a 'slight modification' relating the rate of profit to the cost of wages including therein the profits of the capital goods' producers. In the *Principles*, however, Mill reverts to a view which envisages the cost of wages as consisting entirely of labour (direct and indirect). The problem is a serious one, for it is only by dint of the latter view that Mill was able to relate the cost of wages to labour's proportionate share.

14 Similarly, Mill made explicit the divergence between Ricardian and Smithian theory in the context of taxation of wages:

> On whom, in this case, will the tax fall? According to Adam Smith, on the community generally, in their character of consumers; since the rise of wages, he thought, would raise general prices. We have seen, however, that general prices depend on other causes, and are never raised by any circumstance which affects all kinds of productive employment in the same manner and degree. A rise of wages occasioned by a tax, must, like any other increase of the cost of labour, be defrayed from profits.
>
> (830)

15 The issue was also taken up in correspondence of 13 September 1865 (XVI: 1102); 15 December 1865 (1127); 22 December 1867 (1335); and – in particular – 21 June 1870 (XVII: 1734–5; see text above, pp. 49–50). See also a letter dated 30 May 1872 (1901) on the impossibility of a general tax on profits resulting in an increase in the price level.

16 It should be kept in mind that a Royal Commission on Trade Unions was appointed in 1867; the working-class vote was granted by the Reform Act of 1867, and the unequal Master and Servants Acts were amended in the same year; and complete legal recognition was accorded trade unions in 1871. It has been stated that

> in 1863 began the campaign for the amendment of the Master and Servant Acts which was the true starting point of that remarkable decade of successful pressure from 1866 to 1876 which produced more legislative gains for the working class than all the mass agitations of the preceding half century.
>
> (Perkins 1969: 401)

17 Dr Schwartz asserts that Thornton 'continued to hold that a general rise of wages could be passed on to prices, despite Mill's arguments showing that, in the circumstances of the time, it could only take place at the expense of profits' (1972: 98). In point of fact, Thornton (2nd edn [London 1870]: 299–301) is quite clear that a truly general wage increase will not be passed on to consumers. He may differ from Mill, however, in requiring that the wage increase be (literally) worldwide.

18 While Mill was critical of the Bank Charter Act of 1844, he at no time agreed with Fullarton and Tooke that notes do not affect prices but simply adjust to price movements, or that the money supply is a 'passive' response. Compare Fetter 1965: 190, 226–7.

19   It is a fundamental weakness of the account by Dr Schwartz that, while reference is made to Mill's 'adoption of the Ricardian dictum that "profits depend on wages"', it is implied that Mill took this position only *after* he had rejected the wages-fund theory in 1869 (1972: 101). Compare: 'Mill was to reject the idea of a general rise in prices as impossible' (97). The essence of our argument is that these themes were quite central to Mill from at least 1830, reappearing continuously throughout the essay 'On profits and interests' and the *Principles*.

20   Dr Schwartz asserts that 'it would be unrewarding...to ask whether it was inconsistent of Mill to attempt to build a new political economy on the basis of the Ricardian system', and that

> questions as to the originality or coherence of Mill's economic thought are irrelevant and unimportant, distracting attention from the real problem. Of course he was both original and coherent, but the questions that go to the heart of the matter are others. What were Mill's relations to his teachers? What was Mill aiming at with his 'New Political Economy'? Was he successful? And whether he achieved his goal or no, how valuable is his doctrine from the point of view of today's economics and social philosophy?
>
> (Schwartz 1972: 3–4 [cf. 235])

These latter questions may indeed be the important ones, but I do not see how the matter of Mill's consistency can be thus dismissed in attempting to provide answers. And a mere assurance of Mill's coherence simply begs the question.

21   The point is fairly made by Léon Walras, who contrasted Jevons' failure in this regard with his own achievement:

> Jevons a eu le tort de ne pas dire que le système de Ricardo et Mill est remplacé. Je remplace dans ma *Théorie mathématique de la Richesse Sociale* et dans mes *Eléments d'Economie politique pure* le système de Ricardo et Mill par un système très beau, très simple dans ses éléments et très vaste dans ses details.
>
> (Walras 1965, I: 626)

Walras recognised, however, Jevons' 'ten remarkable pages' (discussed below) which state 'that the formula of the English school, in any case the school of Ricardo and Mill, must be reversed, for the prices of productive services are determined by the prices of the products, and not the other way round' (Walras 1954: 45).

22   In his introduction to Jevons' *Theory of Political Economy* (1970) Professor R. D. C. Black rejects the usual criticism of Jevons that he failed to develop a theory of factor pricing and therefore a full neo-classical perspective. His intention, Black suggests, was Benthamite; he was not concerned with a general pricing system (Black 1970: 17–20).

This interpretation merits careful consideration, for it is by no means self-evident, since Jevons' Preface to the Second Edition does imply a preoccupation with the general pricing problem, both by the suggestions made regarding a 'desirable' approach and by the criticisms of orthodoxy. Jevons' reference to input prices as the *effect* rather than the *cause* of value, on the other hand, lends some support to Professor Black's argument whereby Jevons was not groping towards a general equilibrium system of the Walras–Pareto type. At the same time, it will be recalled that Walras himself applauded this passage; frequently, however, Walras used the term 'cause' in a particular sense – that of 'universal concomitance and exact proportionality' – and it is not certain how much weight to place upon Walras' approbation. On Walras' use of the expression 'rareté is the cause of value', see Jaffé 1972: 398. Professor Black in his most recent contribution suggests that Jevons' adherence to Benthamism may have held him back from developing a full-fledged theory of factor pricing (Black 1972: 373–4). This interpretation would be fully consistent with Jevons' position in his Preface.

23 Professor Stigler does not raise this question, although he envisages Mill as attempting 'to add improvements here and there to the Ricardian system' (1965: 11), a position also adopted by Dr Schwartz (1972: 3, 236).

24 On the significance of this assumption see Hutchison 1972: 457.

25 Mill's emphasis upon interest as a reward for abstinence does not create a problem from the point of view of his consistency. The conception of profit as a residual arising from the productive power of labour (see *CW*, II: 411) is the basis for investment demand, while abstinence relates to the supply side and explains the constraints on the growth of capital (see Blaug 1968: 193; Balassa 1959: 149).

26 See *CW*, III: 701, where Mill refers the reader to his *Essays on Some Unsettled Questions* on a question which 'is too intricate in comparison with its importance, to be further entered into in a work like the present'.

27 Jevons was quite correct to emphasise that the non-Ricardian features which he enumerated were presented in Mill's *Principles* as exceptions to the rule, or special cases. See Jevons 1924: xlviii.

28 And indeed Mill points out that 'wages in different employments do not rise or fall simultaneously, but are, for short and sometimes even for long periods, nearly independent of one another' (*CW*, III: 480).

29 Cf. Sowell 1972: 164; Schumpeter 1954: 530.

30 Schumpter 1954: 569–70:

> J. S. Mill's system . . . absorbed enough of the Say conception – and in addition was sufficiently helped by Senior's notion of abstinence – to be free from any such objection [as Ricardo's inability to deal with simultaneous equations], and it offered all the elements of the complete model that Marshall was to build. But he retained so many Ricardian relics that there is some excuse for Jevons's and the Austrians' not seeing that they were developing his analysis and for believing instead that they had to destroy it.

31 Dr Schwartz refers to the 'merit' of 'writing the history of economic doctrines from the point of view of pure analysis' (1972: 243). It would seem, however, that serious misinterpretations may result from a failure to justify with sufficient care the standard of reference chosen in such an historical approach.

32 '[My] acquaintance with economics commenced with reading Mill . . . and translating his doctrines into differential equations as far as they would go; and, as a rule, rejecting those which would not go' (Marshall, in Pigou 1925: 412).

33 Even G. F. Shove, who commenced his famous study of Marshall's *Principles* with the proposition that the latter 'is nothing more or less than a completion and generalisation, by means of a mathematical apparatus, of Ricardo's theory of value and distribution as expounded by J. S. Mill', conceded that 'if the Ricardian analysis was our starting-point, by the end of the journey we have entered a new world' (cf. Shove 1942).

34 See the references in de Marchi 1972: 345n.

35 See Ricardo 1951, VIII: 379–80; IX: 35, 171–2.

36 Cf. Schwartz 1972: 238.

References

Bailey, Samuel (1825) *A Critical Dissertation on the Nature, Measure and Causes of Value*, London: R. Hunter.

Balassa, Bela A. (1959) 'Karl Marx and John Stuart Mill', *Weltwirtschaftliches Archiv*, 83: 147–65.

Black, R. D. C. (1970) Introduction to Jevons' *Theory of Political Economy*, Harmondsworth: Gregg International.

——(1972) 'W. S. Jevons and the foundation of modern economics', *History of Political Economy*, 4: 364–78.

Blaug, Mark (1958) *Ricardian Economics*, New Haven: Yale University Press.

——(1968) *Economic Theory in Retrospect*, 2nd edn, Homewood: Irwin.

Fetter, F. W. (1965) *The Development of British Monetary Orthodoxy: 1797–1875*, Cambridge MA: Harvard University Press.

——(1969) 'The rise and decline of Ricardian economics', *History of Political Economy*, 1 (Spring): 67–84.

Hollander, S. (1968) 'The role of fixed technical coefficients in the evolution of the wages-fund controversy', *Oxford Economic Papers*, 20: 320–41.

Hutchison, T. W. (1972) 'The "Marginal Revolution" and the decline and fall of English classical political economy', *History of Political Economy*, 4 (fall): 442–68.

Jaffé, W. (1972) 'Léon Walras's role in the "Marginal Revolution" of the 1870s', *History of Political Economy*, 4 (fall): 379–405.

Jevons, W. S. (1871) *Theory of Political Economy*, London: Macmillan.

——(1879) *Theory of Political Economy*, 2nd edn, London: Macmillan.

——(1924) *Theory of Political Economy*, 4th edn, London: Macmillan.

Knight, F. H. (1956) [1935] 'The Ricardian theory of production and distribution', in *On the History and Method of Economics*, Chicago: University of Chicago Press.

de Marchi, N. B. (1972) 'Mill and Cairnes and the emergence of marginalism in England', *History of Political Economy*, 4 (fall): 344–63.

Marx, Karl (1965) [1873] 'Afterword' to the 2nd German edition of *Capital*, I, Moscow: Progress Publishers.

——(1971) [1871] *Theories of Surplus Value*, III, Moscow: Progress Publishers.

——(1973) [1857] *Grundrisse: Foundations of the Critique of Political Economy*, London: Pelican Marx Library.

Meek, R. L. (1967) *Economics and Ideology, and Other Essays*, London: Chapman and Hall.

——(1972) 'Marginalism and Marxism', *History of Political Economy*, 4 (fall): 500–1.

Mill, J. S. (1963–91) *Collected Works of John Stuart Mill*, ed. J. M. Robson, Toronto: University of Toronto Press (herein *CW*).

——(1848) *Principles of Political Economy, Collected Works*, II and III. Last (7th) edition by Mill [1871].

——*Essays on Economics and Society*, in *Collected Works*, IV and V.

——(1869) 'Thornton on labour and its claims', *Fortnightly Review*, new series 5, May: 505–18; June: 680–700; in *Collected Works*, V: 631–68.

——*Later Letters, 1848–1873*, in *Collected Works*, XIV–XVII.

Perkins, Harold (1969) *The Origins of Modern English Society: 1780–1880*, London: Routledge and Kegan Paul.

Pigou, A. C. (ed.) (1925) *Memorials of Alfred Marshall*, London: Macmillan.

Ricardo, David (1951–73) *Principles of Political Economy*, in P. Sraffa (ed.) *Works and Correspondence of David Ricardo*, I, Cambridge: Cambridge University Press.

Robbins, L. C. (1970) *The Evolution of Modern Economic Theory*, London: Macmillan.

Schumpeter, J. A. (1954) *History of Economic Analysis*, New York: Oxford University Press.

Schwartz, P. (1972) *The New Political Economy of J. S. Mill*, London: Weidenfeld and Nicolson.

Shove, G. F. (1942) 'The place of Marshall's *Principles* in the development of economic theory', *Economic Journal*, 52: 294–329.

Sowell, Thomas (1972) *Say's Law*, Princeton: Princeton University Press.

Stigler, G. J. (1965) *Essays in the History of Economics*, Chicago: University of Chicago Press.

Walras, Léon (1954) *Elements of Pure Economics* [4th definitive edn 1926], translated and edited by William Jaffé, London: George Allen and Unwin.

——(1965) *Correspondence of Léon Walras and Related Papers*, I, ed. W. Jaffé, Amsterdam: North-Holland.

Winch, Donald (1970) Introduction to Mill's *Principles of Political Economy*, Harmondsworth: Gregg International.

Chapter 4

On John Stuart Mill's defence of Ricardian economics[1]

This paper offers a solution to a conundrum discerned by students of the political economy of J. S. Mill. The problem has been set forth neatly thus: 'it seems remarkable, how with [J. S. Mill's] intellectual sympathies and extensive understanding, he was prepared to lend his immense influence and prestige' to the 'non-historical and non-historiate' economics of Ricardo (Hutchison 1978: 55). Even commentators who read Mill's early essay on method as an attempt to escape from the trammels of his heritage raise a similar problem:

> one may have to conclude that the break was not far-reaching enough. . . . We can observe a certain rigidity in his unwavering acceptance of the main tenets of Ricardian and Utilitarian doctrine. His new political economy was based on wider premises than his father's was, and reached conclusions more in tune with his time, but basically it consisted of a series of variations (some very original and interesting) on themes present in Bentham, James Mill and Ricardo. John Stuart could not or would not complete his intellectual emancipation.
>
> (Schwartz 1972: 49)

Or yet again (regarding the essay) 'perhaps the most interesting fact' is that Mill 'ended up far closer to his father's position than might have been expected' (Winch 1966: 370); and, more generally, allusion is made to Mill's 'remarkable ingenuity in admitting evidence adverse to Ricardo's predictions while preserving the essential position embodied in the theory', and to his 'delicate balancing act' of 'reaffirming and expanding the Ricardian framework, while at the same time generously incorporating new ideas and taking account of evidence which others considered to be damaging or antagonistic to the Ricardian system' (Winch 1970: 28–9).

To state the problem is to imply that Mill's self-proclaimed adherence to Ricardo was fanciful and superficial – that in some objective sense he ought to have achieved independence. Schumpeter is quite explicit on this matter:

> the economics of the *Principles* are no longer Ricardian. This is obscured by filial respect and also, independently of this, by J. S. Mill's own belief

that he was only qualifying Ricardian doctrine. But this belief was erroneous. His qualifications affect essentials of theory, and still more, of course, of social outlook.

(Schumpeter 1954: 529; cf. Bharadwaj 1978: 269)

And it is to the psychiatrist's couch that some have recourse as explanation: 'The key to this continuing servitude no doubt lies in Mill's psyche' – in 'a profound imbalance in the emotional side of his nature' (Schwartz 1972: 49–50).

It is my argument in this paper that J. S. Mill's self-proclaimed identification with Ricardo can be accounted for without recourse to psychiatry. There is general evidence pointing to Mill's 'eminently sober, balanced and disciplined mind', a view not affected by the episode of his breakdown and subsequent recovery (Hayek 1951: 15, 35; cf. Wolfe 1975: 33). And there is certainly nothing 'unbalanced' about a refusal to innovate for the sake of innovation. This is the essence of the matter. Mill insisted (and rightly so) that Ricardian method had wide applicability, extending far beyond the specific frame of reference pertinent to a capitalist-exchange system; there was therefore nothing 'non-historical' or 'non-historiate' about the method as such. Moreover, the specific axiomatic framework of Ricardian theory retained, in Mill's estimation, its empirical relevance in contemporary circumstances. It is not difficult to demonstrate Mill's strictly limited vision of early prospects for significant institutional change – the established frame of reference was likely to retain its empirical validity for a long time ahead; and this despite the conspicuous differentiation of the 'temporary' laws of distribution from the 'permanent' laws of production. Thus while Mill's sentiments regarding the provisional nature of the institutional and behavioural assumptions must be taken seriously, the fact remains that a healthy degree of scepticism assured against 'visionary enthusiasm'.

Most significant is the fact that the key theorem derived on the basis of the standard axiomatic framework – the inverse wage-profit relation – served as a potent reply to critics of union activity during the 1860s. Ricardianism provided Mill with a powerful weapon in the battle for social reform, and there is no cause for wonderment at his fidelity.

It follows from our argument that Mill's insistence upon the principles of institutional and behavioural relativity in the essay on method of 1836 (and his organisation of the *Principles* to reflect this characteristic), far from constituting a divergence from the methodology of Ricardian economics, amounted rather to an attempt to specify the legitimate scope of the discipline, and thereby to protect it from a range of unfair charges. There is truth in Ashley's statement that Mill did not abandon abstract science but rather placed it 'in a new setting', that 'he kept it intact, but he sought to surround it . . . with a new environment' (Ashley 1909: ix), but I would qualify it by suggesting that the 'new' setting constituted a formal spelling out of the scope of Ricardian political economy rather than true novelty. There is, I believe, common ground between the mature J. S. Mill and Ricardo, while James Mill is odd-man-out.[2] The breakaway of the early 1830s was from his father.

As I have shown elsewhere (Hollander 1979) Ricardo's 'strong cases' constituted analytical simplifications introduced to clarify the argument for better comprehension, but to be appropriately modified in the treatment of real-world problems. The 'principles' of political economy *as such* could provide but limited guidance in applied economics where a variety of conflicting causal influences is at play, and where allowance is required for time-lags and frictions.[3]

Two examples only will be given here of Ricardo's balanced position — relating specifically to his concern with the 'short run' implications of policy, which diluted markedly the political effectiveness of arguments based on the 'principles' of political economy and thus differentiated his use of theory sharply from that of James Mill. First, his approach to corn law reform.

Ricardo rejected liberalisation in time of depression because it could only worsen immediate employment opportunities:

> We all have to lament the present distressed situation of the labouring classes in this country, but the remedy is not very apparent to me. The correcting of our errors in legislation with regard to trade would ultimately be of considerable service to all classes of the community but it would afford no immediate relief: on the contrary I should expect that it would plunge us into additional difficulties.
>
> (Ricardo 1951–73, VIII: 103)

He only called for legislation in 1821 after the return of prosperity in the manufacturing sector. Moreover, repeal was not to be total, and was to be brought about by gradual steps and after due warning, and with allowance made for compensation.

The foregoing passage is cited by Professor Hutchison as evidence of 'great wisdom ... in the realization of ignorance and the scepticism regarding conclusions deduced from long-run, rapidly self-equilibrating models' (Hutchison 1978: 49–50n). But it is read as an exception to the rule: 'It amounts to an extreme contrast with the more typical kinds of Millian-Ricardian policy analysis'. It is not clear why at this particular point, and nowhere else, Ricardo should have 'entertained doubts', and Hutchison offers no suggestions. But on my reading of the record there is nothing to account for. Ricardo's position on the corn laws was no exception. He was typically preoccupied with the appropriate timing of proposed reforms.

Thus it is that one can easily appreciate his case for devaluation to avoid the severe deflationary effects of a return to gold: 'I never should advise a government to restore a currency, which was depreciated 30 pct., to par; I should recommend . . . that the currency should be fixed at the depreciated value by lowering the standard' (Ricardo 1951–73, IX: 73–4).

Ricardo, furthermore, was keenly conscious of the limitations imposed upon political economy by the very nature of its data; he shared with Smith the view that 'disturbing causes' disqualified the subject as a predictive science. He was aware too of the historical relativity of the institutional and behavioural axioms adopted in the treatment of the capitalist-exchange system. And he insisted upon the formal distinction between 'science' and 'factual' economics. Ashley suggested that while 'it may be possibly open to question how far James Mill was a trustworthy interpreter of Ricardo . . . what cannot be doubted is the extent and penetrating character of his influence' (Ashley 1909: vii). But it is precisely this latter aspect of the relationship that is open to serious question. For the distinction between 'science' and 'factual' economics and the conscious use of strong cases as an analytical device only, limited to 'scientific' work; the distrust of over-simplified models for policy pronouncement; the rejection of universally valid axioms; the allowance for disturbing causes, and the view of theoretical economics as a set of investigative tools, rather than a body of descriptive truths or a set of moral exhortations, characterise Ricardo's position alone.

In these respects there is much common ground between Ricardo and J. S. Mill. And although the extent to which the latter was fully aware of the commonality admittedly remains an open question, we cannot neglect his own representation of his methodological principles as the standard or orthodox position *at its best*. In any event, Mill's evaluation of sound 'Ricardian' method turns out to have been accurate and objective.

We must also have in mind the representation of Ricardo (not James Mill) as one of the great teachers of theoretical economics: 'I doubt if there will be a single opinion on pure political economy in the [*Principles*] which may not be exhibited as a corollary from his doctrines' (22 February 1848, *CW*, XIII: 731). Shortly after, he referred to the 'just appreciation of the great teachers of political economy, particularly Ricardo' (5 April 1852, *CW*, XIV: 88).[4] Now these statements of loyalty are not merely lip-service designed to avoid 'stirring up divisions'. For we need only contrast them with an evaluation of the *Elements* in 1833, which makes it clear that Mill did not consider his father to be one of the 'great masters': '[James] Mill's powers of concatenation and systematic arrangement qualified him to place in their proper logical connexion the elementary principles of the science as established by its great masters, and to furnish a compact and clear exposition of them' (1833, *CW*, I: 593). There is too the description of the *Elements* as 'a very useful book when first written, but which has now for some time finished its work' (1833, *CW*, I: 213). Nothing of the kind was ever said of Ricardo's *Principles*. Mill was quite frank about the contrast.

The commonly encountered charges of inconsistency on theoretical grounds – particularly Mill's allowance for both 'Ricardian' and 'neo-classical' conceptions of value and distribution – are poorly grounded; Mill was quite correct to represent various apparent theoretical innovations as corollaries from Ricardian doctrine (see Hollander 1982). What, however, of Mill's so-called 'remarkable ingenuity' in dealing with evidence adverse to Ricardo's 'predictions'? This matter has also been treated elsewhere: Ricardo (like Adam Smith before him) did not design his economic models with an eye upon *specific* predictions (Hollander 1979). And this was precisely the position adopted by Mill in his formal writings on method. Nothing in British economic experience (particularly the movements of wage and profit rates) reflected adversely on Ricardian doctrine, and there was nothing 'ingenious' about Mill's response. Ricardianism provided general tools of analysis, and more specifically a fundamentally important theorem of distribution, which proved indispensable to Mill in his social preoccupations quite independently of the actual path of agricultural productivity and real wage rates.

Mill certainly found fault with the 'old school of political economy', and it is one of our tasks to define precisely what he had in mind by his criticisms. The evidence suggests that while even the master economists were taken to task for an excessive preoccupation with the capitalist-exchange system, this fault was not seen to be inherent in the method as such – at least that of the best teachers. In any event, Mill's harshest criticisms, it is easy to show, were directed at irresponsible and second-rate practitioners who misused political economy for apologetic ends by representing, for example, the subject merely as a set of formulae justifying extreme *laissez-faire*.[5] These were criticisms which Mill expressed from the 1830s; there is reason to doubt the recently expressed opinion that only in the last years of his life, under the influence of Cliffe Leslie, was he becoming aware of the irresponsibility of extreme deductive procedure and 'moving towards a historical and inductive approach' (Hutchison 1978: 55).

Notes

1 This chapter is a summary of a paper read at the Eighth International Economic History Congress, Budapest, August 1982. (An earlier version of this paper was presented at the History of Economic Society Conference, Exeter College, Oxford, September 1981.) For their advice and comments my warmest thanks to Bob Coates, Spencer Davis, Robert Fenn, Scott Gordon, Rick Kleer and Neil de Marchi.

2 A good case can be made out whereby Mill's essay was formulated as a reaction against his father's 'chemical' constructions in economics – the failure to recognise the conditional or hypothetical nature of the assumptions which rendered the conclusions of the economist true in the abstract, and requiring therefore allowance in application for 'disturbing causes' and an appropriate 'summing-up of effects'.

That this is so is further suggested by the distinction made in the essay between the 'science' and the 'art' of political economy, and the allowance for an extensive empirical or inductive dimension at various stages of the deductive

process, positions with which it is doubtful whether James Mill would have sympathised. For his approach was 'to construct the social science *more geometrico*; starting from self-evident premises, and by a chain of syllogisms working down to universally-valid conclusions' (Schwartz 1972: 59f).
3 See also de Marchi 1970: 266 – 'J. S. Mill's methodological position was no different from Ricardo's. Mill only formally enunciated the "rules" which Ricardo implicitly adopted'.
4 Cf. also Mill's remark of 1869 regarding his father: 'One of his minor services was, that he was the first to put together in a compact and systematic form, and in a manner adapted to learners, the principles of Political Economy as renovated by the genius of Ricardo' (Mill 1869, I: xiv).
5 For an excellent discussion in line with our own, see de Marchi 1978.

References

Ashley, W. J. (1909) Introduction to J. S. Mill, *Principles of Political Economy*, London: Longmans, Green.
Bharadwaj, K. (1978) 'The subversion of classical analysis: Alfred Marshall's early writing on value', *Cambridge Journal of Economics*, 2: 253–71.
von Hayek, F. A. (1951) *John Stuart Mill and Harriet Taylor: Their Friendship and Subsequent Marriage*, London: Routledge and Kegan Paul.
Hollander, S. (1979) *The Economics of David Ricardo*, Toronto: University of Toronto Press.
——(1982) 'On the substantive identity of the Ricardian and neo-classical conceptions of economic organization: the French connection in British classicism', *Canadian Journal of Economics*, 15 (November): 586–612.
Hutchison, T. W. (1978) *On Revolutions and Progress in Economic Knowledge*, Cambridge: Cambridge University Press.
de Marchi, N. (1970) 'The empirical content and longevity of Ricardian economics', *Economica*, 37: 257–76.
——(1978) 'The success of J. S. Mill's principles', *History of Political Economy*, 6 (summer): 119–57.
Mill, J. S. (1869) Preface to James Mill, *Analysis of the Phenomena of the Human Mind*, 2nd edn, London: Longmans, Green, Reade and Dyer.
——(1963) *Earlier Letters, 1812–1848*, in *Collected Works of John Stuart Mill*, XIII, Toronto: University of Toronto Press.
——(1967) [1836] *Essays on Some Unsettled Questions in Political Economy*, in *Collected Works*, IV, V.
——(1972) *Later Letters, 1848–1873*, in *Collected Works*, XIV.
——(1981) [1873] *Autobiography and Literary Essays*, in *Collected Works*, I.
Ricardo, D. (1951–73) *The Works and Correspondence of David Ricardo*, 11 vols, VIII: *Letters 1819–21*; IX: *Letters July 1821–1823*, Cambridge: Cambridge University Press.
Schumpeter, J. A. (1954) *History of Economic Analysis*, New York: Oxford University Press.
Schwartz, P. (1972) *The New Political Economy of John Stuart Mill*, London: Weidenfeld and Nicolson.
Winch, D. (1966) *James Mill: Selected Economic Writings*, Edinburgh: Oliver and Boyd.
——(1970) Introduction to J. S. Mill, *Principles of Political Economy*, Harmondsworth: Penguin.
Wolfe, W. (1975) *From Radicalism to Socialism: Men and Ideas in the Formation of Fabian Socialist Doctrines, 1881–9*, New Haven and London: Yale University Press.

Chapter 5

William Whewell and John Stuart Mill on the methodology of political economy[1]

Introduction

William Whewell, in his *Philosophy of the Inductive Sciences* (1840) dealing with the progress of scientific knowledge, portrayed induction as a process of discovery of increasingly comprehensive systems of explanation leading to the isolation of explanatory laws of nature of universal and necessary validity. On his view, science progresses from low-order empirical generalisations of observed particulars to more and more comprehensive and inclusive theoretical generalisations such as Newton's Gravitational Law. It is essential to be clear on the central place accorded deduction in the inductive programme: 'each of the lower order generalizations is derivable deductively from the one of next highest order, and is the inductive evidence for that higher order generalization' (Butts 1968: 17).[2] Whewell's celebrated 'Table of Induction' (his stratification of individual hypotheses) can be read downwards to indicate 'the *deductive* movement from higher-level to lower-level hypotheses, and from the latter towards the data' (Buchdahl 1971: 345). Indeed Buchdahl represents Whewell as deductivist *par excellence* in the sense that his basic procedure is the fitting of hypotheses to the data in which all 'logical' movement is unidirectional, from hypotheses to the data which are demonstrated to be their deductive consequence; 'inductive inference' for Whewell means no more than that 'verifiable deductions have been successfully fitted to the corresponding hypotheses' – no further 'proof' of the hypothesis is required. On the other hand, hypotheses (at least at the upper reaches) are generated under the guidance of what Whewell called 'Fundamental Ideas'; or 'conceptions' existing apart from empirical evidence and implying an *a priori* intuitional dimension – although as Strong points out, such conceptions are historically conditioned, occurring to minds 'variously conditioned and equipped in particular ways within epochs or stages of the progress of scientific knowledge' (Strong 1955: 231).[3] And the 'colligations' of facts by the formulation of hypotheses – into which the intuitive element intrudes – are subject to controversy and trial by prediction, so that in the course of scientific advance erroneous hypotheses are transformed and the body of true propositions augmented. Accordingly,

Strong too is led to play down the peculiarly *inductive* dimension; it was unnecessary even for Whewell to have called his general philosophy of discovery an inductive philosophy, since all he intended was the '*modus operandi* of discovery' (231). And, to repeat what was said at the outset, his philosophy is a progression towards the arrival (with the aid of fundamental ideas) at axioms which reflect 'substantial general truths' or 'universal or necessary truths'; since associated with Whewell's fundamental ideas are his necessitarian axioms (Buchdahl 1971: 352–3; cf. 360).

It has been observed that any conflict between Whewell's 'ideas' and his falsification had little practical import (351, cf. 367). The metaphysical dimension, though ever present, does not interfere with the requirements of hypothesis testing; the 'fundamental ideas' behind the laws are after all historically relative and thus subject to modification (especially simplification) – scientific advance is a progressive exercise. Yet J. S. Mill took the very strongest umbrage at the intuitive dimension of the exposition, for it seemed to him to imply that the axioms of physical science (e.g. two straight lines cannot enclose a space or two straight lines which intersect cannot be parallel to a third; the indestructibility of matter; the chemical combination of bodies) are not represented by Whewell as generalisations from experience, which alone would be valid, but rather as universal and necessary truths resting 'on evidence of a higher and more cogent description than any which experience can afford' (Mill, *CW*, VII: 238).[4] Mill expressed in his *System of Logic* full agreement with J. F. W. Herschel's criticism of Whewell in 1841, which 'maintains, on the subject of axioms, the doctrine . . . that they are generalizations from experience' (248n).[5]

Whether or not Mill in his *System of Logic* (1843) did full justice to Whewell's position, envisaged as a concern with the process of discovery rather than the logic of induction,[6] is not our immediate concern here. It is the fact of his strong hostility to the *a prioristic* element in Whewell's analysis that we shall bear in mind in what follows. For all that, there is a counterpart in Mill's analysis to Whewell's 'Fundamental Ideas' – sufficient in some accounts to justify his categorisation as 'inductivist' (Buchdahl 1971: 346–7) – namely his insistence upon 'inductive validity', or logical proof that the hypothesis is true, proof extending beyond successful prediction. As is well known, Mill insisted that in every deductive procedure 'there must be a direct induction as the basis of the whole' (*CW*, VII: 454). But the three stages of induction, ratiocination and verification did not have to be undertaken in that precise order. What is referred to as the Hypothetical Method of Deduction 'suppresses the first of the three steps, the induction to ascertain the law; and contents itself with the other two operations, ratiocination and verification; the law which is reasoned from, being assumed, instead of proved'. The Hypothetical Method – insofar as we are concerned to prove 'the truth' of the hypothesis – could be justified only if the final step of verification 'shall amount to, and fulfil the condition of, a complete induction' (492).[7] For this to be so, it is no longer sufficient that the process generates results (by way of ratiocination) which are 'verified' by the evidence; the ability of the model based on hypothesised causes to anticipate and predict did not by itself confirm the causes as *vera causa*, since even 'false' and conflicting hypotheses might account for known phenomena (500–1). Stringent conditions had to be satisfied.[8] Essentially, the hypothesis, if it is to represent a '*vera causa*', must not entail mere supposition; its existence must be detected by 'independent evidence' (495–6). And Whewell was taken to task for his belief to the contrary in the strongest terms (503).

The Whewell–Mill relation is confusing in part at least because less doctrinal metaphysics attaches to universal and necessary axioms for Whewell than first meets the eye; and conversely because Mill sought to arrive at *vera causa*, a desideratum bearing a necessitarian connotation of some kind. Moreover, in any confrontation regarding lower-level generalisation the scope for a clash of opinion is *a fortiori* minimised, since the question of the universality and necessity of axioms and thus the role of intuition in their selection or their 'inductive proof', does not arise. And a conflation of their positions emerges in the present study which is specifically concerned with the research programme in political economy as envisaged by Whewell and Mill at an early period, the early 1830s. I shall demonstrate that despite the appearance of *Methodenstreit*, Whewell and Mill were at one regarding appropriate procedure – the immediate tasks in economics.

It is, nonetheless, a story of mutual misunderstanding, in the clarification of which there emerge aspects of the later formal clash of position in the contexts of the sciences in general – particularly Mill's objections to Whewell on 'Fundamental Ideas'. For while it may well be true of the full-fledged version that the practical import of Whewell's 'Fundamental Ideas' with their (at least apparent) intuitional and extra-experiential dimension should not be exaggerated, it is also the case, as far as concerns political economy, that Whewell initially had hopes for a special inductive procedure designed to yield universal and necessarily valid axioms, and amounting to something other than or more than the selection and testing of hypotheses. Only reluctantly did he concede a role for 'verifiable' deduction (Mill's ratiocination) on the basis of locally relevant and directly observed axioms – at which low level of generalisation metaphysical issues were scarcely pertinent – thus arriving at Mill's general position of appropriate procedure.

A brief summary of the argument may prove helpful. Whewell adhered in the 1820s and 1830s to a polemical campaign by various Cambridge writers and their allies (including the economist Richard Jones) – described by themselves as an *inductive* campaign be it noted – to disparage 'Ricardian' political economy represented by them as entailing hasty and illegitimate generalisations, derived deductively from axioms supposedly of universal and comprehensive coverage and permanent validity – this in itself a legitimate objective and ideal – but in actuality resting on the most casual observation and even introspection. But severe ambiguities run through Whewell's expositions. In the first place, after a period of enthusiasm for a special inductivist programme designed to derive comprehensive and universal generalisations in political economy (which apparently ruled out a role for deduction) he came to have grave doubts about what the programme entailed – doubts which he only expressed privately. Second, he himself engaged in deductive economics (mathematically formulated) based on locally relevant axioms.[9] There is evidence that he recognised a positive case for deductive economics as a useful and legitimate operation, within an appropriately constrained empirical environment – a case (as a first approximation) for a specialist political economy which, for example, abstracts economic considerations ('wealth maximisation') from other determinants of human behaviour, the Ricardo–Mill case. Yet he so surrounded his early accounts of deductive economics (including his own) with disparaging remarks, and so exaggerated the inductive task, that it is easy to understand him as denying a significant role for a specialist political economy even as a first step – deductive exercises ('downward reasoning') on locally valid assumptions, would be premature – and as proposing as the immediate task the construction by 'induction' of a small number of universally valid axioms somehow encapsulating the net effect of a wide variety of what, on a less ambitious programme, would have to be treated as 'disturbing causes'. Only then – at some distant stage – would deduction come into its own.

The problem which the record poses is the absence in Mill's essay on the methodology of political economy,[10] or in his correspondence of the early 1830s, or in the retrospective account devoted to the period in the *Autobiography*, of any reference to Whewell's papers on political economy, despite the fact that there is considerable common ground, particularly the insistence upon a careful empirical justification for the axioms and the complementarity of inductive and deductive procedures. The answer, I shall suggest, may lie in the tone of, and the ambiguity surrounding, Whewell's formulations – a reflection of his public enthusiasm for 'induction'. Mill may have failed to recognise the common ground, understanding Whewell as engaging in a general condemnation of economic theory, a denial of the usefulness of deductive exercises until the 'inductive' task, in the sense of the construction of universally valid axioms, had been completed or had achieved much more significant advance. But there is also a closely related issue to which we have alluded already, namely Whewell's notion of induction as entailing more than the mere analysis of empirical evidence. At the time he composed his essay, Mill would have been well aware of the perspective, for it is apparent in Whewell's contribution to the *Bridgewater Treatises* of 1833; the message of the chapter 'On induction' would have utterly repelled him. More generally, the entire Cambridge intellectual *milieu* was anathema – and the sentiment was a mutual one. It would have been difficult for him to give credit to Cambridge in these circumstances even if (and this is not certain) he had been fully conscious of the extensive common ground on the narrower technical issues relating to economics.

My reading of the record suggests that the substantive implications deriving from Whewell's 'Kantian' perspective for his research programme in economics were negligible. But the intuitive or *a prioristic* dimension to his account of the process of discovery did encourage a flirtation with the notion of a special inductive approach (which he soon realised led nowhere); and it set the tone which implied a *Methodenstreit* in economics. As we shall see, Whewell himself was later to try to repair the damage.

In what follows, we shall proceed thus: the second section summarises reactions to Herschel's *Preliminary Discourse on the Study of Natural Philosophy* (1830) by Mill and Whewell, for already here apparent differences between them emerge on the methodology of political economy, Whewell adopting a stricter position than either Herschel or Mill. In the third section it becomes clear that Whewell's confidence in a special 'inductive' programme *à la* Jones was indeed rather more apparent than real – he had his doubts. The fourth and fifth sections treat Whewell's specialist papers on political economy of 1829 and 1830 – both his general methodological statements which disparage deduction as an immediate task, and his specific contribution to 'Ricardian' economics. In this latter context, we shall demonstrate his recognition of a positive role for deductive theory within an appropriately constrained environment – on the basis, that is to say, of locally relevant axioms. That this is the position maintained by Mill in his early work on method is the theme of the sixth section, where we offer a rationalisation of Mill's silence on the common ground with Whewell. The penultimate section records Whewell's (later) formal abandonment of an 'inductivist' programme in favour of the Mill approach. We conclude with some comments on the broader significance of Mill's position, specifically the charge that he was guilty of 'scientism'. This charge, I shall argue, proves to be unsubstantiated; indeed, his lasting message to economists is to be ever conscious of the peculiar limitations of their discipline.

Early reactions to Herschel's *Preliminary Discourse*

It proves convenient to commence with some formal reactions by Mill and Whewell to Herschel's celebrated study of scientific method, which appeared at the same time as the Whewell papers and Mill's preliminary work on his essay. A critical tone emerges in Whewell's account which is absent from that of Mill.

A major theme running through Herschel's discourse is the requirement for a judicious blend of induction and deduction in scientific method – the former a process of 'reasoning upward' from specific instances to general principle, and the latter a process of 'reasoning downward' from general principle to particular application: where 'the inductive and deductive methods of enquiry may be said to go hand in hand, the one verifying the conclusions deduced by the other', we have a 'combination of experiment and theory' which forms 'an engine of discovery infinitely more powerful than either taken separately' (Herschel 1830: 179–81). For Herschel, the isolation of 'residual' phenomena (or disturbing causes) results by way of verification in applications of theory to specific cases after allowance for the 'compound effect' of known causes, the latter arrived at possibly by way of deductive reasoning (156). But the process of verification may lead not only to the isolation of a modifying cause (a residual) and the confirmation of the initial model and its axioms; it may reveal the initial model itself to be defective and to require improvement (164–6). And here Herschel introduces his celebrated warning against casual verification of a theory and his recommendation to place oneself 'in the situation of its antagonists', and even 'perversely' to seek its weaknesses (167).

Herschel had no complaints about contemporary political economy on matters of method. On the contrary, in this branch of social science, he suggested, there was occurring an application of the proven methods of natural science – a blending of experience and reasoning:

> The successful results of our experiments and reasonings in natural philosophy, and the incalculable advantages which experience, systematically consulted and dispassionately reasoned on, has conferred in matters purely physical, tend of necessity to impress something of the well weighed and progressive character of science on the more complicated conduct of our social and moral relations. It is thus that legislation and politics become gradually regarded as experimental sciences; and history...as the archive of experiments, successful and unsuccessful, gradually accumulating towards the solution of the grand problem – how the advantages of government are to be secured with the least possible inconvenience to the governed. The celebrated apothegm, that nations never profit by experience, becomes yearly more and more untrue. Political economy, at least, is found to have sound principles, founded in the moral and physical nature of man, which, however lost sight of in particular measures – however even temporarily controverted and borne down by clamour – have yet a stronger and stronger testimony borne to them in each succeeding generation, by which they must, sooner or later, prevail.
>
> (Herschel 1830: 172–3)

Mill's essay of 1836, both its general argument and terminological formulation is, in several major respects, at one with the *Preliminary Discourse*.[11] No mention is made of it in correspondence of the early 1830s, the essay itself contains no references thereto, and in the *Autobiography* Mill explicitly states that he had originally read (and even reviewed) it 'with little profit' (*CW*, I: 215, 217). Yet this statement is belied by the record. For in the review for *The Examiner*, Mill represented the work 'as an example, and the only example, of a vast body of connected truth, gradually elicited by patient and earnest investigation, and finally recognized and submitted to by a convinced and subdued world' (*The Examiner*, 20 March 1831: 179–80). The prejudice (even of scientists) against the study of methodology, despite the general failure to appreciate what scientific discovery entails, was condemned by Mill; for

> with the exception of the analysis of the syllogism which was performed long ago by the ancients, scarcely any thing has yet been contributed towards an accurate dissection of the mode in which the human understanding arrives at the discovery and verification of truth.

Herschel's work, by contrast, contained

> a clearer and less incomplete view of the nature of philosophical truth, of the evidence on which it rests, and the means of discovering and testing it, than is to be found in any work which has yet been produced. . . . We never met with a book so calculated to inspire a high conception of the superiority of science over empiricism under the name of *common sense* – of the advantage of *systematic* investigation, and high general cultivation of the intellect.

The review ends by quoting in full the passage (cited above) relating to political economy, referring to 'the incalculable advantages which experience, systematically consulted and dispassionately reasoned on, has conferred' on physical science and was beginning to confer on the social and moral sciences. And Mill was in fact to use as epigraph for his second volume of the *System of Logic* that passage which champions a *mixed method of induction and deduction* – 'a combination of experiment and theory' forming 'an engine of discovery infinitely more powerful than either taken separately' (*CW*, VII: 484).[12] This passage would have served perfectly as epigraph for the essay of 1836, and Mill's neglect of Herschel is difficult to appreciate considering his approving tone both in 1831 and 1843. We note also that in the manuscript version of the *System of Logic* (and in all editions until the fourth) Mill commended Herschel's formulation in the *Preliminary Discourse* regarding axioms – that they are generalisations from experience (*CW*, VII: 250–1n).[13]

Let us turn next to Whewell's immediate reaction to the *Preliminary Discourse*. We thereby obtain a conception of pertinent aspects of his position regarding scientific method in general at the time he first addressed himself to economics.

The emphasis is upon the *ascending* process of induction and the *descending* process of deduction (terminology borrowed from Bacon):

> Mr Herschel's account of the matter agrees with that which we have

given. After speaking of the importance of classifying facts and objects, he says – 'When we have amassed a great store of such *general facts*, they become the objects of another and higher species of classification, and are themselves included in laws which, as they dispose of groups, not individuals, have a far superior degree of generality, till at length, by continuing the process, we arrive at *axioms* of the highest degree of generality of which science is capable. This process is what we mean by induction.'

When we have attained by this process to propositions of any degree of generality in science, we can often, by pure reasoning, deduce from them, consequences recommended by their curiosity or their utility. Thus, when we have obtained, by induction from observation of which we have given an instance, the laws of the moon's motion in the heavens, we may from these discover at what times, and with what circumstances, eclipses of the sun and moon will occur. And the more general are the truths which we have reached by our inductive ascent, the more copious and varied will be the inferences which we may obtain by reasoning downwards from them. This mutual dependence and contrast of induction and deduction, this successive reasoning up to principles and down to consequences, is one of the most important and characteristic properties of true science. The great legislator of this science ever and anon calls our attention to this feature of his method: 'Neque enim in plano via sita est, sed ascendendo et descendendo; ascendendo ad axiomata, descendendo ad opera.'

(Whewell 1831a: 380–1)

Now the allowance for deduction once the inductive process has arrived 'at propositions of any degree of generality' is revealing. More specifically, it emerges that a legitimate and important function for deduction is allowed in every science but only *'when much advanced'*. And here will be found a veiled critical allusion to political economy, Whewell taking a harsher line than Herschel:

But there is also another process belonging to this philosophy which has made its appearance in our narrative, and on which we must say a word, – that of *deduction*. From such laws as we have described, the circumstances being given, the facts of each particular case may be deduced; and often, the end being proposed, the fittest means may be assigned; and this process belongs to those reasoning faculties of the mind which lead us from definitions and principles to their consequences. This is an important part of every science when much advanced. But it must carefully be recollected that this process of deduction is only so far applicable as we suppose that of induction to be already successfully performed. The two movements are exactly the reverse of each other: one reasons *to* principles, the other *from* them. The one, beginning its progress from the facts of the external world, travels towards propositions successively more and more comprehensive, and commonly more and more simple: the other commences its course from simple and general assumptions, and derives conclusions limited and complicated by the conditions of particular cases. The difference might seem to be sufficiently obvious; yet it has been so often overlooked, or misapprehended, that we feel greatly obliged to Mr Herschel for having stated it so distinctly as he has done; and we would willingly hope that, for the future, the distinction will never be lost sight of; that sciences, whether physical, political, or moral, of which the whole structure consists in the consequences of a few axioms, and the whole process in syllogistic logic, or what is equivalent to it, will not hereafter claim the name of inductive sciences, so as to confound the *organ* of Aristotle with that of his reformer.

(Whewell 1831a: 387–8)

Whewell recognised Herschel's warning against leaping to premature generalisations, but suggested that Herschel did not go far enough:

We refer to [Bacon's] condemnation of the method of *anticipation*, as opposed to that of gradual induction; a judgment indeed which of itself almost conveys the whole spirit and character of his philosophy, and which, therefore, we have been surprised to find not more distinctly touched upon in Mr Herschel's discourse. The way of anticipation *leaps at once* from facts and particulars to the most general axioms, and then, assuming these to be established, deduces from them the laws of particular cases.

'There are, and can be,' says Bacon, 'but these two ways of seeking truth; the former, the anticipatory, is the one now in use; the latter is the true but yet untried path' (Aphorism 19). 'Both begin from sense and from particulars, both rest ultimately in supreme generalizations, yet they are separated by an immense interval; for while one sets up at once certain abstract and useless generalities, the other rises by degrees to general expressions of existing things' (Aphorism 22).

(Whewell 1831a: 399)

Only in well-established sciences was there little danger of 'anticipation', since 'the necessity of verifying our generalizations, or abandoning them, is irresistibly felt and acted on' (400).

The outcome of this brief review is that Whewell – unlike Mill and Herschel – regarded deduction in political economy, which he surely included amongst the infant sciences (see below), as premature, and likely to fall into the sin of 'anticipation' or illegitimate leaping from poorly established assumptions to unjustified application, unless much greater attention were paid to the process of 'gradual induction'. But what precisely did this process amount to?

On Whewell's doubts regarding 'induction' in political economy

Richard Jones was looked to as the specialist from whom great things could be expected in political economy. It is appropriate, therefore, to have before us some of Jones' methodological statements regarding the 'defective' generalisations of the orthodox political economists on the one hand, and the 'correct' approach on the other:

> It wants no great deal of logical acuteness to perceive, that in political economy, maxims which profess to be universal, can only be founded on the most comprehensive views of society. The principles which determine the position and progress, and govern the conduct, of large bodies of the human race, placed under different circumstances, can be learnt only by an appeal to experience. He must, indeed, be a shallow reasoner, who by mere efforts of consciousness, by consulting his own views, feelings and motives, and the narrow sphere of his personal observation, and reasoning *a priori*, from them expects that he shall be able to anticipate the conduct, progress and fortunes of large bodies of men, differing from himself in moral or physical temperament, and influenced by differences, varying in extent and variously combined, in climate, soil, religion, education and government.
>
> (Jones 1831: xv)

> It must be admitted that political economy must found all maxims which pretend to be universal on a comprehensive and laborious appeal to experience; – it must be remembered steadily, that the mixt causes which concur in producing the various phenomena with which the subject is conversant, can only be separated, examined, and thoroughly understood by repeated observation of events as they occur, or have occurred, in the history of nations; and can never be submitted (except in cases extremely rare) to premeditated experiment; – and we must not shrink from the inevitable conclusion, that the progress of knowledge on such a subject must be difficult and slow; and *that*, almost in exact proportion to the extent of the field to be observed, and the complexity and intricacy of the results presented by it. Still even these considerations, while they afford abundant ground for caution, afford none at all for despair. On the contrary, to a mind well instructed in the ordinary road which inductive science has travelled towards perfection, the very abundance and variety of the materials on which we have to work, give rational ground for steadfast hope.
>
> (Jones 1831: xix–xx)[14]

If we wish to make ourselves acquainted with the economy and arrangements by which the different nations of the earth produce and distribute their revenues, I really know but of one way to attain our object, and that is, to look and see. We must get comprehensive views of facts, that we may arrive at principles which are truly comprehensive. If we take a different method, if we snatch at general principles, and content ourselves with confined observations, two things will happen to us. First, what we call general principles will often be found to have no generality; we shall set out with declaring propositions to be universally true, which, at every step of our further progress, we shall be obliged to confess are frequently false: and, secondly, we shall miss a great mass of useful knowledge, which those who advance to principles by a comprehensive examination of facts, necessarily meet with on their road.

(Jones 1833, in Whewell 1859: xxiv–xxv)

There can be no mistaking Whewell's initial enthusiasm for this kind of stance:

I am quite satisfied [he wrote to Herschel in 1827] of the truth of Jones's general views, and also that they possess the great property of being proved at any step of their induction between the most general and the most particular. You may laugh at this criterion, but it is capable of being exemplified nonetheless.

(Whewell, 23 November 1827, in Todhunter 1876: 86)

He was receptive to Jones' idea for the establishment of an 'inductivist' review:

I like much your aspirations after a reform, or at any rate a trial, in the way of reviewing for ourselves. . . . I have a very strong conviction that taking such a line of moral philosophy, political economy, and science, as I suppose we should, we might partly find and partly form a school which would be considerable in influence of the best kind.

(Whewell, 24 April 1831, in Todhunter 1876: 118)

Whately, Senior and McCulloch figure large as the *bêtes noires* in this episode.[15] And he wrote encouragingly regarding the reception of Jones' book on rent: 'I am bound to say . . . that it is no bad success for a book not deductive like Ricardo's but inductive, and in its inductions, as you must allow far from complete, to obtain as much notice as yours has done' (27 December 1832, in Todhunter 1876: 151).

Now it can be shown that Whewell had his doubts – growing doubts – about the inductivist programme for political economy championed by Jones. We need but compare his warm approval of 1827 with the following revealing letter of 1831 warning against 'vapour[ing]' about the successive steps of generalization' and 'declaiming . . . about generalization' when what was required were positive examples 'to guide and substantiate' the inductive procedure. 'I do not', he frankly admitted, 'yet see my way to anything which I could propound concerning generals':

I shall be glad to see your speculations about induction when they are finished, for among other questions it is certainly an important one how the true faith can best be propagated. I have done what I could in my review of Herschel. . . . Of induction applied to subjects other than Nat. Phil. I hardly know one fair example. Your book is one. A good deal of Malthus's population is a beginning of such a process, excluding of course his anticipatory thesis, the only thing usually talked of. What else can you produce? or how can you expect to lay down rules and describe an extensive method with no examples to guide and substantiate your speculations? You may say a number of fine things and give rules that look wise and arguments that look pretty, but you will have no security that these devices are at all accurate or applicable. . . . It is not that I do not think induction applicable and the examination of its rules important in the notional sciences, but I do not yet see my way to anything which I could propound concerning generals. . . . I cannot imagine, however, that you will do your pupil any great good by treating him to all our wise aphorisms. You may enable him to vapour about the successive steps of generalizations and to call his own opinions inductive, and those he rejects anticipations; but I am persuaded he will have no profitable perception of any valuable truth.

(Whewell to Jones, February 1831, in Todhunter 1876: 115–16)[16]

Whewell's concern that Jones had failed to provide adequate illustrations of the proposed approach grew with the latter's failure to publish the later parts of his work on *Distribution of Wealth*.[17] And we find him soon complaining that Jones was 'lapsing into definitions'.[18] Indeed, in private correspondence he expressed his hope that he would not be misunderstood as taking too 'heterodox' a position regarding the need for theory in statistical studies:

The Statistical Society in London was engaged before the meeting in drawing up a large collection of questions for circulation. They will, I have no doubt, obtain a great deal of information, but my opinion at present is that they would go on better if they had some zealous *theorists* among them. I am afraid you will think me heterodox, but I believe that without this there will be no zeal in their labour and no connexion in their results. Theories are not very dangerous, even when they are false (except when they are applied to practice), for the facts collected and expressed in the language of a bad theory may be translated into the language of a better when people get it; but unconnected facts are of comparatively small value.

(Whewell to M. Quetelet, 2 October 1835, Todhunter 1876: 228–9)[19]

Whewell on political economy, 1829-31

We turn now to Whewell's own formal papers on political economy. In some preliminary remarks to his *Mathematical Exposition of Some Doctrines of Political Economy* (1829) Whewell made out a case for the use of mathematics in the process of 'reasoning downwards from assumed principles' – the complex combination of causal principles by way of deduction, as distinct from that of the establishment of those principles (small in number and of general applicability); the latter a matter for 'the higher department of the science of Political Economy' (a revealing term):

> Such a system of calculation must of course borrow the elements and axioms which are its materials, from that higher department of the science of Political Economy, which is concerned with the moral and social principles of men's actions and relations. These materials thus received, stated in the simplest manner, must be subjected to the processes of a proper calculus, and we may thus obtain all the results to which the assumed principles lead, whatever be the complexity of their combination. And such a mode of proceeding will be of very great advantage to truth; inasmuch as it will make it inevitably necessary to separate the moral axioms and assumptions on which the theories rest, from all other matter which may tend to obscure or confound them. It will also separate entirely the two parts of the subject which it is of immense importance to keep separate; – the business of proving these assumptions, and that of deducing their conclusions. Much ingenuity has been shewn in reasoning downwards from assumed principles. These principles are however so few and general, (we do not now speak of their truth or applicability) that the task of deducing their results is almost entirely a business of the mathematical faculty; and might have been done in a few pages by clothing them in mathematical formulae.
>
> (Whewell 1968 [1829]: 3–4)

Whewell then proceeded to consider an imaginary non-mathematical mechanics discerning therein three dangers all of which had in reality been overcome:

> They might have assumed their principles wrongly; they might have reasoned falsely from them in consequence of the complexity of the problem; or they might have neglected the disturbing causes which interfere with the effect of the principal forces. But the making mechanics into a Mathematical science supplied a remedy for all these defects. It made it necessary to state distinctly the assumptions, and these thus were open to a thorough examination; it made the reasonings almost infallible; and it gave results which could be compared with practice to shew whether the problem was approximately solved or not.
>
> (Whewell 1968 [1829]: 4–5)

An equivalent case is made out for a mathematical political economy. Whewell was particularly careful to insist that the outcome would not constitute 'a near approximation to the business of the world, any more than the doctrines of Mechanics are to actual practice, if we neglect friction and resistance, and the imperfection of materials, and suppose moreover the laws of motion to be questionable'. The problem equivalent to friction in mechanics had thus to be recognised, although Whewell is not clear in his first paper whether this is to be done at the (first) stage of establishment of the axioms or at the (third) stage of allowance for disturbing causes. But his own immediate concern was with the second stage – that of 'the deduction of conclusions from fundamental propositions', and this with particular reference to the alternative analyses of the effects of taxation on distribution undertaken by 'the followers of Mr Ricardo' on the one hand and by T. Perronet Thompson on the other.[20] It was not, he insisted, his concern 'to adduce any new arguments on one side or the other', but to seek for the source of the disagreement by use of the mathematical method, for as 'the principles of the different parties' – the axiomatic base of the respective argument – were nearly identical, the source of the difference must be found in the process of deductive reasoning therefrom.[21]

The reader of the paper of 1829 would not have taken it as an attack on deduction as a matter of principle. The insistence that the small number of general axioms once adequately isolated by 'the higher department of the science' 'must be subjected to the processes of a proper calculus' in order to 'obtain all the results to which the assumed principles lead, whatever be the complexity of their combination', allows a key role for the deductive process – the 'reasoning downwards from assumed principles'. More than that, the reinforcement of deduction by mathematics is apparently allowed (albeit rather obliquely) even prior to the successful isolation of the general axioms as an (indirect) contribution to their establishment by making it necessary 'to state distinctly the assumptions' – the provisional assumptions – thus rendering them 'open to a thorough examination', and by setting the stage for a sound verification against the facts with an eye upon allowance for 'disturbing causes'. But in the background there is the complaint that contemporary political economy was a distorted science with 'much ingenuity' shown in the deductive processes but the proof of the assumptions – 'few and general' – not yet established. And this message is very much reinforced in his second mathematical contribution dealing with Ricardo's *Principles* specifically.[22]

Whewell commenced this paper by maintaining that mathematico-deductive process was appropriate only *after* the establishment of the axiomatic base in the sense of 'a few simple and evident' or 'a few precise and universal principles', thereby playing down even the earlier (rather casual) allowances for the process as a contribution to this exercise. Those who believed that the Ricardians had completed the inductive task were woefully in error:

> Among a number of those who have recently cultivated the study of Political Economy, an opinion appears to prevail that, by the labours of Mr Ricardo and his followers, a large mass of our knowledge on this subject has been reduced to the form of a series of exact logical deductions from a few simple and evident principles. . . . I have already, in a former communication, observed that when our object is to deduce the results of a few precise and universal principles, mathematical processes offer to us both the readiest and safest method; since by them we can most easily overcome all the difficulties and perplexities which may occur in consequence of any complexity in the line of deduction, and are secure from any risk of vitiating the course of our reasoning by tacit assumptions or unsteady applications of our original principles.
>
> (Whewell 1968 [1831]: 1–2)

His complaint against orthodox political economy was that its axiomatic foundation supposedly incorporated 'steady and universal' and 'paramount and predominant' principles, but in fact neglected a variety of principles (possibly of equal significance) which 'oppose and control them' – the 'disturbing causes' of the 1829 paper. The task of building up general (all-inclusive) axioms still remained to be undertaken and was bound to be 'far from either short or easy':

> To extricate such principles from the mass of facts which observation of the world and of ourselves teaches us, – to establish the reality, number, and limits of such laws, – these are offices which belong to a branch of philosophy altogether different from that which the mathematician, in the proper sense of the name, has to deal. Such a task is far from being either short or easy; and it would be very hasty to take for granted that it is already completed, or even that any considerable part of it is performed. For my part, I do not conceive that we are at all justified in asserting the principles which form the bases of Mr Ricardo's system, either to be steady and universal in their operation, or to be of such paramount and predominant influence, that other principles, which oppose and control them, may be neglected in comparison. Some of them appear to be absolutely false in general, and others to be inapplicable in almost all particular cases.
>
> (Whewell 1968 [1831]: 2–3)

And again in his concluding remarks we find the same objections to the presumption that the axiomatic basis of orthodox doctrine incorporated a 'few certain principles', 'universally and strictly true':

> I will not quit the subject without again stating that I by no means wish

to attribute any mathematical certainty, or any extraordinary value, to the preceding results, considered with reference to their application to the real circumstances of human affairs. I must however observe, that if they are useless and inapplicable, the fault resides in the postulates which I have borrowed from Mr Ricardo and others, and not in the mode of deducing the consequences of these principles. If these postulates were universally and strictly true, the results, as above stated, would be exactly, and in all cases, verified: I may add, that if we had reached such a point in the progress of this science – if it were reduced to a few certain principles, and to a long train of deductions from these – (a form which it appears to have been the object of Mr Ricardo and his followers to give to it –) the mathematical method would be the one proper for its treatment, being the most certain, the shortest, and, with a little preparation, the simplest. Mathematics is the logic of quantity, and will necessarily, sooner or later, become the instrument of all sciences where quantity is the subject treated, and deductive reasoning the process employed.

(Whewell 1968 [1831]: 42–3)

In Whewell's stated opinion, the immediate requirement in political economy was thus the establishing of 'the few certain principles' but by a process of 'far higher philosophical dignity and importance' than mathematics – this was the first step. Premature exercises in mathematical reasoning were dangerous:

I am however well aware, that the pretensions of Political Economy to such a scientific character, are as yet entirely incapable of being supported. Any attempt to make this subject at present a branch of Mathematics, could only lead to a neglect or perversion of facts, and to a course of trifling speculations, barren distinctions, and useless logomachies.... And these defects may be incurred, even though common verbal reasoning be substituted for mathematics, if the course adopted be that of assuming principles and definitions, and making these the origin of a system. The most profitable and philosophical speculations of Political Economy are however of a different kind: they are those which are employed not in reasoning *from* principles, but *to* them: in extracting from a wide and patient survey of facts the laws according to which circumstances and conditions determine the progress of wealth, and the fortunes of men. Such laws will necessarily at first, and probably always, be too limited and too dependent on moral and social elements, to become the basis of mathematical calculation: and I am perfectly ready to admit, that the discovery of such laws, and the investigation of their consequences, is an employment of far higher philosophical dignity and importance than any office to which the Mathematician can aspire.

(Whewell 1968 [1831]: 43–4)

It is thus Whewell's position that the task of deriving the basic principles by induction was so immense that little purpose would be served by devoting attention to the subsequent deductive stage. Indeed, there is a strong suggestion in the foregoing passage that the materials of the social sciences might prove intractable and not allow the construction of the requisite body of a small number of universally valid axioms – that the conflicting causal influences (acting, say, on behaviour) could not be assimilated into a simple general rule, in which case, so it is intimated, although without elaboration, there would be no purpose served by mathematico-deductive procedures.

Whewell's mathematical rendition of Ricardo, from this perspective, merely served the *destructive* purpose of demonstrating (indirectly) the inadequacy of the orthodox axiomatic framework (and to a lesser extent its errors of logic), rather than the positive purpose of demonstrating the efficacy, by way of case study, of rigorous mathematical reasoning and its usefulness if applied to a body of empirically suitable axioms. His general methodological remarks, in a review of Jones' work on rent, point to the same conclusion. Political economy, Whewell there insisted, must be an inductive science. A role for deduction is clearly recognised, but only at a later stage: 'It must *obtain* its principles, by reasoning upwards from facts, before it can *apply* them by reasoning downwards from axioms' (1831b: 52) – expressions with which we are by now fully familiar. Orthodox procedures, he complained, provided a 'most illustrious instance of that error which Bacon so long ago stigmatised with the name of anticipations, and perpetually opposed to the true course of inductive philosophy, the interpretation of nature'. This little known passage deserves to be considered in full, for it makes crystal clear that the charge against the Ricardians is of neglecting the inductive state of 'reasoning up' or of 'continuous and gradual ascent', and leaping to generalisations on scanty evidence (see Appendix to this chapter).[23] As in the mathematical papers, Whewell observed of the 'English system' that a theory which merely takes into account the strict assumptions of the model and neglects the many causes at work by which these are 'controlled and checked' may well 'deviate far from the facts' (1831b: 58–9). And he mocked the pretensions of the economists who behaved as if the task of establishing the 'few general and simple laws' constituting the axiomatic base was already completed, when in fact their science was in its infancy – 'the youngest' of all sciences, and 'the most complex, mixed and vast in its subjects, depending on the most subtle, obscure and unmeasurable elements' into the bargain:

There are, no doubt, portions of physical science, which admit of this deductive treatment; in which the whole of our knowledge consists in the complex and ramified results of a few general and simple laws. But all persons who have attended to the nature of science know, that the reduction of any province of knowledge to such a form is the last grand act and *dénouement* of its history: that even in physics not more than two or three branches (physical astronomy and mechanics, and partially optics), have thus reached the fulness of their growth; and in these this progress has been the result of centuries of persevering labour and of the efforts of hundreds of zealous and patient students. Even among the material sciences, by far the greater number have yet to wait for the appearance of their supreme and final legislators; their Newton is still to come. It continues still to be their task to endeavour to reason up to higher and wider rules than they now possess, as well as to trace the consequences of those which the sagacity of past times has already discovered. It will therefore be a most strange and singular circumstance in the history of sciences, if political economy, the youngest of them, the most complex, mixed and vast in its subjects, depending on the most subtle, obscure and unmeasurable elements, should have sprung at once to this ultimate condition, this goal and limit of its possible intellectual progress. We may well wonder if it shall appear that nature, so sparing hitherto of her most splendid gift, the discovering and generalizing intellect, should have poured forth with a prodigality which left nothing to expectation or labour, those minds which were to urge political economy instantly through every stage of its progress up to its supreme principles, and to leave nothing for their successors but to lengthen and brighten the chain of deduction, by which minor truths hang from these summits of knowledge.

(Whewell 1831b: 54–5)

Whewell as 'Ricardian'

We must now allow for the possibility that Whewell's negative tone towards deduction as a useful exercise in the contemporary state of the science reflects an intention to avoid antagonising such close acquaintances as Richard Jones.[24] That his deprecatory statements regarding the utility of mathematical deduction should not be taken at face value is suggested by a qualification that while some of Ricardo's axioms 'appear to be absolutely false in general, and others to be inapplicable in almost all particular cases', nonetheless 'to trace their consequences may be one of the obvious modes of verifying or correcting them' (Whewell 1968 [1831]: 3).[25] And this more positive perspective – the perspective of the first mathematical paper – is confirmed by the details of the analysis which follows, for Whewell registers few complaints against Ricardian deductive procedures (apart from some charges of faulty logic) *provided the axiomatic context is limited to the capitalist exchange system.*[26] To this matter we now turn.

In his representation of the Ricardian system, Whewell designated as the first 'Postulate' that of rent – rent envisaged as the excess over normal profits. (In point of fact he would have done better to have called this a theorem regarding rent, since it is deduced from the assumptions of capitalistic farming and capital mobility which assures uniformity of the rate of profit on capital.) This 'postulate' or 'hypothesis', he conceded,

> is generally allowed to be verified approximately in England: though even here, the reluctance, difficulty and loss which accompany the transfer of farming capital to other employments, the moral and social ties which connect the landlord and tenant, and the numbers of cases in which the cultivator does not live on profits only, very much limit the generality, and obstruct and extend [sic.] the manifestation of the naked principle thus asserted.

There will be more to say regarding the proposed treatment of the various rigidities and qualifications alluded to here. It is outside England that the postulate would not do at all:

> Taking the world at large, it has been shewn, in the admirable work of Mr Jones, that this view and measure of rents is entirely inapplicable, and that none of the suppositions on which it proceeds have the slightest resemblance to the actual state of things. It is to be recollected therefore, that whenever the postulate of rent is introduced, the application of our reasonings can only be made to cases of *farmers' rents*: and that all countries in which *serf, metayer, ryot* or *cottier* rents, or *cultivator-proprietors* prevail, that is 99 hundredths of the cultivated globe, are to be excluded from our conclusions.
> (Whewell 1968 [1831]: 4, emphasis added)

In addition to the major postulate, there were two others regarding rent. That relating to *differentially productive plots* 'which form a continuous decreasing series' such that no-rent land exists at the limit, Whewell observes correctly, is not 'necessarily implied in the measure of rent just mentioned'. Yet he accepted the assumption – 'the fact that there are soils approaching nearly to this limit, may however be conceded' so that rent becomes a differential surplus as well as the excess over normal profits – without formally specifying whether (as is probable) his concession applied solely to English conditions (3–4). The further supposition that each successive dose of capital 'must universally obtain a proportionally smaller return than the preceding' was, however, rejected (following Richard Jones) as 'an assumption without any *a priori* foundation whatever, and not at all consistent with the known history of agriculture' (4–5).[27]

Here, a reference to Whewell's review of Jones' 'Essay on the distribution of wealth' in *The British Critic* for July 1831 is illuminating. There is the criticism of the orthodox pretence that the axioms of the standard models – in this case axioms regarding rent – were universal in coverage:

If it were necessary to point out the very limited applicability of the economist's view of rent, we conceive the state of cultivation in many parts of Ireland would be a case sufficiently decisive. In the districts occupied by cottiers, who pay an extravagant sum for the use of the land, and extract from it a scanty and precarious subsistence of potatoes, in what sense can the rent they pay be said to be the excess of the produce of good over the worst soils? which, according to our modern theorists, is a proposition universally true of all rents whatever. Or what would an Irish peasant say, if we were to set about proving to him that this must be so, by asserting that 'if it were otherwise, he would remove his capital to some other employment'?.... Where is the wisdom of asserting principles as general when almost every case which occurs to us makes the phraseology in which they are expressed unmeaning?

(Whewell 1831b: 49)[28]

But there is also unmistakably the concession that the orthodox axioms were valid in local conditions. And assuming capitalistic farming (and also postulating that 'all mutual good-will' is abolished so that self-interested behaviour reigns), Whewell admitted that 'the rent must constantly tend to become equal to the excess of the produce of the land over that of any other employment of the requisite capital'.[29] The case may have been a limited one in scope – 'prevailing universally only in England, Belgium and Holland, and being found beyond these boundaries only in smaller spots' – but the orthodox theory was valid in that case. It was the generalisation of the rent principle that he found unacceptable: 'This proposition, curious and important in the case to which it belongs, has been constantly asserted to all rents whatever, and is, up to the present day, held by the systematic economists to be indisputably and unexceptionally true' (51–2). It is to methodological weakness – the failure to adopt 'inductive' procedure – to which Whewell looks for an explanation of the orthodox propensity to generalise.

We return to the second mathematical paper and consider the discussion of the axiom relating to general wages. Whewell asserted that the Ricardian system incorporates a given (long-run) real wage – the postulate 'that the labourer's command of food and other necessaries is never permanently augmented or diminished' (1968 [1831]: 5). This axiom hinged upon the Malthusian population mechanism, to which Whewell took strong exception, conceiving it as intended to be of universal relevance: 'the assumption of such a necessary and universal operation of wages upon population, is entirely gratuitous and unfounded . . . there is not the slightest ground for asserting this to be the law of such changes, any more than any other law arbitrarily assumed' (6).[30] More specifically, orthodox theory neglected the negative effects of high wages upon population growth:

the postulates above stated are so far from being adequate properly to represent the general facts, that we can hardly look for any accordance between the calculated and the observed effects. To consider, for instance, the tendency of mankind to increase their numbers as a universal and inevitable law, and to leave out of consideration the co-ordinate and antagonist tendency by which they endeavour to preserve and increase their comforts, is to insure a total dissimilarity between our theory and the actual state of things.

(Whewell 1968 [1831]: 14)

Whewell himself expressed his own doubts about the isolation of an appropriate *general* law:

To obtain such principles as may truly indicate to us the manner in which alterations of wages do really operate upon the habits and numbers of the labourers, is an object of great interest and importance, and one in which, though some progress has been done, much is yet to be done. It seems little likely that any general law, free from all control of time, place and circumstance, will be found of any real use or value.

(7)[31]

We must, he here added, steer clear of 'the propensity of the speculative powers of the human mind to rush forwards and to endeavour to seize on such a general law'.[32]

Consistently with this latter position, Whewell was prepared to accept the assumption of labour mobility – as was the case, we have already seen, regarding capital mobility – within a constrained environment. The outcome was the principle of competitive pricing which

is true so far as the possibility and operation of such a transfer [of labour between occupations] extends; that is, it is true of prices in the same country, and so far as the labour which is embodied in the commodity is, from conditions of time and place, within the reach of this competition.

(9)

Of all the axioms discussed perhaps the most important, because of its pervasive relevance, is the Postulate of Equilibrium. In undertaking the mathematical formulation, Whewell adopted the axiom that all prices are at their natural values, and the structures of wages and profits in equilibrium (11–12).[33]

The assumption is justified on grounds that it simplifies the analytical problem, and also constitutes a valid first approximation, although caution is advised:

along with this simplification we incur a necessary and perpetual, and it may be, a very considerable deviation from the circumstances of actual fact. In reality, this equilibrium is never attained: probably in most cases it is never approximated to. There is a constant tendency towards the state of things in which the elements of wealth are in this exact balance, but... [we cannot] flatter ourselves that we have solved the problem of the course and distribution of the current of wealth, when we have combined the laws according to which an exact balance might be produced.

We are to recollect therefore, that even if our principles were exact, deductions from them made according to the method we are now following, would give us only a faint and distant resemblance of the state of things produced by the perpetual struggle and conflict of such principles with variable circumstances. Such deductions however would probably have some resemblance, in the general outline of their results, to the true state of things. They would offer to us a *first approximation*: and in difficult problems of physics, it is precisely by such a simplification as this, that a first approximation is obtained. Thus in the investigation of the problem of the tides, we have a very complex case of the *motion* of a fluid: but Newton's mode of treating the question was, to consider what would be the form of *equilibrium* of the ocean, acted upon by the forces which produce the tides: and this solution of the problem, though necessarily inexact, was accepted as the best which could easily be obtained. The investigations of Laplace and others who have since treated the problem on its true grounds, as a question of hydrodynamics, have shewn that Newton's solution explains rightly the main features of the phenomenon.

(Whewell 1968 [1831]: 12–13)

There is a further caution. The analysis will only yield a satisfactory first approximation if the 'circumstances and tendencies' which are excluded from the formal axioms are 'of an inferior order to those which we take into account' in consequence of 'their small amount or short duration'. What determines the appropriate axiomatic base, Whewell is saying, is the ruling empirical environment. There may be circumstances where it is *not* legitimate to treat disequilibria as of secondary importance compared to the 'general tendencies':

In order however that solutions of this nature may have any value, it is requisite that the principles, of which we estimate the operation, should include *all* the *predominant* causes which really influence the result. We necessarily reject some of the circumstances and tendencies which really exist: but we can do this with propriety, only when the effects of these latter agents are, from their small amount or short duration, inconsiderable modifications only of the general results. The quantities which we neglect must be of an inferior *order* to those which we take into account; otherwise we obtain no approximation at all. We may with some utility make the theory of the *tides* a question of equilibrium, but our labour would be utterly misspent if we should attempt to consider on such principles the theory of *waves*.

It appears to be by no means clear that the irregular fluctuations and transitory currents by which the elements of wealth seek their natural level may be neglected in the investigation of the primary laws of their distribution. It is not difficult to conceive that the inequalities and transfers produced by the temporary and incomplete action of the equalizing causes, may be of equal magnitude and consequence with those ultimate and complete changes by which the general tendency of such causes is manifested. A panic may produce results as wide and as important as a general fall of profits.

(Whewell 1968 [1831]: 13–14)

Whewell modestly allowed that he was unable to state the extent to which his own representation of the Ricardian model based upon the equilibrium assumption is vitiated (14). What he does insist, as we have seen, is that the Ricardian system fails because the 'co-ordinate and antagonistic tendency' opposing, for example, the Malthusian law is left out of account.

The neglect of technical progress is also said to be unjustified, and to have led Ricardo into conceiving his account of the growth process – involving constant wages and resort to inferior land – as 'the necessary and universal progress of nations'. This he denies, even as representative of British experience. Yet oddly enough, the incorporation of new technology is not represented as an extension of the system of basic axioms, but rather as a correction of logical error, and this is difficult to appreciate:

That this has been the course of events in England seems to be clearly and demonstrably false. After Mr Jones's reasonings (Essay, chap. vii, sect. 6.), I do not conceive that any doubt can remain on the subject. And it is remarkable that Mr Ricardo's error in this instance is not a mistaken assumption of principles, but it is a defect in his deduction from his principles, a part of his task which is generally supposed to be unexceptionable. The error resides in his having neglected altogether the effects of an increase in the power of agriculture, which, in England, has been a change at least as important and as marked, as the increase in the population. This being the case, it is evident that the whole of his assumption of the nature of the economical progress of this country, and the views of the distribution of wealth arising from this assumption, must fall to the ground.

(Whewell 1968 [1831]: 15)[34]

The outcome of the foregoing survey is that Whewell, despite the general tone of the paper of 1831, was not launching a campaign against deductive method as such. He objected to the weak axiomatic base of Ricardian theory supposedly envisaged by its practitioners as turning upon a few universally valid principles (as it should, ideally, be) but in fact incorporating only assumptions which reflect 'circumstances of time and place'. To a modest programme – if it is recognised as such – Whewell does not object; although which axioms were to be formally absorbed into the specialist model, and which were to be excluded as a first approximation and subsequently dealt with as 'disturbing causes', was an empirical matter regarding which he had little to suggest himself.

Mill's *Essay on Method*: the problem posed

Space limitation necessitates that in this section we proceed in assertive fashion regarding Mill's early essay on the methodology of political economy.[35] The essential message of that work, as I read it, is that while nature nowhere presents us with pure economic data, a positive and strong case can yet be made for a socially useful specialist science of political economy, to the extent that the economic determinants of behaviour are distinguishable from others – albeit a science of limited and provisional scope in consequence of the local and temporary status of the behavioural axioms. Mill's case was made out in practical terms; for strategic purposes he saw great merit in a lowering of sights, although for him (as for Whewell) the construction of a unified social science, incorporating a wide range of behavioural patterns and extending far beyond the investigation of wealth, was the ultimate ideal.

The process would entail a complementarity of 'inductive' and 'deductive' procedures, more accurately a 'mixed method of induction and ratiocination'. It is the method of the mechanical sciences which on Mill's account provides the basic model for social science. Although specific experience is quite useless in the face of complex causality ('composition of causes'), this source of evidence is essential in the derivation of individual axioms, and thus constitutes the *sine qua non* for deductive exercises. Second, as in the physical sciences, allowance was to be made for model improvement in consequence of the procedures of 'verification' – the correction not only of logical error, but of empirical deficiencies in the axiomatic framework. But verification does not mean prediction; the inability of economic models to serve as predictive instruments is a key feature of Mill's methodology – his Ricardian methodology – and of profound importance to this day.

It is necessary to insist upon the extensive empirical dimension to political economy envisaged by Mill in his early essay – a dimension he attributed to his illustrious forebears – for it is disguised by his representation of the subject as a 'hypothetical' science reasoning 'from assumptions not facts' (including an 'arbitrary' definition of man justified in part by reference to 'introspection'), and by his formal exclusion of the verification process from the science. Despite the apparent championship of an 'a priori' procedure designed to yield universally applicable generalisations based upon unobservable motivation,[36] Mill's case for a specialised political economy is in fact made on empirical grounds, and reflects a confirmed hostility to any representation of the wealth-maximisation assumption as of 'universal' relevance. He proceeded by emphasising the empirical justification for the behavioural axiom within a specific institutional environment and range of activities, while warning at the same time of the need for vigilance in application of deductive theory even within that constrained environment – for it is average or normal behaviour only that is covered by the axiom, so that in any particular application there would inevitably be at play 'disturbing causes' not allowed for by the model. It is this very attempt at precision that disguised the fact that the axiom itself was justified in empirical terms.

The analysis of Mill's essay reveals close parallels with Whewell's position. For both there are the stages of *induction* (a building up of axioms), *deduction* (a logical combination of complex cause/effect relations) and *verification*. As for the discussion of the inductive stage, both insisted that the premises of a model must have a firm empirical justification, and that the axiomatic foundation be subject to improvement and development by way of continual verification against the facts – the changing facts. From this point of view Mill's essay might be said to have been deliberately designed as a reply to Whewell's charges against orthodox methodology. In effect it constitutes a defence of the subject, as envisaged by the great masters, in which he too criticised irresponsible championship by a variety of so-called 'Ricardians' (lesser lights) of an axiomatic foundation of 'universal' relevance on the basis of scant evidence.

The Ricardian theorems were valid only within a specific institutional and social framework. But a general theory of wealth covering a wider range of institutional frameworks was, Mill believed, conceivable in principle. It would incorporate a variety of differential behavioural and technological assumptions – although even the axiomatic base of the science as it existed allowed for 'composition of causes' to some extent. But such a 'synthesis' of causal influences was still a matter for the future, and this we have seen was Whewell's position also. In the interim, political economy served a useful purpose, having in mind that some or all of the causal influences formally excluded from the model (the 'disturbing causes') had to be taken into account in applications of the theorems, and this even in applications to problems of policy generated within the relatively narrow institutional frame of reference to which the model was specifically designed – namely, the capitalist exchange system of contemporary Britain.

There is little to distinguish Whewell from Mill in all this, apart (possibly) from the evaluation of the 'usefulness' of the deductive exercise when carried out with reference to a single country or (a few countries) at a specific period of its development. Even here the difference is not conspicuous. The theorist was said by Mill to be duty bound to carry out a verification 'upon every new combination of facts as it arises' to assure 'that any residuum of facts which his principles do not lead him to expect, and do not enable him to explain, may become the subject of a fresh analysis, and furnish the occasion for a consequent enlargement or correction of his general views' – a formulation very close to that of Herschel. And Whewell referred to mathematics as allowing a sound deduction of the consequences of principles, as one of the most obvious modes of 'verifying or correcting' the general principles.[37]

Why then did Mill not refer in his essay to Whewell and the commonality of position? It seems to me that allowance must be made for a strong possibility that Mill failed to note Whewell's allowances for a deductive economics constructed on a narrowly based axiomatic foundation appropriate for a local environment. For these allowances emerge only during the course of his detailed analysis of the Ricardian models, whereas his general observations on methodology in the economic pamphlets and the review of Jones give a very different impression – that the task at hand was the building up of general axioms (incorporating the full range of 'causes'), a task of 'far higher philosophical dignity and importance' than mere deduction, and which might last for generations, and even fail because of the peculiar complexity of social data to yield the requisite small number of universal axioms – in which case no use at all for deduction could be envisaged.

Let us recall also the major theme relating to the derivation of axioms in Whewell's later works on the history of science to which Mill was to object. In the *System of Logic*, we have seen (above, pp. 70, 75), Mill expressed full agreement with Herschel's criticism of Whewell's *a prioristic* view of the axioms of the mathematical and physical sciences. But it is also clear (above, pp. 74–5) that even in the early 1830s, at the time of composition of the methodological essay, Mill recognised much common ground with Herschel's *Preliminary Discourse*; whereas Whewell adopted a rather more critical attitude towards Herschel as far as concerns the social sciences. And there is no mistaking the notion of an inductive process involving much more than a combination of logic and experience in Whewell's economic papers – the representation of the discovery of the principles which constitute the 'origin of a system', as 'an employment of far higher philosophical dignity and importance than any office to which the Mathematician can aspire', or the reference to 'the higher department of the science of political economy'. There is in short a 'metaphysical' dimension to Whewell's championship of induction in the social as well as the physical sciences.

This perspective pervades Whewell's contribution to the celebrated *Bridgewater Treatises*, which appeared precisely during the preparation of Mill's essay (Whewell 1834).[38] A few extracts from the chapters 'Inductive habits' and 'Deductive habits' will give the flavour of a central message of that work. Especially striking are Whewell's references to 'the constitution of the mind' and to 'scientific perceptions', which bear an *a prioristic* or intuitive connotation, in the inductive exercise:

> It will readily be conceived that it is no easy matter, if it be possible, to analyse the process of thought by which the laws of nature have thus been discovered; a process which...has been in so few instances successfully performed.... But... we conceive it may be shown that the constitution and employment of the mind on which such discoveries depend, are friendly to that belief in a wise and good Creator and Governor of the world, which it has been our object to illustrate and confirm;... the true scientific perception of the general constitution of the universe, and of the mode in which events are produced and connected, is fitted to lead us to the conception and belief of God.
>
> (Whewell 1834: 304)

The essence of induction for Whewell is its yielding of entirely new knowledge:

> when Newton conceived and established the law [gravitation] itself, he added to our knowledge something which was not contained in any truth previously known, nor deducible from it by any course of mere reasoning. And the same distinction, in all other cases, obtains, between those processes which establish the principles, generally few and simple, on which our sciences rest, and those reasonings and calculations, founded on the principles thus obtained, which constitute by far the larger portion of the common treatises on the most complete of the sciences now cultivated.
>
> (Whewell 1834: 329)

The entire tone of these chapters is one which relegates deduction to a lower sphere. Yet more significant, Whewell alludes to the 'moral sciences' and warns of the uselessness of mathematical reasoning when prematurely undertaken:

> It is certain...that the mathematician and the logician must derive from some process different from their own, the substance and material of all our knowledge, whether physical or metaphysical, physiological or moral. This process, by which we acquire our first principles, (without pretending here to analyse it), is obviously the general course of human experience, and the natural exercise of the understanding; our intercourse with matter and with men, and the consequent growth in our minds of convictions and conceptions such as our reason can deal with, either by her systematic or unsystematic methods of procedure. ...If the mathematician is repelled from speculations on morals or

politics, on the beautiful or the right, because the reasonings which they involve have not mathematical precision and conclusiveness, he will remain destitute of much of the most valuable knowledge which man can acquire. And if he attempts to mend the matter by giving to treatises of morals, or politics, or criticism, a form and a phraseology borrowed from the very few tolerably complete physical sciences which exist, it will be found that he is compelled to distort and damage the most important truths, so as to deprive them of their true shape and import, in order to force them into their places in his artificial system.

(Whewell 1834: 336–7)

We have here also a clear statement that the task at hand in the social sciences was the seeking for a 'First Cause of the Moral and Material World', a task impeded not by deficiencies of logical habits of mind, but deficiencies of 'the habit of apprehending truth of other kinds' – that of 'ultimate truths and efficient causes' (340). This is precisely the message which Whewell conveys in his general statements regarding method in the economic pamphlets. And taking into account his formal participation in the concerted programme against Ricardian political economy – and its polemical tone – it is not stretching things far to suggest that, despite our demonstration of extensive common ground on methodological matters, Mill understood Whewell's position to be opposed to deduction as a matter of principle – including him amongst those charged in the 1828 review of Whately with failing to appreciate Bacon and wishing 'to discard the syllogism which they thought was one method of reasoning, and confine [themselves] to induction which they imagined was another'. S. G. Checkland (1951) has written of an 'ambiguity' in the public mind regarding Whewell's position;[39] it may well be that this too was Mill's judgement.

It may be helpful to place the entire issue in broader intellectual perspective. We must not lose sight of the fact that the Cambridge 'inductivist' group included leading churchmen and professors opposed to Ricardianism – their conception of Ricardianism – the population and rent principles in particular.[40] To render the tone of their hostility, we may refer to Jones' bitter denunciation of the birth control notions said to be implicit in the former doctrine – 'vile', 'degrading' and the work of the devil – and of the notion that the interests of the landlord are opposed to those of society as a whole (Jones 1831: xiii–xiv, x–xi, xxxi–xxxii).

Mill himself entered the lists in a review of Adam Sedgwick's discussion of the Cambridge University programme. Here *inter alia* he attacked the old universities as second-rate and blamed them for the low cultural state of the community: 'all is right so long as no one speaks of taking away their endowments, or encroaching upon their monopoly'.[41] Sedgwick's comments on natural philosophy, the utilitarian theory of morals in particular, were described as 'a few trite commonplaces' (Mill, *CW*, X: 39); his conception of the theory of utility was condemned as 'misrepresentation in voluntary ignorance' (72; also 51f, 62f); and the whole work was said to be on a 'level with a lower class of capacities' (73).

Whewell referred to Mill's (anonymous) review as the work either of a demagogic scoundrel or an idiot:

> I am somewhat puzzled, not being able to make out whether the reviewer is a scoundrel, who, by bringing together ferocious expressions knowingly, endeavours to excite people's passions against an antagonist, or whether he is a real *bonâ fide* example of that silliness which belongs to Benthamites and the like; and which can see nothing but moral horrors in all persons of opposite opinions.
>
> (Whewell to Jones, 9 May 1835, in Todhunter 1876: 212)

Mill obviously did not know of this particular comment, but he was perfectly aware of Whewell's connections – that he was enmeshed in the 'Cambridge Network'.[42]

The conflict is quite evident. But nowhere is Mill's hostility towards Whewell better expressed than in a comment made subsequently, which envisages Whewell's perspective on induction – his 'necessary truths' – as an invitation to social apologetics:

> We do not say the intention, but certainly the tendency, of his efforts, is to shape the whole of philosophy, physical as well as moral, into a form adapted to serve as a support and a justification to any opinions which happen to be established. A writer who has gone beyond all his predecessors in the manufacture of necessary truths, that is, of propositions which, according to him, may be known to be true independently of proof; who ascribes this self-evidence to the larger generalities of all sciences (however little obvious at first) as soon as they have become familiar – was still more certain to regard all moral propositions familiar to him from his early years as self-evident truths. His *Elements of Morality* could be nothing better than a classification and systematizing of the opinions which he found prevailing among those who had been educated according to the approved methods of his own country; or, let us rather say, an apparatus for converting those prevailing opinions, on matters of morality, into reasons for themselves.
>
> (Mill, *CW*, X: 169–91)[43]

In the light of all this, it cannot be precluded that Mill's neglect of Whewell's economic papers in 1836 is, at least in part, explicable by a sharp division of social attitude whether or not Mill realised the extent of Whewell's allowance regarding deductive theory in economics within an appropriately limited environment. Common ground on this matter – and it is far from certain that Mill recognised it as such – would have paled in significance compared with the broader issues at stake.

We must allow also for the fact that it was not in Mill's character to advertise differences between political economists. While his essay alludes to certain fallacious perspectives, including those of his own father, it constitutes largely a positive defence of the subject as envisaged by the great masters. To emphasise agreement with Whewell and Cambridge with their critical tone, albeit valid when directed at some of the lesser lights amongst the economists, would without question have suggested a *Methodenstreit* within economics, and was therefore to be avoided.

On Whewell's formal abandonment of the 'inductive' programme

We have discerned a duality in Whewell's approach in his essays on economics, and have suggested that Mill may have seen one aspect only – the championship of induction of an unacceptable order. The allowances Whewell made regarding the legitimacy of a deductive science based on local axioms as a first approximation justified in empirical terms – the Ricardian procedure as envisaged by Mill – Mill himself may not have recognised in Whewell's writings. And he certainly would have been unaware of Whewell's own privately expressed doubts regarding Jones.[44]

Now, in a discussion of Mill's *System of Logic* first published in 1849, Whewell conceded frankly that deductive procedure took precedence in the research programme of political economy, that little more could be achieved from further elaboration of the inductive establishment of axioms:

> But there is another reason which, I conceive, operates in leading Mr Mill to look to Deduction as the principal means of future progress in knowledge, and which is a reason of considerable weight in the subjects of research which, as I conceive, he mainly has in view. In the study of our own minds and of the laws which govern the history of society, I do not think that it is very likely that we shall hereafter arrive at any wider principles than those of which we already possess some considerable knowledge; and this, for a special reason; namely, that our knowledge in such cases is not gathered by mere external observation of a collection of external facts, but acquired by attention to internal facts, our own emotions, thoughts, and springs of action; facts are connected by ties existing in our own consciousness, and not in mere observed juxtaposition, succession, or similitude ... many of the principles which regulate the material wealth of states, are obtained, if not exclusively, at least most clearly and securely, by induction from large surveys of facts. Still, however, I am quite ready to admit that in Mental and Social Science, we are much less likely than in Physical Science, to obtain new

truths by any process which can be distinctively termed *Induction*; and that in those sciences, what may be called *Deductions* from principles of thought and action of which we are already conscious, or to which we assent when they are felicitously picked out of our thoughts and put into words, must have a large share; and I may add, that this observation of Mr Mill appears to me to be important, and, in its present connexion, new.

(Whewell 1860: ch. xxii, 284–5)[45]

This is a quite remarkable passage. It implies a profoundly significant *volte face*. Whereas in the earlier papers Whewell had formally presumed that the social sciences shared with the physical sciences the requirement of a building-up of universally valid axioms from the facts, albeit supplemented by an intuitive element, it is now urged, in the light of the 'internal' nature of evidence in the social sciences, that such axioms were at hand without the need for as strong a factual input as in the physical sciences. The weight placed on the evidence of 'our own consciousness' – which still smacks of intuition – is increased at the expense of factual evidence involving 'observed juxtaposition, succession, or similitude'. His earlier doubts (above, pp. 79–80) regarding Jones' scheme were now, it seems, out in the open. But what also strikes the eye is the attribution of this same perspective to Mill – a total failure to appreciate the central place assigned in the *System of Logic* (which incorporates the substance of the early essay on definition and method) to an on-going process in which the axioms of political economy are subject to continual improvement and modification in the light of factual evidence. It is Whewell who in the end emerges as champion of a procedure which he and his inductivist colleagues originally attributed to the economists in hostile terms as involving 'anticipation', or premature leaping to generally valid axioms which at best had locally valid relevance.

Yet we are not allowed to rest. There still remains a degree of ambiguity regarding Whewell's final position. For in a chapter of the *Philosophy of Discovery* (1860) entitled 'Political economy as an inductive science' immediately following the review of Mill's *System of Logic* just cited, he repeats much of what he had written in the early 1830s regarding 'hasty and premature generalizations' on the part of the political economists – the sin of 'anticipation' – insisting anew so it seems, as he had been wont to do, upon the true method:

And what is the sounder and wiser mode of proceeding in order to obtain a science of such things? We must classify the facts which we observe, and take care that we do not ascribe to the facts in our immediate neighbourhood or specially under our notice, a generality of prevalence which does not belong to them. We must proceed by the ladder of Induction, and be sure we have obtained the narrower generalizations, before we aspire to the widest.

(Whewell 1860: 295–6)

And again he recommends Jones' work on rent as an exemplar.

For all that, when we attend to the details of Whewell's recommendation it transpires that he does not have in mind a special inductivist programme at all, despite his reference to 'the ladder of Induction'. These were so many words. His concern – and he is merely reproducing in summary his 'Ricardian' stance of 1831 – was the need to avoid unjustified generalisation on the basis of locally valid axioms. There is nothing here at odds with Mill, to whom indeed Whewell paid tribute as being free from guilt:

> Mr Mill has much more distinctly characterized the plan and form of Political Economy in his system [*Logic*, vi. 3]. He regards this science as that which deals with the results which take place in human society in consequence of the desire of wealth. He explains, however, that it is only for the sake of convenience that one of the motives which operate upon man is thus insulated and treated as if it were the only one: – that there are other principles, for instance, the principles on which the progress of population depends, which co-operate with the main principle, and materially modify its results: and he gives reasons why this mode of simplifying the study of social phenomena tends to promote the progress of systematic knowledge.
>
> (Whewell 1860: 294)

And even with regard to the 'speculators' he ended on a less critical note than had been his earlier practice:

> And thus those precepts of the philosophy of discovery which we have repeated so often, which are so simple, and which seem so obvious, have been neglected or violated in the outset of Political Economy as in so many other sciences: – namely, the precepts that we must classify our facts before we generalize, and seek for narrower generalizations and inductions before we aim at the widest. If these maxims had been obeyed they would have saved the earlier speculators on this subject from some splendid errors; but, on the other hand, it may be said, that if these earlier speculators had not been thus bold, the science could not so soon have assumed that large and striking form which made it so attractive, and to which it probably owes a large part of its progress.
>
> (Whewell 1860: 298–9)[46]

Concluding note: Mill and 'scientism'

The term 'scientism' has been coined to designate the belief that an extension of scientific and engineering techniques can legitimately be made to the study of society with the promise of similarly impressive results. The term is due to Hayek, who was particularly incensed by the 'historicism' of the Saint-Simonians – their attribution to the social sciences of the task of discovering the 'natural laws' of the progress of civilisation, supposedly as 'necessary' as that of gravitation, from which perspective derived a penchant for collectivist social engineering (Hayek 1941; 1942–4). For Hayek, the characteristic 'subjectivism' of the social sciences – the role of motive, knowledge, expectation, and so forth – ruled out the parallel and precluded, above all, long-term historical prediction. It was Hayek's view that Mill had been early on infected by Saint-Simon and subsequently by Comte, and he cites the motto (from Condorcet) to Book VI of the *System of Logic* to that effect:

> The only foundation for the knowledge of the natural sciences is the idea that the general laws, known or unknown, which regulate the phenomena of the Universe, are necessary and constant; and why should that principle be less true for the intellectual and moral faculties of man than for the other actions of nature.
>
> (Hayek 1941 [February]: 13)[47]

Yet this view of Mill's position does not ring true. It is certainly not suggested by our analysis of Mill's methodology as formulated in the early essay. On the contrary: that specific prediction was ruled out, even in the specialist social sciences such as political economy, is a key theme of that work, and much attention is paid to the complexities of application. But there is also to be found in the early correspondence – a letter to Gustave d'Eichthal of October 1829 – a beautiful formulation of some of the special problems in social science (and it is a statement which Whewell would surely have applauded) which, in Mill's view, the Saint-Simonians had failed completely to appreciate, a criticism engendered especially by Comte's *Traité de Politique Positive* (1823):

> it is only the *partie critique* which appears to me sound, *the partie organique* appears to me liable to a hundred objections ... it is a great mistake, a very common one too, which this sect [the Saint-Simonians, to which group Comte was then attached] seem to be in great danger of falling into to suppose that a few striking and original observations, are sufficient to form the foundation of a *science positive*. M. Comte is an exceedingly clear and methodical writer, most agreeable in style, and concatenates so well, that one is apt to mistake the perfect coherence and logical consistency of his system, for truth. This power of systematising, of tracing a principle to its remotest consequences, and that power of clear and consecutive exposition which generally accompanies it, seem to me to be the characteristic excellencies of all the good French writers; and are nearly connected with their characteristic defect, which seems to me to be this: They are so well satisfied with the clearness with which their conclusions flow from their premises, that they do not stop to compare the conclusions themselves with the fact though it is only when

they will stand this comparison that we can be assured the premisses have included all which is essential to the question. They deduce politics like mathematics from a set of axioms & definitions, forgetting that in mathematics there is no danger of partial views: a proposition is either true or it is not, & if it is true, we safely apply it to every case which the proposition comprehends in its terms: but in politics & the social science, this is so far from being the case, that error seldom arises from our assuming premisses which are not true, but generally from our overlooking other truths which limit, & modify the effect of the former.

(Mill, *CW*, XII: 35–6)

Now, the criticism proceeds immediately with the fundamentally important observation that Comte's error flowed from his preclusion of the characteristic problem in social science – that of choice between ends. He had transformed the social into a purely technological problem by this procedure:

It appears to me therefore that most French philosophers are chargeable with the fault ... of insisting upon only seeing *one* thing when there are many, or seeing a thing only on one side, only in one point of view when there are many others equally essential to a just estimate of it ... [this fault] ... pervades [Comte's] whole book; & it seems to me, it is this fault which alone enables him to give his ideas that compact & systematic form by which they are rendered in appearance something like a *science positive*. To begin with the very first and fundamental principle of the whole system, that government and the social union exist for the purpose of concentrating and directing all the forces of society to some one end.

(Mill, *CW*, XII: 36)

In the *System of Logic* the major problems of applied social science are further elaborated following the lines established in the essay. In particular, there could be no practical maxims of general application even if social phenomena conformed to *known* causal relationships, thus precluding the problem of 'disturbing' causes. Social phenomena

might not only be completely dependent on known causes, but the mode of action of all these causes might be reducible to laws of considerable simplicity, and yet no two cases might admit of being treated in the same manner. So great might be the variety of circumstances on which the results in different cases depend, that the art might not have a single general precept to give.

(Mill, *CW*, VIII: 877)

The problem was that of weighing in the balance the relative force of the numerous (supposedly known) causal influences playing upon the condition and progress of society – influences

> innumerable, and perpetually changing; and though they all change in obedience to causes, and therefore to laws, the multitude of the causes is so great as to defy our limited powers of calculation. Not to say that the impossibility of applying precise numbers to facts of such a description, would set an impassable limit to the possibility of calculating them beforehand, even if the powers of the human intellect were otherwise adequate to the task.
>
> (878)

The primary conclusion drawn from these characteristics is that

> Sociology, considered as a system of deductions *a priori*, cannot be a science of positive predictions, but only of tendencies. We may be able to conclude, from the laws of human nature applied to the circumstances of a given state of society, that a particular cause will operate in a certain manner unless counteracted; but we can never be assured to what extent or amount it will so operate, or affirm with certainty that it will not be counteracted; because we can seldom know, even approximately, all the agencies which may coexist with it, and still less calculate the collective result of so many combined elements.
>
> (Mill, *CW*, VIII: 898)

Social science, to the extent that it was 'insufficient for prediction', had to be distinguished from astronomy, the data of which were relatively few and stable.

Now Mill of course devoted attention in the *System of Logic* to the Inverse Deductive or Historical Method, and it is these chapters which most preoccupy those who charge him with 'scientism'. The problem defined here was to 'ascertain [the empirical laws of progress], and connect them with the laws of human nature, by deductions showing that such were the derivative laws naturally to be expected as the consequence of those ultimate ones' (916).[48] And the exercise was designed to yield genuine causal laws of progress extending beyond empirical generalisation, with which

> we may . . . be prepared to predict the future with reasonable foresight; we may be in possession of the real *law* of the future; and may be able to declare on what circumstances the continuance of the same onward movement will eventually depend.
>
> (791)

Yet it is unlikely whether Mill meant by the foregoing, positive prediction; he probably intended *tendencies* as he certainly did in the simpler specialist branches – secular tendencies extending beyond the limits of individual countries and periods, knowledge of which would permit policy makers to exercise intelligent judgement.[49] Moreover, he had no illusions about the magnitude of the task. For one thing, the programme could scarcely proceed without development of the 'science of human character formation' or *ethology*, whereby to arrive at the requisite principles of human nature and he was perfectly aware of the absence of such foundation (906).[50] We certainly know how impatient he was with Comte's presumptions:

> You may well call Comte's a strange book. I agree...that it is well calculated to stir the mind and create a ferment of thought...because it is the first book which has given a coherent picture of a supposed future of humanity with a look of possibility about it, and with enough of *feature* for the reason and imagination to lay hold of it by....[But] with all his science he is characteristically and resolutely ignorant of the laws of the formation of character; and he assumes...all these [character] differences as ultimate, or at least necessary facts, and he grounds universal principles of sociology on them.
>
> (Mill, *CW*, XIII: 738–9)[51]

Most important is Mill's position that

> the more highly the science of ethology is cultivated, and the better the diversities of individual and national character are understood, *the smaller, probably, will the number of propositions become, which it will be considered safe to build on universal principles of human nature.*
>
> (*CW*, VIII: 906, emphasis added)

Accordingly, there always existed a danger of claiming too much for empirical generalisations – 'the common wisdom of common life'. For example,

> when maxims...collected from Englishmen, come to be applied to Frenchmen, or when those collected from the present day are applied to past or future generations, they are apt to be very much at fault. Unless we have resolved the empirical law into the laws of the causes on which it depends, and ascertained that those causes extend to the case which we have in view, there can be no reliance placed in our inferences. For every individual is surrounded by circumstances different from those of every other individual; every nation or generation of mankind from every other nation or generation: and none of these differences are without their influence in forming a different type of character. There is, indeed, also a certain general resemblance; but peculiarities of circumstances are continually constituting exceptions even to the propositions which are true in the great majority of cases.
>
> (Mill, *CW*, VIII: 864)

The significance of the chapters on historical progress thus lies in the warning that in the absence of genuine causal laws of a secular order, there was the greatest danger of attributing excessive predictive power to the specialist social sciences (such as political economy), based as they are on locally relevant and impermanent axioms. With all this Whewell would have agreed. Mill's warnings of the limited scope of economics bear repeating to this day.

Appendix

Extract from Whewell's review of Jones' Distribution of Wealth, *in* The British Critic, *X (July 1831), 52–3*

In recent times, and especially since the publication of Mr Ricardo's treatise, the science has been put altogether in a deductive form, and made to consist intirely of the results of two or three axioms variously applied and combined. Thus Mr Ricardo's work in its original form (for the manifest monstrosity of some of his conclusions induced him afterwards to attempt to avoid them by a compromise of scientific consistency) was merely a development of three principles, namely, 'the principle of population', stated and applied with a mathematical severity, of which the promulgator of the principle had always pointed out the folly; 'the doctrine of rent', applied in the same manner as a universal and fundamental truth; and Mr Ricardo's own measure of exchangeable value by the capacity of labour employed on the article. These three principles were not only laid down as being certain and infallible, like the laws of motion, but it was also assumed that they were so far the sole or leading principles which govern production and distribution, that all interferences with and exceptions to them might be neglected as casual and short-lived anomalies. From these principles there was deduced, as of course might be done from any such axioms whether true or false, a train of connected (and it might easily have been consistent) conclusions, in the contemplation of which minds of logical propensities found an agreeable employment. Undoubtedly very extraordinary errors were committed in the process of this deduction, and remain up to the present time part of the received creed of the economists; but with these we do not at present meddle, as our professed business is with the vices of their method.

The mode in which the above sweeping and exclusive principles were obtained was by some transient and cursory reference to a few facts of observation or of consciousness. From such grounds, without any extensive comparison or systematic course, a spring was at once made to these highest and most comprehensive generalities. And this feature in their career of investigation it is, which we are compelled to declare to be an utter violation of all the precepts, and invasion of all the examples, which indicate the true road to the attainment of philosophical truth.

It is in short the most recent and most illustrious instance of that error which Bacon so long ago stigmatized with the name of *anticipation*, and perpetually opposed to the true course of inductive philosophy, the *interpretation of nature*. Anticipation *leaps*, he says, from particulars to the most general axioms; Induction passes by a continuous and gradual ascent through intermediate generalities. The former may produce assent from its consistency, for if men were to be insane, according to one fixed common manner, they might still agree perfectly well. But no possible exercise of human ingenuity can in this way produce a philosophy which shall be verified in the occurrences of the world, or which shall enable us to predict and control the future.[52]

Notes

1 Several friends and colleagues have greatly helped with advice and criticism: Spencer Davis, Tom Kompas, Trevor Levere, Margaret Schabas, Francis Sparshott and Tim Tutton. I am much indebted to them. Research funds were provided by a Lady Davis Fellowship held at the Hebrew University, Jerusalem (1979–80), and by the Canada Council. Their support is gratefully acknowledged.

2 Cf. also de Marchi and Sturges (1973: 380) who observe that deduction 'takes general principles as given, and is concerned only with how they apply or are combined in particular cases. It is of prime importance therefore to ensure that one's premisses are well founded.'

3 Cf. 218, 223f. Strong observes of fundamental ideas that they are 'not truths in science but the grounds or conditions for systematic formulation of theory' or intuitive conceptions 'consciously sought and reflected upon by scientists in search of comprehensive and consistent systems of explanation' (221). But he also refers to a wavering by Whewell

> between a Kantian doctrine of *a priori* relations of thought, and a Christian Platonism of eternal, rational forms in the Mind of God, the view expressed in the Bridgewater Treatise. Thus he sometimes argues that a 'Fundamental Idea' is an *a priori* mental structure, but at other times that it is an eternal rational ordering of nature in the mind of God.
>
> (222)

(Cf. note 18, paragraph 2, for an example of Whewell's requirements of 'Fundamental Ideas'.)

4 On Mill's hostility to the intuitional philosophy of the German metaphysicians and its bearing upon his debate with Whewell, see further: Nagel 1950: xxvii f; Randall 1965: esp. 64f; McRae in Mill, *CW*, VII: xxi f; Ryan in Mill, *CW*, IX: x f.

5 Indeed Mill felt it necessary to add that he had arrived at this position quite independently of Herschel. See too Mill to John Austin, 7 July 1842 (XIII: 528): '[Herschel's] review of Whewell contains so much that chimes with my comments on the same book that he would probably like to lend a helping hand to a writer on the same side with him' – an allusion to Mill's preference for Herschel as *Quarterly* reviewer of his forthcoming *System of Logic*. On

5 October 1844, Mill wrote to Comte that he found Whewell's (privately circulated) reply to Herschel's review 'très faible' (XIII: 639).

6 It is Strong's theme that he did not (1955: 226f, 231). Also Nagel 1950: xxxiii–xxxiv.

7 In principle, there would be no reason to rule out any hypothesis imaginable and account for an effect by 'some cause of a kind utterly unknown, and acting according to a law altogether fictitious'. But such hypotheses would be implausible and would 'not supply the want which arbitrary hypotheses are generally invented to satisfy by enabling the imagination to represent to itself an obscure phenomenon in a familiar light'. Accordingly there probably never existed a hypothesis involving both a fictitious 'agent' and a fictitious law of operation; 'either the phenomenon assigned as the cause is real, but the law according to which it acts, merely supposed; or the cause is fictitious, but is supposed to produce its effects according to laws similar to those of some known class of phenomena' (Mill, CW, VII: 490).

8 For a critical perspective on Mill, cf. Buchdahl 1971: 350–1, 354–5, 359, 364; Strong 1955: 210, 224, 228, 230.

9 Whewell's first paper entitled 'Mathematical Exposition of Some Doctrines of Political Economy' was read before the Cambridge Philosophical Society on 2 and 14 March 1829, and immediately sent to press (Whewell to Richard Jones, 2 April 1829, Whewell Papers, Cambridge [hereinafter WPC], Add.Mss. C51.[63]). It was then distributed privately to various persons: 'I send you some copies of my paper on Polit. Econ.', Whewell wrote to his friend John William Lubbock. 'I shall be much obliged to you if you will employ a porter for me to carry them to the persons to whom they are directed' (Whewell to Lubbock, 30 April 1829, WPC: 0.15.47.[178]). T. R. Malthus, for one, acknowledged receipt on 26 May, and T. P. Thompson on 12 June; cf. Malthus to Whewell, 26 May 1829, in de Marchi and Sturges 1973: 387; Thompson to Whewell, 12 June 1829, WPC: Add.Ms. 2.213.[114]. Dionysius Lardner and Richard Jones were other recipients.

We cannot be sure whether Mill or other 'Ricardians' were amongst the recipients in 1829, although this cannot be ruled out since Whewell had written to Jones of his intention to have the paper printed and sent 'to the Economists whom I know, by way of challenge' which perhaps implies economists from whom he expected objections (5 March 1829, WPC: Add.Mss. c.51.[62]). But in any event, the paper appeared the following year in the *Transactions of the Cambridge Philosophical Society* III (1830) (I), 191–230.

Whewell's second paper – 'Mathematical exposition of some of the leading doctrines in Mr Ricardo's "Principles . . . "' – was read on 18 April and 2 May 1831 and immediately printed (Dionysius Lardner acknowledged receipt on 31 May [WPC: Add.Ms. a.208.[4]]). See also Whewell to J. D. Forbes, 14 July 1831 in Todhunter 1876: II, 122). The paper also appeared in the *Transactions of the Cambridge Philosophical Society*, IV (1833) (I), 155–98.

10 'On the definition of political economy and on the method of philosophical investigation in that science', *London and Westminster Review* (October 1836); reprinted (with some revision) as Essay V in *Essays on Some Unsettled Questions of Political Economy* (1844), CW, IV: 309f. The Preface to the *Unsettled Questions* gives the date of writing as 1829 and 1830; but Mill's bibliography gives it as Autumn 1831 (Ney MacMinn et al. [eds] *Bibliography of the Published Writings of John Stuart Mill* [Evanston, 1945] 47). See also Mill to John Stirling, 20–22 October 1831, CW, XII: 79–80. Mill also refers to a rewriting of the essay in the summer of 1833 (*Bibliography*, 47), and we find him in early 1834 asking

for suggestions of 'all manner of further developments, clearer explanations, and apter illustrations' (Mill to J. P. Nichol, 17 January 1834, *CW*, XII: 211). In his *Autobiography* Mill also alludes to a partial rewriting of the essay in 1833 (*CW*, I: 189).

11   In the passage just cited, however, Herschel seems to confound the 'science' and 'art' of political economy by conceiving the subject as concerned with the solution to a particular problem in policy. Mill in his essay warned against this type of confusion.

12   Mill also drew in the *System of Logic* upon Herschel's detailed analysis of the four methods of experimental investigation and his cautions regarding the limited scope of 'empirical laws' (cf. *CW*, VII: 405–6, 414f, 426–8).

See also the friendly remarks regarding Herschel's book, in Mill to Herschel, 1 May 1843, *CW*, VIII: 583–4.

See also Mill's earlier analysis of Richard Whately's *Elements of Logic* for the *Westminster Review* of 1828 where – by and large following Whately on the principle involved – Mill took issue with those 'inductive philosophers of modern times' who (misunderstanding the criticisms of the schoolmen by 'their idol' Bacon) believed that 'it was necessary to discard the syllogism which they thought was one method of reasoning, and confine ourselves to induction, which they imagined was another' ('Whately's *Elements of Logic*', *Westminster Review*, IX, January 1828, in *CW*, XI: 12–14). On Mill's early speculations regarding induction and deduction see Pappé 1979; Sparshott 1978, in *CW*, XI: Introduction.

13   Regarding *Preliminary Discourse*, 95–6.

14   See also vii, xii, xxii–xxiii, xxvii, xxix–xl for the failure of the orthodox economists to build up general principles in responsible fashion.

15   For Whewell's comments on Whately and Senior, see letters to Jones, February 1831 and 15 July 1831, in Todhunter 1876: 115, 123; and his review of Jones for *The British Critic, Quarterly Theological Review and Ecclesiastical Record*, X (July 1831): 56.

Whewell complained in the *British Critic* (58) of McCulloch's review of Jones' *Distribution of Wealth*, for the *Edinburgh Review* (1831: 84–99), that McCulloch 'has not been ... at all induced to retract his assertion of the universality of the principles which belong to farmers' rents alone'; and that he confused *metayer* and *ryot* rents. Apart from this, Whewell objected (on religious grounds) to McCulloch's representation of man as a 'machine' (60). See too letter to Jones, 27 December 1832, in Todhunter 1876: 152.

16   See also Whewell to Jones, 23 July 1831: 'you will give us illustrations and examples of the ascending method applied to moral sciences, we shall have no difficulty in fighting the "downward road" people' (125).

17   'People care so little about all matters of method abstractly considered, that I should be better satisfied of obtaining notice if we had more to shew in the way of example of the right method – in short if you would get your Wages published' (Whewell to Jones, 15 July 1831, 123). Also Whewell to Herschel, 8 June 1831: 'I hope he [Jones] will work, for the part he is now employed upon is of more importance both from its novelty and its applicability than the former' (WPC: 0.15.97[129]).

18   In a paper 'On the use of definition', *Philological Museum*, II (1833), Whewell had maintained that definition is not the starting point in the process of discovery but the last stage. Malthus responded (1 April 1833):

I confess I was a little alarmed at it at first; and thought it was an attack upon my definitions in Political Economy, which I certainly do not consider as useless. I agree with you in thinking that new definitions of terms are not always necessary to get at truth; and that the most exact definitions are not so much the causes as the consequences from our advances in knowledge. At the same time, I should say, that in regard to this latter position, they act and react upon each other, and that without some understanding as to the meaning of the words used the advances in knowledge would be very slow, though it might still be quite true that you would not arrive at the very best definitions, till a very great progress had been made.

(On this matter see Todhunter 1876: I, 66.)

See also a comment to Jones, 19 February 1832, Todhunter 1876: 141, which is potentially of great interest in the light of the later formulations discussed in the Introduction: 'conceptions must exist in the mind in order to get by induction a law from the collection of facts' because of 'the impossibility of inducting or even of collecting without this'.

19 A rift developed in the 1830s between Jones and Whewell on the role of mental constructs, Jones (siding with Herschel) allowing for 'conceptions of the mind' only in the abstract sciences such as geometry, but not in the natural sciences. Cf. de Marchi and Sturges 1973: 381n: 'This rift may have been quite as important as the better-known fact of Jones's delays in publishing in preventing the development of an effective inductivist alliance against the Ricardian School'.

20 The reference is to Thompson, *The True Theory of Rent in Opposition to Mr Ricardo and Others*. Whewell had at hand the third edition (1828), cf. Todhunter 1876: 93–4. (Thompson, it may be noted, had addressed himself to the version of the rent doctrine formulated by James Mill in his *Elements of Political Economy* [1820].) Whewell was much taken with Thompson's criticism, based on the nature of infinite series, of the Ricardian rejection of Adam Smith's proposition that taxes on wages result in a higher general level of prices.

21 Cf. Whewell to Jones, 5 March 1829:

> my object is to shew the *mode* of applying mathematics so as to extract difficulties of calculation from difficulties of moral reasoning – to keep apart the business of reasoning *up to principles & down from* them. The former is inductive & belongs to you, the latter is *deductive* & may, I am sure, be managed best by my implements.
>
> (WPC: Add.Mss. c.51.[62])

22 For technical analyses see Cochrane 1970; Henderson 1973.

23 The supposed 'errors of reasoning' by orthodox theorists include the rent doctrine, particularly the notion that an increase in aggregate rents proves the interests of the landlord to be opposed to those of society; favourable reference is made to Jones 1831: ch. vii (cf. Whewell 1831b: 59f). Whewell also refers to Jones' attempt to show that a falling profit rate, and an increase in the price of raw produce relative to manufacturing prices and foreign corn prices, 'are entirely insufficient to prove such a diminution of agricultural efficiency' as the 'Ricardists' believed.

24 Whewell was much prone to downplay his own contribution to mathematical economics, e.g. to Herschel, 8 June 1931: 'You will find in the last N° of the Transactions a paper of mine on the Mathematics of Political Economy. I hope to see the day when the Ricardist system will be considered as good for no other use' (WPC: 0.15.97[129]); to Jones, 23 April 1849: 'People will not mind

me when I write Political Economy, except indeed I join to it mathematics, and make nonsense of it' (Whewell in Todhunter 1876: 353).

25   In an interesting letter (Whewell to Jones, 2 April 1829) there seems to be an expression of a more positive attitude towards deduction on Whewell's part than that of Jones:

> I have not much more expectation than you have that mathematics will for a long time to come be an important instrument in advancing political economy, but I think that we hope it will prevent people from drawing wrong conclusions from the data they have got and may systematize and illustrate some of the course of reasoning which the Ricardists consider to be important *though you do not*. They certainly have gone wrong in some instances of bad calculation alone....I do hope that it will prevent my friends the young mathematicians from looking with too profound and unquestioning an awe upon the crasser dogmatizing of the Millians.
>
> (WPC: Mss. c.51.[63], emphasis added)

26   His statement in correspondence of 1831, to J. D. Forbes, 14 July (Todhunter 1876: II, 122) that 'I profess only to trace the consequences of Ricardo's principles – principles which I am sure are insufficient and believe *to be entirely false*' is belied by the texts.

27   Precisely the same position is adopted on these matters in Whewell 1968 [1829]: 8–9).

28   Cf. also 51:

> It is surely worth notice, as a remarkable circumstance, that our modern political economists, up to the present time, should have shut their eyes upon all the forms of rent which have been explained in the previous part of our review, and should have selected farmers' rents, and their conditions, as the materials of a doctrine necessarily and universally applicable.

29   Cf. a specific observation by Herschel in correspondence with Whewell which also implies a far less critical approach than that of Jones:

> In Jones's exposé of Ricardo & Malthus's doctrine he has hardly kept strongly enough in his readers view the circumstance that, in an extensive country where much inferior land exists uncultivated the same course of events which raises rents by the more efficient cultivation of the old soils & outlays of Capital on them, will, though not necessarily, yet, by a practical certainty, cause some portion of Capital to flow over on new soils of inferior quality. It will still then remain practically true that [?] of rent is [?] in country – on the long run – accompanied with a resort to inferior soil. Ricardo's error on W[h.] Jones dwells so strongly seems to me to consist mainly in mistaking this almost sure concomitant of rents for their cause whereas their real cause is *that quality of the soil by which its cultivation replaces the outlay on it by a larger return than the average profits of Capital & ∴ other branches of trade*.
>
> (Herschel to Whewell, [15, 18?] February 1831, WPC: Add.Ms. a.207.[19])

30   Oddly enough, Whewell recognised that the level of 'subsistence' was, for Ricardo, not a *physiological* matter but proceeded with his criticism in only slightly modified form: 'The assumption that the *habits* of the labourers cannot change from period to period, so as to accommodate themselves to different

amounts of real wages, appears to be quite unsupported by reason, and in direct contradiction to all known history' (1968 [1831]: 7).

31 A similar position had already been expressed several years earlier, cf. Whewell to Jones, December 1826, in Todhunter 1876: 81:

> What I have to say about [the principle of population] is in sum this – that the false induction consists in generalizing the impulse to increase, and not generalizing, to a coordinate extent and with corresponding views of their bearing, the moderating and controlling influences which the nature of society and of man contain.

32 He proceeded to use the fix-wage assumption in his mathematical rendition of Ricardo's model, which he took to task regarding taxation:

> We assume still the postulate of wages, although, as has been said, it appears to be unfounded, and consequently the inferences to which it leads, as to the incidence of taxes, will not be verified in fact. But, granting the principle, there appears to be some difficulty in tracing its results, and Mr Ricardo, in attempting to do so, has been led into an arithmetical fallacy, as was pointed out by Col. Thompson, and as I have shewn in a preceding Memoir. (Ricardo, p. 301, and *Camb. Trans.*, Vol. III, p. 192.) Mr Ricardo's opinion was, that taxes upon wages fall entirely on profits, while other writers maintain that they will affect prices and rent. Calculations such as we have already employed will enable us to obtain the true result in this case.
> (Whewell 1968 [1831]: 27; see also note 20 above)

33 Although the average wage rate is at subsistence the general profit rate is on the decline; the economy is not in a stationary state.

34 He seems to contradict himself when he adds:

> It may however still be curious to see the exact consequences of the assumptions now referred to; and moreover, our formulae will be applicable with no great modification, to the case in which the powers of production are supposed to have increased.

35 For a full treatment see my 'J. S. Mill's methodology of economics: on "economic man" and the empirical dimension to deductive theory' (unpublished ms, 1981).

36 There is an extensive tradition in the economic literature that this was indeed Mill's position. Cf. Ingram 1888: 150; Keynes 1891: 19; Viner 1917, in E. J. Hamilton *et al.* 1962: 108f; Marshall 1920: 823–4; Schumpeter 1954: 537; O'Brien 1975: 73; Koot 1975: 322; Hutchison 1978: 55, 63–4.

See, however, Schwartz 1972, *The New Political Economy of John Stuart Mill*, thus called to reflect 'the repercussions of Mill's reactions against the Utilitarians on his methodology of economics', reactions discernible in the essay (59); and Ryan 1970, for an emphasis upon an 'empiricist' dimension to Mill's methodology: 'he rejects also the excessively abstract and hypothetical approach to Economics, which was typified by what he named the "geometrical" method of James Mill's *Essay on Government*' (xviii); cf. also:

> Mill takes care to point out that *a priori* does not mean altogether independent of experience; the principles of human nature from which we reason are obtained by inductive inquiry. In the light of Macaulay's jibes at James Mill, this is an essential point to make.
> (Ryan 1970: 140)

37   There are also, a careful comparison reveals, numerous specific instances of linguistic similarity between the two formulations.

38   Cf. Strong 1955: 222.

39   We have shown Whewell's ambiguity to lie in his simultaneous condemnation of and allowance for Ricardian deductive theory. Checkland, however, sees things a little differently: Whewell was not

> averse to political economy *per se*. Richard Jones provided the escape from the apparent dilemma with his Baconian injunction to 'look and see'. It was to him that Whewell, Sedgwick, Herschel, and other leading Cambridge scientists gave their blessing. Political economy was to some a long, perhaps indefinite, apprenticeship to the facts. This meant, of course, that to the public their attitude appeared ambiguous, involving acceptance of political economy, but rejection of the leading school, at a time when the two appeared to the indiscriminating to be coterminous.
>
> (Checkland 1951: 61)

40   See on all this Checkland 1951, esp. 52–3; and also 60f regarding opposition to utilitarianism.

See also Rashid 1980 (esp. 289–91) on the Cambridge opposition to 'Ricardian' economics on the ground that ethics could not be separated from theology or based on materialistic premises. In the battle against Utilitarianism, Ricardian economics was seen as the ally or associate of Benthamism.

41   'Professor Sedgwick's *Discourse on the Studies at the University of Cambridge*', *London Review* (April 1835); *CW*, X: 35. Sedgwick's *Discourse* was based on a lecture delivered in the Chapel of Trinity College in December 1832. The published version was dedicated to the 'Master of Trinity' (Whewell). Mill reviewed the 3rd edition (1834) (see *CW*, XII: 235, 238).

42   Cf. Cannon 1964. Whewell had published in defence of mandatory daily attendance at college chapel service (cf. J. M. Douglas [Mrs S. Douglas], *The Life and Selections from the Correspondence of William Whewell* [London, 1881], 165, 173).

43   'Whewell's moral philosophy', *Westminster and Foreign Quarterly Review*, October 1852. Cf. *CW*, X: 168–9 – 'in the English Universities no thought can find place except that which can reconcile itself with orthodoxy'.

44   We have, however, shown how even in his published works some of these doubts came into the open.

45   See also his praise of Mill's Book VI:

> though I have myself restrained from associating moral and political with physical science in my study of the subject, I see a great deal which is full of promise for the future progress of moral and political knowledge in Mr Mill's sixth Book, 'On the Logic of the Moral and Political Sciences'. Even his arrangement of the various methods which have been or may be followed in 'the Social Science', – 'the Chemical or Experimental Method', 'the Geometrical or Abstract Method', 'the Physical or Concrete Deductive Method', 'the Inverse Deductive or Historical Method', though in some degree fanciful and forced, abounds with valuable suggestions, and his estimate of 'the interesting philosophy of the Bentham school', the main example of 'the geometrical method' is interesting and philosophical.
>
> (Whewell 1860: 290–1)

46   Cf. also the positive statement regarding equilibrium in economics treated as 'tendency' in 'Mathematical exposition of some doctrines of political economy.

Second memoir', read before the Cambridge Philosophical Society, April 1850;
cf. Whewell 1968 [1829]: 22.

47   Cf. *CW*, VIII: 912.
   Cf. Knight 1956 [1947]: 227–47. And Popper 1963: II, 87, citing Mill:
   'The fundamental problem . . . of the social science, is to find the law according
   to which any state of society produces the state which succeeds it and takes its
   place' (*CW*, VIII: 912). Also 322, regarding the historical method:

> By its aid we may hereafter succeed not only in looking far forward into the
> future history of the human race, but in determining what artificial means
> may be used, and to what extent, to accelerate the natural progress as far as it
> is beneficial.
>
> (*CW*, VIII: 930)

48   The normal sequence appropriate in specialist branches of social science was
   inapplicable because of the complexity involved – namely, to set out from
   principles of human nature and 'determine the order in which human
   development must take place, and to predict consequently, the general facts of
   history up to the present time' (*CW*, VIII: 915–16).
   In his *Autobiography*, Mill attributes the inverse deductive method to Comte
   and defines it thus:

> instead of arriving at its conclusions by general reasoning and verifying
> them by specific experience (as is the natural order in the deductive branches
> of physical science), it obtains its generalizations by a collation of specific
> experience, and verifies them by ascertaining whether they are such as would
> follow from known general principles.
>
> (*CW*, I: 219)

49   Cf. *CW*, VIII: 930. The passage cited by Popper (above, note 47) does not
   necessarily bear an authoritarian connotation any more than similar statements
   in the context of the specialist social sciences.
50   Cf. also 914–15.
51   Mill to J. P. Nichol, 30 September 1848, regarding Comte's *Discours sur
   l'Ensemble du Positivisme* (1848).
52   The reference to Bacon is to *Novum Organum*, Book I, Aphorism 26: 'We are
   wont, for the sake of distinction, to call that human reasoning which we apply
   to nature the anticipation of nature (as being rash and premature), and that
   which is properly deduced from things the interpretation of nature'. Aphorism
   19 contains the reference to induction as a process of gradual ascent:

> There are and can exist but two ways of investigating and discovering truth.
> The one hurries on rapidly from the senses and particulars to the most
> general axioms, and from them, as principles and their supposed
> indisputable truth, derives and discovers the intermediate axioms. This is
> the way now in use. The other constructs its axioms from the senses and
> particulars, by ascending continually and gradually, till it finally arrives at
> the most general axioms, which is the true but unattempted way.

References

Buchdahl, G. (1971) 'Inductivist versus Deductivist approaches in the philosophy of
   science as illustrated by some controversies between Whewell and Mill', *The
   Monist*, 55 (July): 343–67.

Butts, R. E. (ed.) (1968) *William Whewell's Theory of Scientific Method*, Pittsburgh: University of Pittsburgh Press.

Cannon, W. E. (1964) 'Scientists and broad churchmen: an early Victorian intellectual network', *Journal of British Studies*, 4 (November): 65–88.

Checkland, S. G. (1951) 'The advent of academic economics in England', *The Manchester School of Economic and Social Studies*, 19 (January): 43–70.

Cochrane, J. L. (1970) 'The first mathematical Ricardian model', *History of Political Economy* 2 (fall): 419–31.

Hamilton, E. J., Rees, A. and Johnson, H. G. (eds) (1962) *Landmarks in Political Economy*, Chicago: University of Chicago Press.

von Hayek, F. A. (1941) 'The counter-revolution of science', *Economica*, 8 (February): 9–36; (May): 119–50; (August): 281–320.

——(1942–4) 'Scientism and the study of society', *Economica*, 9 (August 1942): 267–91; 10 (February 1943): 34–63; 11/12 (February 1944): 27–39.

Henderson, J. P. (1973) 'William Whewell's mathematical statements of price flexibility, demand elasticity and the Giffen Paradox', *The Manchester School* (September): 329–42.

Herschel, J. F. W. (1830) *Preliminary Discourse on the Study of Natural Philosophy*, London: Longman.

——(1841) Review of Whewell, *History of the Inductive Sciences from the Earliest to the Present Times* (1837), *Philosophy of the Inductive Sciences Founded upon Their History* (1840), in *Quarterly Review*, 68 (June): 177–238.

Hutchison, T. W. (1978) *On Revolutions and Progress in Economic Knowledge*, Cambridge: Cambridge University Press.

Ingram, J. K. (1888) *A History of Political Economy*, London: A & C Black.

Jones, R. (1831) *An Essay on the Distribution of Wealth and the Sources of Taxation: Part I – Rent*, London: John Murray.

——(1833) 'An introductory lecture on political economy, delivered at King's College, London, 27 February 1833', cited in W. Whewell 'Prefatory notice', *Literary Remains Consisting of Lectures and Tracts on Political Economy by the Late Rev. Richard Jones* (London, 1859), xxiv–xxv.

Keynes, J. N. (1955) [1891] *Scope and Method of Political Economy*, 4th edn, New York: Kelley and Millman.

Knight, F. H. (1956) [1947] 'Salvation by science: the gospel according to Professor Lundberg', in *On the History and Method of Economics*, Chicago: University of Chicago Press, 227–47.

Koot, G. M. (1975) 'T. F. Leslie, Irish social reform, and the origins of the English Historical School of Economics', *History of Political Economy* 7 (fall): 312–36.

McRae, R. F. (1973) Introduction, *System of Logic: Ratiocinative and Inductive*, VII, *Collected Works of John Stuart Mill*, Toronto: University of Toronto Press.

de Marchi, N. B. and Sturges, R. P. (1973) 'Malthus and Ricardo's inductivist critics: four letters to William Whewell', *Economica*, 40 (November): 379–93.

Marshall, A. (1920) *Principles of Economics*, 8th edn, London: Macmillan.

Mill, J. S. (1963–91) *Collected Works of John Stuart Mill*, Toronto: University of Toronto Press. Herein *CW*.

——(1967) *Essays on Economics and Society, Collected Works*, IV.

——(1969) [1852] 'Whewell's moral philosophy', *Westminster and Foreign Quarterly Review* (October): 169–91, in *Essays on Ethics, Religion, and Society, Collected Works*, X.

——(1973) [1872] *A System of Logic, Ratiocinative and Inductive*, 8th edn, in *Collected Works*, VII., viii.

——(1978) [1828] 'Whately's *Elements of Logic*', *Westminster Review*, IX (January): 3–35, in *Essays on Philosophy and the Classics, Collected Works*, XI.

——(1981) *Autobiography and Literary Essays, Collected Works*, I.

Nagel, E. (1950) *John Stuart Mill's Philosophy of Scientific Method*, New York: Hafner.

O'Brien, D. P. (1975) *The Classical Economists*, Oxford: Clarendon Press.

Pappé, H. O. (1979) 'The English Utilitarians and Athenian democracy', in R. R. Bolgar (ed.) *Classical Influences on Western Thought AD 1650–1870*, Cambridge: Cambridge University Press, 295–308.

Popper, K. R. (1963) *The Open Society and its Enemies*, New York: Harper and Row.

Randall, J. H. (1965) 'John Stuart Mill and the working-out of empiricism', *Journal of the History of Ideas*, 26: 59–88.

Rashid, S. (1980) 'The growth of economic studies at Cambridge, 1776–1860', *History of Education Quarterly* 20 (fall): 281–94.

Ryan, A. (1970) *The Philosophy of John Stuart Mill*, London: Macmillan.

——(1979) Introduction, *An Examination of Sir William Hamilton's Philosophy*, in *Collected Works of John Stuart Mill*, IX, Toronto: University of Toronto Press.

Schumpeter, J. A. (1954) *History of Economic Analysis*, New York: Oxford University Press.

Schwartz, P. (1972) *The New Political Economy of John Stuart Mill*, London: Weidenfeld and Nicolson.

Sparshott, F. E. (1978) Introduction, *Essays on Philosophy and the Classics, Collected Works of John Stuart Mill*, XI, Toronto: University of Toronto Press.

Strong, E. W. (1955) 'William Whewell and John Stuart Mill: their controversy about scientific knowledge', *Journal of the History of Ideas*, 16: 209–31.

Thompson, T. P. (1828) *The True Theory of Rent in Opposition to Mr Ricardo and Others*, 3rd edn, London: Heward.

Todhunter, I. (ed.) (1876) *William Whewell, D.D.: Master of Trinity College, Cambridge*, II, London: Macmillan.

Viner, J. (1962) [1917] 'Some problems of logical method in political economy', *Journal of Political Economy*, 25, in E. J. Hamilton *et al.* (eds) (1962), *Landmarks in Political Economy*, Chicago: University of Chicago Press, 101–24.

Whewell, W. (1831a) 'Herschel – a preliminary discourse on the study of natural philosophy', *Quarterly Review*, 45 (July): 374–407.

——(1831b) 'Jones – on the distribution of wealth', *The British Critic, Quarterly Theological Review and Ecclesiastical Record*, 10 (July): 41–61.

——(1834) *Astronomy and General Physics Considered with Reference to Natural Theology*, III of the *Bridgewater Treatises*, London: W. Pickering.

——(1840) *Philosophy of the Inductive Sciences*, London: Parker.

——(1860) *On the Philosophy of Discovery*; 'Of induction, with especial reference to Mr J. S. Mill's System of Logic' (1849); 'Political economy as an inductive science' (1860); London: Parker.

——(1968) [1829] *Mathematical Exposition of Some Doctrines of Political Economy*, Cambridge, 1829; reprinted 1968, Farnborough: Gregg International (also reprinted 1971, New York: Kelley).

——(1968) [1831] *Mathematical Exposition of Some of the Leading Doctrines in Mr Ricardo's 'Principles of Political Economy and Taxation'*, Cambridge, 1831; reprinted 1968, Farnborough: Gregg International (also reprinted 1971, New York: Kelley).

Chapter 6

'Dynamic equilibrium' with constant wages

J. S. Mill's Malthusian analysis of the secular wage path

Introduction

In the Ricardian growth model, which utilises the axiom of diminishing agricultural returns, the real wage rate tends downwards, the profit rate falling notwithstanding this decline. The 'subsistence' wage rules in the stationary state alone and is reached simultaneously with that rate of profit corresponding to zero net capital accumulation (Hicks and Hollander 1977; Samuelson 1978; Hollander 1983a). There are differences of detail between these versions: For Samuelson the downward wage path is a 'dynamic equilibrium' path (the rates of growth of capital and labour proceeding in line) assuming regular positive relationships between growth of capital and population and their respective returns. (The subsistence wage path is a limiting theoretical case though consistent with balanced factor growth.) In the Hicks–Hollander version the system moves with wages declining on the average to the subsistence level, the wage movement resulting from deviations between the growth rates of capital and labour. The Hicks–Hollander version captures one aspect of Ricardo, but a case can also be made for the stronger (dynamic equilibrium) version considering Ricardo's subscription to Malthus' analysis and the basic Smithian growth principle discussed in the following paragraphs.

The first clear exposition of a general 'dynamic equilibrium' growth model was by Malthus. In his *Principles of Political Economy* (1820) we have a splendid statement of the presumption that in a system involving ongoing population growth the real wage must exceed the subsistence level but the impossibility (because of land scarcity) of such excess remaining unchanged throughout the course towards stationariness; and moreover the impossibility also of the (common) factor growth rates remaining at a constant level:

> the supposition ... of a constant uniformity in the real wage of labour is not only contrary to the actual state of things, but involves a contradiction.
>
> The progress of population is almost exclusively regulated by the

quantity of the necessaries of life actually awarded to the labourer; and if from the first he has no more than sufficient to keep up the actual population, the labouring classes could not increase, nor would there be any occasion for the progressive cultivation of poorer land. On the other hand, if the real wages of labour were such as to admit of and encourage an increase of population, and yet were always to remain the same, it would involve the contradiction of a continued increase of population after the accumulation of capital, and the means of supporting such an increase had entirely ceased.

We cannot then make the supposition of a *natural* and *constant* price of labour, at least if we mean by such a price, an unvarying quantity of the necessaries of life. And if we cannot fix the real price of labour, it must evidently vary with the progress of capital and revenue, and the demand for labour compared with the supply.

We may, however, if we please, suppose a uniform progress of capital and population by which is not meant in the present case the same *rate* of progress permanently, which is impossible; but a uniform progress towards the greatest practicable amount, without temporary accelerations or retardations.

(Malthus 1820: 297)[1]

In his *Essay on Population*, on the other hand, Malthus outlined an alternative growth model wherein even in circumstances of land scarcity and diminishing returns, wages may remain constant, although not at the 'subsistence' level in the sense of a wage at which population size remains unchanged. The constancy of the wage is not, however, subject to the objection made by Malthus himself in the *Principles*; for a change in axiom is involved, namely, the divorce of the rate of population growth from the level of wages, or the abandonment of the fundamental Smithian relationship whereby

the demand for labour, according as it happens to be either increasing, stationary, or declining; or to require an increasing, stationary, or declining population, regulates the subsistence of the labourer, and determines in what degree it shall be, either liberal, moderate, or scanty.

(Smith 1937: 815)

On this latter view, a deceleration of the capital growth rate during the course of expansion will entail a reduction in the real wage even though population growth decelerates in line; indeed, it is precisely in consequence of a lower wage that the population growth rate is brought into line. Malthus' alternative, by contrast, recognises the possibility that labourers exert a deliberate effort to keep long-run wages unchanged by appropriately reducing the rate of population growth – by way of prudential reduction in the marriage rate (and thus the birth rate) – in the face of a falling rate of accumulation. It follows from this change in behavioural axiom that the 'burden' of diminishing returns is no longer shared between capitalists and labourers in the form of a decline in both profit and wage rates; what occurs is a decline in the profit rate and a sharper decline in the population growth rate than in the alternative case until stationariness is achieved (for a full account see Hollander 1983b, 1984).

The two Malthusian versions were effectively utilised in response to a proposal by Arthur Young 'so to adjust the wages of day-labour as to make them at all times equivalent to the purchase of a peck of wheat' (1890: 583). This proposal 'in its general operation, and supposing no change of habits among the labouring classes', Malthus objected,

> would be tantamount to saying that, under all circumstances, whether the affairs of the country were prosperous or adverse; whether its resources in land were still great, or nearly exhausted; its population ought to increase exactly at the same rate – a conclusion which involves an impossibility.

Here we have an application of the 'standard' model – the wage path *must* fall to assure the appropriate deceleration in the population growth rate. But allow for prudence and the picture is transformed, as Malthus proceeds to show:

> If, however, this adjustment, instead of being enforced by law, were provided by the increasing operation of the prudential check to marriage, the effect would be totally different, and in the highest degree beneficial to society. A gradual change in the habits of the labouring classes would then effect the necessary retardation in the rate of increase, and would proportion the supply of labour to the effective demand, as society continued to advance ... without the pressure of a diminishing quantity of food, but under the enjoyment of an increased quantity of conveniences, and luxuries.
>
> (Malthus 1890: 583)

Our concern in this paper is with J. S. Mill. We shall demonstrate that Mill followed Malthus in all major respects, and adopted the analysis according to which the profit rate declines with the real wage proceeding unchanged, although not, of course, along the subsistence path. We shall also consider some specific applications. Mill (like Malthus) did not concern himself with simplification for pedagogical purposes. His model carried a fundamentally important policy message – to encourage emulation by the unskilled of the 'prudential' behaviour already practised by skilled industrial workers. The object was to forestall the fall in wages which *must* occur upon any decline in the rate of accumulation, should population growth continue at its maximum physiological capacity irrespective of the wage (the polar opposite case to that of prudential behaviour designed to maintain the wage). The warning, it transpires, applied to the future. For the striking feature of Mill's account of contemporary British manufacturing is constancy of the profit rate and of wages (perhaps even an upward trend) notwithstanding rapid population growth. This confluence of circumstances is possible only where land scarcity is not yet manifest (as in North America) or where its effects are counterbalanced by new technology. It is the latter situation that applied in Britain, and Mill's warning to labour was with an eye to a possible future drying-up of the sources of new technology.

Before proceeding to our task, reference should be made to a brilliant investigation of the features of the constant-wage model by Caravale and Tosato (1980). The authors attribute the model to Ricardo, basing themselves on a passage in the *Essay on Profits* – that he would assume 'that capital and population advance in the proper proportion, so that the real wages of labour, continue uniformly the same' (Ricardo 1951, IV: 12; in Caravale and Tosato 1980: 11, 113–14). But Ricardo immediately thereafter himself explains why he proceeded thus: 'that we may know what peculiar effects are to be ascribed to the growth of capital, the increase of population, and the extension of cultivation, to the more remote, and less fertile land'. It is merely a simplifying assumption made for a particular expository purpose; the analysis in the *Principles* proceeds otherwise, although in all probability Ricardo would have welcomed the prudential model.[2] The formal model is the work of Malthus and Mill.[3]

Capital and labour supply conditions

We commence by brief reference to the capital and labour supply conditions presupposed in the *Principles of Political Economy*. Mill formulated a regular functional relation between savings and the profit (interest) rate. There is no ambiguity regarding this matter: 'The greater the profit that can be made from capital, the stronger is the motive to its accumulation' (Mill 1965: 161); 'when profits fall, increase of capital is slackened' (344); 'it is . . . an almost infallible consequence of any reduction of profits, to retard the rate of accumulation' (843; cf. 827, 844). A minimum return on capital is also defined:

Any accumulation . . . by which the general capital is increased, requires as its necessary condition a certain rate of profit; a rate which an average person will deem to be an equivalent for abstinence, with the addition of a sufficient insurance against risk.

(Mill 1965: 737)

When this rate (which may vary geographically and temporally) rules, 'no further increase of capital can for the present take place' (738).

Mill approached the population variable by insisting upon the continued usefulness of the Malthusian conception of a maximum physiological capacity of a human population to double itself in approximately two decades, drawing for evidence upon 'the most favourable circumstances known to exist, which are those of a fertile region colonized from an industrious and civilized community' (Mill 1965: 155). Under usual conditions this geometrical ratio is not, however, encountered and it is with the nature of the 'checks' that Mill is preoccupied in his chapter on the 'Law of the increase of labour' (Book I.10) – 'the unlimited extent of its natural powers of increase and the causes owing to which so small a portion of that unlimited power is for the most part actually exercised' (Mill 1965: 159).

The check to the maximum population growth rate was not necessarily imposed by the death rate ('only' by the death rate was added in 1852) – war and disease, and insufficiency of food – the birth rate achieving the maximum level physiologically possible. Human reproduction was also to a greater or lesser degree 'restrained by the fear of want rather than by want itself', so that even where starvation was not an issue, 'many' ('most' in the manuscript and editions 1848, 1849) were yet influenced by 'the apprehension of losing what have come to be regarded as the decencies of their situation in life'; acting from motives of 'prudence' or the 'social affections', people married at such age and had that number of offspring 'consistent with maintaining themselves in the condition of life which they were born to, or were accustomed to consider as theirs' (Mill 1965: 157).[4]

The constraints on population growth by way of deaths, and of prudential control of births designed to maintain living standards, are said to be the sole forces 'hitherto . . . found strong enough, in the generality of mankind, to counteract the tendency to increase' – that is, the tendency to increase at the maximum rate possible. Limitation of family size to the end of actually raising living standards is conceded amongst members of the middle class; but 'such a desire is rarely found, or rarely has that effect, in the labouring classes. If they can bring up a family as they were themselves brought up, even the prudent among them are usually satisfied' (Mill 1965: 157). And although Mill adds that 'too often they do not even think of that, but rely on fortune, or on the resources to be found in legal or voluntary charity', implying an absence of 'prudence', he concludes by contrasting contemporary Asian conditions or those of medieval Europe, where population was held down by starvation, with modern societies wherein 'few, even among the poorest of the people, are limited by actual necessaries, and to a bare sufficiency of those; and the increase is kept within bounds, not by excess of deaths, but by limitation of births' (Mill 1965: 157) – again a reference to restrictions on the growth rate of population below its maximum.

These were generalities. We shall see presently that the practice of 'prudential' behaviour in contemporary Britain was limited to the class of skilled labourers. Reproduction on the part of the unskilled was at the maximum physiological rate possible without regard to the maintenance of living standards.

A further essential preliminary for what follows is the formal contrast between circumstances where land scarcity is not yet manifest, and where an increase in population at its 'maximum' potential rate (namely a doubling in a single generation) can proceed with no downward pressure on the real wage rate, and situations where this possibility is ruled out. The former included specifically North America and the Australian colonies, which enjoyed advanced European technology and savings habits and were not subject to land scarcity, so that the rate of accumulation proceeded at least as rapidly as population at its maximum and the real wage was maintained above subsistence at a steady, perhaps increasing, level:

> In countries like North America and the Australian colonies, where the knowledge and arts of civilized life, and a high effective desire of accumulation, co-exist with a boundless extent of unoccupied land, the growth of capital easily keeps pace with the utmost possible increase of population, and is chiefly retarded by the impracticability of obtaining labourers enough. All, therefore, who can possibly be born, can find employment, without overstocking the market: every labouring family enjoys in abundance the necessaries, many of the comforts, and some of the luxuries of life.
>
> (Mill 1965: 343–4)

In the absence of this special confluence of circumstances, it would be impossible for population to expand at the maximum rate without downward pressure on wages, and this because of impediments to the rate of accumulation. These impediments might act directly:

> those circumstances . . . in which population can with impunity increase at its utmost rate, are rare, and transitory. Very few are the countries presenting the needful union of conditions. Either the industrial arts are backward and stationary, and capital therefore increases slowly; or the effective desire of accumulation being low, the increase soon reaches its limit.

But even where these direct constraints on accumulation are absent, the effects of land scarcity – a falling marginal product – will bear upon the rate of accumulation: 'The increase of capital is checked, because there is not fresh land to be resorted to, of as good quality as that already occupied' (Mill 1965: 344).

The constant-wage growth model

We turn now to our case that Mill recognised the possibility of ongoing factor expansion with the wage constrained to a level exceeding subsistence strictly defined. A version of the argument is found in the chapter on the 'Influence of progress...' (Book IV.3). Here, technology assumed given, population and capital are presumed to proceed at the same rate, implying a constant commodity wage: 'We shall suppose them... to increase with equal rapidity; the test of equality being, that each labourer obtains the same commodities as before, and the same quantity of those commodities' (Mill 1965: 723). The assumption of equal growth rates is made, since a more rapid expansion of either factor can be analysed in terms of one or other of the simpler hypothetical disturbances dealt with earlier in the chapter – population increasing with capital stationary, which implies a falling wage; or capital increasing with population stationary when wages rise. Mill then proceeded to trace out the consequences of a growth path entailing a given commodity wage:

> Population having increased, without any falling off of the labourer's condition, there is of course a demand for more food. The arts of production being supposed stationary, this food must be produced at an increased cost. To compensate for this greater cost of the additional food, the price of agricultural produce must rise.... Rent will rise both in quantity of produce and in cost [labour embodied]; while wages, being supposed to be the same in quantity, will be greater in cost. The labourer obtaining the same amount of necessaries, money wages have risen; and as the rise is common to all branches of production, the capitalist cannot indemnify himself by changing his employment, and the loss must be borne by profits.
>
> (Mill 1965: 723)

It is thus Mill's view that capital accumulation and population growth can proceed at the same rate with the return on capital declining – so that, considering the savings-interest relationship always insisted upon, the common factor growth rate must also be decelerating – and the wage rate constant.

Mill's formulations in the chapter 'Of taxes on commodities' (Book V.4) prove to be highly pertinent to the growth theme, particularly the deceleration of the capital growth rate during the course of expansion – a central feature of a comparison made between two economies identical in all respects bar the imposition of a tithe in one alone:

> Though the untithed island is always verging toward the point at which the price of food would overtake that in the tithed island, its progress toward that point naturally slackens as it draws nearer to attaining it; since – the difference between the two islands in the rapidity of accumulation depending upon the difference in the rates of profit [higher in untithed] – in proportion as these approximate, the movement which draws them closer together, abates of its force. The one may not actually overtake the other, until both islands reach the minimum of profits: up to that point, the tithed island may continue more or less ahead of the untithed island in the price of corn: considerably ahead if it is far from the minimum, and is therefore accumulating rapidly; very little ahead if it is near the minimum, and accumulating slowly.
>
> (Mill 1965: 845)

Nothing is here said of a declining real wage during the course of ongoing expansion, and this despite the slowing down in the rate of accumulation, so that on Mill's own terms one must suppose population growth to be declining in line with capital. The absence of a falling real wage is clear in a statement, shortly before, that 'the effect of accumulation, when attended by its usual accompaniment, an increase of population, is to increase the value and price of food, to raise rent, and to lower profits' (843).

That a falling real wage is not a *sine qua non* of the growth process, despite a slowing down in capital accumulation, similarly comes to the fore in the earlier chapter (Book V.3) 'Of direct taxes':

> Even in countries which do not accumulate so fast as to be always within a short interval of the stationary state, it seems impossible that, if capital is accumulating at all, its accumulation should not be in some degree retarded by the abstraction of a portion of its profit; and...it is inevitable that a part of the burthen will be thrown off the capitalist, upon the labourer or the landlord. One or other of these is always the loser by a diminished rate of accumulation. If population continues to increase as before, the labourer suffers: if not, cultivation is checked in

its advance, and the landlords lose the accession of rents which would have accrued to them.

(Mill 1965: 828)

Here it is apparent that a slackening in the population growth rate – presumably to keep in line with that of capital – ensures against any fall of wages; only to the extent that population growth proceeds unchecked will wages fall.

The famous chapter specifically devoted to the 'Tendency of profits to a minimum' (Book IV.4) is also relevant to our theme. The chapter provides a splendid illustration of the sense of the notion 'tendency' to refer not to a necessarily observable trend but rather to a force (amongst other and possibly conflicting forces) acting on a particular variable:

> We now arrive at the fundamental proposition which this chapter is intended to inculcate. When a country has long possessed a large production, and a large net income to make savings from, and when, therefore, the means have long existed of making a great annual addition to capital; (the country not having, like America, a large reserve of fertile land still unused;) it is one of the characteristics of such a country, that the rate of profit is habitually within, as it were, a handsbreadth of the minimum, and the country therefore on the very verge of the stationary state. By this I do not mean that this state is likely, in any of the great countries of Europe, to be soon actually reached, or that capital does not still yield a profit considerably greater than what is barely sufficient to induce the people in those countries to save and accumulate. My meaning is, that it would require but a short time to reduce profits to the minimum, if capital continued to increase at its present rate, and no circumstances having a tendency to raise the rate of profit occurred in the meantime. The expansion of capital would soon reach its ultimate boundary, if the boundary itself did not continually open and leave more space.
>
> (Mill 1965: 738–9)

In the foregoing passage the downward trend of profits is related to capital growth proceeding at an *unchanged* rate. Similarly, in commenting on the contemporary British case: 'the mere continuance of the present annual increase of capital, if no circumstance occurred to counteract its effect, would suffice in a small number of years to reduce the rate of net profit to one per cent' (739) again:

> in such a country as England, if the present annual amount of savings were to continue, without any of the countervailing circumstances

which now keep in check the natural influence of those savings in reducing profit, the rate of profit would speedily attain the minimum, and all further accumulation of capital would for the present cease.

(741)

But although Mill neglected to make explicit the deceleration in accumulation that can be expected as profits fall, he certainly did not reject this repeatedly reiterated relationship (indeed the full savings function is again reiterated [747]). It is simply that the particular purpose of the exposition – to show that in the absence of 'counteracting circumstances' even the *same* rate of accumulation as experienced in actuality, *and no greater*, must soon force profits to the minimum – did not call for a full specification of the savings function. This task Mill assuredly left to his readers.

What assumption is being made regarding population growth and the wage rate? A slower growth rate of population than capital would certainly reduce the rate of profit, assuming given technology and a given distribution of productive and unproductive labour (yet a further condition added to the *ceteris paribus* basket):

an augmentation of capital, much more rapid than that of population, must soon reach its extreme limit, unless accompanied by increased efficiency of labour (through inventions and discoveries, or improved mental and physical education), or unless some of the idle people, or of the unproductive labourers, become productive.

(740)

But the main point is that even 'if population did increase with the increase of capital, and in proportion to it, the fall of profits would still be inevitable' in consequence of the rising price of agricultural produce. More specifically this holds true, Mill proceeds to clarify, 'unless the labourer submits to a deterioration in his condition', a possibility that is immediately set aside:

If both these avenues to an increased supply of food were closed [domestic technological change, easier food imports] and population continued to increase, as it is said to do, at the rate of a thousand a day, all waste land which admits of cultivation in the existing state of knowledge would soon be cultivated, and the cost of production and price of food would be so increased, that, if the labourers received the increased money wages necessary to compensate for their increased expenses, profits would very soon reach the minimum. The fall of profits would be retarded if money wages did not rise, or rose in a less degree; but the margin which can be gained by a deterioration of the labourers' condition is a very narrow one: in general they *cannot* bear much reduction; when they can, they have also a higher standard of necessary requirements, and *will* not.

(Mill 1965: 740–1)

That wages are above subsistence in the strict sense of the term is obvious – how else could population be growing at 'the rate of a thousand a day'? And yet a declining wage is not a necessary part of the story.

Mill's summary statement: the stationary state

Mill's famous chapter 'Of the stationary state' (Book IV.6) contains a passage which conveniently encapsulates the entire argument to this point. Most significant is the sharp awareness of the need for prudence in a growing system as well as in a state of stationariness. It is noteworthy, too, that Mill suggests that appropriate restraint might be more easily generated in a slowly growing economy or even a zero-growth economy:

> Even in a progressive state of capital, in old countries, a conscientious or prudential restraint on population is indispensable, to prevent the increase of numbers from outstripping the increase of capital, and the condition of the classes who are at the bottom of society from being deteriorated. Where there is not, in the people, or in some very large proportion of them, a resolute resistance to this deterioration – a determination to preserve an established standard of comfort – the condition of the poorest class sinks, even in a progressive state, to the lowest point which they will consent to endure. The same determination would be equally effectual to keep up their condition in the stationary state, and would be quite as likely to exist. Indeed, even now, the countries in which the greatest prudence is manifested in the regulating of population, are often those in which capital increases least rapidly. Where there is an indefinite prospect of employment for increased numbers, there is apt to appear less necessity for prudential restraint. If it were evident that a new hand could not obtain employment but by displacing, or succeeding to, one already employed, the combined influences of prudence and public opinion might in some measure be relied on for restricting the coming generation within the numbers necessary for replacing the present.
>
> (Mill 1965: 753)

The contemporary labour market: sectoral differences

In Mill's various accounts of contemporary British industrial conditions, sharp differences are manifest between the population mechanism in the case

of the skilled and unskilled workers. It transpires that 'prudential' behaviour
was practised only by the skilled class – that

> the restraining principle lies in the very great proportion of the
> population composed of the middle classes and the skilled artizans, who
> in this country almost equal in number the common labourers, and on
> whom the prudential motives do, in a considerable degree, operate.
>
> (Mill 1965: 346)

Furthermore, the maintenance of high and steady wages, which applied only
in the manufacturing centres, was possible despite uncontrolled population
growth on the part of the unskilled only because of the high and steady rate
of capital accumulation in those centres.[5] In brief, contemporary Britain,
albeit an 'old' country, enjoyed some of the characteristic features of North
America, where land scarcity was not yet manifest, permitting a growth rate
of capital at least equal to the maximum physiological growth rate of
population, and the maintenance of the real wage at a high (and even rising)
level. For in consequence of an extraordinary rate of accumulation in British
cotton-manufacturing centres, a consequence of new technology, it had been
possible for wages to be there maintained over several decades, despite
unchecked (urban) population growth (and even for agricultural wages in
areas near the cities to be pulled up):

> A similar advantage [to that experienced in North America], though in
> a less degree, is occasionally enjoyed by some special class of labourers in
> old countries, from an extraordinarily rapid growth, not of capital
> generally, but of capital employed in a particular occupation. So gigantic
> has been the progress of the cotton industry since the inventions of Watt
> and Arkwright, that the capital engaged in it has probably quadrupled
> in the time which population requires for doubling. While, therefore, it
> has attracted from other employments nearly all the hands which
> geographical circumstances and the habits or inclinations of the people
> rendered available; and while the demand it created for infant labour has
> enlisted the immediate pecuniary interest of the operatives in favour of
> promoting, instead of restraining, the increase of population; never-
> theless wages in the great seats of manufacture are generally ['still' prior
> to 1865 editions] so high, that the collective earnings of a family
> amount, on an average of years, to a very satisfactory sum; and there is,
> as yet, no sign of permanent [added, 1865 edition] decrease, while the
> effect has also been felt in raising the general standard of agricultural
> wages in the counties adjoining.
>
> (Mill 1965: 344)

The high rate of accumulation and constancy of wages proceeded 'consistently with not forcing profits to a lower rate':

> [Rapid accumulation] is shown by the increasing productiveness of almost all taxes, by the continual growth of all the signs of national wealth, and by the rapid increase of population, while the condition of the labourers is certainly not declining, but on the whole improving [1867; till 1862: 'certainly is not on the whole declining']. These things prove that each commercial revulsion, however disastrous, is very far from destroying all the capital which has been added to the accumulations of the country since the last revulsion preceding it, and that invariably, room is either found or made for the profitable employment of a perpetually increasing capital, consistently with not forcing down profits to a lower rate.
>
> (Mill 1965: 742)[6]

'Prudential' behaviour was, in contemporary circumstances, practised only by the skilled class of labourers, as already remarked. Evidence of prudential behaviour in the British case consistent with an attempt to maintain living standards is found in 'the diminished number of marriages in the manufacturing districts in years when trade is bad' (149), a cyclical phenomenon; conversely, 'according to all experience, a great increase invariably takes place in the number of marriages, in seasons of cheap food and full employment' (342). But Mill also alluded to evidence of a changing minimum standard, implying attempts on the part of labour by restraint on population growth to *raise* average real earnings. Such restraint reflects both wage-induced and 'exogenous' alterations in the conception of the minimum.

French data since the Revolution are referred to often and cited as evidence that the actual experience by labour of an improvement in living standards may itself stimulate an altered conception, a higher conception, of the 'minimum' wage in the event that the improvement is sufficiently marked to affect significantly the rising generation:

> To produce permanent advantage, the temporary cause operating upon them must be sufficient to make a great change in their condition – a change such as will be felt for many years, notwithstanding any stimulus which it may give during one generation to the increase of people. When, indeed, the improvement is of this signal character, and a generation grows up which has always been used to an improved scale of comfort, the habits of this new generation in respect to population

become formed upon a higher minimum, and the improvement in their condition becomes permanent.

(Mill 1965: 342)

The same phenomenon, though less conspicuous, is said (following Malthus) to have characterised the English case in the years 1715–65, a period experiencing a succession of remarkably good harvests:

So considerable an improvement in the condition of the labouring class, though arising from an accident of seasons, yet continuing for more than a generation, had time to work a change in the habitual requirements of the labouring class; and this period is always noted as the date of 'a marked improvement in the quality of the food consumed, and a decided elevation in the standard of their comforts and conveniences'.

(343n)

But such cases were rare, and Mill played down

the repeal of the corn laws, considered merely as a labourer's question, or... any of the schemes... for making the labourers a very little better off. Things which only affect them a very little, make no permanent impression upon their habits and requirements, and they very soon slide back into their former state.

(342)

And even major improvements need not have the desired effect (cf. 188).

Drawing again upon illustrations from the British and French cases, Mill alluded also to the consequences of exogenous changes in the minimum standard, that is, changes unrelated to the actual experience of higher wages:

Every advance they make in education, civilization, and social improvement, tends to raise this standard; and there can be no doubt that it is gradually, though slowly, rising in the more advanced countries of Western Europe. Subsistence and employment in England have never increased more rapidly than in the last forty years, but every census since 1821 showed a smaller proportional increase of population than that of the period preceding; and the produce of French agriculture and industry is increasing at a progressive ratio, while the population exhibits in every quinquennial census, a smaller proportion of births to the population.

(Mill 1965: 159)

The reference to forty years of particularly rapid growth of labour demand was inserted in 1862 (correcting appropriately the figure in the two preceding editions, 1852 and 1857); but the manuscript and the first two editions (1848 and 1849) read '16 years' placing the rapid increase in 'subsistence and employment' only from the early 1830s, and suggesting a realisation in about 1850 that the particularly striking upward trend in capital accumulation commenced earlier (dating at least to the early 1820s) than Mill had originally imagined. That the census data revealed a declining population growth rate since 1821 appears unchanged throughout all editions (on the French data see also 152, 287f, 342).

The recognition of a slackening in the growth rate of population relative to that of capital, and this over an extended period of at least four decades, is striking and comes as a surprise considering a statement in the same context that attempts to raise living standards are 'rarely found' in the labouring classes, and that 'hitherto' restraints on population expansion had reflected at best the insistence upon unchanged standards but no more (157; cf. above). And that the contemporary upward trend in real wages, reflecting a deliberate constraint on population growth relative to that of capital, was not adequately reflected in the textual formulations, is clear from the fact that the only (potential) sources formally isolated to account for the 'trend' to stationariness are land scarcity and constraints on the growth of capital; labour is not thus represented as a 'scarce' factor:

the impediments to the increase of population do not arise from the first of these elements [labour]. On the side of labour there is no obstacle to an increase of production, indefinite in extent and of unslackening rapidity. Population has the power of increasing in a uniform and rapid geometrical ratio. If the only essential condition of production were labour, the produce might, and naturally would increase in the same ratio; and there would be no limit, until the numbers of mankind were brought to a stand from actual want of space.

(Mill 1965: 160)

the limit to the increase of production is two-fold; from deficiency of capital, or of land. Production comes to a pause, either because the effective desire of accumulation is not sufficient to give rise to any further increase of capital, or because however disposed the possessors of surplus income may be to save a portion of it, the limited land at the disposal of the community does not permit additional capital to be employed with such a return, as would be an equivalent to them for their abstinence.

(Mill 1965: 186)

What reasons can be offered for Mill's apparent hesitation to allow formally for the evidence of secular real wage increase which indicates that labour supply may indeed act as a constraint on expansion?[7] To the extent that the improvements reflect an 'exogenous' change in standards, there is, formally speaking, no problem; cultural or sociological changes of this nature are on a par with technological changes, and it is legitimate to set them aside for some analytical purposes. And setting aside technological change allows a focus upon land scarcity; setting aside cultural change allows a focus on labour reproducibility. In any event, the contemporary British case indicated only a 'gradual' change in the minimum standard. It is endogenous changes, reflecting a functional relation between the magnitude of the wage and the long-run growth rate of population, that are more problematic.

Yet even here the problem is only apparent. Mill does not, after all, propose a regular functional relation whereby a rising real wage acts to raise the minimum standard; the wage increase must be a discrete one and significantly so, and such cases were few and far between. Relevant too is the fact, already alluded to, that prudential behaviour characterised only skilled labourers in the British case. For the high earnings of the unskilled town workers had not encouraged a noticeable alteration in their conception of the minimum standard so that any future slackening in the growth rate of capital would lead to a fall in wages, possibly to the level of the common farm labourer. This was the ever-present shadow, and it is scarcely surprising that Mill minimised labour scarcity – albeit manifested in the class of skilled workers – under these conditions.[8]

The shadow was also cast over the agricultural sector where to the extent wages had been kept up above 'subsistence', it was due to the attraction of labour into the towns, and without which attraction wages were likely to fall to the Irish level (351). And we must keep in mind Mill's fear that it is 'much more difficult to raise than to lower, the scale of living which the labourer will consider as more indispensable than marrying and having a family' (342). There was thus always the danger of a deterioration in the subsistence minimum itself, a danger leading Mill to question 'all propositions ascribing a self-repairing quality to the calamities which befall the labouring classes'.

Summary

Mill's model of a growth path entailing constant wages above 'subsistence', despite a deceleration in the rate of accumulation, applies only where 'prudential' motives on the part of labour are at play. This model was inapplicable to contemporary Britain as far as concerns the unskilled manufacturing workers, for their high and steady wages depended upon accumulation proceeding unchecked at a rate equivalent to an unrestricted growth rate of population – a possibility due to ongoing technical progress.

There existed, however, a potential danger that in the event of a decline in the growth rate of labour demand, wages would fall. The model provides an account of the manner in which by prudential behaviour – as already practised by the class of skilled workers – any such fall could be prevented: 'the great and growing intelligence of the factory population would, it may be hoped, avert [the calamity], by an adaptation of their habits to their circumstances' (351). It had less a descriptive than an exhortatory purpose. And here we also see very clearly that Mill's theorising is not designed for prediction. In the event of a deceleration in accumulation (and this was by no means certain, given continued improvements in technology) wages would fall only if the habits of the unskilled remained unchanged.

Notes

1 The reference to 'the demand for labour compared with the supply' in the penultimate paragraph is an apparent allusion to divergencies from the secular path. A full section is devoted to the issue – that 'the supplies of labour and the supplies of capital do not always keep pace with each other' (Malthus 1820: 306). This makes it certain that on the path the factor growth rates *are* in line.

2 That Ricardo would have subscribed to this analysis is clear from his famous pronouncement that 'the friends of humanity cannot but wish that in all countries the labouring classes should have a taste for comforts and enjoyments.... There cannot be a better security against a superabundant population' (1951, I: 100).

3 Malthus was prepared to rely on individual self-interest to assure the prudential outcome, whereas Mill was conscious of the free-rider dilemma, and looked to public opinion to counteract 'selfish' behaviour which might undermine the desirable outcome.

   In Caravale a possible rationalisation for the prudential hypothesis is offered whereby '*la crescita della popolazione è funzione decrescente del livello assoluto della popolazione stessa; una sorta di spontaneo e collettivo controllo delle nascite motivato ad esempio da ragioni ecologiche*' (1981: 10).

   The speed of adjustment to equilibrium, which will depend partly upon the degree of foresight by workers, will not be discussed in this paper. But if allowance is made for a lag in the response of population growth behind that of capital, one might expect (assuming an initial situation of equal growth rates) an actual wage path which 'sags' below the horizontal dynamic equilibrium path.

4 Cf. 'There is a condition to which the labouring people are habituated; they perceive that by having too numerous families, they must sink below that condition, or fail to transmit it to their children; and this they do not choose to submit to' (Mill 1965: 157–8, also 287, 341–2).

5 A word regarding agriculture. Here because of the absence of the 'prudential' motive, population was constrained by variation in the death rate alone (Mill 1965: 346). Indeed, 'the checks to population' in the case of the common agricultural labourer – prudential checks acting on the birth rate – 'may almost be considered as non-existent' and the living conditions in the southern counties were consequently 'painful to contemplate'. The labourers of these counties, with large families, and eight or perhaps nine (seven or eight till

1857) shillings for their weekly wages when in full employment, have for some time been ('lately became' till 1857) one of the stock objects of popular compassion: 'it is time that they had the benefit also of some application of common sense' (351).

6   Cf. also 'the growing demand [for food] of so rapidly increasing a population as that of Great Britain'; and 'our population and capital' increasing 'with their present rapidity' (Mill 1965: 745).
Logically we must presume the innovations, albeit in cotton, to be (indirectly) land-augmenting; cf. Samuelson:

> Mill went on to emphasize that technological innovation, continued in the long-run steady state, would imply *rising output forever*; we can show on Mill's behalf that, if the technical change is *land-augmenting* at a steady exponential rate, then labor and capital will grow forever at the same balanced exponential rate, just enough to match the growth of land measured in 'efficiency units' and with the long-run wage rate and profit rate each just high enough above their respective bare minima to elicit the implied growth rates of the factors.
>
> (Samuelson 1978: 1416)

7   Cf. Samuelson (1978: 1417):

> Even Mill is not realistic enough in his modelling of innovation and the lagging supply of population in advanced economies. What observers like Kuznets have observed this past century is that the growth of technology has been enough *to keep the real wage growing at something like an exponential rate*, with the growth in population and saving not being fast enough to wipe out the rising trend in real wages.

8   Mill at one point went so far as to argue that (in 'old' countries) not even technical improvement at its most rapid conceivable rate could prevent a fall in real wages, except a population growth restrained below the physiological maximum. Thus though 'improvement may during a certain space of time keep up with, and even surpass the actual increase of population' (190), as indeed was the case in Britain, where technical advance (even prior to corn-law repeal) had 'so materially lightened, for the time being, the pressure of population on production', yet 'it assuredly never comes up to the rate of increase of which population is capable; and nothing could have prevented a general deterioration in the condition of the human race, were it not that population has in fact been restrained'. But here he must have been somewhat carried away, for there had been no restraint on the supply of unskilled labour in the towns, and yet wages had not declined.

References

Caravale, G. A. (1981) 'Note sulla teoria Ricardiana del valore, della distribuzione e dello sviluppo', paper read at Ricardo Colloquium, Perugia.

Caravale, G. A. and Tosato, D. A. (1980) *Ricardo and the Theory of Value, Distribution and Growth*, London: Routledge and Kegan Paul.

Hicks, J. R. and Hollander, S. (1977) 'Mr Ricardo and the moderns', *Quarterly Journal of Economics*, 91, 3: 351–69.

Hollander, S. (1983a) 'On the interpretation of Ricardian economics; the assumption regarding wages', *American Economic Review, Papers and Proceedings*, 73 (May): 314–18.

——(1983b) 'The population principle and social reform: Malthus revisited', unpublished manuscript. Since published as 'On Malthus' population principle and social reform', *History of Political Economy*, 1986, 18: 187–236.

——(1984) 'The wage path in classical growth models: Ricardo, Malthus and Mill', *Oxford Economic Papers*, 36: 200–12.

Malthus, T. R. (1820) *Principles of Political Economy*, London: John Murray

——(1890) *Essay on the Principle of Population*, reprinted from the last edition revised by the author (1826), London: Ward, Lock.

Mill, J. S. (1965) *Principles of Political Economy*, II, III, *Collected Works of John Stuart Mill*, ed. J. M. Robson, Toronto: University of Toronto Press.

Ricardo, D. (1951–73) *The Works and Correspondence of David Ricardo* (11 vols) ed. P. Sraffa; I: *Principles of Political Economy*; IV: *Pamphlets, 1815–1823*, Cambridge: Cambridge University Press.

Samuelson, P. A. (1978) 'The canonical classical model of political economy', *Journal of Economic Literature*, 16 (December): 1415–34.

Smith, A. (1937) [1776] *The Wealth of Nations*, New York: Modern Library.

Appendix

Canonical growth

Paul A. Samuelson

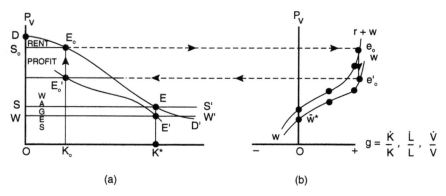

(a)   (b)

Figure 6.1 Labour and capital grow in concert from initial E_0. But now competition determines a fractional breakdown of the dose's surplus return between both components of the dose, $w(t)-\bar{w}*$ as well as $r(t) - \bar{r}*$, at those fractions that just succeed in evoking the same balanced growth in the supplies of the respective factors $L(t)$ and $K(t)$. The $E_0'E'$ locus in (a) gives the breakdown of the fruits of transient progress between capitalists and labourers: the faster the relative supply responsiveness of population, the nearer will $E_0'E'$ be to WW' and the greater profit's transient share; the steeper is $E_0'E'$ northwest of E', the greater the transient share of labour in the above-subsistence surplus. (Short-run distribution of total product, of OK_0E_0D, is shown by the rent triangle S_0E_0D; the dose's remaining rectangle $OK_0E_0S_0$ is divided between profit share and wages share by E_0' on the $E_0'E'$ locus.)

. (b) shows exactly how the $E_0'E'$ locus is determined. The locus ww shows the real wage needed to elicit each algebraic growth rate of labour in balance with the composite dose, $g = \dot{K}/K = \dot{L}/L = \dot{V}/V$ (where $\dot{L} = dL/dt$, etc.). The $r + w$ locus shows the p_v composite returns needed for the combined dose to grow, its needed wage rate plus needed profit rate, to induce balanced growth g – with $w(t)$ read from the lower curve and $r(t)$ from the interval between the curves. One begins at the computational cobweb E_0 in (a) then moves horizontally to e_0 in (b) and down to e'_0. Going back to (a) gives the appropriate height of E_0' in (a) and appropriate short-run distribution of non-rent income between profit and wages, thus filling in at each new time any logical gaps in the 'wage-fund' palaver of the classicists.

Source: Figure 3 in P. A. Samuelson (1978) 'The Canonical Classical Model of Political Economy', *Journal of Economic Literature*, 16 (December): 1415–34.

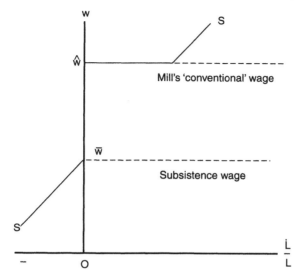

Figure 6.2a The classical supply schedule relating growth rate of labour supply to real wage is redrawn here to give Mill his conventional wage level that is above the subsistence wage level: ŵ being above w̄ gives the ss schedule its vertical and horizontal stretches.

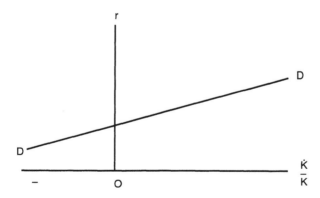

Figure 6.2b The growth rate of capital has the normal single-valued shape of Samuelson's ss 1978 canonical classical model.

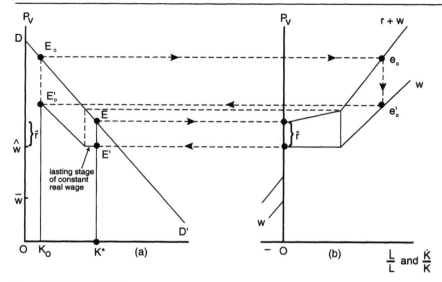

Figure 6.3 6.3a and 6.3b are constructions exactly like Samuelson's 1978 Figs. 3a and 3b, our Figure 6.1, but with the *ww* schedule on the right made to have vertical and horizontal stretches in accordance with Mill's alleged conventional wage rate at a level above his subsistence wage rate. The $E_o'E'$ path of dynamic equilibrium for the transition-stage wage rate is constructed by the cobweb device just as in the 1978 diagram. But now one sees the lasting stage of constant real wage, at Mill's conventional level $\hat{w}$, as shown by the final horizontal phase of $E_o'E'$. Though labour and capital grow transitionally in balance, their common growth must decelerate if the falling profit rate lowers $\dot{K}/K$ along the unchanged schedule of Figure 6.2b.

Chapter 7

J. S. Mill on 'derived demand' and the wages-fund theory recantation

It is inviting to regard J. S. Mill's formal arrangement of the *Principles of Political Economy* – the discussion of 'production', 'distribution' and 'exchange' in separate books – as indicating a failure to define distribution in terms of the pricing of scarce factor services, or to appreciate the relation between factor pricing, the technical conditions of production and allocation (Knight 1956: 42; Schumpeter 1954: 543). But Mill had reasons, which involve matters other than pure theory, for the decision to organise his work as he did – a concern to distinguish those economic relationships which do from those which do not vary between alternative societal organisations; an interest in comparative economic development; and a pedagogical concern for simplicity. It is certainly true that the formal treatment of production, distribution and exchange, in that order, left its mark on the substantive matter itself; serious confusions were created which a more satisfactory package from a theoretical perspective would probably have avoided. As an obvious example, placing the contrast between 'demand for commodities' and 'demand for labour' – the fourth fundamental proposition on capital – before either the analysis of distribution (particularly the wages-fund theory) or the analysis of exchange, courted misunderstanding. Moreover, Mill's social preoccupations sometimes led him to bring the discussion of difficult technical problems to a close rather too hastily for the analytically conscientious reader (Marshall 1920: 824). Yet for all that, his position can be unravelled, and it is clear that the organisation of the *Principles* did not derive from any intention to divorce production and distribution from exchange in a technical sense. The general perspective is, in fact, one of a tight interconnection between these aspects of the economic problem (following the lines laid out by Ricardo).

As a typical instance of misdirected criticism, we may refer to G. P. Scrope's objections to Mill's fourth fundamental proposition on capital – 'demand for commodities is not demand for labour':

> Can Mr. Mill really believe that the labour spent by the whole building trade of London . . . has not been paid for by the vast sums of money for

which these houses have been sold? Can he suppose that the builders have built them all out of their own pockets, instead of acting merely as intermediate agents between the working tradesmen and the purchaser, paying out with one hand what they receive with the other?

(Scrope 1873: 120)

This indeed was precisely the substance of W. S. Jevons' complaint that, according to the fourth proposition – which he rightly observed originated with Ricardo – capitalists 'maintain and pay for labor whether or not there is a demand for the commodities produced', and 'production goes on independently of the use to which the produce is to be put' (Jevons 1905: 127).[1]

I shall show that there is nothing in the proposition which denies the validity of derived demand for inputs (imputation); on the contrary, Mill specifically stated his adherence to the imputation principle without, of course, providing a watertight analysis thereof. In the first section, I present the evidence of Mill's acceptance of the concept of derived demand, evidence that proves essential for an appreciation of the fourth proposition on capital. This proposition, I show in the second section, was not designed to explain the return to labour at the industry level, and in no way conflicts with the principle of imputation. With this behind us, we will be in a position to consider formally aspects of the wages-fund doctrine. In the third section, the doctrine is taken up in terms of Mill's conception of economic process. A picture emerges which is far removed from a simple agricultural economy wherein the wages fund may be interpreted as a (real) wage bill, made up of commodities sharply distinguished from 'luxury' goods, and 'predetermined' in magnitude at the commencement of the period of production. Mill (like Ricardo) did not take seriously the conceptual framework of an annual agricultural cycle governing the demand for labour, and allowed for rapid alterations in the flow of real wages.

This demonstration sets the stage for an attempt to clarify what must surely constitute one of the most difficult interpretive problems in the classical literature, Mill's famous recantation from the wages-fund theory in 1869. The fourth section offers our interpretation of this most peculiar episode – Mill's new insistence upon a labour demand 'curve' of zero elasticity. His case, we shall argue, turns upon derived demand presuming zero elasticity of demand for final product in the short run – an argument pertinent at the industry level but extended too hastily to the economy as a whole.

The principle of derived demand

I shall deal first with the pricing of inputs in particular industries, although the classical economists paid far less attention to micro-economic problems of this order than to the determination of the general wage rate. I shall demonstrate the presence in Mill's work of an appreciation of derived demand, in the sense that the ultimate source of factor remuneration is in sales proceeds, and the motive for factor employment is the (expected) added revenue product. The argument is obviously not technically watertight because a clear marginal principle is absent.

We encounter a brief suggestion of the relationship in question in Mill's reference in the *Principles* to 'the present system of industrial life, in which employments are minutely subdivided, and all concerned in production depend for their remuneration on the price of a particular commodity' (*CW*, III: 455). The principle was further elaborated in a chapter dealing with indirect inputs of labour in lengthy processes of production:

> All these persons ultimately derive the remuneration of their labour from the bread, or its price: the plough-maker as much as the rest; for since ploughs are of no use except for tilling the soil, no one would make or use ploughs for any other reason than because the increased returns, thereby obtained from the ground, afforded a source from which an adequate equivalent could be assigned for the labour of the plough-maker. If the produce is to be used or consumed in the form of bread, it is from the bread that this equivalent must come.
>
> (*CW*, II: 31)

It is presumably the expectation of future yield that provides the motive for the use of the input.

In the case of materials which are 'destroyed as such by being once used', 'the whole of the labour required for their production, as well as the abstinence of the person who supplied the means of carrying it on, must be remunerated from the fruits of that single use'. By contrast,

> implements ... being susceptible of repeated employments, the whole of the products which they are instrumental in bringing into existence are a fund which can be drawn upon to remunerate the labour of their construction, and the abstinence of those by whose accumulations that labour was supported. It is enough if each product contributes a fraction ... towards the remuneration of that labour and abstinence, or towards indemnifying the immediate producer for advancing that remuneration to the person who produced the tools.
>
> (37, cf. 32)

The general principle also covers workers involved in transportation of a product 'from the place of its production to the place of its destined use ... its final consumption'; they too 'derive their remuneration from the ultimate product' (32–3). The wholesale and retail functions of the 'Distributing Class, whose agency is supplementary to that of the Producing Class', are similarly treated: 'the produce so distributed, or its price, is the source from which the distributors are remunerated for their exertions, and for the abstinence which enabled them to advance the funds needful for the business of distribution' (40). It is indeed in consequence of the 'increased utility' afforded by these functions that the product 'could be sold at an increased price proportional to the labour expended in conferring it' (48).

Although in the above citations the 'distributive' functions are formally separated from the strictly 'productive', it is quite clear that the process of production in any meaningful economic sense was envisaged as coming to an end upon sale to the final consumer. It is essential to note that this applies also to wage-goods. For Mill distinguished labourers' accommodation from industrial structures which have what he termed a 'protective' function in production – 'manufactories, warehouses, docks, granaries, barns, farm buildings devoted to cattle, or to the operations of agricultural labour' – on the grounds that the housing of workers is 'destined for their personal accommodation: these, like their food, supply actual wants, and must be counted in the remuneration of their labour' (38). Similarly, coal may be employed 'not only in the process of industry, but in directly warming human beings. When so used, it is not a material of production, but is itself the ultimate product' (35). The point at stake is an important one, since the formal inclusion of wage-goods within capital, to be discussed in the next section, may leave the impression that such commodities were envisaged as intermediate products reflecting a sort of 'production of commodities by means of commodities'. That 'the finished products of many branches of industry are the materials of others' (36) was an irrelevant consideration in the case of workers' consumables, which were treated on a par with all other final goods.

There is also to be found in the *Principles* (*CW*, III: 474) a passage of potential significance for Mill's intentions by his 'recantation' in 1869 of the wages-fund doctrine. It contains an observation drawn from Thomas De Quincey focusing upon the implications of the fact that input use is characterised by the properties of derived demand and joint demand. The perspective is one of microeconomics involving particular industries.[2]

'Demand for commodities is not demand for labour'

We turn next to the theory of distribution from a macro-economic perspective. To set the stage we must have in mind aspects of Mill's discussion of capital.

The formal definition of capital is that of 'a stock previously accumulated, of the products of past labour', the function of which in production is 'to afford the shelter, protection, tools and materials which the work requires, and to feed and otherwise maintain the labourers during the process. These are the services which present labour requires from past, and from the produce of past, labour' (*CW*, II: 55). In the same context Mill also defined capital as 'wealth appropriated to reproductive employment'; and yet more generally, as 'whatever of the produce of the country is devoted to production' (57).

The first of Mill's four propositions respecting capital – all of which are part and parcel of Ricardian doctrine – asserts that 'industry is limited by capital':

> There can be no more industry than is supplied with materials to work up and food to eat. Self-evident as the thing is, it is often forgotten that the people of a country are maintained and have their wants supplied, not by the produce of present labour, but of past. They consume what has been produced, not what is about to be produced. Now, of what has been produced, a part only is allotted to the support of productive labour, and there will not and cannot be more of that labour than the portion so allotted (which is the capital of the country) can feed and provide with the materials and instruments of production.
>
> (Mill, *CW*, II: 63–4)

It is not always clear whether Mill intended his proposition to relate solely to a dependency of productive employment upon 'circulating capital' (wage-goods and materials). So it might appear but for the closing sentence, which specifically refers also to fixed capital. In the latter case, the 'dependency' of productive employment on capital has a dual implication unless we assume – and this is probably a fair attribution in the present context – constancy of the real wage rate, so that circulating capital can be treated on a par with technological capital in its relationship to labour. The weight of emphasis, however, is such as to suggest a very general statement more concerned with circulating than with fixed capital, for which there were good reasons, as we shall presently see.

The proposition on capital which primarily concerns us here is Mill's fourth, which does not, strictly speaking, constitute a distinct proposition at all but is rather a direct corollary of the first (Hayek 1941: 433; Taussig 1896: 219–20; Marshall 1920: 828). Thus 'what supports and employs productive labour, is the capital expended in setting it to work, and not the demand of purchasers for the produce of the labour when completed'; the demand for commodities 'determines in what particular branch of production the [existing] labour and capital shall be employed' (*CW*, II: 78). Similarly, 'it is not the money paid by the purchaser, which remunerates the labour; it is the capital of the producer; the demand only determines in what manner that capital shall be employed, and what kind of labour it shall remunerate' (88).

Clearly, the notion that demand for commodities is not demand for labour does not relate to the demand for particular kinds of labour, or labour in particular industries. For Mill did not deny that a demand for a particular kind of commodity gives rise to a demand for labour to make that commodity; as we have seen: 'all concerned in production depend for their remuneration on the price of a particular commodity'. What Mill had in mind by the fourth proposition was *aggregate* wages: 'The general principle, now stated is that demand for commodities determines merely the direction of labour, and the kind of wealth produced, but not the quantity or efficiency of labour, or the aggregate of wealth' (87).

Mill himself had difficulty in expressing his precise intentions. But one particular formulation reveals the essence of the matter and confirms the preoccupation with aggregative employment and earnings. I have in mind the criticism of those economists who argued 'as if a person who buys commodities, the produce of labour, was an employer of labour, and created a demand for it as really, and in the same sense, as if he bought the labour itself directly, by the payment of wages'. On the contrary,

> if by demand for labour be meant the demand by which wages are raised, or the number of labourers in employment increased, demand for commodities does not constitute demand for labour. I conceive that a person who buys commodities and consumes them himself, does no good to the *labouring classes*; and that it is only by what he abstains from consuming, and expends in direct payment to labourers in exchange for labour, that he benefits the *labouring classes*, or adds anything to the amount of their employment.
>
> (*CW*, II: 80; emphasis added)

Both Ricardo and J. B. Say were said to have fully appreciated this position; this is important, for the latter also went some way towards an appreciation of the theory of imputation, indicating thereby that there is no necessary conflict between this approach to distribution and the approach implied by the fourth proposition on capital, since each pertains to a distinct area of discourse (cf. Hollander 1979: 373–5).

The wages-fund theory and economic organisation

It is usual to attribute to the classical economists a conception of economic activity which runs in terms of discontinuous output, so that advances out of past produce are required for the maintenance of current activity. The wages-fund theory is said to fall into this category of models. Contrasting with such conceptualisations are those which emphasise the continuity of production – synchronised activity.

There is, of course, no question that the time-consuming character of economic activity caught the eye of the classical economists, Mill among them (*CW*, II: 33, 58–9). Their models imply the need for accumulated advances to tide over producers. Yet the fact is that many of Mill's utterances on substantive matters relating to capital, investment and production point towards a model much more consistent with synchronised activity. It is my impression that his formal accounts involving discontinuities were designed to bring to the fore as clearly as possible the time-consuming character of economic activity. But it must not be overlooked that synchronisation economics does not gainsay this particular aspect (although it certainly tends to disguise its presence), since it remains true that the flow of current input is responsible for the flow of future production, and decisions regarding the current use of input must be made on the basis of expectations regarding the future; similarly, it remains true that the current flow of output is the consequence of input use in the past. These facts, of course, only become conspicuous within the terms of the model when consideration is given to an expansion of capacity from period to period when the (real) proceeds of past activity prove inadequate to 'finance' the current flow of input. If what I have asserted is a legitimate representation of Mill's position – the evidence will presently be laid out – the greatest care is required in understanding what he had in mind by the wages-fund doctrine. To this matter we now turn.

It will be convenient to have before us that strong version of the doctrine wherein a specific annual wage bill is 'destined' – no more and no less – to be paid out to labour, upon which assumption the celebrated labour demand curve of unitary elasticity is based. The most explicit statement is by Mill himself at the time of his retraction of belief in the doctrine in 1869. In his review of Thornton on labour, Mill laid out what he conceived to be the received doctrine:

> The theory rests on what may be called the doctrine of the wages fund. There is supposed to be, at any given instant, a sum of wealth, which is unconditionally devoted to the payment of wages of labour. This sum is not regarded as unalterable, for it is augmented by saving, and increases with the progress of wealth; but it is reasoned upon as at any given moment a predetermined amount. More than that amount it is assumed that the wages-receiving class cannot possibly divide among them; that amount, and no less, they cannot but obtain. So that, the sum to be divided being fixed, the wages of each depend solely on the divisor, the number of participants. In this doctrine it is by implication affirmed, that the demand for labour not only increases with the cheapness, but increases in exact proportion to it, the same aggregate sum being paid for labour whatever its price may be.
>
> (Mill, *CW*, V: 643–4)

For Mill, this is a characteristically ambiguous statement, since it is not specified whether the 'circulating capital' is in real or money terms (Taussig 1896: 230f). But it appears that the latter was intended, for while Mill found the rationale for this conceptualisation of the labour market in the notion of a form of *discontinuous* production, reference is also made to 'the capitalist's *pecuniary* means':

> In the common theory, the order of ideas is this. The capitalist's

pecuniary means consist of two parts – his capital, and his profits or income. His capital is what he starts with at the beginning of the year, or when he commences some round of business operations: his income he does not receive until the end of the year, or until the round of operations is completed. His capital, except such part as is fixed in buildings and machinery, or laid out in materials, is what he has got to pay wages with. He cannot pay them out of his income, for that he has not yet received. When he does receive it, he may lay by a portion to add to his capital, and as such it will become part of next year's wages-fund, but has nothing to do with this year's.

(Mill, *CW*, V: 644; cf. *CW*, IV: 301)

Let us now gather evidence from Mill's *Principles* to evaluate the accuracy of this retrospective view. The picture which emerges bears little resemblance to that portrayed in 1869.

Statements relating to wage-rate determination in the *Principles* are relatively few and surprisingly ambiguous. The most important appears at the outset of the chapter 'On wages', and deals with the general return to labour (including service or unproductive labour):

Wages, then, depend mainly upon the demand and supply of labour; or as it is often expressed, on the proportion between population and capital. By population is here meant the number only of the labouring class, or rather of those who work for hire; and by capital only circulating capital, and not even the whole of that, but the part which is expended in the direct purchase of labour. To this, however, must be added all funds which, without forming a part of capital, are paid in exchange for labour, such as the wages of soldiers, domestic servants, and all other unproductive labourers. There is unfortunately no mode of expressing by one familiar term, the aggregate of what has been called the wages-fund of a country: and as the wages of productive labour form nearly the whole of that fund, it is usual to overlook the smaller and less important part, and to say that wages depend on population and capital. It will be convenient to employ this expression, remembering, however, to consider it as elliptical, and not as a literal statement of the entire truth.

With these limitations of the term, wages not only depend upon the relative amount of capital and population, but cannot under the rule of competition be affected by anything else. Wages (meaning, of course, the general rate) cannot rise, but by an increase of the aggregate funds employed in hiring labourers, or a diminution in the number of the competitors for hire; nor fall, except either by a diminution of the funds devoted to paying labour, or by an increase in the number of labourers to be paid.

(Mill, *CW*, II: 37–8)

This is the most important formal statement of the principle of wage-rate determination in the entire work. Its crude inadequacies are such that it is hardly unfair to say that, from a theoretical viewpoint, we are scarcely carried beyond the assertion that 'wages are what wages are'. For it begs a host of questions, most important of which is the precise determination of the breakdown of aggregate capital between its components by reference to some kind of production function. Yet Mill evidently believed, and perhaps justifiably so, that the formulation sufficed for his purposes, basing upon it a veritable barrage of conclusions regarding labour policy. It is difficult to avoid the impression that the theoretical details relating to the demand for labour simply did not concern him deeply in this context; it was application, based upon a minimal theoretical structure, that was the major preoccupation, the intention being to demonstrate that the condition of the labouring class 'can be bettered in no other way than by altering that proportion [between capital and populations] to their advantage; and every scheme for their benefit, which does not proceed on this as its foundation, is, for all permanent purposes, a delusion' (343, cf. 354). It is pertinent that the larger part of the chapter 'On wages' itself, apart from two subsequent chapters on 'Popular remedies for low wages', focuses upon the implications of the Malthusian population doctrine – labour supply – rather than the nature of the demand for labour. Thus a change in the cost of wage-goods works its effects upon wages first by impinging upon labour supply. There can be little question that Mill's primary concern was with issues of this order.

A second formal statement of the doctrine, again in the context of the equilibrating function of wage movements, is equally vague:

> Goods can only be lowered in price by competition, to the point which calls forth buyers sufficient to take them off; and wages can only be lowered by competition until room is made to admit all the labourers to a share in the distribution of the wages-fund. If they fell below this point, a portion of the capital would remain unemployed for want of labourers; a counter-competition would commence on the side of capitalists, and wages would rise.
>
> (Mill, *CW*, II: 356)

This passage might be read as assuming a rigidly predetermined wages bill; but it is also not inconsistent with a totally different version of the wages-fund theory, wherein the wages bill is not a predetermined sum but the equilibrium outcome of a market-clearing process (about which more below). Once again, there is too little theoretical detail to be sure of Mill's intention regarding strict analysis. The formulation served the purpose of an elementary exposition of the notion of an equilibrium wage rate designed to counter popular remedies for low wages (such as minimum-wage legislation) in which context precisely the extract appears.

Yet for all that there comes to light, upon closer examination of the qualifications allowed by Mill to the main statement, some profoundly interesting theoretical insights. I have in mind his qualifications in the present context to the 'law of markets'. Mill recognised the possibility of slack periods in particular trades when available capital is kept idle – a circumstance which could still be formally absorbed into the doctrine, for 'Capital which the owner does not employ in purchasing labour, but keeps idle in his hands, is the same thing to the labourers, for the time being, as if it does not exist' (338). More significant, the allowance is extended to the aggregate labour market:

> When there is what is called a stagnation...then work people are dismissed, and those who are retained must submit to a reduction of wages: though in these cases there is neither more nor less capital than before.... If we suppose, what in strictness is not absolutely impossible, that one of these fits of briskness or of stagnation should affect all occupations at the same time, wages altogether might undergo a rise or a fall. These, however, are but temporary fluctuations: the capital now lying idle will next year be in active employment, that which is this year unable to keep up with the demand will in its turn be locked up in crowded warehouses; and wages in these several departments will ebb and flow accordingly: but nothing can permanently alter general wages, except an increase or a diminution of capital itself (always meaning by the term, the funds of all sorts, devoted to the payment of labour) compared with the quantity of labour offering itself to be hired.
>
> (Mill, *CW*, II: 338–9)

Further allowances for excess capacity will be found in the formal discussion of capital in the first Book. Thus

> a fund may be seeking for productive employment, and find none, adapted to the inclinations of its possessor: it then is capital still, but unemployed capital. Or the stock may consist of unsold goods, not susceptible of direct application to productive uses, and not, at the moment, marketable: these, until sold, are in the condition of unemployed capital.
>
> (57; cf. 65)

Idle capital in these contexts apparently refers not only to unsold stocks of goods, but also to money funds available for investment in wage payments or other disbursements. What is involved is a well-considered and fundamental qualification to the proposition that 'industry is limited by capital' (a matter already alluded to in the previous section), from which it is apparent that Mill intended to supplement the basic doctrine regarding aggregate employment by some function relating to the state of aggregate demand for final goods – or what is equivalent, some function of the net excess demand for money.

The significance of the qualification extends beyond its linkage of monetary and employment theory, important though this is. Most relevant is that the qualification points away from any notion of an aggregate sum of wealth, in real or money terms or both, *unconditionally* 'destined' for the payment of wages. In the light of all this it appears that the wages-fund doctrine was, as Mill himself put it in one of our foregoing citations, a theory relating to 'permanent' wages – assuming full equilibrium as far as concerns aggregate demand for commodities – and particularly relevant for an appreciation of the general problems of population or the inability to generate increased employment by protective measures.

There is much else pointing to this conclusion. What we have to say next is pertinent to the question of a strict upper boundary to the real wage bill (and *a fortiori* the money wage bill).

The function of capital, as we have seen, is 'to afford the shelter, protection, tools and materials which the work requires, and to feed and otherwise maintain the labourers during the process'. But Mill was very careful to specify that the fraction of capital whose function it is to fulfil the tasks of 'maintaining' labour need not actually take the form of stocks of wage-goods:

> What then is his capital? Precisely that part of his possessions, whatever it be, which is to constitute his fund for carrying on fresh production. *It is of no consequence that a part, or even the whole of it, is in a form in which it cannot directly supply the wants of labourers.*
>
> (*CW*, II: 56; emphasis added)

The reason for this position lies in the supposed flexibility of the system which permits, by exchange or by production, the easy and rapid generation of commodities suitable for workers' consumption.

Thus a decision by a capitalist to increase investment implies a fall-off in his demand for luxuries ('plate and jewels') – hitherto financed from the sale of his product (for example, iron goods) – and a corresponding increase in expenditure upon productive labour; this entails appropriate increases in money wages and accordingly in the demand by labour for food (*CW*, II: 57). What of expanded production of food to meet the new demand? Increased food supplies might, we are told, be obtained immediately by importation, presumably in exchange for the luxuries hitherto consumed by capitalists, or at least for goods produced by means of the resources made available by the reduction in luxury consumption. If increased importation is not possible, then

> labourers will remain for a season on their short allowance: but the consequences of this change in the demand for commodities, occasioned by the change in the expenditure of capitalists from unproductive to productive, is that next year more food will be produced, and less plate and jewellery. So that . . . without having had anything to do with the

food of the labourers directly, the conversion by individuals of a portion of their property, no matter of what sort

– in this case stocks of iron goods –

from an unproductive destination to a productive, has had the effect of causing more food to be appropriated to the consumption of productive labourers.

True enough, in the absence of increased food imports it may take a 'season' for food supplies to be expanded, but there is little question that Mill intended to minimise the significance of any such delay. The ease of achieving expansions of the food supply explains the conclusion that what distinguishes capital goods from others

does not lie in the kind of commodities, but in the mind of the capitalist – in his will to employ them for one purpose rather than another; and all property, however ill adapted in itself for the use of labourers, is a part of capital, so soon as it, or the value to be received from it, is set apart for productive reinvestment. The sum of all the values so destined by their respective possessors, composes the capital of the country. Whether all those values are in a shape directly applicable to productive uses, makes no difference. *Their shape, whatever it may be, is a temporary accident: but once destined for production, they do not fail to find a way of transforming themselves into things capable of being applied to it.*
(Mill, *CW*, II: 57, emphasis added; cf. 67–8, 82–3; *CW*, IV: 266–7)

The less significant is the distinction between wage-goods and luxury-goods, of course, the greater the flexibility of the productive system and the ease of expanding the former at the expense of the latter. In point of fact, the notion of a sharp distinction between the two categories broke down at an early stage in Mill's exposition, as is clear from the discussion of the 'unproductive' consumption of productive labourers (*CW*, II: 58). Workers normally earn a 'surplus' over subsistence requirements which can best be seen in terms of the case of increased investment with given labour supply. Assuming the workers to be 'already sufficiently supplied with necessaries', they now will

become consumers of luxuries; and the capital previously employed in the production of luxuries, is still able to employ itself in the same manner: the difference being, that the luxuries are shared among the community generally, instead of being confined to a few.
(68)

From all this there emerges a rather clear picture of Mill's vision of economic process in an advanced capitalist-exchange system. It is far removed from a primitive agricultural economy for which a rigidly interpreted wages-fund theory might be appropriate, namely one wherein workers consume a distinct class of commodities, produced in annual jets, and opportunities for carry-over from period to period are limited (for an alternative view see Ekelund 1976). Workers are paid in money, not in kind, and enter the market to purchase commodities at retail like any other consumers; there is no distinction in this regard between consumption by labourers, capitalists or landlords. The 'wages fund' is thus expressed in money, but has a real counterpart in the flow of wage-goods currently made available at retail outlets (our reading is consistent with that of Taussig 1896: 233).

The recantation of the wages-fund doctrine (1869) begins, we have seen, with a criticism of what Mill claimed to be received doctrine – his own original position, namely the technological inability, deriving from the discontinuity of the production process, to alter the magnitude of the wages bill (apparently even the 'pecuniary' wages bill) during the course of the 'year'. This criticism, I have argued, appears unjustified if directed against the position actually developed in the *Principles*, where there is little to suggest any such rigidity of the wages bill – in either money or real terms. Yet there is a sense in which the wages bill can be said to be 'predetermined' – the sense implied by any determinate solution to a problem of competitive pricing: the demand and supply curves must be stable for such solution to be meaningful, their stability reflecting investment plans by capitalists and plans regarding work and leisure by labourers. It would seem that Mill erred in 1869 by confusing the two senses in his description of his original position.

The wages-fund theory: the recantation interpreted

Mill's precise position in 1869 concerning the wages-fund doctrine constitutes one of the most difficult problems in the history of economics. It is to this matter that we now turn.

After rejecting the case of unitary demand elasticity, Mill focused upon that of completely inelastic and apparently coincidental schedules of supply and demand, where 'neither sellers nor buyers are under the action of any motives, derived from supply and demand, to give way to one another'; in this case,

> which the law of equality between demand and supply does not provide for, because several prices all agree in satisfying that law... the question between one of those prices and another will be determined by causes which operate strongly against the labourer, and in favour of the employer... nothing but a close combination among the employed can

give them even a chance of successfully contending against the employers.

(*CW*, V: 642–3)

Let us then trace out the argument made for zero elasticity of labour demand. The precise order of the argument must be carefully followed.

The case begins, as noted, with the account of the wages-fund doctrine in terms of a unitary elastic demand curve for labour as a whole – the theory was applied to aggregate wages. At the next stage, however, Mill referred to the motives of an individual employer of labour in making what seems to be his main argument against the notion of unitary elasticity.

> Does the employer require more labour, or do fresh employers of labour make their appearance, merely because it can be bought cheaper? Assuredly, no. Consumers desire more of an article, or fresh consumers are called forth, when the price has fallen: but the employer does not buy labour for the pleasure of consuming it; he buys it that he may profit from its productive powers, and he buys as much labour and no more as suffices to produce the quantity of his goods which he thinks he can sell to advantage. *A fall of wages does not necessarily make him expect a larger sale for his commodity, nor, therefore, does it necessarily increase his demand for labour.*

(Mill, *CW*, V: 644; emphasis added)

Mill's case thus relates to the *derived demand* for labour. Since a fall in wage costs does not 'necessarily' lead to expectations of greater final sales for the product it does not 'necessarily' lead to an increase in demand for the factor.

Now, whereas Thornton believed that commodity markets are typically characterised by totally inelastic demand – at least over significant ranges – Mill did not. Moreover, he had just written a few pages earlier that 'it is the next thing to impossible that more of the commodity should not be asked for at every reduction of price' (637), and the response of quantity demanded to price played an important role in Mill's general economics. But in the *Principles* Mill had alluded to the properties of 'derived' and 'joint' demand with regard to input use. These characteristics were the source of rigidities of production and consumption which tended to delay the fall of price to new cost levels (*CW*, III: 474). It is not unlikely then that when Mill stated in 1869 that 'a fall of wages does not necessarily make [the employer] expect a larger sale for his commodity, nor, therefore, does it necessarily increase his demand for labour' he had in mind so short a period that an expansion of sales may not be taken seriously by employers who, in such an event, refrain from immediately increasing their demand for labour. This position does not, however, rule out expanded demand for an input when a longer period is allowed. And, indeed, in Part II of the review Mill recognised such reaction. The logic of the argument, strictly speaking, is of the partial-equilibrium variety. It implies therefore a concern with a variation in the wages paid to a particular category of labour in a single industry, other wage rates and product prices held constant. Yet the wages-fund doctrine under attack involves the aggregate demand for labour, and suggests a concern with a variation in general wages. Mill was on dangerous ground when he (implicitly) shifted from the former to the latter context. In short, he based his case for a zero elasticity of aggregate labour demand upon an argument not strictly applicable to that area of discourse. But he was probably troubled by the issue; for he himself raised the possibility that while the demand for labour by an employer in a particular industry may be totally inelastic upon wage reductions – a rendition suggesting a *partial* wage change – yet the capital released may be invested elsewhere in the system, so that 'the whole of the wages-fund will be paying wages as before' (*CW*, V: 644).

No direct answer to the foregoing problem was given; but precisely at this juncture Mill denied the existence of a 'predetermined' aggregate wages bill: 'Exists there any fixed amount which, and neither more nor less than which, is destined to be expended in wages?' The wages bill 'cannot exceed the aggregate means of the employing classes' (after allowance for their personal maintenance), but 'short of this limit, it is not, in any sense of the word, a fixed amount'. The capitalist is under no obligation to spend a specific sum upon labour; each employer (and therefore presumably all employers) can be obliged to spend more than expected on wages, or may enjoy a windfall gain even during the brief period before old plans can be revised and new plans put into operation:

> In short, there is abstractly available for the payment of wages, before an absolute limit is reached, not only the employer's capital, but the whole of what can possibly be retrenched from his personal expenditure; and the law of wages, on the side of demand, amounts only to the obvious proposition, that the employers cannot pay away in wages what they have not got.
>
> (*CW*, V: 645)

We are now in a position to draw the threads of the argument together. On close inspection it will be seen that there are two distinct aspects to Mill's case. First, the argument that in the very short run firms may not respond to a fall (or, presumably, a rise) in the wage rate, because of low expectations of increased (decreased) final sales. *This, in fact, was the only rationale offered for zero demand elasticity for an input*; and while the argument implies a partial wage change, it was clearly Mill's intention to make a case for zero elasticity of the *aggregate* demand for labour, in the short period, upon variation in *general* wages – a rather too casual extension.

In the event of zero elasticity, a variation in the wage rate entails a variation in the total industry wage bill. The second part of Mill's case, which also applies to the short-run period, urges that such alterations in the wage bill are indeed conceivable, since the notion of a technical inability to vary its size is groundless.

Notes

1 For an account of these and other criticisms see Thompson 1975: 174–92. Thompson falls into the same trap as these early critics when he writes (188) that Mill himself was 'oblivious to the fact that without consumption there would be no demand for resource inputs, labour included'. For an accurate perspective see Schumpeter 1954: 644.
2 Ricardo had never spelled out as clearly as did Mill adherence to the general notion of imputation in the context of the return to particular inputs, but the evidence suggests that he did not reject J. B. Say's version of the doctrine. In approaching the classical theorems on capital, the greatest care must be taken to keep this in mind (see Hollander 1979: 670–1).

References

Ekelund, R. B. Jr (1976) 'A short-run classical model of capital and wages: Mill's recantation of the wages fund', *Oxford Economic Papers*, 28 (March): 66–85.
von Hayek, F. A. (1941) *The Pure Theory of Capital*, Chicago: University of Chicago Press.
Hollander, S. (1979) *The Economics of David Ricardo*, Toronto: University of Toronto Press.
Jevons, W. S. (1905) *Principles of Economics*, revised edn, London: Macmillan.
Knight, F. H. (1956) *On the History and Method of Economics*, Chicago: University of Chicago Press.
Marshall, Alfred (1920) *Principles of Economics*, 8th edn, London: Macmillan.
Mill, J. S. (1963–91) *Collected Works of John Stuart Mill*, Toronto: University of Toronto Press. Herein *CW*.
——(1965) *Principles of Political Economy, Collected Works*, II, III.
——(1967) [1869] 'Thornton on labour and its claims', *Fortnightly Review*, new series, 5, in *Collected Works*, V, 631ff.
Schumpeter, J. A. (1954) *A History of Economic Analysis*, New York: Oxford University Press.
Scrope, G. P. (1873) *Political Economy for Plain People*, London: Longmans, Green and Co.
Taussig, F. W. (1896) *Wages and Capital: An Examination of the Wages Fund Doctrine*, New York: Appleton and Company.
Thompson, J. H. (1975) 'Mill's fourth fundamental proposition: a paradox revisited', *History of Political Economy*, 7: 174–92.

Chapter 8

Exogenous factors and classical economics[1]

Introduction

In this paper, John Stuart Mill (1806–73) is taken as our primary representative 'classic'. Not only did he bring the classical line of thought (the economics of Adam Smith and David Ricardo) to fruition, but no other nineteenth-century economist did more to define the scope and method of economics. Indeed, it is Mill who argued a case of the kind made out by the present Project.

We proceed in the second section to a statement of the case argued by Mill for a specialist science of economics. Economics, largely based upon rational calculation of costs and returns, was not envisaged as the 'science of wealth', but as one branch of such an investigation. The decision to proceed by way of quasi-independent disciplines turned upon a strategic evaluation of a higher likelihood of insightful results relating to causal process by an 'analytical' (as distinct from a 'synthetical') treatment, with an eye to the problem of 'disturbing causes'. The synthesis of causal influences in their entirety was, however, the ideal, while in the interval the very greatest care had to be taken to avoid casual application to policy of the conclusions drawn from necessarily incomprehensive models.

In the third section we lay out the essentials of classical micro-economics, and in the fourth and fifth those of classical macro-economics. We shall then be in a position to deal with the specific concerns of the present Project. The treatment of exogenous factors from the perspectives of pricing and growth is taken up in the sixth section. The final section elaborates further on exogenous factors in the growth context.

The case for specialisation and the problem of 'disturbing causes'

The outstanding characteristic of natural and of social phenomena was, in Mill's account, that of 'Composition of Causes' where 'the effects of different causes are...not dissimilar, but homogeneous, and marked out by no assignable boundaries from one another; A and B may produce not *a* and *b*, but different portions of *a'* (Mill, *CW*, VII: 434). The composition of causes was responsible for an optical illusion. While each (separate) cause/effect relationship continued to operate, it might not, at first sight, appear to be in operation at all. To underscore the continuous operation of the individual 'causes', Mill supported use of the term 'tendency' (443–4).

The primary tasks of science were to determine the effect that will follow a certain combination of causes, and conversely the combination of causes that would produce a given effect (458, 460). Inductive procedures – even when based on well-established experimental methods of empirical enquiry – could not deal with this kind of problem. In the presence of 'mutual interference of causes, where each cause continues to produce its own proper effect according to the same laws to which it conforms in its separate state', deduction alone was 'adequate to unravel the complexities', and the empirical methods had the task of supplying premises for, and verification of, deductions (439).

The social sciences dealt with a subject matter characterised more than any other (with the exception of physiology) by plurality and composition of causes. Social phenomena are pre-eminently of a nature requiring deductive treatment, based upon an axiomatic foundation. But there existed practical limits to the complexity of deductive models. The solution was to limit the range of applicability of the models to classes of social phenomena 'which, though influenced ... by all sociological agents, are under the *immediate* influence, principally at least, of a few only' (Mill, *CW*, VIII: 900). This practical objective dictated the location of disciplinary boundaries, the basic presumption being that different classes of social fact depended 'immediately and in the first resort ... on different kinds of causes', allowing therefore for 'distinct and separate, though not independent, branches of sociological speculation'. As far as it concerned economics, the class of relevant social phenomena was that

> in which the immediately determining causes are *principally* those which act through the desire of wealth; and in which the psychological law *mainly* concerned is the familiar one, that a greater gain is preferred to a smaller. I mean, of course, that portion of the phenomena of society which emanates from the industrial, or productive operations of mankind; and from those of their acts through which the distribution of the products of those industrial operations takes place insofar as not effected by force, or modified by voluntary gift.
> (*CW*, VIII: 901, emphasis added)

The separate science of political economy, with its basis in wealth-maximisation, was conceived as part of the first stage of construction of a general theory of wealth. A general theory would, ideally, combine a variety of specialist scientific treatments each based on alternative motivation –

those behavioural assumptions involving motives other than wealth maximisation, which constitute 'disturbing causes' from the perspective of political economy, belonged 'to some other science' (Mill, *CW*, IV: 331) – and would thus incorporate into its axiomatic base a wide range of behavioural patterns.

For the specialist procedures of economics to be legitimate, it must be the case empirically that the range of specialist study encompasses a sufficiently homogeneous pattern of behaviour:

> Those portions alone of the social phenomena can with advantage be made the subjects, even provisionally, of distinct branches of science, into which the diversities of character between different nations or different times enter as influencing causes only in a secondary degree.
>
> (Mill, *CW*, VIII: 906)

The specialist exercises are 'liable to fail in all cases in which the progressive movement of society is one of the influencing elements', 'for this movement is implicitly frozen within *ceteris paribus* conditions' (916).

'Causes' formally incorporated in the economic model are distinguished from those excluded (as 'disturbing' or 'modifying') by their predominating influence in the sense that the class of phenomena under investigation (the production and distribution of wealth in our case) depends largely upon them, and by their ubiquity – that they are causes 'common to the whole class of cases under consideration' (Mill, *CW*, IV: 326). Allowance for modifying circumstances at a subsequent stage of investigation was particularly desirable 'as certain fixed combinations' of the influences common to all cases were 'apt to recur often, in conjunction with ever-varying circumstances' of the class of the less important or less ubiquitous influences (*CW*, VIII: 901).

The formal demarcation line between those 'causes' to be incorporated within economics and those which are to be treated as 'disturbances' and the subject matter of other sciences was, for Mill, far from rigid. In fact, a disturbing cause 'which operates through the same law of human nature out of which the general principles of the science arise ... might always be brought within the pale of the abstract science, if it were worthwhile', thereby adding a 'supplementary theorem' thereto (*CW*, IV: 331). The axiomatic foundation of contemporary economics even included behavioural assumptions in conflict with wealth maximisation:

> in a few of the most striking cases (such as the important one of the principle of population) [these corrections] are ... interpolated into the expositions of Political Economy itself; the strictness of purely scientific arrangement being thereby somewhat departed from, for the sake of practical utility.
>
> (323)

Similarly, the science allowed for 'two perpetually antagonizing principles' to the desire for wealth – namely 'aversion to labour' and 'the desire for the present enjoyment of costly indulgencies' (321).

Mill failed to specify the particular specialisations which would (in principle) complement economics. But it is probable that when he distinguished between 'competition' and 'custom', and argued that 'only through the principle of competition has political economy any pretension to the character of a science' (*CW*, II: 239) he had in mind the character of an *independent* science, custom being the subject of complementary sciences based upon alternative axiomatic bases. An investigation of wealth founded on altruistic behaviour might provide a second example.

It is sometimes suggested that J. S. Mill introduced the notion of 'disturbing causes'. But in fact it was a view central to both Smith and Ricardo. It reflects a belief that economics is not a predictive science (such as astronomy) amenable to test by the measure of accuracy of prediction, and this because of the almost inevitable intervention of disturbing causes. For example, Ricardo adopted an analytical framework incorporating the principle of diminishing agricultural returns, although he was conscious of the historical and prospective intervention of technological change. This was because technological progress takes the form of random shocks and so might be accorded secondary status compared to diminishing returns – a force in 'constant operation':

> The causes, which render the acquisition of an additional quantity of corn more difficult are, in progressive countries, in constant operation, whilst marked improvements in agriculture, or in the implements of husbandry are of less frequent occurrence. If these opposite causes acted with equal effect, corn would be subject only to accidental variation of price, arising from bad seasons, from greater or less real wages of labour, or from an alteration in the value of the precious metals, proceeding from their abundance or scarcity.
>
> (Ricardo 1951, IV: 19n)

A similar notion is implied in the monetary context, where Ricardo explained his insistence that note reduction would tend to lower the value of gold despite apparent refutations: 'Because, in commerce, it appears to me that a cause may operate for a certain time without our being warranted to expect that it should continue to operate for a much greater length of time' (Ricardo 1951, V: 377). Again, the disturbance to a clearcut relation between note contraction and the value of gold is envisaged to be of a random nature.

As noted, a principal outcome of the classical perspective is the rejection of the notion of economics as a predictive science. It had, rather, an explanatory function, and in this exercise, theorists were duty bound to fight against the natural reluctance 'to admit the reality or relevancy of any facts which they have not previously either taken into account, or left a place open for, in their system' (Mill, *CW*, IV: 336). Paul Samuelson (1972: 780) was struck by Charles Darwin's advice to 'always study your residuals' – in his case by writing down arguments *against* the theory of evolution. For us, J. S. Mill is closer to home (the same recommendation was made by Sir John Herschel). The ultimate function, however, is prescriptive:

> The aim of practical politics is to surround any given society with the greatest possible number of circumstances of which the tendencies are beneficial and to remove or counteract, as far as possible, those of which the tendencies are injurious. A knowledge of the tendencies only, though without the power of accurately predicting their conjunct result, gives us, to a considerable extent, this power.
>
> (Mill, *CW*, VIII: 898)

Classical micro-economists

Boundaries

Classical economists distinguished between the production of scarce commodities capable of storage (a necessary condition for designation as 'wealth') and of services, or between the production of capital in some form or other, and pure services leaving behind directly or indirectly no lasting sources of enjoyment. By 'productive labour' they intended labour productive of 'wealth'. It is the flow of future utilities embodied in a (scarce) material product that renders it an item of wealth, wealth constituting a store of utilities.

The non-accumulatability of services posed problems for Mill from the perspective of human capital. But it was still possible to consider as 'productive', labour which yields material product only indirectly, covering thereby labour involved in acquiring industrial skill. Also included is police protection of industry, and transportation and other distributive services and (logically) some medical services. For Adam Smith, by contrast, all service workers earn derivative incomes. Still excluded from wealth are theatrical and musical skills, however 'valuable' they might be.

A surplus-yielding requirement of productive labour supplements the accumulatability requirement. This too has a Smithian pedigree; in the *Wealth of Nations* only labour bestowed on the production of material goods is said to be capable of 'adding value' – service labour 'adds to the value of nothing' (Smith 1937: 314). For Mill, productive labour is not restricted to the private sector, yet his primary concern was with the capitalist, not the government sector; and if we can set aside the problem of the capitalistic employment of opera singers and make the appropriate allowances for distributive personnel and the like, we are left with the broad classical distinction between labour engaged in the capitalist sector with an eye to profit, and service labour engaged for purposes of final consumption.

Derived demand

Ricardo subscribed to J. B. Say's notion of derived demand or imputation (Hollander 1979: ch. 6; 1982). Similarly, Mill appreciated the notion that the ultimate source of factor remuneration is in sales proceeds, and the motive for factor employment is the added revenue-product expected.

That the process of production in the capital-exchange system ends with sale to the final consumer applies also in the case of wage goods. But while in the micro-economic context workers' consumables are treated on a par with all other final goods, for other purposes wage goods (or at least that part constituting 'subsistence') are treated as intermediate products.

The law of demand

The negative price–quantity relationship is standard in classical economics, notwithstanding the absence of a marginal-utility concept: 'The demand . . . varies with the value, being generally greater when a thing is cheap than when it is dear' (Mill, *CW*, III: 497).

The argument for a negative slope runs in terms of the 'income effect' generated by price variation. Depending upon the kind of commodity involved, more or less of any increase in purchasing power generated by a fall in price will be devoted to the commodity in question rather than to others. From this perspective 'absolute necessaries' were demand-inelastic (467). The elasticity of the market-demand curve will be higher, the higher the opportunities to attract additional purchasers by further price reductions (607). Like the income effect, this had been recognised by Ricardo, who had noted that the degree of attraction varies with the range of prices in question (cf. Hollander 1979: 275f).

Short-run price formation

The analysis of short-run price formation, well clarified by Smith, runs in terms of the equation of quantity demanded and supplied. The exposition involves the role played by the negative slope of the 'demand curve' in the process of correction of excess demand and supply, allowance made also for the withdrawal of supply into stocks upon price reductions as part of the adjustment mechanism.

Cost price and profit-rate equalisation

The classical appreciation of the relativity of exchange value and the allocative underpinnings of the process of equilibration is clearly expressed in Mill's discussion of production costs: 'Value is a relative term, not a name for an inherent and substantive quality of the thing itself' (*CW*, III: 479). As Ricardo had further clarified,

> in considering ... the causes of *variations* in value, quantity of labour is the thing of chief importance; for when that varies, it is generally in one or a few commodities at a time, but the variations of wages (except passing fluctuations) are usually general, and have no considerable effect on value.
>
> (481)

Nonetheless, wage differentials will be reflected in the cost-price structure (as well as relative labour inputs) and changes thereof will generate changes therein. The same principles apply to profits: 'It is only by entering in a greater degree into the cost of production of some things than of others, that they can have any influence on value' (482).

The foregoing qualification allows for profit-rate differentials reflecting unequal risk and so forth, and also for differential time periods of production from industry to industry (differential factor proportions). Even general wage changes will then influence the structure of prices.

Long-run competitive or cost prices afford equal expectation of return on capital. This result hinges upon the capital-mobility axiom. In the event of a return exceeding the going rate, 'capital rushes to share in this extra gain, and by increasing the supply of the article, reduces its value'; conversely in the reverse case, output is restricted (*CW*, III: 471–2). Adjustment processes are not instantaneous, so that it is always expectation of return that is relevant in stating the profit-rate equalisation theorem. Appropriate allowance is made for sluggish adjustments; before capital can be extricated from a declining trade (or increased in the case of expansion) the returns thereon are in the nature of Marshallian 'quasi-rent', a notion already firmly established by Ricardo.

Mill appreciated that while

> the cost to society as a whole, of any production, consists in the labour and abstinence required for it ... as concerns individuals and their mutual transactions, wages and profits are the measure of that labour and abstinence, and constitute the motives by which the exchange of commodities against one another is immediately determined.
>
> (*CW*, XVII: 1894–5)

Here we have a conscious distinction between aggregative and micro-economic theorising. The theory of costs was treated from a micro-economic perspective involving relative value and the motives underlying allocation.

We may consider rent from this perspective. Land is distinguished from the other factor returns on the basis of aggregate supply conditions, rent reflecting scarcity in the case of an 'agent' subject to 'engrossment and appropriation' (*CW*, II: 29). Thus far the aggregative perspective is in line with Ricardo. When Mill focused upon individual sectors – and in this he reverted to Adam Smith – the picture was different: 'when land capable of yielding rent in agriculture is applied to some other purpose, the rent which it would have yielded is an element in the cost of production of the commodity which it is employed to produce' (*CW*, III: 498).

Long-run adjustment

Mill also approaches the issue of long-run price and output adjustment in unconventional terms from the perspective of the modern reader. Taking as the standard case the adjustment to a new equilibrium following a technological change that reduces natural price, Mill's novel approach allows a price-setting role to individual (competitive) entrepreneurs who act to forestall entry into the industry by firms in response to super-normal profit. It is, therefore, not always increase in supply that works to reduce price to the lower cost level, but price that is lowered directly at a rate depending upon the estimate of the immediate danger of entry made by existing entrepreneurs, who calculate the risks of entry as viewed by prospective entrants (*CW*, III: 473–4). In the usual case of non-zero elasticity of demand, existing firms will be faced by larger markets which they can serve at the going (economy-wide) profit rate. In the limiting case of zero demand elasticity (characterising basic foodstuffs) there will be no such opportunities; here price falls to cost without industry expansion.

Variable-cost conditions

In the event of increasing costs, variations in conditions of demand lead to changes in long-run cost price as well as output. Agriculture provides the main example. The 'law of value', in this case, is that natural price 'is determined by the cost of that portion of the supply' – 'even the smallest' – 'which is produced and brought to market at the greatest expense' (Mill, *CW*, III: 490). Decreasing cost conditions are also recognised (*CW*, II: 131f). It is allowed that an increase in industry output is compatible with a larger number of small firms, but high output is said to encourage the establishment of large firms – concentration increases with industry size – though this is not stated as a 'law'.

The wage and profit structures

The recognition of heterogeneous labour led both Adam Smith and Ricardo to abandon the pure labour theory, even prior to allowance for capital and land, and have recourse to a labour cost theory. Smith recognised certain institutional impediments, which in the Britain of his day tended to hinder the transfer of labour from one occupation to another. Apart from these artificial constraints, a market process assured that earnings in different occupations tend to keep in line, so that different monetary returns in long-run equilibrium reflect the varying degrees of attractiveness attached to each occupation. Free competition assured that monetary and non-monetary returns together were equalised between occupations.

Mill was dissatisfied with the Smithian analysis in two respects: general unemployment and the existence of 'natural and artificial monopolies' both distorted the structure (*CW*, II: 383, 386–7).

Characteristically for the classics and contrasting with modern analysis, the structure analysis takes into account the population variable and is not limited to the allocation of a given work force. Population growth in any sector, if relatively excessive, will force down the wage below the due competitive level; conversely, a relatively restrained growth is required to maintain a 'monopoly' return. Thus the maintenance of monopoly returns requires control of supply *internal* to the group, even in the absence of upward mobility and increase of supply from outside. Conversely, 'prudence' on the part of the skilled will not suffice to maintain their 'monopoly' returns in the event of a disintegration of barriers.

Mill's population and wage-structure analyses together imply that in the absence of non-competing groups, population growth rates across sectors cannot get out of line and that a stable wage structure emerges. In a state of full stationariness, and assuming full mobility, there will be groups of workers earning more than the 'base' subsistence wage, which excess will not stimulate expansion on their part. This dual condition of equalising money-wage differentials yet zero population growth in each sector must be modified for a growing system, a competitive wage structure then emerging around a 'base' wage appropriate for a particular positive growth rate of population.

The analysis of non-competing groups also has implications for the theory of value. Mill is clear that the 'monopoly return to skill is limited by the price which purchasers are willing to give for the commodity they produce', whereas entry sufficing to reduce the wage to the competitive level would entail a price which reflects (*inter alia*) wage costs (*CW*, II: 387) – a nice illustration of 'cost' envisaged in terms of alternative opportunities.

Within gross profits Mill included interest or 'the remuneration of abstinence', wages of superintendence or the return to the 'assiduity and skill' of management, and compensation for risk or insurance (*CW*, II: 401). The profit rate varies according to the nature of the trade – mainly differences in risk, but also in 'the circumstances which render one employment more attractive or more repulsive, than another' (403). Allowing for these variations, and setting aside monopoly, profit rates tend to an equality, understood as referring to employments not individuals; for (excluding pure interest) profit which (in equilibrium) varies little between employments will still vary greatly between individuals, depending on 'the knowledge, talents, economy, and energy of the capitalist himself, or of the agents whom he employs; on the accidents of personal connection; and even on chance' (406).

Classical macro-economics

Capital and employment capacity

By 'saving', the classics intended the employment, by the provision of appropriate equipment and wage goods, of productive labour in which venture these capital goods are used up or 'consumed' more or less rapidly. The term is also used to mean the creation of new capital goods. A change in expenditure from luxury consumption to investment (or to services for personal use or otherwise) redirects currently utilised resources towards the production of goods which will sooner or later be placed at the disposal of workers in the form of wages or technological capital, increasing the aggregate demand for labour. This is the sense of the classical theorem that 'demand for commodities is *not* demand for labour'; micro-economic employment decisions *do* hinge on final demands.

In the polar extreme case of a given labour supply, an expansion of investment at the expense of 'luxury' consumption will simply imply a higher aggregate wage bill; there may not even be required any transfer of resources from the 'luxury' sector. Only in the event of expanded employment does the requirement for technological capital arise. Assuming an available labour supply at constant wages, the positive effect of net investment upon employment manifests itself only after newly created (technological) capital goods have been installed. The programme is thus accomplished in two stages: first, a transfer of resources from 'luxury' industries to capital-goods industries, which involves no net effect upon employment (and thus none on aggregate wages), and second, the operation of the capital goods by new entrants into the labour market. It is at this second stage that the aggregate wage bill rises, implying an expansion in the demand, on the part of the newly employed, for wage goods.

Instead of envisaging a *change* in the pattern of outlay from consumption to investment, we may compare *alternative* expenditure patterns. The higher the rate of investment per period, the higher the rate of expansion of capacity, and thus of employment of 'productive' labour.

The classics allowed for idle capital – not only unsold stocks of goods, but also money funds available for investment in wage payments or other disbursements – qualifying the proposition that 'industry is limited by capital' by a function describing the state of aggregate demand for final goods – the net excess demand for money. The qualification belies any notion of an aggregate sum of wealth unconditionally 'destined' for the payment of wages; variations in the aggregate demand for commodities can lead to variations in capacity usage. The wages-fund doctrine was, in fact, not designed for the short run; it related to 'permanent' wages – assuming full equilibrium as far as concerns aggregate demand for commodities – and was designed to treat long-run population growth and such questions as the ability to generate increased employment by protective measures.

Capital-supply conditions and the minimum rate of return

The source of savings is in the 'surplus' which defines the maximum 'ability to save' (including wage income exceeding subsistence). The 'abstinence' involved in saving need not entail 'privation'; additions to capital might be financed out of a surplus increased by technical change (Ricardo 1951, IX: 127). Actual savings out of the maximum sum potentially available depend in part on prospective yield – 'the greater the profit that can be made from capital, the stronger is the motive to its accumulation' (*CW*, II: 161). A positive interest rate was seen to be a necessary feature of the full stationary state. As a factual matter, Mill (*CW*, V: 734) assumed that the minimum at which savings would cease was approximately 1 per cent.

The rate of profit allows not only for 'the effective desire to accumulate savings' but also for the productive application of those savings; the minimum profit rate at which net investment is reduced to zero exceeding the minimum rate of interest by a risk premium. The minimum profit rate in the stationary state thus exceeds the return required by savers. (The fact that some insurance against risk is required even on investment by the capitalist 'on his own account' implies that at low ranges of the interest rate savings will occur which may not be absorbed into industrial projects.)

On machinery

The classical problem of 'machinery' involves exogenous technological improvements of the capital-absorbing type – the 'conversion' of circulating into fixed capital – reducing the global 'wages fund' and, therefore, employment or per capita wages or both. The extent and speed of adoption of such technologies relative to the rate of net capital accumulation becomes the key issue.

Mill, like Ricardo, was optimistic even assuming ongoing population expansion:

> Although . . . the labouring classes must suffer, not only if the increase of fixed capital takes place at the expense of circulating, but even if it is so large and rapid as to retard the ordinary increase to which the growth of population has habitually adapted itself; yet, in point of fact, this is very unlikely to happen, since there is probably no country whose fixed capital increases in a ratio more than proportional to its circulating.
>
> (Mill, *CW*, II: 97)

This contrasts with Marx's 'prediction' of a declining growth rate of labour demand due to an increase in the ratio of 'constant' to 'variable' capital in the face of ongoing population expansion (cf. Hollander 1984a). Further reason for optimism lies in the stimulus to the 'ability' and 'motive' to save generated by the innovation itself:

> [improvements] increase the return to capital; and of the increase the benefit must necessarily accrue either to the capitalist in greater profits, or to the customer in diminished prices; affording, in either case, an augmented fund from which accumulation may be made, while enlarged profits also hold out an increased inducement to accumulation.
>
> (*CW*, II: 98)

Labour-supply conditions: effort-income

It is usually assumed in classical economics that higher per capita wages engender increased effort – at least in the case of developed economies. Some allowance is made for a backward-bending supply curve, although it was not yet seen as a practical issue. An interpersonal dimension enters to complicate the wage-effort relationship. Thus:

> a state of complete equality of fortunes would not be favourable to active exertion for the increase of wealth. Speaking of the mass, it is as true of wealth as of most other distinctions – of talent, knowledge, virtue – that those who already have, or think they have as much of it as their neighbours, will seldom exert themselves to acquire more.
>
> (Mill, *CW*, III: 890)

By implication, an across-the-board increase would have a different impact on labour supply than a more localised increase.

Labour-supply conditions: population growth

Mill approached the population variable by insisting upon the continued usefulness of the Malthusian conception of a maximum physiological capacity of a human population to double itself in approximately two decades (*CW*, II: 155). But under usual conditions this geometrical ratio is not encountered, and it is with the nature of the 'checks' that Mill was preoccupied.

The check to the maximum population growth rate was not necessarily imposed by the death rate (war and disease, and insufficiency of food), with the birth rate achieving the maximum level physiologically possible. Human reproduction was also to a greater or lesser degree 'restrained by the fear of want rather than by want itself', so that even where starvation was not an issue, 'many' were influenced by 'the apprehension of losing what have come to be regarded as the decencies of their situation in life'; acting from motives of 'prudence' or the 'social affections', people married at a certain age and had that number of offspring 'consistent with maintaining themselves in the condition of life which they were born to, or were accustomed to consider as theirs' (157).

So much for a static state where the (culturally determined) subsistence wage rules. But considering the context of a growing system with wages exceeding culturally determined 'subsistence', as in contemporary Britain, Mill (like Ricardo) presumed in fact that the unskilled propagated at the maximum physiological rate (or at least at a constant rate irrespective of the wage). As Ricardo recognised, at a range close to 'subsistence' wage, deceleration in the growth rate necessarily occurs upon further wage reduction.

Productivity and scale

The role of 'cooperation' or 'the combined action of numbers' as a determinant of productivity is a conspicuous classical theme. Mill's discussion (*CW*, II: Book 1, ch. 8) commences with Wakefield's distinction between simple and complex cooperation, the former entailing several individuals working together on the same set of operations, and the latter, a division of labour between tasks undertaken simultaneously. It proceeds to the issue of exchange between town and country, and thence to instances of higher degrees of division of labour. Thereafter the precise nature of the advantages of specialisation are taken up, including Smith's conception of specialisation as a stimulus to invention, and the savings which flow from classification of workers according to their differential physical capacities and from the increased utility derived from specialised tools. The limitations to division of labour imposed by the extent of the market, and by the nature of the particular employment, are discussed, the latter with special reference to agriculture.

At the enterprise level, opportunities for specialisation hinge on firm size, but even when specialisation has reached a technical maximum, output expansion can lead to higher productivity as the labour force is used to capacity. Other determinants of large scale include the technological need for expensive machinery, and opportunities created for economy of superintendence. There is a presumption (again following Smith) that competitive *industry* supply-price declines with expansion, notwithstanding the fact that the scale economies alluded to relate to the *firm*.

The weight of evidence suggested that small scale was not detrimental to agricultural productivity except if carried to extreme lengths as in France. Given the organisation of agriculture, output expansion is subject to diminishing returns, a reflection of land scarcity. This manifests itself at the extensive and intensive margins. The latter is not rationalised in terms of 'variable proportions' as in modern formulations.

A classical 'growth' model

Classical growth theory focuses upon the trend paths of the wage- and profit rates (for full details see Hollander 1984b). A formal model captures several of the main characteristics:[2] land scarcity manifested in diminishing agricultural returns at least beyond a certain labour/land ratio; a positive functional relation between the return on capital (r) and the capital growth rate (g_K) for r exceeding some minimum (r^*); a labour growth rate (g_L) possibly irresponsive to wage reductions at high ranges but responsive at levels close to 'subsistence' (w_S):

$$Q = F(L) \qquad F'(L) > 0 \qquad F''(L) \leq 0$$

$$g_K = \frac{\dot{K}}{K} = \theta_1(r) \qquad \begin{array}{l} \theta_1(r) > 0 \\ \theta_1(r^*) = 0 \text{ for some } r^* > 0 \end{array}$$

$$g_l = \frac{\dot{L}}{L} = \theta_2(w) \qquad \begin{array}{l} \theta_2(w) > 0 \text{ at } w \text{ close to } w_s \\ \theta_2(w_s) = 0 \text{ for some } w_s > 0 \end{array}$$

The outcome of the growth process is a downward path of wages until the 'subsistence' level (w_S) where (g_L) has fallen to zero. The profit rate falls simultaneously until the minimum return (r^*) at which g_K is zero. The 'subsistence' wage and the equivalent 'subsistence' return on capital are thus attained only in the state of stationariness.

Panel A in each diagram below portrays the marginal product curve generated by variable labour on given land (HH'). MM' depicts the maximum wage, w_{max}, that is obtainable when the minimum feasible return on capital rules. MM' is thus the marginal product less a constant percentage. (For simplicity, wages are measured in commodity and not in value terms; we proceed as if wage goods are a single good; and fixed capital is neglected.)

In formal terms, the wage per worker, w, plus profits per worker, wr (in circulating capital models where wages are paid one period in advance of the sale of the product), exhausts the marginal product of labour, $F'(L)$, so that:

$$w + wr = F'(L)$$

therefore:

$$w = \frac{F'(L)}{1 + r}$$

If w_{max} is the wage such that $r = r^* > 0$, then $w_{max} < F'(L)$, the shortfall reflecting the minimum return on capital (r^*).

In each diagram, panel B portrays the wage on the vertical axis and g_K and g_L on the horizontal axis, and the g_K–w relationship it depicts is derived from panel A. For any (absolute) labour supply, MM′ indicates the maximum wage (w_{max}) that reduces r to r* and therefore g_K to zero. A lower wage at the same marginal product of labour will be associated with a higher r and therefore a higher g_K: thus at any given marginal product, the lower the wage the higher the rate of profit and the higher the rate of growth of capital; this generates a negative g_K–w relationship, the curve emanating from the y axis at the appropriate level given by the height of MM′. At the same time, at any given w, a declining marginal product along HH′ implies a decline in r and thus in g_K, and this effect will be reflected by a continual inward shift of the g_K–w function in panel B.

Population growth in conditions of land scarcity generates inward shifts of the g_K curves and a fall in the (secular) wage, as shown by the arrowed line in panel A, until w_S – the 'subsistence' wage at population size L_4; simultaneously the profit rate falls to r* where net capital accumulation ceases.

In Ricardo's version the secular wage movements are governed by deviations between the capital and labour growth rates (Ricardo 1951, I: 98, 101). Malthus, by contrast, developed a 'dynamic-equilibrium' wage path where the falling wage trend (see Figure 8.1) emerges notwithstanding equality of the capital and population growth rates. The wage path is represented as a 'supposition', implying thereby a hypothetical reference path. This path cannot be achieved in a competitive world where capitalists and labourers act independently. For since the return on capital (r) = F′(L)/w - 1 (r moves inversely to proportional not absolute wages) it follows that, in an expanding system, the initial impact of diminishing returns at the going wage is on capitalists alone inducing a fall in g_K relative to g_L; and, assuming a regular decline in the marginal product, the deficiency g_K < g_L is continually reconstituted notwithstanding the wage decline. The dynamic-equilibrium path is a construct of the mind derived by asking what the wage path would be if it is assumed that g_L = g_K under conditions of diminishing returns. The return to the 'joint' factor evidently declines; but the share of the incidence of declining productivity can be calculated by reference to the capital-supply and labour-supply growth functions, namely the g_K–r and the g_L–w relationships. There is a unique wage rate for each marginal product which is consistent with balanced factor growth.

Mill followed Ricardo rather than Malthus insofar as his downward wage trend results from deviations between the factor growth rates to labour's disadvantage. For 'the test of equality' between the factor growth rates is that 'each labourer obtains the same commodities as before, and the same quantity of those commodities' (CW, III: 723).

Where land scarcity is not yet manifest, population can increase at its 'maximum' potential rate (namely a doubling in a single generation) with no

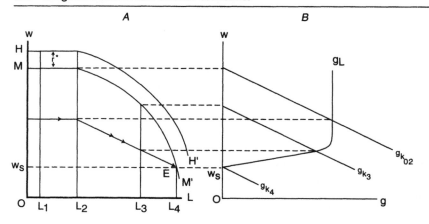

Figure 8.1 The falling wage trend. The stationary state is achieved at population size L₄.

downward pressure on the real wage, provided that capital accumulates at that rate. Such was said to be the case in North America and the Australian colonies, which enjoyed advanced European technology and savings habits so that the rate of accumulation proceeded at least as rapidly as population at its maximum, and the real wage was maintained above subsistence at a steady, perhaps increasing, level (Mill, *CW*, II: 343–4). In the absence of this special confluence of circumstances, it would be impossible for population to expand at the maximum rate without downward pressure on wages, and this because of impediments to the rate of accumulation, reflecting land scarcity – a falling marginal product: 'The increase of capital is checked, because there is not fresh land to be resorted to, of as good quality as that already occupied' (344).

The model can accommodate an increasing wage trend under conditions of constant returns, assuming an initial excess $g_K > g_L$. Alternatively, an upward wage path can be allowed for in terms of increasing returns, even if initially $g_K = g_L$.

Exogenous factors: pricing and growth

In the sphere of micro-economics, *exogenous structural impacts* predominate. The analysis of pricing turns on the rule that 'only through the principle of competition has political economy any pretension to the character of a science' (*CW*, II: 239), for only so far as prices are competitively determined 'can they be reduced to any assignable law' (*CW*, III: 460). On these grounds the analysis – based on 'the axiom ... that there cannot be for the same article, of the same quality, two prices in the same market' – is limited to the wholesale sector, for Mill represents individual consumers as typically failing to act in maximising fashion, the 'axiom' actually constituting a second-stage deduction from more basic behaviour postulates which do not apply in the retail sector: 'the feelings which come into play in the operation of getting, and in that of spending... income, are often extremely different' (*ibid.*).

> Either from indolence, or carelessness, or because people think it fine to pay and ask no questions, three-fourths of those who can afford it give much higher prices than necessary for the things they consume; while the poor often do the same from ignorance and defect of judgment, want of time for searching and making inquiry, and not unfrequently, from coercion, open and disguised.
>
> (*ibid.*)

Considering this position on consumer behaviour, one might be justified in supposing that the negative slope of the market demand curve based on individual maximisation principles is inapplicable in the retail sector. But this is not so; the rationale in question (income effects) refers to final consumers. Mill evidently uses the methodological distinction between 'scientific' economics based on the standard maximisation axiom – and 'applied' economics which allows for qualifications, the subject matter of 'other sciences'. At all events, the outcome, in practice, is a failure of competitive market pricing at the retail level.

Search costs can (logically) be incorporated within maximisation economics, but this is less true of 'ignorance', 'defective judgment' and 'coercion'. As for the wealthy, the issue here is that of conspicuous consumption resulting in an upward sloping demand curve (*CW*, III: 869). In effect, in the case of low-income earners, sociological factors prevent the attainment of positions on the utility frontier; in that of high-income earners, they 'distort' the frontier.

In some cases 'custom' – again an exogenous structural impact – encourages forms of price discrimination. In others the impact manifests itself as a fixing of (retail) prices with free entry resulting in reduced markets for individual sellers who operate at less than full capacity – the 'monopolistic competition' model (*CW*, II: 243). The monopolistic competition model emerges also in the discussion of professional remuneration and banking.

Technological considerations also are recognised as influencing market structure. In the context of increasing returns Mill observed that 'where competitors are so few, they always end up agreeing not to compete. They may run a race of cheapness to ruin a new candidate, but as soon as he has established his footing they come to terms with him' (142). The implication is that, *ceteris paribus*, price will be higher the smaller the number of independent firms in the industry (*CW*, III: 927–8).

'Strict' or 'absolute' monopoly – a single seller – was easily dealt with as the limiting case. Mill (following Smith) provided a statement of the total revenue function, which implies revenue rather than profit maximisation as the objective (468); cost of production determines the minimum. The formal restriction of the 'scientific' treatment of pricing to the competitive case was thus qualified: monopoly, whether natural or artificial, is designated as a 'disturbing cause', but it was one which had 'always been allowed for by political economists' and (as in the case of monopolistic competition) Mill applies to it the tools of economic analysis. It is in markets characterised by 'small numbers' that problems arise which were not perceived to be subject to 'assignable law'.

Further exogenous structural impacts, reflecting social and financial obstacles to upward mobility, are conspicuous in the analysis of the wage structure. Thus the recognition that the costs even of a minimal education and of maintenance during the training period 'exclude the greater body of the labouring people from the possibility of any such competition' as would reduce the 'monopoly' return of the skilled (372). Even within the basic Smithian framework, a wide variety of social attitudes will govern labour and capital supplies to particular industries, and thus the pattern of wage and profit rates.

The key feature of classical growth economics is the technological principle of diminishing agricultural returns which formally relates the labour force as an independent variable to marginal productivity as dependent variable. Here arise openings for *exogenous independent-variable plug-ins* in the guise of manpower quality: 'A day's labour of a Hindoo or a South American... cannot be compared with that of an Englishman' (Ricardo 1951, II: 272). This in turn limits the range of applicability of the theory of profits; in relating the profit rate to the proportion of the work-day devoted to the production of wage goods, we take for granted a specific social, productive, and geographic context defining the 'quality' of labour: 'I should not estimate profits in England by the labour of a Hindoo... unless I had the means of reducing them to a common standard'.

Mill gave precedence to manpower quality over natural advantages (including location); areas with the 'best climate and soil' had 'few incentives' for sustained labour and little concern for 'remote objects' (Mill, *CW*, II: 102–3). (In these terms he even explained backwardness in the creation of good political institutions, including those for the protection of property.) British industrial predominance is attributed partly to the energy of its work force – a consequence rather of climatic conditions than original temperament – intending by 'energy' not the efforts people are 'able and willing to make under strong immediate incentives', for in this there was comparatively little distinction between nations, but rather 'the capacity of present exertion for a distant object; and... the thoroughness of... application to work on ordinary occasions' (103–4).

The impact of exogenous independent-variable plug-ins is extensive.

Thus regarding the general level of intelligence: 'there is hardly any source from which a more indefinite amount of improvement may be looked for in productive power than by endowing with brains those who now have hands', an observation covering superintendence and non-routine as well as routine tasks (Mill, *CW*, II: 105f). Trustworthiness of labour, and friendly industrial relations — which themselves have sociological sources — are weighed on a par with intelligence as affecting labour quality. And much weight is placed upon 'security' — 'no improvements operate more directly upon the productiveness of labour, than those in the tenure of farms, and in the laws relating to landed property' (183). The French Revolution is described as having been 'equivalent to many industrial inventions' — a Ricardian proposition which Mill illustrates in terms of the strengthening of redress against injury to person and property by people of rank (183).

There is also an exogenous impact on the quality of manpower peculiarly pertinent to underdeveloped economies — the potential stimulus to effort provided by 'new wants and desires' (104) — in contrast to advanced societies where 'indulgence tends to impoverish'. The opening of foreign trade, by

> making a [people] acquainted with new objects, or tempting them by the easier acquisition of things which they had not previously thought attainable, sometimes works a sort of industrial revolution in a country whose resources were previously underdeveloped for want of energy and ambition in the people: inducing those who were satisfied with scanty comforts and little work to work harder for the gratification of their new tastes.
>
> (Mill, *CW*, III: 593–4)

In the absence of such stimuli, Mill suggests that the pressure of numbers (in semi-barbarous countries) helps break the habit of indolence (*CW*, II: 102f).

The issue is crucial to the scope of the model in a further sense. The assumption of 'insatiability of human wants' was used to support the view that there can be no long-run deficiency of aggregated demand — the law of markets — which is taken for granted in construction of the growth model. But the assumption was not universally valid: Only in developed countries such as England was it 'not necessary that . . . new tastes and new wants should be generated — the old tastes are sufficient for the purpose. Tastes and wants exist already in a sufficient degree, give but the means of satisfying them and demand follows' (Ricardo 1951, IV: 344). Even in developed economies, 'satiation' might in principle pose a problem for the future, although workers would then choose to enjoy higher real incomes in the form of increased leisure, so that 'overproduction . . . could not . . . then take place in fact, for want of labourers' (Mill, *CW*, III: 574). The classical growth model presupposes a particular 'character'.

It is desirable to distinguish *exogenous independent-variable plug-ins* from *exogenous parameter plug-ins* — in the present instance changes in the 'quality' of labour from changes in the technology (possibly embodied in fixed capital) with which it operates, and which affect productivity of labour of given 'quality'. The 'laws of production' – which include the principle of diminishing agricultural returns but also increasing returns in manufacturing, the constraint imposed on industry by capital, and the differential impact of productive and unproductive consumption (Mill, *CW*, II: 199) – are formally said by Mill to be 'immutable' in contrast with the 'malleable' laws of distribution. But this holds good with the state of knowledge given; and knowledge indeed is sometimes placed on a par with 'the properties of nature', as a datum from the perspective of economics (*CW*, II: 3, 20–1). A change in the state of knowledge then acts to shift HH′ (and accordingly MM′) with stimulatory effects on the wage and/or the profit rate (see Figure 8.1).

We turn to the labour-supply function, where the scope for exogenous intervention is particularly extensive. It is fair to say that the *raison d'être* of classicism resides just here, namely in a concern with the inculcation of 'prudential' demographic behaviour patterns.

'Prudence' can be *purely* exogenous, wherein the g_L curve shifts leftward in consequence of ongoing educational-propaganda programmes. It is conceivable that steady-state wages might be generated notwithstanding land scarcity and its impact on g_K (see Figure 8.2).

Here we have a prime instance of a *'Type II' or exogenous parameter plug-in* affecting the magnitude of the parameters of the equation.

But equally an education programme might succeed in altering the elasticity of the curve as in Figure 8.3.

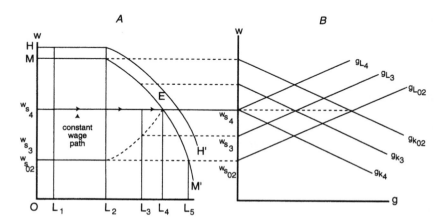

Figure 8.2 A 'Type II' or exogenous parameter plug-in affecting the magnitude of the parameters of the equation. Stationariness is achieved at population $L_4 < L_5$ the 'original' stationary state. In effect the 'subsistence' wage rises from w_{s_0} to w_{s_4}: originally the actual wage declined from w_{s_4} to w_{s_0}

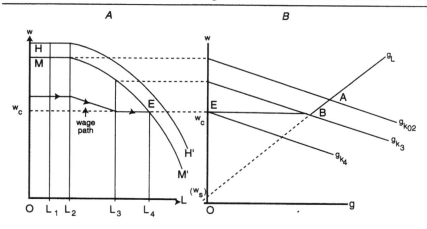

Figure 8.3 The population growth rate constrained by workers

Here workers (as a class) constrain the population growth rate to prevent the wage falling below some designated 'conventional' level as g_K decelerates. In effect, the labour supply function becomes horizontal at w_c, and this wage traces out the 'dynamic equilibrium' path. This process implies ascribing to labour prescience of the steady decline in g_K. Since the classical growth model was designed to portray the effect of an instillation of responsible habits, this assumption makes considerable sense. There will, however, be problems of the 'free-riding' type. It is important to note the role of organisation in this regard; free-riding will be a lesser problem under peasant-proprietorship than under a wage system, since the impact of excess numbers will be much clearer.

Reference is also made to societies where the exercise of foresight is imposed by the state, particularly control of the minimum age of, and the material conditions to be satisfied prior to, marriage. Eighteenth-century Britain provided an instance of prudential behaviour imposed by 'accidental habit', the customary need for private cottages by married couples and the unwillingness of landowners to provide them, circumstances transformed by the Revolutionary Wars and the encouragement given on 'patriotic grounds' to a large population.

In some versions, experience of high wages (due say to a short-run spurt in demand for labour) if extensive enough, may serve to alter *long-run* supply conditions by influencing the conception of a minimum standard on the part of the new generation of workers. This is a case of *non-economic mediated feed-back* acting on the parameter of the supply equation.

Exogenous impacts upon the magnitude of the parameter and possibly the elasticity are equally conspicuous in the case of the g_K function. For savings out of surplus depends not only on the return to capital, but also on a variety of personal, sociological and institutional considerations, including the state of national security and life expectation, intellectual development and consciousness of the future, and the strength of other- as distinct from self-regarding interests. In our diagram an increase in the 'effective desire to accumulate' appears as an upward shift of MM' towards (given) HH'.

The import of the sociological conditions that lie behind the savings schedule is enhanced by recognition of divergencies between the paths taken by the interest and the profit rates. Thus Mill (CW, XIV: 91; IV: 305) recognised a decline in the interest rate since 1840 unrelated to deteriorating agricultural productivity, having in mind features of the social structure pertinent to the relationship between the lending and borrowing classes of the community – a perspective reminiscent of that of A. R. J. Turgot (1770).

A striking instance of a *spill-over effect* occurs in the growth context, namely the psychological implications of secular expansion, the consequences of the falling profit rate:

> By the time a few years have passed over without a crisis, so much additional capital has been accumulated, that it is no longer possible to invest it at the accustomed profit. . . . But the diminished scale of all safe gains, inclines people to give a ready ear to any projects which hold out, though at the risk of loss, the hope of a higher rate of profit; and speculations ensue

with cyclical implications (CW, III: 742). These implications include 'capital loss' and thus a corrective to the falling profit rate – providing an instance of *NE (non-economic)-mediated variable feed-back.*

The impact of biological constraints – the differential demand elasticities for food and other goods – is the source of our earlier observation that the downward wage path cannot involve full micro-economic equilibrium even in the absence of technological progress. For per capita demand for food remains constant upon real wage reductions, but that for other goods declines; accordingly, increases in market demands with population growth necessarily diverge for the different products. In the preclusion of full micro-economic equilibrium patterns arises an instance of *exogenous structural impact.*

Various purely technological characteristics imply that the rate of productivity change is partly governed by the distribution of activity (itself to some degree a matter of exogenously given taste patterns) between manufacturing, agriculture and mining. Again, these impose constraints of a structural order on the values economic variables can attain. For there is a particular amenability of manufacturing to 'improvement', whereas agricultural skill and knowledge are of slow growth, and still slower diffusion (Mill, CW, III: 729). Mining shares with agriculture the characteristic that it 'yields an increase of produce at a more than proportional increase of expense'. There is the further problem of exhaustibility. But conversely, the antagonizing agency, that of improvements in production, also applies in a still greater degree. Mining operations are more susceptible of mechanical improvements than agricultural: the first great application of the steam-engine was to mining; and there are unlimited possibilities of improvement in the chemical processes by which the metals are extracted.

(*CW*, II: 184–5)

One of the *ceteris paribus* conditions in the analysis of the declining profit-rate trend is the distribution of the work force between the unproductive and productive classes – any transfer from the former to the latter counteracting the decline. Again, there is scope for an exogenous impact upon a key economic variable by way of the distribution of activity.

Classical growth theory: some further considerations

Our version of classicism, which perceives of 'subsistence' wages as a limit, contrasts sharply with that by W. A. Lewis:

> The classics, from Smith to Marx, all assumed, or argued, that an unlimited supply of labour was available at subsistence wages. They then enquired how production grows through time. They found the answer in capital accumulation which they explained in terms of their analysis of the distribution of income. Classical systems thus determined simultaneously income distribution and income growth, with the relative prices of commodities as a minor byproduct.
>
> (Lewis 1958: 400)

It is sometimes claimed that the productive-unproductive dichotomy reflects a concern for the liquidation of the primitive sector of the economy in which menial servants are maintained on a feudal basis, and for the development of the advanced industrial sector where well-managed and well-disciplined workers would be employed at higher wages (Bladen 1965: xlii). But concern with 'development' in this sense cannot alone or even primarily explain the classification. Physical commodities are distinguished from services because of an insistence that satisfaction as such be divorced from its source. As earlier explained, the annual product measures sales of producer and consumer goods envisaged as the *source* of utilities and not utilities as such, while final services are excluded since in their case the source and the utilities cannot be separated.

The growth model outlined above appears highly constrained at first sight by its preoccupation with the agricultural sector. But the purpose must be kept in mind – namely to trace out the implications for the distributive returns in an advanced capitalist-exchange system, of land scarcity, *specifically* taking account of the high profile of food in the wage basket. In underdeveloped economies the problem was seen primarily to be one of motivation. The policy implications were totally different. In the one case the key to satisfactory living standards for the masses – the main object of the classicists – lay (broadly speaking) in new technology and/or higher savings propensities and/or population control; in the other, overcoming 'indolence' was the first order of business. The formal model served its purpose well.

Sir John Hicks (1985) has argued that Mill's notions on the stationary state influenced the whole structure of his work in that the investigation of 'equilibrium positions', for which static theory is appropriate, takes precedence over the 'path to equilibrium', a weighting reflected in his concern for a desirable pattern of distribution as an end in itself. Mill's concern with equilibrium positions and desirable distribution is not in question; but it is going much too far to conclude that he 'disposed of the old growth economics'. The stationary state was, of course, closer with population control than without – a fact that comes out very clearly in terms of our prudential wage path. Yet Mill was fully aware that both technological progress and increases in the 'effective desire for accumulation' were in practice proceeding apace, so that stationariness was not in sight; indeed, in the Britain of his day steady-state wages (in fact a constant return on capital) were possible even without population control because of the extremely high rate of capital accumulation permitted by new technology. We must here emphasise Mill's recognition that new industrial and transport technology was responsible for sustaining ongoing aggregate expansion without pressure on wage- and profit rates, partly by way of its impact on agriculture. He feared for living standards in the event that the sources of new technology should dry up before adequate population control had been achieved – an unlikely possibility.

Criticisms of Mill for having played down labour productivity and the rate of technical progress, and for underestimating the importance of applied knowledge and modern technical education (e.g. Spengler 1960), are invalid. These matters were of the essence. In our account above, technology was treated purely as a shift parameter, neglecting the *economic* determinants of invention and innovation. Invention, however, is said to be sometimes 'undergone... in the prospect of a remuneration from the produce' (Mill, *CW*, II: 42). Market structure is pertinent (*CW*, III: 928). And size of establishment and organisation play a role (*CW*, II: 147; III: 902–3). While Mill was unprepared to designate as a 'law' increased manufacturing productivity due simply to scale economies, he did so describe an observed upward secular trend allowance made for new technology (*CW*, III: 713). This positive relation between manufacturing productivity and scale (allowing for innovation) turns partly on the Smithian linkage of invention to specialisation (*CW*, II: 182) but also on the observation that experiments 'can seldom be made with advantage except by rich proprietors or capitalists'

(147). What Mill has to say regarding joint-stock organisation is also relevant; such firms are in a position to attract management of a quality particularly suitable for the undertaking of projects 'out of the ordinary routine' (139).

Most important in the growth context, a falling profit rate is said to act as a stimulus both to investment and innovation: 'The curtailment of profit, and the consequent increased difficulty in making a fortune or obtaining a subsistence by the employment of capital, may act as a stimulus to inventions, and to the use of them when made' (827). Mill in fact wrote of the profit-technology relation as a 'tendency', thus according it the same methodological status as the pressure on profits of scarce land. The treatment of technical progress entirely as a non-economic exogenous factor is clearly inappropriate.

Theoretical science, however, is said to be a purely exogenous matter: the 'material fruits [of speculative thought] are seldom the direct purpose of the pursuit of savants, nor is their remuneration in general derived from the increased production which may be caused, incidentally, and mostly after a long interval, by their discoveries' (*CW*, II, 43). Science, therefore, 'does not, for most of the purposes of political economy require to be taken into consideration'. It is allowed only that:

> when (as in political economy one should always be prepared to do) we shift our point of view, and consider not individual acts, and the motives by which they are determined, but national and universal results, intellectual speculation must be looked upon as a most influential part of the productive labour of society, and the portion of its resources employed in carrying on and remunerating such labour, is a highly productive part of its expenditures.
>
> (43)

Accordingly:

> In a national or universal point of view, the labour of the savant, or speculative thinker, is as much a part of production in the very narrowest sense, as that of the inventor of a practical art; many such inventions having been the direct consequences of theoretic discoveries, and every extension of knowledge of the powers of nature being fruitful of applications to the purposes of outward life.
>
> (42)

The same distinction between the 'individual' and the 'national' points of view is made regarding elementary education and health expenditures (41). From the former perspective such outlays are said not, in the main, to reflect economic decision making, whereas:

> to the community at large the labour and expense of rearing its infant

population form a part of the outlay which is a condition of production, and which is to be replaced with increase from the future produce of their labour. By the individuals, this labour and expense are usually incurred from other motives than to obtain such ultimate return, and, for most purposes of political economy, need not to be taken into account as expenses of production.

The assertion that wealth-maximising motivation is generally not at play in matters pertaining to theoretical science, elementary education and health, is of crucial import. It is all the more regrettable that Mill – who was so keenly conscious of the significance to the growth process of the fraction of the community's resources devoted to technological advance, health and education – failed to carry out an investigation of the topic as a whole. Clearly, the incorporation within economics of the determinants of pure science was a mere 'proposal', albeit flowing from a realisation that (even though maximisation motivation might be irrelevant) the topic could not safely be legated to 'some other science'. Yet the allowance is crucial; for it indicates strikingly that economics, narrowly defined as based on purely economic rationality, was not a predictive science.

This characteristic is particularly noticeable in the context of the 'Influence of the progress of society on production and distribution', a context where the *spill-over effects* from the economic domain, with probable *feed-backs*, are most conspicuous.

Mill takes for granted as characteristic of 'civilized' countries, the 'progress of wealth' in the sense of 'growing material prosperity' – an allusion to aggregate wealth and population (*CW*, III: 705–6) – and spells out three 'tendencies' which characterise this 'progressive economical movement': Advances in technology, in security and in 'cooperation'. These are treated as causal phenomena responsible (directly or indirectly) for expanding aggregate output, but in turn played upon by economic growth. In each case the range of determinants governing the force in question is unstated, except for the impact of economic progress itself.

Thus allusion is made to 'the changes which the progress of industry causes or presupposes in the circumstances of society' (710) with reference to technological advance, implying a mutual cause–effect relation. Mill is very explicit about the multi-causal character of knowledge creation, including the state of wealth:

These remarkable differences in the state of different portions of the human race, with regard to the production and distribution of wealth, must, like all other phenomena, depend on causes. And it is not a sufficient explanation to ascribe them exclusively to the degrees of knowledge, possessed at different times and places, of the laws of nature and the physical arts of life. Many other causes cooperate; and *that very progress and unequal distribution of physical knowledge are partly the effects, as well as partly the causes, of the state of the production and distribution of wealth.*

(Mill, *CW*, II: 20; emphasis added)

We know that, for example, size of productive unit has an impact on knowledge creation; but 'the other causes' are left unexplained.

The second change, 'which has always hitherto characterized, and will assuredly continue to characterize the progress of civilized society', namely 'a continual increase of the security of person and property', is also not explained; we have merely a panegyric to the phenomenon with optimistic observations regarding the future (*CW*, III: 706). And again, a mutual relation is asserted: 'progress' – in this case social progress in the large as well as economic progress – is encouraged by increased security (706) but is also itself responsible for improvements in that regard: 'one of the acknowledged effects of that progress is an increase of general security. Destruction by wars, and spoliation by private or public violence, are less and less to be apprehended' (737).

The third tendency refers to 'cooperation'. Here the mutual linkage is better justified. The impact of specialisation characterising civilised society is said to have 'a debilitating effect upon intelligence and efficiency of the individual' – his ability to adapt means to ends – but not upon collective intelligence and efficiency: 'What is lost in the separate efficiency of each, is far more than made up by the greater capacity of united action', an increased capacity for cooperation reflected in better industrial discipline, adherence to plan, 'subordination of individual caprice', and so forth (708). (This same set of issues had been raised by Adam Smith in the context of invention.) Such capacity reinforces itself, for 'this, like other faculties, tends to improve by practice, and becomes capable of assuming a constantly wider sphere of action'.

The reverse linkage from wealth may be illustrated from the discussion of joint-stock organisation. Despite a negative evaluation of hired workers in general, Mill rejected Adam Smith's low evaluation of joint-stock organisation; Smith had overplayed

> the superior energy and more unremitting attention brought to a business in which the whole stake and the whole gain belong to the persons conducting it; and he overlooked various countervailing considerations which go a great way towards neutralizing even that great point in superiority.
>
> (*CW*, II: 138)

The disadvantages might be reduced by resort to some form of profit-sharing relating the 'interest of the employees with the pecuniary success of the concern', but also, where size permits it, by attraction of 'a class of candidates superior to the common average in intelligence', thereby raising 'the quality of the service much above that which the generality of masters are capable of rendering to themselves' (140).

The pervasive impact of general 'progress' in the sense of advances in technology can be illustrated from our discussion of retailing. A major source of market imperfection, in addition to the rigidities imposed by 'custom', was seen to lie in the ability to practise price differentiation – by location if not by product. This ability, Mill argues, was increasingly weakened by the development of 'great emporia of trade' where retail business could be conducted on a large scale – a consequence in part of the transport revolution which breaks down dependency on local dealers (*CW*, II: 141, 243, 410).

When we extend the scope of progress to incorporate 'opinion', the impact on pricing widens considerably to the correction by appropriate education of such 'deformities' as conspicuous consumption. The phenomenon of non-competing industrial groups was considered by Mill to be in the course of disintegration, in consequence of broader educational opportunities and changes 'so rapidly taking place in usages and ideas' (386f).

Notes

1   This paper was presented at the second meeting, in November 1984, of Project IDEA (Interdisciplinary Dimensions of Economic Analysis) held at the Maison des Sciences de l'Homme, Paris, and jointly sponsored by the International Social Science Council and the Bank of Sweden Tercentenary Foundation.

    References in this paper to various types of plug-ins, spill-overs and feedbacks are based on the definitions and concepts adopted in the Project.

2   There are limitations. For example, there is no formal place for non-agricultural wage goods (though the classics were very much aware that the general profit rate will be affected by changes in the real cost of such commodities). Second, 'fixed capital' is excluded notwithstanding the high profile of the so-called 'machinery' issue. Third, the allocative underpinnings of the inverse wage-profit relation have no explicit place. The model must be 'interpreted' with these limitations in mind.

References

Bladen, V. W. (1965) 'Introduction', in *Collected Works of John Stuart Mill*, II, III, Toronto: University of Toronto Press.

Hicks, Sir John (1985) 'Sraffa and Ricardo: a critical view', in G. Caravale (ed.) *The Legacy of Ricardo*, Oxford: Blackwell.

Hollander, S. (1979) *The Economics of David Ricardo*, Toronto: University of Toronto Press.

——(1982) 'On the substantive identity of the classical and neoclassical conceptions of economic organization: the French connection in British classicism', *Canadian Journal of Economics*, 15 (November): 586–612.

——(1984a) 'Marx and Malthusianism: Marx's secular path of wages', *American Economic Review*, 74 (March): 139–51.

——(1984b) 'The wage path in classical growth models: Ricardo, Malthus and Mill', *Oxford Economic Papers*, 36: 200–12.

Lewis, W. A. (1958) 'Economic development with unlimited supplies of labour', in A. N. Agarwala and S. P. Singh (eds) *The Economics of Underdevelopment*, Bombay: Oxford University Press, 400–49.

Mill, J. S. (1963–91) *Collected Works of John Stuart Mill*, Toronto: University of Toronto Press. Herein *CW*.

——(1965) *Principles of Political Economy, Collected Works*, II, III.

——(1967) *Essays on Economics and Society, Collected Works*, IV, V.

——(1969) *Essays on Ethics, Religion and Society, Collected Works*, X.

——(1972) *Later Letters, 1848–73, Collected Works*, XIV–XVII.

——(1973) *System of Logic: Ratiocinative and Inductive, Collected Works*, VII, VIII.

Ricardo, D. (1951–73) *Works and Correspondence of David Ricardo*, 11 vols, ed. P. Sraffa, Cambridge: Cambridge University Press.

Samuelson, P. A. (1972) 'Economic forecasting and science', in *Collected Scientific Papers*, III, 774–80, Cambridge MA: MIT Press.

Smith, A. (1937) [1776] *The Wealth of Nations*, New York: Modern Library.

Spengler, J. J. (1960) 'John Stuart Mill on economic development', in B. F. Hoselitz *et al. Theories of Economic Growth*, New York: Free Press, 113–54.

Turgot, A. R. J. (1963) [1770] *Reflections on the Formation and Distribution of Riches*, New York: Kelley.

Chapter 9

The relevance of John Stuart Mill

Some implications for modern economics[1]

Introduction

Sir John Hicks has recently lamented that John Stuart Mill 'as an economist, seems to have been de-throned' (Hicks 1983: 60). It is my contention that his under-evaluation has been at a great cost – intellectual and social. Professor Phelps-Brown, in his Presidential Address to the Royal Economic Society in 1971, charged that the profession had contributed little by its sophisticated theoretical and econometric techniques to the most pressing economic problems of our age, and explained this discrepancy by the argument that our models are 'built upon assumptions about human behaviour that are plucked from the air', rather than drawn from observation – 'that the behaviour posited is not known to be what obtains in the actual economy' (Phelps-Brown 1972: 3–4). The President of the American Economic Association in 1971 made precisely the same point, that the 'consistently indifferent performance in practical applications is . . . a symptom of a fundamental imbalance in the present state of our discipline. The weak and all too slowly growing empirical foundation clearly cannot support the proliferating superstructure of pure, or . . . speculative economic theory.' What is needed, considering that by the nature of social systems the structural relationships (both their form and the parameters) are subject to continuous change, is 'a very difficult and seldom very neat assessment and verification of these assumptions in terms of observed facts'. In this context he characterised much econometric work 'as an attempt to compensate for the glaring weakness of the data base available to us by the widest possible use of more and more sophisticated statistical techniques' designed 'to stretch to the limit the meager supply of facts' – techniques 'which themselves are based on convenient assumptions of fact which can be seldom verified' (Leontief 1971: 1–3).

These laments portray the type of consequence against which J. S. Mill had sought to protect economics from 1830 onwards. His own counsel – and also his practice – justified a specialist economics, but specifically on empirical grounds, and thus provisionally; it implied a very modest estimate of the subject's forecasting or predictive potential; it demanded model improvement by way of verification against factual evidence; it disdained any notion of the universal validity of economic principles; it focused attention upon the mechanics of pricing in the real world of business rather than some ideal world; and it invited consideration of how economic mechanisms might operate under a variety of alternative institutional arrangements. His position took a stand against professional arrogance and narrow-mindedness. Most striking is Mill's remarkable prescience – he himself warned of the probable consequences of adopting the kind of hyper-specialist mathematical research programme in the air, indeed already on the ground, during his last years.

We can trace the deflection of the subject to which I allude to the revolt against classicism in the early 1870s. Professor Black has argued that it is Jevons' emphasis upon 'the importance of the mathematical method' rather than the development of marginal utility theory as such, wherein lies 'the essence of his break with the classical tradition' (Black 1972a: 5). And this indeed seems to hit the nail on the head (compare Schabas 1983a). Jevons' programme was the mathematisation of economic theory: 'Economics, if it is to be a science at all, must be a mathematical science' (Jevons 1924: 3) treating specifically *the mechanics of utility and self-interest* (21) – that is, a science of economising behaviour (Black 1972b: 372). Jevons' hope was for the transformation of economics from a 'mathematical' into an 'exact' science permitting application of statistical method; but economists were to proceed boldly 'in developing their mathematical theories in advance of their data' (Jevons 1924: 6). For the 'mechanical' theory itself 'must be the true one'. Indeed, in a remarkable statement Jevons asserted that 'its method is as sure and demonstrative as that of kinematics or statics, nay, almost as self-evident as are the elements of Euclid, when the real meaning of the formulae is fully seized' (21); similarly, 'the first principles of political economy are so widely true and applicable that they may be considered universally true as regards human nature' (Jevons 1905: 197).

Jevons by no means disdained the efforts of the historicists such as Cliffe Leslie. He observed in 1876:

> I am far from thinking that the historical treatment of our science is false or useless. On the contrary, I consider it to be indispensable. The present state of society cannot possibly be explained by theory alone. We must take into account the long past out of which we are constantly emerging. Whether we call it sociology or not, we must have some scientific treatment of the principles of evolution as manifested in every branch of social existence.
>
> (Jevons 1905: 195)

But theoretical work was to proceed unencumbered, for Jevons insisted firmly on division of labour: 'it will no longer be possible to treat political economy as if it were a single undivided and indivisible science' (Jevons 1905: 197); '[it] is only by subdivision...that we can rescue our science from its confused state' (Jevons 1924: 20–1). And, in any event, historical economics (which apparently entailed different 'scientific' procedures from those appropriate in pure economics) would have a rather limited confirmatory function: 'so far from displacing the theory of economy, [historical economics] will only exhibit and verify the long-continued action of its laws in most widely different states of society' (Jevons 1905: 197).[2]

In what precise ways did Mill differ from Jevons? There are obvious similarities. Mill too distinguished (as Ricardo had done) the 'science' from the 'art' of economics; and for him, too, scientific economics involved a form of maximisation theory. In fact, we must be quite clear that any revolutionary connotation attached to general pricing doctrine has to be avoided when treating the events of the 1870s. For the 'Ricardian' economics of Mill comprises in its essentials an exchange system consistent with the neoclassical elaborations (Hollander 1979, 1985).

But even when we limit our perspective to pricing[3] there is a fundamental difference. The marginalists based their deductions on an assumed psychology acting within an assumed environment. From the limited number of hypothetical postulates relating to human psychology, and the social environment, was to be derived the entire body of economic doctrine; model improvement by the introduction of new material in the form of postulates, axioms, definitions and hypotheses derived by testing against real-world evidence played no part. This perspective threatened a reversion to the severe abstractions of James Mill, which had been undertaken on the basis of axioms adopted without serious empirical study – the state of affairs which induced J. S. Mill in 1829 and 1830 to compose in protest his celebrated essay on scope and method (Mill 1836).[4] For, like Ricardo, he was concerned with the real world of business, not some laboratory experiment. It is a failure of the profession to heed his warnings that delayed for decades the recognition of monopolistic competition, engendered ludicrous accounts of competitive price formation, and pushed such phenomena as conspicuous consumption into the footnotes. In these respects the 1870s encouraged intellectual regression.

I shall take for granted in what follows Mill's case (presented in his early essay on definition and method [Mill 1836] and the *System of Logic* [Mill 1843]) for a specialist economics – the empirical validity of the maximisation axiom, the role accorded 'verification' in model improvement, and the limitations imposed on the scope of economic science by empirical considerations – limitations which preclude 'prediction'. But one matter relating to formal method requires closer attention: Mill's famous assertion regarding the 'universality of the method of political economy', before we turn to the substance of our presentation. This concerns the empirical dimension of the *Principles of Political Economy* (Mill 1848) with special reference to the analysis of price formation and the marginal utility issue. Mill's balanced and highly pertinent position regarding mathematical economics brings the paper to a close.

The universality of the method of political economy

In the course of a criticism in 1834 of English political economists who:

> attempt to construct a permanent fabric out of transitory materials ... [and] presuppose in every one of their speculations, that the produce of industry is shared among three classes, altogether distinct from one another – namely, labourers, capitalists, and landlords; and that all these are free agents, permitted in law and fact to set upon their labour, their capital, and their land, whatever price they are able to get for it
>
> (Mill 1834, *CW*, IV: 225)

– Mill added a qualification which withdraws the barbs as far as concerns the method itself:

> It must not, however, be supposed that the science is so incomplete and unsatisfactory as this might seem to prove. Though many of its conclusions are only locally true, its method of investigation is applicable universally; and as he who has solved a certain number of algebraic equations, can without difficulty solve all others, so he who knows the political economy of England, or even of Yorkshire, knows that of all nations actual or possible; provided he have sense enough not to expect the same conclusions to issue from varying premises.
>
> (cited in the *System of Logic* (*CW*, VIII: 904); a similar position is taken in a reaction to Auguste Comte in 1865 [*CW*, X: 305–6])

This claim regarding the universal applicability of the method of political economy has been said to conflict with the position laid down in the *Principles* that 'only through the principle of competition has political economy any pretension to the character of a science' (Winch 1972: 340). Edgeworth (1910, II: 757), Winch observes,

> drew attention to this inconsistency when he pointed out that it was not really possible for Mill to retain belief in the *a priori* deductive method once 'he began to doubt the universality of the principle of self-interest, which he once regarded as the foundation of economic reasoning'.
>
> (Winch 1972: 340)

Now the fact is that Mill had 'doubted' the universality of the principle of maximising behaviour from 1830 onwards. Are we then obliged to charge him with a self-contradiction throughout the essay?

The formulation relating to the applicability of the method of economics to 'all nations actual or possible' appears indeed to be too strongly stated on Mill's own terms. However, in his paper of 1834 Mill is quite explicit regarding his specific intentions. He insisted that:

> The conclusions of the science, being all adapted to a society thus constituted, require to be revised whenever they are applied to any other. They are inapplicable where the only capitalists are the landlords, and the labourers are their property; as in the West Indies. They are inapplicable where the universal landlord is the State, as in India. They are inapplicable where the agricultural labourer is generally the owner both of the land itself and of the capital, as in France; or of the capital only, as in Ireland. We might greatly prolong this enumeration.
>
> (Mill, *CW*, IV: 226)

In the *System of Logic* (1843) Mill pointed out that

> the deductive science of society will not lay down a theorem, asserting in an universal manner the effect of any cause; but will rather teach us how to frame the proper theorem for the circumstances of any given case. It will not give the laws of society in general, but the means of determining the phenomena of any given society from the particular elements or data of that society.
>
> (*CW*, VIII: 899–900)

To this he adds that

> whoever has mastered with the degree of precision which is attainable the laws which, under free competition, determine the rent, profits, and wages, received by landlords, capitalists, and labourers, in a state of society in which the three classes are completely separate, will have no difficulty in determining the very different laws which regulate the distribution of the produce among the classes interested in it, in any of the states of cultivation and landed property set forth in the foregoing extract.

(Mill was here alluding to the specific institutional arrangements listed in Harriet Martineau's *Political Economy* [1834]. The argument is referred to with enthusiasm by Torrens [1844: xif] in his defence of Ricardian economics.)

The strong statements regarding the applicability of the method of political economy 'to all nations and all times' do not, therefore, extend maximisation principles to all possible cases including (say) those involving custom or gift or force – alluded to in the *System of Logic* (*CW*, VIII: 900–1) as well as the *Principles* – which, Mill maintained, were not amenable to economic analysis and would have to be dealt with by 'some other' science. Mill was pointing rather to the working out of the maximisation hypothesis within a wide variety of specific institutional arrangements in addition to the capitalist-exchange system. This might be illustrated by reference to the treatment of peasant proprietorship, cooperation and the stationary-state issue, but the exercise would extend our present argument too far.

The empirical dimension in the principles: some case studies

The roles accorded 'induction' in the derivation of individual axioms and in model improvement are central to the early essay, and that essay Mill intended his readers to have at hand in 1848. It will be useful to take a brief overview of Mill's actual practice in the *Principles* from this perspective, with particular reference to the self-interest axiom. We must first set aside an unnecessary terminological complexity, turning on the technical usage of 'wealth' to exclude services. This usage has led some commentators to assert that Mill's maximising individuals concern themselves solely with material goods (e.g. Bowley 1937: 46–7, 61, 63). In fact Mill had in mind nothing more than the rule that individuals seek to sell goods and services at the highest price attainable and to buy at the lowest price attainable, and possess the knowledge to do so (*CW*, III: 460, cited below). The consequence of such behaviour combined with other assumptions relating to large numbers and free entry is a single price for the same good (or service) in one market – the so-called 'Jevons rule' which characterises competition; and 'only through the principle of competition has political economy any pretension to the character of science', subject to 'principles of broad generality and scientific precision' (*CW*, II: 239).

That the maximising man in the *Principles* refers to the real man in the market-place rather than a psychological fiction, comes to light with stark clarity in Mill's restriction of the economic analysis of pricing to the wholesale sector:

> The values and prices . . . to which our conclusions apply, are mercantile values and prices; such prices as are quoted in price-currents; prices in the wholesale markets, in which buying as well as selling is a matter of business; in which the buyers take pains to know, and generally do know, the lowest price at which an article of a given quality can be obtained. . . . Our propositions will be true in a much more qualified sense, of retail prices; the prices paid in shops for articles of personal consumption.
>
> (Mill, *CW*, III: 460)

This restriction turns on the observation that buyers at retail outlets do not typically make their purchases 'on business principles' – a reflection of their indolence, carelessness, satisfaction derived from paying high prices, ignorance, defective judgement and coercion, apart from high search costs (*CW*, III: 460). Equally conspicuous is the discussion of the motives governing employers of domestics (and of clerks), which explains why more is often paid than the 'competitive' wage in terms of 'ostentation' and a variety of 'more reasonable motives', all of which turn on the personal contact between employee and employer (*CW*, III: 398–9). This case-study provides a very clear indication that the assumption of wealth maximisation is pertinent to the anonymous market-place where personal contacts are reduced to a minimum, precluding the range of considerations in question. Quite clearly, Mill was fully at one with Smith regarding the supposed empirical accuracy of the maximising assumption in the capitalist-exchange environment, and more specifically the limitations imposed by that environment on a range of 'self-interested' forms of behaviour (but see Blaug 1980: 61, for a quite different perspective).

Marshall maintained of Ricardo and his followers that they 'often spoke as though they regarded man as a constant quantity, and they never gave themselves enough trouble to study his variations' (Marshall 1920: 762). While little harm was done in the contexts of money and trade, they were 'led astray' particularly in that of distribution; they

> attributed to the forces of supply and demand a much more mechanical and regular action than is to be found in real life: and they laid down laws with regard to profits and wages that did not really hold even for England in their own time.
>
> (Marshall 1920: 762–3)

Marshall did not include Mill of the *Principles* in this charge; it was rather Mill of the essay (1836) who was supposedly guilty, Marshall presuming mistakenly that it was written under the influence of James Mill (Marshall 1920: 764–5n). As for the *Principles*, Marshall was right in that Mill did not there apply the principles of supply and demand 'mechanically', either in the context of commodity or of service pricing. Yet he took great pains to avoid disparaging competitive pricing, and in so doing *reinforced* the importance of classical theorising, even from an empirical perspective.

His course of action involves the matter of 'disturbing causes' so central to the formal discussion of method. Consider the declaration that

> while there is no proposition which meets us in the field of political economy more often than this – that there cannot be two prices in the same market . . . yet every one knows that there are, almost always two prices, in the same market.
>
> (*CW*, II: 242)

The solution adopted by Mill, in effect, is to treat non-maximising behaviour in the retail sector as involving 'disturbing causes' in pricing – in principle the responsibility of 'some other science'. But this, it must be emphatically stressed, has an empirical justification, in so far as the primary force at work – that governing the determination of the underlying wholesale price – remained pecuniary maximisation.

The latter procedure can be further illustrated by reference to the allowance in the essay that the 'perpetually antagonistic principles to the desire of wealth', namely 'aversion to labour, and desire of the present enjoyment of costly indulgencies', are in practice taken into account by economics 'to a certain extent' precisely because of their empirical pervasiveness (*CW*, IV: 322). This matter is much amplified in the *Principles*, where it is clarified that by desire of wealth is intended pecuniary maximisation, and by the two antagonistic forces in question a willingness to by-pass an opportunity to increase the return per hour or per unit of capital by movement between sectors, or to forego a bargain in commodity markets. Thus Mill observed regarding Continental Europe,

> that prices and charges, of some or of all sorts, are much higher in some places than in others not far distant, without its being possible to assign any other cause than that it has always been so: the customers are used to it, and acquiesce in it.
>
> (*CW*, II: 244)

Similarly,

> an enterprising competitor, with sufficient capital, might force down the charges, and make his fortune during the process; but there are no enterprising competitors; those who have capital prefer to leave it where it is, or to make less profit by it in a more quiet way.

The same could be said of labour. Now in the British case too, where 'the spirit of competition' is the strongest, custom was still a 'powerful influence'; but in other environments people were 'content with smaller gains, and estimate their pecuniary interest at a lower rate when balanced against their ease or their pleasure'. Clearly Mill intended more than a quantitative difference between Britain and the Continent. In the latter kind of environment the force of the wealth-maximisation motive was swamped by the antagonistic motives, so that little could be said of the response to a newly created wage or profit differential or a reduction in price; havoc was wrought as far as concerns 'predictions' regarding labour and capital flows, or rates of consumption with price change. In the British case, there were strong empirical presumptions favouring the process of equalisation of returns to labour and to capital, and also the negative slope to the demand curve and thus a tendency to stable equilibrium in competitive markets – at least up to the wholesale stage.

Thus it is also that Mill appeals to the empirical accuracy of the behavioural axiom in his discussion of profit-rate equalisation (cost pricing):

> If the value of a commodity is such that it repays the cost of production not only with the customary, but with a higher rate of profit, capital rushes to share in this extra gain, and by increasing the supply of the

article reduces its value. This is not a mere supposition or surmise, but a fact familiar to those conversant with commercial operations.

(*CW*, III: 472)

We recall too (below, pp. 195–6) the appeal to the real world of business and the complexity of entrepreneurial decision-making in the context of what we shall call 'internal adjustment' to cost variation.

The same perspective emerges in Mill's general analysis of the wage structure with special reference to his allowance for non-competing groups. A variety of features of the real world, conspicuously the impediments to mobility of a financial and social order, underlay his dissatisfaction with Smithian analysis, and it was his growing optimism regarding a breakdown of the impediments that ultimately led him to conclude that while 'there are few kinds of [skilled] labour of which the remuneration would not be lower than it is, if the employer took the full advantage of competition', yet competition 'must be regarded, in the present state of society as the principal regulator of wages, and custom or individual character only as a modifying circumstance, and that in a comparatively slight degree' (*CW*, II: 337).

Moreover, the existence of unusual cases is never denied. The most striking are the instances of excessive entry, as in the literary professions (*CW*, II: 392) or the Canadian timber trade (*CW*, II: 383–4) generating negative returns even in equilibrium – a consequence of that 'principle of human nature' whereby a few great prizes stimulate miscalculation. But this principle too was treated as a 'modifying circumstance' in going conditions.

That the primary behaviour axiom holds good as a first approximation is thus justified on purely empirical grounds, as we are led to expect from the essay. But here we must note the fundamentally important caution regarding the allowances that have to be made in practice, a caution that appears following recognition of possible cases of permanent inequalities in the return on capital:

> These observations must be received as a general correction to be applied whenever relevant, whether expressly mentioned or not, to the conclusions contained in the subsequent portions of this treatise. Our reasonings must, in general, proceed as if the known and natural effects of competition were actually produced by it, in all cases where it is not restrained by some positive obstacle. Where competition, though free to exist, does not exist, or where it exists, but has its natural consequences overruled by any other agency, the conclusions will fail more or less of being applicable. To escape error, we ought, in applying the conclusions of political economy to the actual affairs of life, to consider not only what will happen supposing the maximum of competition, but how far the result will be affected if competition falls short of the maximum.
>
> (Mill, *CW*, III: 244)

Again, this too reflects what is said in the essay, namely that verification of the hypothesis is 'no part of the business of science, but of the application of science'. But it must be understood with qualification.[5]

As in the essay, so in the *Principles* we find that Mill allows the absorption into his economic models of market forms that do not fit the purely competitive case. What we have to say on this matter is pertinent to an evaluation of the view that, from Mill's perspective, 'we never test the *validity* of theories, because the conclusions are true as one aspect of human behaviour by virtue of being based on self-evident facts of human experience' (Blaug 1980: 77). That the notion of 'self-evident' facts is suspect we know already; what emerges, however, is the further circumstance that Mill does attempt model improvement based upon testing against the record; much more is involved than 'a search...for sufficient supplementary causes to close the gap between the facts and the causal antecedents laid down in the theory' (Blaug 1980: 75).

Model improvement as defined in the essay is the hoped-for consequence of the process of testing against the evidence. In some instances a new disturbing cause would be discovered which in future use of theory has to be kept in mind – as instanced by the obstacles to wage-rate equalisation which Mill's empirical studies brought to light. But model improvement in consequence of verification might be more substantive, taking the form of 'inserting among its hypotheses a fresh and still more complex combination of circumstances, and so adding *pro hâc vice* a supplementary chapter or appendix, or at least a supplementary theorem to the abstract science'. Thus the exclusion of monopoly from the scientific domain and its treatment as disturbing cause turns out to be purely a formal matter; in practice Mill admitted that it had 'always been allowed for by political economists' and himself applied the tools of analysis to this case (Hollander 1985: 300–1). Even more striking, he allows in practice for the absorption of custom – again formally a 'disturbing cause' – where custom establishes prices yet competition acts to reduce profits to the economy-wide rate by reducing market size – the 'monopolistic competition' model (*CW*, II: 243, 409–10). Here, then, we have two splendid illustrations of the observation in the essay that 'a disturbing cause...which operates through the same law of human nature out of which the general principles of the science arise...might always be brought within the pale of the abstract science, if it were thought worthwhile'.[6]

Equally striking is Mill's recognition of (short-run) excess demand for money to hold. This too illustrates model improvement, in this case a consequence of the 'anomaly' of contemporaneous excess labour and capital which forced itself on his attention after his escape from his father's influence. And the idea of an endogenous trade cycle is better developed by Mill than any contemporary and clearly related to real-world events.[7]

On price formation

Much of the apparent ambiguity surrounding Mill's formulations of cost price in its relation to demand-and-supply dissipates on a close inspection of the texts. For it becomes apparent that it arises from an impressive attempt to get a grip on the notoriously complex issue of long-run price and output adjustments in unconventional terms from the perspective of the modern reader, precisely because Mill is attempting to deal with the complexity of real-world business.

We take as the standard case the adjustment to a new equilibrium following a technological change that reduces natural price. Mill's approach allows a price-setting role to individual (competitive) entrepreneurs who, aware of the likelihood of entry into the industry by firms in response to super-normal profit, act to forestall them. It is, therefore, not increase in supply that works to reduce price to the lower cost level, but price that is lowered directly, at a rate depending upon the estimate of the immediate danger of entry made by existing entrepreneurs who calculate the risks of entry as viewed by prospective entrants, a calculation which turns partly upon demand elasticity (*CW*, III: 473–4).

It is expectation of increased supply that brings about the price reduction to cost, for which reason precisely 'if the supply *could* not be increased no diminution in the cost of production would lower the value'. Next to be noted is the actual output expansion, in the usual case of non-zero elasticity of demand, by existing firms who will be faced by larger markets which they can serve at the going (economy-wide) profit rate. In the limiting case of zero demand-elasticity (characterising basic foodstuffs) there will, of course, be no such opportunities at all; this possibility Mill emphasised in order to counter the view that there necessarily occurs an output expansion to assure that price falls to cost.

There arise a number of complications. Before these expansions have been accomplished there will be excess demand at cost price, and one must suppose that consumers or perhaps retailers, for their part, will put upward pressure on the price. This kind of complexity is actually raised by Mill in his treatment of a tax:

> Again, reverse the case, and suppose the cost of production increased.... The value would rise; and that probably immediately. Would the supply be diminished? Only if the increase of value diminished the demand. Whether this effect followed, would soon appear, and if it did, the value would recede somewhat, from excess of supply, until the production was reduced, and would then rise again.
>
> (*CW*, III: 474)

In this case, as before, price changes 'immediately' (although the counterpart to the logic of fear of entry is not clarified). At the higher price, in the first instance, supply exceeds demand in the event that demand contracts, generating some downward pressure on the price, although it seems that the market does not fully clear until the adjustment is completed; only after output is actually reduced can the higher price level be permanently maintained. The implication is that, in our case of technological change, prices will rise somewhat from the initial (lower-cost) level, although firms would be reluctant to accept improved offers for fear of attracting new entrants, and would be engaged in attempting to expand capacity to meet the expected demand at the cost price, even if current price should be held somewhat above it. But again, the market does not actually clear until the adjustment process is completed. (That a degree of trial and error is involved is also clarified by the remark that 'the permanent tendency of supply is to conform itself to the demand which is found by experience to exist for the commodity when selling at its natural value'.)

There are, of course, complexities. Mill's firms are supposed to engage in a passive form of collusion to satisfy what amounts to an implicit market division arrangement. A characteristic of the analysis is its failure to indicate the long-run optimum size of the firms, each of which is apparently presumed to have the technical ability to expand at constant cost without limit; what constraint exists is self-imposed.[8] Second, it would be going too far to attribute to Mill sole reliance on internal adjustment. That mechanism applies where the disturbance is amenable to treatment in partial-equilibrium terms, where the economy-wide profit rate can be taken by firms in a particular industry as given. It would not apply to a disturbance such as a general wage change. And it is difficult to see how it would operate effectively alone in variable-cost industries where there is no unambiguous level of costs to which firms can attempt to adjust price. Even in the standard case of adjustment to technological change in a constant-cost industry, the smaller the success of existing firms in maintaining price near the new cost level, the greater will be the attraction for newcomers. And the mechanism will be irrelevant in the case of newly established industries. Yet despite all this we have here a remarkable attempt, of which we have simply lost sight in the literature, to get to grips with an exceedingly complex issue. This case illustrates my contention that even in their own domain of price theory, the marginalists failed to build on their predecessors – a failure accountable by their model-building in isolation from the real business world.

Mill and marginal utility

We proceed to the marginal utility issue – the fact that the classical approach to the law of demand (the negative slope to the demand curve) eschewed reference to the principle of satiability of wants. How to explain what, from a neo-classical perspective, is often represented as a 'failing' (cf. de Marchi 1972: 350). Is the marginal utility episode not a case of unambiguous progress?

It is possible that the marginal utility concept itself was long familiar to Mill (de Marchi 1972: 347; Bowley 1972; Hollander 1977); in fact, Mill utilised a version of diminishing utility in his case for income redistribution (Hollander 1985: 880). That Mill 'inherited from Ricardo a bias against giving consumption a place equal to that held by production and distribution in the schema of economic science' (de Marchi 1972: 350, cf. 354, 363) is also true, provided that this is not understood as downplaying the law of demand itself which was so central to Ricardian economics, or as a blanket denial that the ultimate motive governing production and employment is final purchase. By his statements in the essay regarding consumption Mill merely intended to convey that the 'laws of consumption' – which are identified with the 'laws of human enjoyment' – fall outside the domain of the economist (CW, IV: 318n). The existence of such laws, however, seems to be conceded. Indeed, Mill removes some potential roadblocks along the path. There is his insistence in *Utilitarianism* (1861) that 'rules of arithmetic are applicable to the valuation of happiness, as of all other measurable quantities' (CW, X: 258). In *A System of Logic* he took strong issue with Comte and others who

> prefer dogmatically to assume that the mental differences which they perceive, or think they perceive, among human beings, are ultimate facts, incapable of being either explained or altered, rather than take the trouble of fitting themselves, by the requisite process of thought, for referring those mental differences to the outward causes by which they are for the most part produced, and on the removal of which they would cease to exist.
>
> (CW, III: 859)

He maintained that

> the commonest observation shows that different minds are susceptible in very different degrees to the action of the same psychological causes. The idea, for example, of a given desirable object, will excite in different minds very different degrees of intensity of desire.
>
> (CW, VIII: 865, cf. 857)

but he was ready enough to allow the usefulness of 'approximate generalizations', albeit that they constituted the lowest kind of empirical law: 'that which is only probable when asserted of individual human beings indiscriminately selected, being certain when affirmed of the character and collective conduct of masses' (CW, VIII: 847).

There is, then, no categorical rejection of an investigation of the 'laws of human enjoyment'. And the question would have arisen for Mill whether it might be fruitful to seek a basis in psychology for the law of demand.

As a matter of principle, Mill maintained (in a famous letter to Cairnes) that 'the wants of the time' required 'that scientific deductions should be made as simple and as easily intelligible as they can be made without ceasing to be scientific' (letter of 5 December 1871; CW, XVII: 1863). Now the law of demand had already been rationalised in terms of the income effect by Ricardo, and more than that may not have been found necessary. We can be rather more specific. Our researches have shown that when pressed to consider the details of consumer reaction to relative price variation, purchasing power held constant, Mill applied brilliantly and effortlessly a 'revealed preference' analysis, thereby confirming a liking for as simple a rationale as possible – eschewing psychologism in favour of the pure logic of choice (Hollander 1985: 270–1). This illustrates nicely his complaint to Cairnes in the letter just referred to regarding Jevons' 'mania for encumbering questions with useless complications' (CW, XVII: 1862). Jevons, for his part, simply asserted that 'it is surely obvious that Economics does rest upon the laws of human enjoyment; and that, if those laws are developed by no other science, they must be developed by economists' (Jevons 1924: 39). Mill probably did not see the *Theory* (Schabas 1983a: 39); but he was closer to the truth than Jevons by his realisation that recognition of the need for a theory of demand does not necessarily imply need for a psychological theory of consumption.[9]

But the appeal for simplicity alone might not have led to a refusal to follow through along a route which otherwise promised a more profound comprehension of behaviour. There is a further consideration – Mill's appreciation that consumer goods are usually characterised by some degree of durability imposing a 'capital' dimension upon decisions to purchase. For the production process comes to a halt when things are 'in place where they are required for use' (CW, II: 48); to focus on psychology to explain the stage of acquisition would have appeared inappropriate without the further complication of a discount factor, since the 'laws of human enjoyment' come into play only with the *use* of (durable) consumer goods.

There is also the belief that much consumer activity at the retail level is governed by non-maximising motivation. (From this point of view, it is doubtful whether Mill would have accorded diminishing marginal utility the status even of 'empirical law'.)[10] To the extent that consumer behaviour is not undertaken on terms of 'business principles', economics had nothing much to say. It is not that Mill was 'prevented' from defining optimum consumption patterns because he lacked the principle of marginal utility (de Marchi 1972: 356–7); rather, maximising behaviour was, empirically speaking, an inappropriate axiom in the first place. But to the extent that the consumer was envisaged as a maximiser – or at least as behaving consistently – an 'objective' approach was preferable. Important matters of principle govern Mill's neglect of diminishing marginal utility; to refer to it as a 'failure' and imply that the contributions of the 1870s were an unambiguous advance is inappropriate.

Mill and mathematical economics

Schwartz maintains that 'Mill was no mathematician, either by training or, which is more important, by inclination', and accordingly 'resisted the trend towards the formalization of new knowledge' (Schwartz 1972: 238). As an indication of this perspective he cites the letter to Cairnes regarding Jevons' *Theory of Political Economy* (1871) already referred to:

> I have not seen Mr Jevons's book, but as far as I can judge from such notices of it as have reached me, I do not expect that I shall think favourably of it. He is a man of some ability, but he seems to me to have a mania for encumbering questions with useless complications, and with a notation implying the existence of greater precision in the data than the questions admit of. His speculations on logic, like those of Boole and De Morgan, and some of those of Hamilton, are infected in an extraordinary degree with this vice.
>
> (Mill, *CW*, XVII: 1862)

The notion that Mill's mathematics were inadequate can be dismissed (de Marchi 1972: 347; Schabas 1983a: 283). A key to Mill's reaction to Jevons will rather be found in an observation by Cairnes regarding *The Theory of Political Economy* (Jevons 1871) in the letter which elicited the foregoing citation – 'I own', Cairnes wrote, that 'I have no faith in the development of economic doctrines by mathematics. What you have said on the subject of nomenclature in the second vol. of your Logic seems to me decisive upon this point' (23 October 1871, cited by Schwartz 1972: 295). Cairnes is here referring to Mill's generalisation in *A System of Logic* that

> whenever the nature of the subject permits our reasoning processes to be, without danger, carried on mechanically, the language should be constructed on as mechanical principles as possible; while in the contrary case, it should be constructed that there shall be the greatest possible obstacles to a merely mechanical use of it.
>
> (*CW*, VIII: 707)

This is followed by a statement of presumption against the widespread applicability of mathematical language suitable only for the 'mechanical' approach:

> [The] admirable properties of the symbolic language of mathematics have made so strong an impression on the minds of many thinkers, as to have led them to consider the symbolic language generally; to think that

names in general, or (as they are fond of calling them) signs, are fitted
for the purposes of thought in proportion as they can be made to
approximate to the compactness, the entire unmeaningness, and the
capability of being used as counters without a thought of what they
represent, which are characteristic of the *a* and *b*, the *x* and *y* of algebra.
This notion has led to sanguine views of the acceleration of the progress
of science by means which, I conceive, cannot possibly conduce to that
end, and forms part of that exaggerated estimate of the influence of
signs, which has contributed in no small degree to prevent the real laws
of our intellectual operations from being understood.

(Mill, *CW*, VIII: 708)

It is likely that this perspective governed at least in part the allusion to
Jevons' 'use of a notation implying the existence of greater precision in the
data than the questions admit of'. The observation extends far beyond the
application of mathematics to consumption theory. Quite generally, Mill's
fear was that the inappropriate use of mathematical language would act as a
positive hindrance to scientific progress; Jevons' mathematical programme
for economics must have seemed to Mill an invitation to set out on a false
trail.

Of crucial import here is the reaction to the argument that the adoption
of a mathematical approach to the deductive sciences 'would reduce all
reasonings to the application of a technical form, and enable their
conclusiveness to be rationally assented to after a merely mechanical process,
as is undoubtedly the case in algebra' (*CW*, VIII: 709). This case could only
be applied 'where the practical validity' of the reasoning derives from the
reasoning itself as in geometry and the 'science of number'. But where there
arises the problem of 'composition of causes' involving propositions valid
only in the absence of countervailing causes and thus having only
'hypothetical certainty' – the key problem in economics – what is called
for is an attitude of mind alert to the specifics of the case and the empirical
'meaning' of the axioms:

A conclusion . . . however correctly deduced, in point of form, from
admitted laws of nature, will have no other than an hypothetical
certainty. At every step we must assure ourselves that no other law of
nature has superseded, or intermingled its operation with, those which
are the premises of the reasoning; and how can this be done by merely
looking at the words? We must not only be constantly thinking of the
phenomena themselves, but we must be constantly studying them;
making ourselves acquainted with the peculiarities of every case to
which we attempt to apply our general principles.

(Mill, *CW*, VIII: 710)

Mill's fear that a mathematical programme would encourage a perspective deflecting attention from 'the meaning of our signs' is very nicely illustrated from the theory of consumption. I refer again to his approach towards the retail sector – consumers, in many cases, were not, he believed, maximisers. The science of economics based upon maximising behaviour had much to offer regarding the determination of outputs and prices up to the wholesale level, but not beyond; the assumption of marginal calculation by final consumers might be totally inappropriate from an empirical perspective.

From this viewpoint, the transformation of economics into a mathematical subject would entail an episode in scientific regression. And, in point of fact, the marginal treatment of consumption did throw overboard Mill's sophisticated empirical approach to demand – the recognition of 'disturbing causes' which generate failures of the 'law of demand' – in favour of Jevons' excessive simplification in the interest of mathematisation, such as the assumptions of independent goods and independent consumers. More generally, Mill's potentially fruitful approach to competitive price formation involving the relation between firm and industry, and expectation regarding entry, fell on unreceptive soil, Jevons and Walras resorting to totally artificial expedients in order to proceed. This loss of 'realism' is particularly conspicuous in the case of Walras, who, as Jaffé has strenuously argued, was concerned with the workings of an 'ideal' system, not a 'real' capitalist economy, and whose *tâtonnement* process was unrelated to price adjustments in actual markets (Jaffé 1980; but see the counter-argument by Walker 1984).

Mill's warnings were remarkably prescient considering the fact that he was unfamiliar with the writings of the early 1870s. And equally striking, some of the dangers of over-simplified models had been long before formulated in a letter of 1829 to d'Eichthal. There he had emphasised that French procedure, by neglecting 'disturbing causes', distorted the operation even of those causes allowed for:

> They deduce politics like mathematics from a set of axioms & definitions, forgetting that in mathematics there is no danger of partial views: a proposition is either true or it is not, & if it is true, we may safely apply it to every case which the proposition comprehends in its terms: but in politics & the social science this is so far from being the case, that error seldom arises from our assuming premises which are not true, but generally from our overlooking other truths which limit, & modify the effect of the former.
> (Mill, *CW*, XII: 35–6; cf. *A System of Logic*, *CW*, VIII: 894)

There is an interesting parallel here with Keynes' celebrated warnings of 1939 regarding econometrics, in his paper on 'Professor Tinbergen's method'.[11]

This is not the end of the matter. There are various pronouncements in *A System of Logic* which together amount in effect to a case against mathematical 'forecasting' in economics – an exercise that requires precise numerical data – and which also may have played a part in Mill's actual (or potential) response to Jevons. First, consider the positive overview in the case of the physical sciences:

> The immense part which those laws ['which are the peculiar subject of the sciences of number and extension'] take in giving a deductive character to the other departments of physical science, is well known; and is not surprising, when we consider that all causes operate according to mathematical laws. The effect is always dependent on, or is a function of, the quantity of the agent; and generally of its position also. We cannot, therefore, reason respecting causation, without introducing considerations of quantity and extension at every step; and if the nature of the phenomena admits of our obtaining numerical data of sufficient accuracy, the laws of quantity become the grand instrument for calculating forward to an effect, or backward to a cause.
>
> (Mill, *CW*, VII: 620)[12]

Here the reader is referred to volumes I and II of Auguste Comte's *Cours de Philosophie Positive* for further elaboration, and to volume III for the 'limits to the applicability of mathematical principles' – limits which cover economics:

> Such principles are manifestly inapplicable where the causes on which any class of phenomena depend are so imperfectly accessible to our observation, that we cannot ascertain, by a proper induction their numerical laws; or where the causes are so numerous, and intermixed in so complex a manner with one another, that even supposing their laws known, the computation of the aggregate effect transcends the powers of the calculus as it is, or is likely to be; or lastly, where the causes themselves are in a state of perpetual fluctuation; as in physiology, and still more, if possible, in the social science. The solutions of physical questions become progressively more difficult and imperfect in proportion as the questions divest themselves of their abstract and hypothetical character, and approach nearer to the degree of complication actually existing in nature; insomuch that beyond the limits of astronomical phenomena, and of those most nearly analogous to them, mathematical accuracy is generally obtained 'at the expense of the reality of the inquiry'.
>
> (Mill, *CW*, VII: 620–1; cf. 459)

Mill concludes that the application of mathematical principles would be 'chimerical' in chemistry and physiology and in 'the still more complex inquiries, the subjects of which are phenomena of society and government'.

There are thus two conceptually distinct but complementary cases pointing away from the fruitful applicability of mathematics to economics –

one based on the danger of attributing a bogus precision to symbols, thereby opening the door for excessively simple 'geometric' procedures; the other turning upon the paucity of numerical data and the complexity of causal relations which rule out precise computation of the combined effect of causes.

In her account of the reaction to Jevons by Cairnes and Mill, Dr Schabas has remarked upon Mill's own recognition that, in so far as scientific knowledge involves the pursuit of causal laws, it is 'ultimately quantitative and thus mathematical in principle', so that, she concludes, 'Mill would have to concede, given this claim, that political economy, as the study of the causes which regulate wealth, was in the very same sense as it was for Jevons, inextricably mathematical. Mill, however, did not reach these conclusions' (Schabas 1983a: 291). Yet as Schabas proceeds to show, Mill went a long way along the Jevonian path. I take issue only with her representations of Mill's position as 'inconsistent' (Schabas 1983a: 293). A word of explanation.

Concern with the excessive simplifications characterising French geometrical procedure, and doubts regarding mathematical forecasting, do not necessarily rule out the use of mathematics in aid of clear logical thought. Mill himself, after all, had engaged in elementary algebraic formulations (*CW*, III: 611). A formal statement of his recognition of a legitimate role for mathematics appears in the *System of Logic* itself, where reference is made to 'the value of mathematical instruction as a preparation for those more difficult investigations' (chemistry, physiology, social science and government, and aspects of astronomy) 'in the applicability not of its doctrines, but of its method', by providing training in the deductive procedure of employing 'the laws of simpler phenomena for explaining and predicting those of the more complex' (*CW*, VII: 621). In *An Examination of Sir William Hamilton's Philosophy* (Mill 1865), in the chapter containing Mill's reply to a hypercritic of the study of mathematics, the contrast appears very strikingly. Here (following Comte) Mill defends mathematical instruction as an 'indispensible first stage of all scientific education worthy of the name', on the grounds that it sets high standards of 'proof', encourages precise logical thought based upon given axioms, postulates and definitions, and teaches 'the importance of quantities' (*CW*, IX: 472f).[13] Thus even though

> in the achievements which still remain to be effected in the way of scientific generalization it is not probable that the direct employment of mathematics will be to any great extent available [Mill here includes the moral and social sciences] the nature of the phenomena [precluding] such an employment for a long time to come – perhaps for ever, [yet (applied) mathematics] affords the only sufficiently perfect type.
>
> (*CW*, IX: 480–1)

For

the process itself – the deductive investigation of Nature; the application of elementary laws, generalized from the more simple cases, to disentangle the phaenomena of complex cases – explaining as much of them as can be so explained, and putting in evidence the nature and limits of the irreducible residuum, so as to suggest fresh observations preparatory to recommencing the same process with additional data: *this* is common to all science, moral and metaphysical included; and the greater the difficulty, the more needful is it that the enquirer should come prepared with an exact understanding of the requisites of this mode of investigation, and a mental type of its perfect realization.

(Mill, *CW*, IX: 481; cf. also *CW*, XXI: 235–7)

But there was a danger. Once again the perspective of 1829 is reiterated:

And here we come upon the one really grave charge which rests on the mathematical spirit, in respect of the influence it exercises on pursuits other than mathematical. It leads men to place their ideal of Science in deriving all knowledge from a small number of axiomatic premises, accepted as self-evident, and taken for immediate intuitions of reason. . . . Nearly everything that is objectionable, along with much of what is admirable, in the character of French thought, whether on metaphysics, ethics, or politics, is directly traceable to the fact that French speculation descends from Descartes instead of from Bacon. All reflecting persons in England, and many in France, perceive that the chief infirmities of French thinking arise from its geometrical spirit; its determination to evolve its conclusions, even on the most practical subjects, by mere deduction from some single accepted generalization: the generalization, too, being frequently not even a theorem; but a practical rule, supposed to be obtained directly from the fountains of reason: a mode of thinking which erects one-sidedness into a principle, under the misapplied name of logic, and makes the popular political reasoning in France resemble that of a theologian arguing from a text, or a lawyer from a maxim of law.

(Mill, *CW*, IX: 485)

Thus unlike Cliffe Leslie – indeed unlike Cairnes (Checkland 1951: 166) – Mill warned only against the abusive use of mathematics, not mathematics *per se*. This is further confirmed by his defence of political economy against Comte's low opinion, in the course of which he insisted on the applicability to the social sciences of the methods designed for the natural sciences – the 'scientific artifice familiar to students of science, especially for the application of mathematics to the study of nature':

When an effect depends on several variable conditions, some of which change less, or more slowly, than others, we are often able to determine either by reasoning or experiment, what would be the law of variation of the effect if its changes depended only on one of the conditions, the remainder being supposed constant. The law so found will be sufficiently near the truth for all times and places in which the latter set of conditions do not vary greatly, and will be a basis to set out from when it becomes necessary to allow for the variations in those conditions also. Most of the conclusions of social science applicable to practical use are of this description.

(Mill, *CW*, X: 309)

Comte's system, Mill complained, 'makes no room for them. We have seen how he deals with the part of them which are the most scientific in character, the generalizations of political economy.'

By his various allowances, Mill is certainly not 'inconsistent'; his balanced perspective defining the role of mathematics in economics bears consideration in our own day. For it is one thing to doubt the usefulness of 'calculating forward' to a precise numerical forecast, or to condemn the application of maximisation principles without discrimination, however empirically inappropriate the exercise may be. It is quite another to employ mathematics as a check to sound reasoning. Mill's position was in effect taken up by Marshall, who certainly allowed for mathematics as an aid to 'clear thought' while at the same time he objected to contrived 'appearance[s] of lucidity' (Marshall 1920: 357n, 368; cf. also 781f).

Our discussion helps lighten a further grey area in the literature – the notion that the adoption of algebra requires for Mill that the science in question afford precise numerical data (compare J. N. Keynes 1955 [1891]: 249; Schabas 1983a: 288; 1983b: 27). This view was strongly opposed by Jevons in his Preface:

Many persons entertain a prejudice against mathematical language, arising out of a confusion between the ideas of a mathematical science and an exact science. They think that we must not pretend to calculate unless we have the precise data which will enable us to obtain a precise answer to our calculations.

(Jevons 1924: 5)

But Mill recognised the quantitative dimension to economic phenomena notwithstanding the absence of precise data – their basis in 'the psychological law...that a greater gain is preferred to a smaller' (*CW*, VIII: 901) – and more specifically, he was prepared to countenance the (limited) use of algebra in economics, notwithstanding the absence of precise data; indeed, he himself supplemented his verbal account of price formation in the trade context by an attempt to generalise in algebraic terms. The pronouncement that mathematical 'solutions of physical questions became progressively more difficult and imperfect in proportion as the questions divest themselves of their abstract and hypothetical character, and approach nearer to the degree of complication actually existing in nature' (see above, p. 202) creates no difficulty for us. He intended thereby the ambitious task of mathematical forecasting and the derivation of axioms à la Newton (cf. note 12); much easier is the more mundane task of formulating causal relations of the order 'more or less'.

Concluding remarks

Mill himself was suspicious of Jevons' approach. But to be fair we must allow for Jevons' own realisation of the limits of mathematics in the 'dynamical' branches of economics (Black 1972a: 7–8), and recall his own brilliant inductive contributions. The true danger of a specialist programme for mathematical economics divorced on principle from applied economics has proved to be a long-term liability from the perspective of professional trends – an 'objective' result (to use a Marxian term) of the kind of recommendation characterising the 'innovators' of the early 1870s.

Mill's awareness of the danger has been our topic. But we must at all costs avoid any notion of Mill as averse to deductive theory as such. Professor Winch has argued that Walter Bagehot carried further Mill's 'conciliatory stance' towards the historicists – which 'provided an opportunity to undermine claims to universality' – 'by restricting the science to "a single kind of society – a society of grown-up competitive commerce, such as in England"' (Winch 1972: 340). Mill certainly warned of unjustified applications of theory, and this even *within* the advanced British system – these instances illustrate his insistence on the non-universality of the standard axioms of economics. But it is also true that he demonstrated the empirical relevance of the science to a far broader range of institutions – both existing and prospective – than those allowed by Bagehot. There is no 'conciliation' here. We must not, for example, presume (as Winch presumes) that Mill's observations on cooperation or the stationary state imply the 'replacement' of competition. The same holds for the study of peasant proprietorship. Competition, and thus economic theory, is accorded a very extensive (though not universal) scope.[14]

Some like to call Mill self-contradictory. But this is gratuitous. His strength lay precisely in his demonstration that the range of applicability of economic science – in terms of the empirical accuracy of the maximisation axioms – was narrower than 'extremist' deductivists imagined, but broader than 'extremist' opponents of theory imagined. This balanced attitude cannot but encourage a habit of mind which, while ready to seek out and experiment with alternative institutional arrangements, yet retains, in their consideration, a healthy awareness of possible limits – flowing from behavioural as well as physical constraints – to what can be accomplished. Unfortunately this lesson has always, so it seems, to be learned the hard way.

Notes

1 A version of this paper was delivered at the Third History of Economic Thought Society of Australia Conference held at La Trobe University, Melbourne, 17–20 May 1985. I am grateful to the participants, particularly to Philip Williams and Michael White, for their criticisms.

2 Similar recommendations were made by Walras. He too championed a sharp demarcation between pure, applied and social economics, confining the first – represented as 'a science which resembles the physico-mathematical science in every respect' – to the 'theory of the determination of prices under a hypothetical regime of perfectly free competition' (Walras 1954: 71, 40); and representing 'any value in exchange' as 'partak[ing] of the character of a natural phenomenon, natural in its origins, natural in its manifestations and natural in its essence', a reference to the scarcity property (Walras 1954: 69).

   Menger in Austria was unenthusiastic about mathematics, but went even further than his confrères in insisting firmly on the independent status of pure theory. For he denied, on methodological grounds, any meaning to the verification of the principles of rational action (compare Winch 1972: 330, 343).

3 The notion that a classicism without the population-growth mechanism cannot be conceived (Winch 1972: 336) is questionable. The inverse wage-profit relation, turning on principles of allocation theory, applies even with population treated as a constant. And although population plays so large a part in Mill's work, 'the strictness of purely scientific arrangement [is] thereby somewhat departed from for the sake of practical utility' (CW, IV: 323) since a variety of motives apart from wealth maximisation are at play. There are other similar enlargements relating to knowledge creation and health.

   Note: Throughout this chapter *CW* stands for *Collected Works of John Stuart Mill* and the references to this are written in the form *CW*, IV (vol.): 225 (page).

4 Mill was quite at one with those members of the Historical School who did not object to deduction as such – on the contrary – but insisted that 'deductions should be made from categorical premises obtained from historical material' (Viner 1962: 109); Roscher's work on 'historicism' reads like Mill's (Roscher 1878: I, 110).

   In an account of the marginalist developments, Professor Winch refers to Mill's 'concessions' to the 'prevailing intellectual tide' of the second half of the century – the evolutionist and inter-disciplinary critics of economic theory (1972: 341); similarly, 'Mill went further than any of his immediate neoclassical successors were willing to go in meeting the historical and sociological critics of political economy' (340). These formulations, by alluding to Mill's 'concessions', fail to recognise that the later British historicists, such as Cliffe Leslie, were themselves nourished by Mill's *Principles* (Hollander 1985: 926); and that Mill's own positive objections on 'historical' lines to Jevons' type of approach to theory extend back to the early 1830s.

   My reaction is similar to the formulation by Hutchison, which assumes a belated response by Mill to the historical critics (Hutchison 1978: 55n).

5 The stage of *verification* in the deductive process, although it may indeed contribute towards establishment of the axioms or correction of the logical process of deduction, is not itself a device for the derivation of complex causal relations; that remains the function of '*ratiocination*'. Verification contributes only indirectly by indicating the need for improvement in the axiomatic

foundation (or in the logical process itself). It would, therefore, not be misleading to say that the present axiomatic framework, perhaps incorporating refinements shown to have been required by an *earlier* verification, constitutes the first stage for any *subsequent* ratiocination; and to describe the scientific work at hand as involving ratiocination on the basis of the axiomatic framework – again without reference to the possibility that the framework owes something to a preceding verification, or that further modifications might be proven necessary by a new verification as additional evidence accumulates.

We will not enter into the details of Mill's position on the proof of hypotheses, except to say that he took a stricter line than did William Whewell, objecting to the latter's 'Friedmanesque' position whereby the verification of predictions flowing from a hypothetically based theory constituted a proof of the 'truth' of that theory; in Mill's view this was insufficient, since the 'condition of accounting for all the known phenomena is often fulfilled equally well by two conflicting hypotheses' (*CW*, VII: 501).

6   It is scarcely surprising that Mill excluded 'small numbers' market structures from the domain of political economy. Edgeworth later observed regarding indeterminacy that

> among those who would suffer by the new regime ... would be ... the abstract economists, who would be deprived of their occupation, the investigation of the conditions which determine value. There would survive only the empirical school, flourishing in a chaos congenial to their mentality.
>
> (Edgeworth 1925: I, 138–9)

7   Allowance for varying quality is a further interesting illustration; compare Mill's explanation of the failure of prices to rise as expected in consequence of gold inflows, which runs in terms of a deterioration of the quality of commodities (letter of 15 September 1863, *CW*, XV: 882).

8   In some contexts Mill implies a ∪-shaped or possibly a ⊔-shaped cost curve. Compare his proposal for a test of scale economies (*CW*, II: 133, 140, 141; on this matter see Williams 1978: 54–5; 1982); and his treatment of monopolistic competition (*CW*, II: 243, 409–10; Williams 1978: 56–7).

9   It is most regrettable that the profession cannot be shaken from the opinion that Ricardo and Mill were unable to resolve the paradox of value; and that the utility contributions of the 1870s were required to break the deadlock. For the latest example of this error see Cooter and Rappoport (1984: 510).

If there is any doubt of the sophistication of classical analysis, consider the fact that as early as 1825 Mill, in a study of the corn tariff, effortlessly applied the 'compensation' principle of welfare economics published by Nicholas Kaldor in 1939 in formal utility terms (Stigler 1968: 97).

10   de Marchi (1972: 352–3) characterises the law of diminishing marginal utility as an empirical law; and argues that Mill's associationist psychology would not have provided an adequate underpinning for that law. He concludes that an adherence to associationist psychology made it unlikely that Mill would enunciate even this 'empirical law' for himself (de Marchi 1972: 354).

11   Keynes 1973, xiv: 308:

> Am I right in thinking that the method of multiple correlation analysis essentially depends on the economist having furnished, not merely a list of the significant causes, which is correct as far as it goes, but a *complete* list? For example, suppose three factors are taken into account, it is not enough that

these should be in fact *verae causae*; there must be no other significant factor. If there is a further factor, not taken account of, then the method is not able to discover the relative quantitative importance of the first three.

12 Cf. also 'Inaugural address to the University of St Andrews' (Mill 1867) regarding the potential of applied mathematics in the appropriate physical sciences:

> We are able, by reasoning from a few fundamental truths, to explain and predict the phenomena of material objects: and what is still more remarkable, the fundamental truths were themselves found out by reasoning, for they are not such as are obvious to the senses, but had to be inferred by a mathematical process from a mass of minute details, which alone came within the direct reach of human observation. When Newton, in this manner, discovered the laws of the solar system, he created, for all posterity, the true idea of science.
>
> (Mill, *CW*, XXI: 236)

13 Ricardo's famous complaint against Malthus' opinion that political economy 'is not a strict science like mathematics' (Ricardo 1951: VIII, 331) has been read as evidence of 'dogmatic, *a priori* deductivism' (Hutchison 1978: 56n). But this is doubtful. Ricardo's statement proceeds to specify that Malthus, in consequence of his viewpoint, 'thinks he may use words in a vague way, sometimes attaching one meaning to them, sometimes another and quite different'. Mill pleaded against dogmatic, *a priori*, deductivism throughout his career, yet saw a place for mathematics in deductive theory, basing himself partly on precision of thought; his position, as usual, was fully in line with Ricardo's.

14 See also the misleading reference by Professor George Stigler to the 'astonishing and absurd deficiencies which [Mill] assigned to private enterprise' (Stigler 1982: 14–15).

References

Black, R. D. C. (1972a) 'Jevons, marginalism and Manchester', *The Manchester School of Economic and Social Studies*, 40 (March): 2–8.
——(1972b) 'W. S. Jevons and the foundation of modern economics', *History of Political Economy*, 4 (fall): 364–78.
Blaug, M. (1980) *The Methodology of Economics*, Cambridge: Cambridge University Press.
Bowley, M. (1937) *Nassau Senior and Classical Economics*, London: George Allen & Unwin.
——(1972) 'The predecessors of Jevons: the revolution that wasn't', *The Manchester School*, 40 (March): 9–29.
Checkland, S. G. (1951) 'Economic opinion in England as Jevons found it', *The Manchester School*, 19: 143–69.
Comte, A. (1830–42) *Cours de Philosophie Positive*, 6 vols, Paris: Bachelier.
Cooter, R. and Rappoport, P. (1984) 'Were the ordinalists wrong about welfare economics?', *Journal of Economic Literature*, 22: 507–30.
Edgeworth, F. Y. (1910) 'John Stuart Mill', in R. H. I. Palgrave (ed.) *Dictionary of Political Economy*, II, London: Macmillan, 756–63.
——(1925) *Papers Relating to Political Economy*, London: Macmillan.
Hicks, J. (1983) *Collected Essays on Economic Theory III: Classics and Moderns*, Oxford: Blackwell.

Hollander, S. (1977) 'The reception of Ricardian economics', *Oxford Economic Papers*, 29 (July): 221–57.

——(1979) *The Economics of David Ricardo*, Toronto: University of Toronto Press.

——(1985) *The Economics of John Stuart Mill*, Toronto: University of Toronto Press.

Hutchison, T. W. (1978) *On Revolutions and Progress in Economic Knowledge*, Cambridge: Cambridge University Press.

Jaffé, W. (1980) 'Walras's economics as others see it', *Journal of Economic Literature*, 18 (June): 528–49.

Jevons, W. S. (1905) *The Principles of Economics*, revised edn, London: Macmillan.

——(1924) [1871] *The Theory of Political Economy*, 4th edn, London: Macmillan.

Keynes, J. M. (1973) *The General Theory and After*, Part II, in D. Moggridge (ed.) *Collected Writings*, XIV, London: Macmillan.

Keynes, J. N. (1955) [1891] *Scope and Method of Political Economy*, New York: Kelley.

Leontief, W. (1971) 'Theoretical assumptions and nonobserved facts', *American Economic Review*, 61: 1–7.

de Marchi, N. (1972) 'Mill and Cairnes and the emergence of marginalism in England', *History of Political Economy*, 4 (fall): 344–63.

Marshall, A. (1920) *Principles of Economics*, 8th edn, London: Macmillan.

Martineau, H. (1832–4) *Illustrations of Political Economy*, London: Fox.

Mill, John Stuart (1963–91) *Collected Works of John Stuart Mill*, Toronto: University of Toronto Press. Herein *CW*.

——(1834) 'Miss Martineau's summary of political economy', *Monthly Repository*, in *CW*, IV, *Essays on Economics and Society*, 223–8.

——(1836) 'On the definition of political economy and on the method of investigation proper to it', in *CW*, IV: 309–39.

——(1843) *A System of Logic: Ratiocinative and Inductive*, *CW*, VII, VIII.

——(1848) *Principles of Political Economy*, *CW*, II, III.

——(1861) *Utilitarianism*, in *CW*, X, *Essays on Ethics, Religion and Society*, 203–59.

——(1865) *An Examination of Sir William Hamilton's Philosophy*, *CW*, IX.

——(1867) 'Inaugural address delivered to the University of St Andrews', in *CW*, XXI, *Essays on Equality, Law, and Education*, 215–57.

——*The Earlier Letters, 1812–48*, *CW*, XII, XIII.

——*The Later Letters, 1848–73*, *CW*, XIV–XVII.

Phelps-Brown, E. H. (1972) 'The underdevelopment of economics', *Economic Journal*, 82: 1–10.

Ricardo, D. (1951–73) *The Works and Correspondence of David Ricardo*, 11 vols, VIII, Cambridge: Cambridge University Press.

Roscher, W. (1878) *Principles of Political Economy*, 2 vols, ed. J. J. Lalor, New York: Holt.

Schabas, M. L. (1983a) 'W. S. Jevons and the emergence of mathematical economics in Britain', Ph.D. thesis, Toronto: University of Toronto.

——(1983b) 'J. S. Mill to W. S. Jevons: an unpublished letter', *The Mill Newsletter*, 18: 24–8.

Schwartz, P. (1972) *The New Political Economy of John Stuart Mill*, London: Weidenfeld and Nicolson.

Stigler, G. J. (1968) 'Mill on economics and society', *University of Toronto Quarterly*, 38: 96–101.

——(1982) *The Economist as Preacher and Other Essays*, Chicago: University of Chicago Press.

Torrens, R. (1844) *The Budget*, London: Smith, Elder.

Viner, J. (1962) [1917] 'Some problems of logical method in political economy', in

E. J. Hamilton, A. Rees and H. G. Johnson (eds) *Landmarks in Political Economy*, Chicago: University of Chicago Press, 101–24.

Walker, D. A. (1984) 'Is Walras's theory of general equilibrium a normative scheme?', *History of Political Economy*, 16: 445–69.

Walras, L. (1954) *Elements of Pure Economics*, 4th definitive edn (1926), trans. W. Jaffé, London: George Allen & Unwin.

Williams, P. L. (1978) *The Emergence of the Theory of the Firm: From Adam Smith to Alfred Marshall*, London: Macmillan.

——(1982) 'Welfare and collusion: a comment', *American Economic Review*, 72: 272–5.

Winch, D. (1972) 'Marginalism and the boundaries of economic science', *History of Political Economy*, 4 (fall): 325–43.

Chapter 10

John Stuart Mill as economic theorist

John Stuart Mill was born on 20 May 1806 to James and Harriet (Burrow) Mill in Pentonville, London; and died on 7 May 1873 in Avignon. He was educated privately by his father on Benthamite pedagogic principles. At seventeen he joined his father at the East India Company as junior clerk, retiring as Chief Examiner in 1858. In 1824 appeared the first of many contributions to the *Westminster Review*. Mill directed the *London Review* (*London and Westminster Review* 1836) from 1834 till 1840. He sat as Member of Parliament for Westminster from 1865 to 1868.

The Ricardian paradigm

J. S. Mill insisted on the Ricardian character of his economic theory: 'I doubt if there will be a single opinion (on pure political economy) in the book [*Principles of Political Economy* (1848)] which may not be exhibited as a corollary from his [Ricardo's] doctrines' (letter of 22 February 1848; *CW*, XIII: 731). He did not ignore the criticisms of the preceding quarter-century by 'dissenting' critics of Ricardo, but (quite correctly) did not believe them to be destructive of the main Ricardian theoretical structure (1845b: 395–6, cf. Hollander 1977). From Mill's perspective, the core of the Ricardo doctrine amounted to the proposition that an increase in the general wage rate generates a fall in the general rate of profit on capital rather than an overall increase in manufacturing prices (and reduced rent in agriculture) as Adam Smith had maintained (letter of 4 October 1872; *CW*, XVII: 1909–10).

In Ricardo's formulation of this inverse wage-profit relation, a role is played by the 'absolute standard of value' – a commodity ('gold') produced by a constant quantity of labour, and acting therefore as a labour-measuring device. An increase in the labour embodied in the wage-basket will be reflected in an increase in the gold wage, and will necessarily entail an increase in the share of wages in any given value of output (output produced by a given labour input) available for distribution between labourers and capitalists. (The return to landlords is excluded by treating rent as a differential surplus and attending to the marginal product in agriculture; land is presumed not to contribute to manufacturing.) Ricardo's attention was upon per capita wages: an increase in per capita 'gold' wages implies an increase in the (proportionate) share of wages in per capita output which is of constant 'value' since it is the result of a specific input of labour, and a corresponding decrease in the (proportionate) share of profits. The rate of profit on capital is taken to be a direct function of the latter. The Ricardian scheme thus relates the rate of return on capital to the labour embodied in per capita wages – i.e. to the proportion of the work-day devoted to the production of wages, a proposition which has a strong Marxian flavour (Hollander 1979: ch. 5).

Ricardo's analysis applies whether the wage increase reflects an altered wage basket due in turn to altered demand-supply conditions in the labour-market (such as, on the side of labour demand, a change in the rate of saving, or new labour-displacing technology, or an altered pattern of consumer tastes involving products produced by differential factor ratios) with *given* productivity or an unchanged (or even a falling) wage-basket with *decreasing* productivity. It will be noted that though profits appear to be a 'residual' income ('profits depend on wages'), Ricardo allowed that the profit rate acts upon the rate of savings via 'the motive to accumulate'. Accordingly, labour demand and the commodity wage rate are affected by alterations in the rate of profit. Profits are, therefore, a residual only in the formal sense that the sole contractual payment is that to labour, but not in the substantive sense of a 'surplus value'.

The famous application of Ricardian theory to the problem of corn-import restriction, a central policy issue, is but one of various applications of the fundamental theorem. In this particular application, which pertains to a growing (and closed) economy, the commodity wage falls as the rate of capital accumulation (and consequently demand for labour) decelerates because of land scarcity (diminishing agricultural returns), and checks the rate of population growth. But the 'money' wage rises – reflecting increased labour embodied in the smaller basket – thus reducing the general return on capital. The process continues until the commodity-wage and profit rate attain their respective minima, when both population and capital cease to grow – the stationary state (Hicks and Hollander 1977).

As already intimated, the theory of value served as foundation of the analysis of distribution. More precisely: Ricardo sought to define the minimum conditions required of a medium of exchange, which would assure constancy in the value of output to be shared between the income recipients in the face of a change in distribution (cf. Sraffa 1951). Only in the event of uniform capital-labour ratios in all sectors will a simple labour theory of exchange value apply, such that exchange rates are invariable to wage changes. Ricardo appreciated that in the presence of non-uniform factor proportions, a wage-increase impinges differentially on costs, and thus long-run prices, depending upon the labour intensities of various sectors. He frequently proceeded (as in the above account we have proceeded) by implicitly presuming uniformity. On various other occasions he assumed a medium with mean factor proportions, in which case a wage increase would cause some prices to rise and others to fall in terms of that medium, though to the extent that these variations cancel out the basic theorem remains more or less intact. It must at the same time be emphasised that the general conclusion, whereby the rate of return is governed by the proportion of the work-day devoted to the production of wages, was envisaged as holding good quite generally, even where wages and profits are expressed in terms of ordinary money, both metallic and paper. Ricardo's model was designed to throw light on the underlying processes, not always apparent in a modern capitalist-exchange economy, whereby the rate of return is governed by the proportion of the work-day devoted to the production of wage goods.

Ricardo's analysis of the determination of relative prices implies a system of economic organisation directed by price forces, for he assumes the possibility of output expansion and contraction in response to market signals within a competitive framework, adopting Adam Smith's analysis of the relation between (short-run) market prices and (long-run) cost prices, the latter characterised by equality of wage rates and of profit rates across all sectors, such that when market prices everywhere equal cost prices there is no motive for reallocation. In the case of uniform factor ratios, a wage increase generates no factor reallocation and thus no long-run price variation, precisely because 'the cause that operates on one [industry] operates on all; how then can it be said that the relative values of commodities will be affected?' (Ricardo 1951: II, 179). Where factor inputs differ, labour-intensive industries will be impinged upon more than others, the relative profit rates in those sectors will fall (at the original prices) more sharply, and factors will transfer to sectors less severely affected; in consequence of these factor movements, prices rise (in terms of the measure produced with mean factor proportions) in the contracting labour-intensive sectors and fall in the expanding capital-intensive sectors, an outcome hinging upon the standard (Smithian) assumption of negatively sloping demand curves.

To summarise: While Ricardo's major preoccupation was the macro-economic issue of the relation between the *general* wage rate and the *general* profit rate, he was obliged to deal with the structure of the economy, and this problem he approached from a 'general-equilibrium' perspective. This latter perspective explains his explicit subscription to J. B. Say's account (1819) – which has Smithian pedigree – of mutual interdependence between product and factor markets, incorporating both opportunity cost and the imputing of factor values from product values (cf. Ricardo 1951: I, 282). It remains to add that Say's 'Law of Markets' was used to close the Ricardian 'general-equilibrium' system (Hollander 1979: ch. 6).

Mill on value and distribution

We have defined what came to be known after 1817 as the 'New Political Economy' to describe Ricardo's particular contribution. In an essay 'On profits and interest', Mill presents favourably the Ricardian position, with the 'slight modification' that the rate of profit is related not to the value of per capita wages – the direct and indirect labour embodied in the wage bill – but to the 'cost of wages', which includes the profit of the wage-goods producer (Mill 1844c: 293ff). But even this modification is withdrawn in Book II of the *Principles*, where the profit rate is related inversely to the fraction of a man's labour time devoted to the production of his wages. The 'cost of labour' is thus finally identified with labour embodied in per capita wages and with labour's share in per capita output (Mill 1848: 411ff).

This analysis of profits was provisional:

> It will come out in greater fullness and force when, having taken into consideration the theory of Value and Price, we shall be enabled to exhibit the law of profits in the concrete – in the complex entanglement of circumstances in which it actually works.
>
> (Mill 1848: 415)

Throughout his career, Mill insisted upon the relativity of exchange value and, like Samuel Bailey (1825), rejected the notion of a general alteration in exchange value as logically incomprehensible. But he accepted the Ricardian measure of cost of production:

> [Economists] have imagined a commodity invariably produced by the same quantity of labour; to which supposition it is necessary to add, that the fixed capital employed in the production must bear always the same proportion to the wages of the immediate labour, and must be always of the same durability: in short, the same capital must be advanced for the same length of time, so that the element of value which consists of profits, as well as that which consists of wages, may be unchangeable.
>
> (Mill 1848: 'Of a measure of value', Book III, xv: 579)

(Missing here is the condition that the metal be produced by average factor proportions, but Mill may have been presuming uniform factor ratios.) Now such a measure of cost, 'though perfectly conceivable', would not probably be found in practice because of the high likelihood of changes in the production cost of any commodity chosen. Nevertheless, gold and silver 'are the least variable' and, if used, the results obtained must simply be 'corrected by the best allowance we can make for the intermediate changes in the cost of the production itself'.

The full analysis of the effects of wage-rate changes is undertaken in the important chapter 'Distribution, as affected by exchange' (ch. xxvi). Much is made by commentators of Mill's treatment of production, distribution, and exchange in three consecutive books, as indicative of a failure to envisage any relation between value theory and distribution. This is a misunderstanding. The initial discussion of distribution in Book II was provisional only; in the chapter at hand the order is reversed, and the problem of distribution is analysed in the light of the theory of exchange value.

When the distribution of national income occurs via the mechanism of exchange and money, the 'law of wages' remains unchanged insofar as the determination of commodity wages is concerned, for this depends upon 'the ratio of population and capital' (695). But (as Mill has already explained) from the perspective of the employer it is not merely commodity wages that are relevant, but the 'cost of labour'; the added point is that this cost will be reflected by the money wages paid when money constitutes 'an invariable standard':

> Wages in the second sense [cost of labour], we may be permitted to call, for the present, money wages; assuming, as it is allowable to do, that money remains for the time an invariable standard, no alteration taking place in the conditions under which the circulating medium itself is produced or obtained. If money itself undergoes no variation in cost, the money price of labour is an exact measure of the Cost of Labour, and may be made use of as a convenient symbol to express it.
>
> (696)

Assuming money to be such an invariable measure, the rate of money wages will depend upon the commodity wage and the production costs (and accordingly the money prices) of wage goods, particularly agricultural produce, which vary with 'the productiveness of the least fertile land, or least productive agricultural capital' (697). Since the cost of labour is equated with the proportionate share of the labourer in per capita output, Mill had fully subscribed to the fundamental Ricardian theorem on distribution involving a 'proportions-measuring' money, in terms of which a rise of wages implies an increased share of the labourer in the 'value' of his output and a reduced profit share and rate of return:

> If the labourers really get more, that is, get the produce of more labour, a smaller percentage must remain for profit. From this Law of Distribution ... there is no escape. The mechanism of Exchange and Price may hide it from us, but is quite powerless to alter it.
>
> (479–80)

The 'Marxian' flavour of this formulation may be reinforced by Mill's proposition that 'the cause of profit' can be traced to surplus labour time – the fact that labourers 'in addition to reproducing their own necessaries and instruments, have a portion of their time remaining, to work for the capitalist' (411; first introduced in the fourth edition of 1857). For Mill, however, as for Ricardo, the rate of accumulation (and therefore the demand for labour and the commodity wage) responds to variations in the profit (interest) rate, since savers must be compensated for the psychic cost of abstaining from present consumption ('abstinence'). The breakdown between 'necessary' and 'surplus' labour time is, therefore, a variable dependent upon the supply conditions of capital as well as of labour (population).

As in Ricardo's formulation, the proposition that an increase in the labour embodied in wages is necessarily accompanied by an inverse movement in the rate of return, holds good irrespective of the satisfaction by the medium of exchange of the necessary properties required to guarantee its theoretical suitability as invariable standard. Thus even were prices to rise following an increase of wages, producers would not benefit therefrom, since all their expenses rise (479). More significantly, the gold standard mechanism assured that wage increases are non-inflationary: 'There cannot be a general rise of prices unless there is more money expended. But the rise of wages does not cause more money to be expended' (1869: 661).

Mill and the theory of allocation

As in Ricardo's case, allocation theory provided the primary rationale for the operation of the inverse wage-profit relation. To this matter we turn next.

The theory of costs was treated by Mill, in Ricardian fashion, from a micro-economic perspective involving relative value: 'Value is a relative term, not a name for an inherent and substantive quality of the thing itself' (1848: 479). Accordingly, he defended Ricardo's emphasis upon labour-quantity on the grounds that

> In considering . . . the causes of variations in value, quantity of labour is the thing of chief importance, for when that varies, it is generally in one or a few commodities at a time, but the variations of wages (except passing fluctuations) are usually general, and have no considerable effect on value.
>
> (481)

Nonetheless, wage differentials as well as differential labour input are reflected in the price structure, and changes in wage differentials will generate changes in the price structure (480, also 692). Moreover, in consequence of differential factor proportions, even general wage changes might influence the structure of prices (484).

Notwithstanding Malthus' early interpretation to the contrary (1824), Mill insisted that, in the opinion of 'the Ricardo school', long-run cost prices are arrived at by way of supply variation (1825a: 33–4). In the *Principles*, he cautioned that while 'the value at any particular time is the result of supply and demand, unless that value is sufficient to repay the Cost of Production, and to afford, besides, the ordinary expectation of profit, the commodity will not continue to be produced'. Necessary price, in brief, includes a return on capital 'as great . . . as can be hoped for in any other occupation at that time and place'; and in the event of a return in excess of the going rate, 'capital rushes to share in this extra gain, and by increasing the supply of the article, reduces its value'; in the reverse case output is restricted (1848: 471–2). By his reference to 'a law of value anterior to cost of production, and more fundamental, the law of demand and supply' (583), Mill did not, any more than Ricardo, deny that cost of production works its influence by way of supply variation; but maintained that demand-supply analysis applied to all cases, even where cost analysis is irrelevant.

The central role of supply variation in the establishment of cost price is scarcely surprising, considering that the pertinent perspective in cost-price analysis is one involving 'the motives by which the exchange of commodities against one another is immediately determined' (letter of 15 May 1872; CW, XVII: 1895).

Following Ricardo, Mill employed this perspective in the rationalisation of the inverse wage-profit relation. In contrast to a wage increase affecting one sector, where price will rise to assure equality of profit rates across the board (or a general wage increase in the case of non-uniform factor proportions), there exists no allocative mechanism whereby general prices would be forced upwards in the event of an economy-wide wage increase, should all firms be affected equally by the change: 'There is no mode in which capitalists can compensate themselves for a high cost of labour, through any action on values or prices. It cannot be prevented from taking its effect in low profits' (1848: 479).

The Ricardo–Mill allocation mechanism implies negatively sloped market demand curves. Mill took this for granted: 'It is the next thing to impossible that more of the commodity should not be asked for at every reduction of price' (1869: 637). Mill's formulations constituted an improvement in rigour over Ricardo's – particularly the formal conception of an equation of demand and supply and the distinction between displacements of the demand schedule and movements along the same schedule (1848: 466). But their merit reflects less innovatory content than location at a conspicuous juncture amongst the basic theoretical principles. There are brilliant applications of demand-supply analysis to the joint-production case (582f), and to international trade (1844a; 1848: 587f) – specification of the terms of trade emerging between the limits imposed by the autarkic cost ratios established by Ricardo and the division of the gains from trade, constrained only by a failure to fulfil a promise to show how the range of indeterminateness can be removed in cases of multiple or neutral equilibrium.

The analysis of rent provides a further instance of Mill's elaborations regarding allocation theory. In the aggregate, rent differs from the other factor returns solely in consequence of given land supply (1848: 58). Allowing for qualitative differentials between plots complicated the issue only slightly (429); Mill, following Ricardo, realised that differential rent entails a special case of scarcity value, and that rent might be generated even in the absence of differentials in the event of an absolute constraint on farm output (428). But when he focused upon individual sectors, he spelled out (as Smith and Say had done, but Ricardo had failed to do) the consequence of multi-use land for cost pricing (498, cf. 494), although this perspective plays no part in the analysis of wage and profit rates and their secular movement, where rent is treated entirely as a differential surplus.

Consistent with Mill's 'Ricardian' approach to cost price (exception made for the multi-use land case) is the Smith–Say conception of organisation, which emphasises the ultimate source of factor remuneration in sales proceeds and the motive for factor employment in the revenue product; 'in the present system of industrial life, in which employments are minutely subdivided . . . all concerned in production depend for their remuneration on the price of a particular commodity' (1848: 455), transportation workers 'derive their remuneration from the ultimate product' (33); in consequence of the 'increased utility' afforded by wholesalers and retailers the product is sold 'at an increased price proportioned to the labour expended in conferring it' (48).

The principle that the process of production ends upon sale to the final consumer applies also to wage goods (35, 38). While 'the finished products of many branches of industry are the materials of others' (36), workers' consumables are treated on a par with all other final goods rather than as intermediate goods. In Mill's account (as in Ricardo's) workers are paid in money, not in kind, and enter the market to purchase commodities at retail; there is no distinction to this regard between labourers, capitalists or landlords. The 'wages fund' expressed in money has a real counterpart in the flow of goods currently made available at retail outlets; the fraction of capital whose function it is to fulfil the tasks of 'maintaining' labour need not actually take the form of stocks of wage goods, because the flexibility of the system permits, by exchange or production, the easy and rapid generation of commodities in demand by labour (57, 67–8, 82–3).

The principle of imputation applies to the demand for particular kinds of labour or labour in particular industries. By contrast, Mill's proposition that 'demand for commodities is not demand for labour' (78) relates to aggregate wages and/or employment: 'it is only by what [a person] abstains from consuming, and expends in direct payments to labourers in exchange for labour, that he benefits the labouring classes, or adds anything to the amount of their employment' (80). Both Ricardo and J. B. Say were said to have fully appreciated this position. It is to be noted that when capitalist employers make an investment decision, they abstain from using their own claim to purchase output currently forthcoming at retail outlets, and place this purchasing power at the disposal of labourers (83–4).

Mill on growth, the cycle and the law of markets

In his approach to growth, Mill, following Malthus, supplemented the Ricardian analysis involving a simultaneous decline in both the real wage and the profit rate until their respective minima in circumstances of land scarcity. Mill demonstrated that, in a situation of growing capital and population, the commodity wage need not decline to 'subsistence' if labourers respond to the prospective decline in the rate of accumulation by delaying marriage and reducing procreation. A fall in the wage rate is then no longer necessary to reduce population growth in line with the rate of accumulation. The fall in profits will, however, be more rapid and the stationary state achieved sooner than in the Ricardian version. This model (cf. Hollander 1984; 1985a: 114–51) provides the theoretical backdrop to Mill's reconsideration of the possible merits to zero growth.

The idea of an endogenous trade cycle turning on expectational mood is better developed by Mill than any contemporary. The regularity of cyclical fluctuations was much emphasised in a monetary paper of 1844 (1844d). In the *Principles*, Mill attended to the 'quiescent' period and its place in the cycle. Specifically, a quiescent period entails expansion rather than stationariness, and cyclical fluctuations are partly induced by speculative reactions to the falling return on capital arising from 'the gradual process of accumulation' (1848: 641). The relationship is a mutual one, for while the declining profit-rate trend engenders speculation and the cycle, various losses associated with the cycle play back on the profit rate itself.

In the absence of capital loss, the rate of accumulation would be so great (on Mill's empirical estimate) as to force down the return on capital, since technical progress could not in practice be relied upon to counteract such heavy pressure on scarce land. The first conclusion Mill draws from the fact of a highly active contemporary 'spirit of accumulation' is that 'a sudden abstraction of capital, unless of inordinate amount', need not be feared, for 'after a few months or years, there would exist in the country just as much capital as if none had been taken away' (747). The conclusion altered the perspective towards government expenditure. The standard warnings by orthodox writers against measures which might reduce the capital stock, or its rate of accumulation, were no longer pertinent. Indeed, Mill writes in this context as if capital is no longer to be treated as a scarce factor.

The question arises whether Mill's favourable attitude towards expenditure of public money 'for really valuable, even though industrially unproductive purposes', has genuine Keynesian overtones. The answer must be in the negative. The potential problem is excessive accumulation forcing down the return on capital in the Ricardian fashion – excessive in the sense that the pressure on land exceeds the counteracting force of new technology. Such a decline in the return is in practice temporary, however, in consequence of capital losses – poorly considered 'speculative' additions to the real capital stock which prove untenable in quiescent periods (the speculations induced to some degree by the temporary fall in the profit rate) and the running down of savings for consumption purposes in depression, the inevitable sequel to speculative periods. To this extent there is no question of leakages from the income stream by the non-investment of savings; savings are lost in the sense only of being unproductively used up. Mill's allowance for higher government spending thus amounts to a recommendation to tap the flow of savings, thereby preventing their excessive accumulation, pressure on scarce land and fall in the return on capital, and also the various cyclical consequences of that fall, which include wastage of capital. In effect, Mill was calling for opera houses in place of a superfluous network of railways and 'unproductive' private consumption. This is not a 'Keynesian' perspective.

The orthodox law of markets is in one sense firmly reiterated: there can be no 'overproduction'. But excess capacity and excess supplies of labour and commodities, with a counterpart in an excess demand for money to hold, are fully allowed as a feature of depression (Mill 1844b), a remarkable case of model improvement. At the same time Mill explained why stagnation would be temporary, by reference to a reversal of expectations which encourages a delay of sales wherever possible and a renewal of purchases in response to prospective price increases. This is the basis for Mill's presumption against a Keynes-like 'unemployment equilibrium', and explains partly why government expenditure was not envisaged as a counter-cyclical measure. Only indirectly would government spending be effective, for by imposing a floor to the return on capital, it checks the 'speculative fever' from which depression ultimately proceeds.

It has been well said that Mill's qualifications to the law of markets lead one 'to wonder why so much of the subsequent literature ... had to be written at all' (Baumol and Becker 1952). The recognition of excess demand for money extends to an allowance for active monetary policy to mitigate cyclical pressure. It is regrettable that later economists felt able to brush aside the classical contribution. Mill's warning against over-full employment and his denial of a permanent trade-off between inflation and unemployment (1833) also bear repeating in our day.

Concluding note

John Stuart Mill's methodological perspective (1836) took a stand against professional arrogance and narrow-mindedness. He justified a specialist economics on empirical grounds, and disdained all notion of the universal validity of axioms. He invited consideration of the functioning of an economic system under a variety of alternative institutional arrangements and alternative circumstances, including the 'stationary state', although his concern for equitable distribution did not lead him to dispose of the old growth economics. He maintained a modest estimate of the predictive potential of economic science. He recommended model improvement by way of verification against factual evidence, and focused on the mechanics of pricing in the real world of business rather than some ideal world. He feared the kind of applied mathematical research programme already under way during his last years.

As he, and later Marshall, always insisted, Mill on pure theory (as well as on method) was Ricardian. The analytics of Marshall's *Principles* are in a 'direct line of descent through Mill from Ricardo' (Shove 1942). This generalisation applies preeminently to the theory of value and distribution, for classical cost-price analysis constitutes an analysis of the allocation of scarce resources, with allowance for final demand and the interdependence of factor and commodity markets. Mill's contribution to international trade theory is but an outstanding instance of a broad comprehension of demand theory. The demand-oriented economists of the 1870s exaggerated the innovatory character of their contributions. Similarly, Mill's supply and demand determination of wages and profit is in a line common to Ricardo (and before him Smith) and Marshall.

Mill's perspective on growth – his allowance for progress to the stationary state without depression of the real wage – reflects the perspective of the Philosophical Radicals and, before them, Malthus himself, on desirable social policy. This issue illustrates well the character of classical theory as an exercise in persuasion designed to act on key behavioural patterns, rather than as a 'predictive' device; theory suggested not what will happen, but what, depending on circumstances, can happen (Shackle 1972: 72–3).

References

Selected works

Mill, J. S. (1963–85) *Collected Works of John Stuart Mill*, ed. J. M. Robson, Toronto: University of Toronto Press. Herein *CW*.
——(1824) 'War expenditure', *Westminster Review*, 2 (July): 27–48. In *CW*, IV, 1967: 1–22.
——(1825a) 'The *Quarterly Review* on political economy', *Westminster Review*, 3 (January): 213–32. In *CW*, IV, 1967: 23–43.
——(1825b) 'The Corn Laws', *Westminster Review*, 3 (April): 394–420. In *CW*, IV, 1967: 45–70.
——(1826) 'Paper currency and commercial distress', Parliamentary Review Session of 1826, 630–62. In *CW*, IV, 1967: 71–123.
——(1833) 'The currency juggle', *Tait's Edinburgh Magazine*, 2 (January): 461–7. In *CW*, IV, 1967: 181–92.
——(1834) 'Miss Martineau's summary of political economy', *Monthly Repository*, 8 (May): 318–22. In *CW*, IV, 1967: 223–8.
——(1836) 'On the definition of political economy; and on the method of philosophical investigation in that science', *London and Westminster Review*, 4/26 (October): 1–29 (appears as Essay V in *Essays on Some Unsettled Questions of Political*

Economy, 1844, with title '. . . and on the method of investigation proper to it'). In *CW*, IV, 1967: 309–39.

——(1844a) 'Of the laws of interchange between nations', in J. S. Mill, *Essays on Some Unsettled Questions of Political Economy*, London: Parker. In *CW*, IV, 1967: 232–61.

——(1844b) 'Of the influence of consumption on production', in *CW*, IV, 1967: 262–79.

——(1844c) 'On profits and interest', in *CW*, IV, 1967: 290–308.

——(1844d) 'The currency question', *Westminster Review*, 41 (June): 579–98. In *CW*, IV, 1967: 341–61.

——(1845a) 'The claims of labour', *Edinburgh Review*, 81 (April): 498–525. In *CW*, IV, 1967: 363–89.

——(1845b) 'De Quincey's logic of political economy', *Westminster Review*, 43 (June): 319–31. In *CW*, IV, 1967: 391–404.

——(1848) *Principles of Political Economy with Some of Their Applications to Social Philosophy*, in *CW*, II–III, 1965. Last (7th) edn by Mill, 1871.

——(1869) 'Thornton on labour and its claims', *Fortnightly Review*, new series, 5, May: 505–18; June: 680–700. In *CW*, V, 1967: 631–68.

——(1879) (posthumous) chapters on socialism, *Fortnightly Review*, new series, 25, February: 217–37; March: 373–82; April: 513–30. In *CW*, V, 1967: 705–53.

References

Bailey, S. (1825) *A Critical Dissertation on the Nature, Measure and Causes of Value*, London: R. Hunter.

Baumol, W. J. and Becker, G. S. (1952) 'The classical monetary theory: the outcome of the discussion', *Economica*, 19/76 (November): 355–76.

Hicks, J. R and Hollander, S. (1977) 'Mr Ricardo and the moderns', *Quarterly Journal of Economics*, 91/3 (August): 351–69.

Hollander, S. (1977) 'The reception of Ricardian economics', *Oxford Economic Papers*, 29/2 (July): 221–57.

——(1979) *The Economics of David Ricardo*, Toronto: University of Toronto Press.

——(1984) 'The wage path in classical growth models: Ricardo, Malthus and Mill', *Oxford Economic Papers*, 36/2: 200–12.

——(1985a) *The Economics of John Stuart Mill*, Oxford: Blackwell.

——(1985b) 'On the substantive identity of the Ricardian and neo-classical conceptions of economic organization', in G. Caravale (ed.) *The Legacy of Ricardo*, Oxford: Blackwell.

Malthus, T. R. (1824) 'Political economy', *Quarterly Review*, 30 (January): 297–334.

Ricardo, D. (1951–73) *The Works and Correspondence of David Ricardo*, 11 vols, ed. P. Sraffa, Cambridge: Cambridge University Press.

Say, J. B. (1819) *Traité d'Economie Politique*, 4th edn, Paris: Déterville.

Shackle, G. L. S. (1972) *Epistemics and Economics: A Critique of Economic Doctrines*, Cambridge: Cambridge University Press.

Shove, G. (1942) 'The place of Marshall's *Principles* in the development of economic theory', *Economic Journal*, 52 (December): 294–329.

Sraffa, P. (1951) 'Introduction', in *The Works and Correspondence of David Ricardo*, ed. P. Sraffa, Cambridge: Cambridge University Press.

Chapter 11

Commentary on 'John Stuart Mill interpretation since Schumpeter'

It is most gratifying that Professor de Marchi should see eye to eye with me on so many issues in his account of interpretations of Mill's economics since Schumpeter. However, de Marchi does raise some interesting questions regarding my position that the economics of Ricardo and Mill 'comprises in its essentials an exchange system fully consistent with the marginalist elaborations', and to these I shall devote my comments.

There are first questions of technical detail. 'If market interdependence and the allocative mechanism were really so "central" to the Ricardians, why did they stress the basic distribution theorem in terms of the standard (average) commodity?' asks de Marchi. On several occasions in my studies I have alluded to what I call the 'ambiguous methodological status' of the distribution theorem formulated in terms of the measure (1985: 359; 1979: 304). Rather than spell out the full market mechanism by which a change in the wage generates profit-rate differentials, setting in motion supply adjustments and consequent price variations until a uniformly lower return on capital is achieved in all sectors, Ricardo and Mill frequently chose to identify a fall in the profit rate with the rise in the wage and apply the lower (uniform) rate to calculate the new price structure (e.g. Ricardo 1951, I: 35, 39; Mill 1965: 485).

As for the market-adjustment mechanism itself, we have, for example, Ricardo's statement that all depends on whether 'this inducement [the wage change] act[s] with the same force on all . . . occupations' (1951, I: 28); for 'a rise in the wages of labour cannot fail to affect unequally commodities produced under . . . different circumstances' (32). There is also Mill's elaboration which explains more fully that if the wage has a uniform impact there are no supply adjustments, so that prices remain constant and profits are uniformly squeezed:

> Expenses which affect all commodities equally, have no influence on prices. If the maker of broadcloth or cutlery, and nobody else, had to pay

higher wages, the price of his commodity would rise, just as it would if he had to employ more labour; because otherwise he would gain less profit than other producers, and nobody would engage in the employment. But if everybody has to pay higher wages, or everybody to employ more labour, the loss must be submitted to; as it affects everybody alike, no one can hope to get rid of it by a change of employment, each therefore resigns himself to a diminution of profits, and prices remain as they were.... If wages fall, (meaning here by wages the cost of labour), why, on that account, should the producer lower his price? He will be forced, it may be said, by the competition of other capitalists who will crowd into his employment. But other capitalists are also paying lower wages, and by entering into competition with him they would gain nothing but what they are gaining already.

(Mill 1965: 692)

I beg the reader to ask himself how Mill would have replied had he been asked: 'What now if we assume factor proportions to *differ* so that the impact of the wage increase is unequal?' I cannot imagine any other answer than the one I have given. Let the reader suggest an alternative. As for the 'ambiguous' practice itself, it is not surprising that, once confident of the validity of the inverse wage-profit relation, Ricardo and Mill would use it in analysis, without lengthy discussions of market process. It is a short-cut device and no more.

My position turns, of course, on the appreciation by Ricardo and Mill of supply-demand interactions, and the profit-rate equalisation principle – quite explicit in the Mill extract above. Now de Marchi's hesitations surprise me, since he clearly accepts all of this. Indeed, his agreement extends to the mechanism of adjustment itself in the context of the inverse wage-profit relation. To quote him:

At the risk of repeating myself, I shall comment briefly on the several components of Hollander's case. First, he is able to show convincingly that Mill and Ricardo share the same analysis in all essentials.... He is also successful in demonstrating that Mill (and Ricardo) were thoroughly cognizant of the information-conveying and signalling role of prices, and of the notion of alternative costs. Similarly, they have a clear conception of market interactions, the strictly formal or analytical demonstrations of an inverse relation between wage and profit rates, involving either a corn model or an invariable standard, being just that and nothing more. A useful way to get a sense of all this is to ask, following Ricardo, whether, following upon an increase in the cost of producing wage goods, due to diminishing returns, the farming class can find any way to pass on the increase in their costs. A moment's reflection shows that the constraints on doing so take the form of the common rate of profit that must be earned in both wage goods and nonwage goods sectors, and the need to remain competitive in an open economy. That wages and profits move inversely thus emerges from a consideration of market forces and allocative requirements, with no mention of absolute value or an invariable standard, and no need to confine the analysis to a one-commodity ('corn') world.

(de Marchi 1987: 154–5)

What then, precisely, does bother de Marchi if he travels so far with me? I shall revert to this shortly, after giving my response to his further preliminary questions. First: 'Why did Mill still flirt in the *Principles* with the idea that capital can all be reduced to labour?'. This procedure, which I attributed to Mill in my book, led me to take a cautious position in treating the impact of change in the pattern of final demand on the wage (1985: 362). (McCulloch provides an instance of an economist who specifically denied any long-run impact on the grounds that capital reduces entirely to labour.) Moreover, the differential impact of a wage change in Ricardo's analysis hinges on the allowance for profits in the cost-price of machinery, which Mill seemed to deny (359). After further research, however, I now believe that I was in error in attributing to Mill the non-Ricardian view that capital can be reduced entirely to labour. Space limitations require that this demonstration be made in some other forum [see Chapter 13]. But if I am right, my overall conclusions regarding the powerful allocative dimension to the Ricardo–Mill economics is further reinforced.

I find no difficulty at all with the fourth proposition on capital – 'demand for commodities is not demand for labour'. As I explain on several occasions, this proposition asserts that aggregate labour demand rises in consequence of saving (capital accumulation) rather than consumption (1985: 371; 1979: 373). It is really not surprising that in dealing with this 'macro' issue, the question of non-uniform factor ratios – which would have brought up the possibility of changes in overall labour demand by way of changes in the pattern of activity – should be set aside; the parallel issue of technical change which alters the fixed/wage-fund capital breakdown of the total is, after all, also set aside.

———•❖•———

As previously noted, de Marchi accepts my view that Mill and Ricardo appreciated demand-supply and related allocative analyses. We now come to his basic objection:

Hollander wishes the reader to agree also that there is nothing fundamentally alien to Mill and Ricardo's way of thinking in neo-classical economics. The weak point in this, however, as argued above, lies in the fact that it is insufficient to explain the modelling actually undertaken by the Ricardian on the one hand and by the neo-classicals on the other.

(de Marchi 1987: 155)

The reference here seems to be a challenge which de Marchi earlier addresses to me:

> A test of the usefulness of Hollander's continuity hypothesis is whether, using the supply-and-demand framework and applying it to Ricardo's problem – distribution shares in a growing economy subject to diminishing returns and Malthusian pressures – would yield the characteristic Ricardian propositions. Hollander himself adopts the weaker criterion, that Ricardian and neo-classical economics are not incompatible, the one with the other (e.g. Hollander 1985: vol. 1, 421). It may seem unfair to insist on the stronger test; but the justification is that, as historians, we want to be able to show how distinctive research traditions are driven. Now a set of negative heuristics for the Ricardian research program would surely include a warning against using supply-and-demand models unless possible deeper underlying causes have first been excluded, since such models may lead to error via a setting aside of 'natural and constant' causes. . . . The issue is not at all whether Ricardo and Mill had no appreciation for supply-and-demand analysis, but whether by adopting it we can motivate the particular models they themselves used to give expression to their vision. By this test, I believe Hollander's thesis must be judged historically uninformative, if not positively misleading.

(de Marchi 1987: 147–8)

A similar formulation appears in the conclusion to de Marchi's chapter:

> While being thoroughly appreciative of the ways in which Hollander has enriched our grasp of Ricardian economics, I am unable to share his enthusiasm for seeing in it a nascent form of neo-classicism. Compatibility, certainly, is there; and the supply-and-demand framework was held in common. But demonstrating compatibility is not the same as explaining what caused Ricardian and neo-classical inquirers to take the particular paths that they did; nor is the supply-and-demand framework up to that task. I take the view that as historians we want to be able to motivate the line of inquiry which we see to have been followed. In this light, demonstrating logical compatibility is a more abstract, less historical exercise altogether.

(de Marchi 1987: 159)

If I understand de Marchi in these passages correctly, he argues that *appreciation* by Ricardo and Mill of the allocative mechanism and the *compatibility* of classical and neo-classical economics do not assure that allocation theory 'would yield the characteristic Ricardian propositions'. Now, we have seen that de Marchi accepted the derivation of the fundamental theorem itself in terms of the demand-supply framework. Indeed, this relation, thus based, is defined within a growth context (see earlier quote). I shall, however, face the challenge directly: I shall show that the Ricardian problem of the distributive shares in a growing economy subject to diminishing returns and Malthusian pressures does indeed depend directly on the demand-supply mechanism – indeed, that it is demand which constitutes the primary driving force of the growth process.

In debate with Hutches Trower, Ricardo contrasts a 'control' economy with a market economy and insists that, for the latter, a demand perspective is essential for appreciating the growth process, particularly the characteristic expansion of agriculture:

> The point is dispute in this. Does the supply of corn precede the demand for it, or does it follow such demand? You are of the former – I of the latter opinion. You have not answered one important objection I made to you, namely, that if the supply of corn preceded the demand it must be at a lower price than the grower could afford to produce it – this is the inevitable consequence of supply exceeding demand – who under such circumstances would be induced to grow the surplus quantity of corn? Your mistake appears to me to proceed from considering the case too generally. It is undoubtedly true that if production were wholly under the control of one individual, whose object it was to increase population, he could not better effect his object than by growing more corn in the country than the existing community could consume – it would in that case be at a low price, and the greatest stimulus would be given to population. We might indeed then justly say that it was the abundance of corn which raised up consumers, and that in this respect corn differed from iron, silk or any other commodity[;] but this is not the question under consideration, what we want to know is, whether, in the present distribution of property, and under the influence of the motives which invite to production, corn is produced for any other reason than that iron, silk, wine etc. etc. are produced – whether they are not all produced on account of an actual or expected demand for them, and whether this demand is not always indicated by the relation of the market price to the natural price? If the supply existed one moment previously to the demand, the market price must sink below the natural price, and the manufacturer of the commodity or the grower of the corn, whichever it might be, would not get the usual and general rate of profits, and would therefore be unwilling to produce such a commodity.
> (Ricardo 1951, VIII: 255–6, cf. 235–7)

Lest it be said (I am used to it being said) that my interpretation draws on unrepresentative correspondence, I hasten to point out the centrality of these themes in the *Principles*. The original labour force, following the increase in the demand for labour, devotes its increased money wages (largely if not wholly) to 'luxury' purchases (the prices of which are assumed to remain constant). But in consequence of subsequent population expansion, the demand for 'necessaries' increases, and (in the event of diminishing agricultural returns) their (long-run or cost) prices increase, too. As population expands in response to the initial increase in the money-wage rate and the implied corresponding increase in commodity wages, so a two-way squeeze sets in, the cost prices of necessaries tending upward while the money wage falls from its high level immediately after the disturbance. The population expansion will be brought to a halt sooner – and the money wage corresponding to the equilibrium real wage rate will be higher – than in the case of an unchanged price of necessaries:

> When a high price of corn is the effect of an increasing demand, it is always preceded by an increase of wages, for demand cannot increase, without an increase of means in the people to pay for that which they desire. An accumulation of capital naturally produces an increased competition among the employers of labour, and a consequent rise in its price. The increased wages are not ['not always' in the third edition] immediately expended on food, but are first made to contribute to the other enjoyments of the labourer. His improved condition however induces, and enables him to marry, and then the demand for food for the support of his family naturally supersedes that of those other enjoyments on which his wages were temporarily expended. Corn rises then because the demand for it increases, because there are those in the society who have improved means of paying for it; and the profits of the farmer will be raised above the general level of profits, till the requisite quantity of capital has been employed on its production. Whether, after this has taken place, corn shall again fall to its former price, or shall continue permanently higher, will depend on the quality of the land from which the increased quantity of corn has been supplied. . . . The high wage in the first instance proceeded from an increase in the demand for labour: inasmuch as it encouraged marriage, and supported children, it produced the effect of increasing the supply of labour. But when the supply is obtained, wages will again fall to their former price, if corn has fallen to its former price; to a higher than the former price, if the increased supply of corn has been produced from land of an inferior quality.
>
> (Ricardo 1951, I: 162–3)

This is in fact the mode in which the cultivation of corn is always extended, and the increased wants of the market supplied. The funds for the maintenance of labour increase, and wages are raised. The comfortable situation of the labourer induces him to marry – population increases, and the demand for corn raises its price relatively to other things – more capital is profitably employed on agriculture, and continues to flow towards it, till the supply is equal to the demand, when the price again falls, and agricultural and manufacturing profits are again brought to a level.

(Ricardo 1951, I: 306)

It is by giving the workmen more money, or any other commodity in which wages are paid, and which has not fallen in value, that his situation is improved. The increase of population, and the increase of food will generally be the effect, but not the necessary effect of high wages. The amended condition of the labourer, in consequence of the increased value which is paid him, does not necessarily oblige him to marry and take upon himself the charge of a family – he will, in all probability, employ a portion of his increased wages in furnishing himself abundantly with food and necessaries, – but with the remainder he may, if it please him, purchase any commodities that may contribute to his enjoyments – chairs, tables, and hardware; or better clothes, sugar and tobacco. His increased wages then will be attended with no other effect than an increased demand for some of those commodities; and as the race of labourers will not be materially increased, his wages will continue permanently high. But although this might be the consequence of high wages, yet so great are the delights of domestic society, that in practice it is invariably found that an increase of population follows the amended condition of the labourers; and it is only because it does so, that, with the trifling exception already mentioned, a new and increased demand arises for food. This demand then is the effect of an increase of capital and population, but not the cause – it is only because the expenditure of the people takes this direction, that the market price of necessaries exceeds the natural price, and the quantity of food required is produced; and it is because the number of people is increased, that wages again fall.

(Ricardo 1951, I: 406–7)

Here, then, we see increasing demand for corn as the *sine qua non* of agricultural expansion. Evidently, the principle must be appropriately applied to those versions of classical growth theory entailing continuous population expansion until the stationarity state (cf. Hollander 1984). In these cases agricultural expansion occurs in response to *ongoing* increase in the demand for food.

Even this is not the full story. Ricardo used the principle at hand to counter Malthus' case regarding the possibility of a general glut, for that – Ricardo argued – supposed that capitalists accumulated necessaries without taking into account the pattern of tastes on the part of labour. This supposition was unacceptable, for 'In such a country as England . . . it is difficult to suppose that there can be any disposition to devote the whole capital and labour of the country to the production of necessaries only' (Ricardo 1951, VIII: 293). Ricardo pointed this out to James Mill, who should have used the argument against Malthus:

> during the period of very high wages, food and necessaries would not be produced in such quantities as to occasion a glut, for it would be the interest of the producer to produce such things as were in demand, and suited to the tastes of those who had high wages to expend.
>
> (131)

The role accorded demand and supply is so central to the key Ricardian issues that it fully meets de Marchi's test. It need only be added that Mill took the Ricardian line as I have outlined it. As early as 1828 he had defended the differential-rent theory against the strictures of Senior (1821) and others 'who affect to suppose that Sir Edward West, Mr Malthus, and Mr Ricardo, considered the cultivation of inferior land as the *cause* of a high price of corn'. Rather the reverse: that 'the cultivation of inferior soils' is the *effect* of high price, 'itself the effect of demand', was a doctrine 'explicitly laid down by the distinguished authors previously referred to, and particularly by Mr Ricardo' (Mill 1967: 17). Similarly in the *Principles*: 'Mr Ricardo does not say that it is the cultivation of inferior land' [that is, the 'cause of rent on the superior'], 'but the *necessity of cultivating* it from the insufficiency of the superior land to feed a growing population' (Mill 1965: 428) – the latter certainly an allusion to a rising demand for food (cf. Mill 1965: 745, and the reference to the 'growing demand [for food] of so rapidly increasing a population as that of Great Britain'). Mill applies the principle to that version of the classical growth model entailing equal growth rates of capital and population, thus assuring a constant per capita wage:

> Population having increased without any falling off in the labourer's condition, there is of course a demand for more food. The arts of production being supposed stationary, this food must be produced at an increased cost. To compensate for this greater cost of the additional food, the price of agricultural produce must rise.
>
> (Mill 1965: 273)

De Marchi's 'challenge' relates not only to growth theory. He refers also to Mill's treatment of distribution in Book II and of value in Book III as indicating that 'Mill clearly allows "value" to be created (as commodities) in the production sphere first, and then, as it were, shares it out according to the specific circumstances of the market' (de Marchi 1987: 155). This Marx-like attempt to reconcile 'value' and price is 'very different...from seeking the explicit conditions for optimal factor employment and factor-price determination in a general competitive equilibrium'.

On this matter my position is not so far from de Marchi's, for the 'Marxian' dimension to Mill – especially the source of profits in surplus labour time – is a central feature of my book (1985: 341–2). The transformation too figures widely in the Ricardian literature (e.g. McCulloch 1825: 312–13, cited in Hollander 1981: 150). All this has indeed no counterpart in the post-1870 period. Nevertheless, for the classics (Marx included), it is the market process that assures the transformation of values into prices, such that the rate of profit is everywhere equalised. Moreover, the 'neo-classical' allocative mechanisms are central for the *macroeconomic* dimension of classicism – the magnitude of profits and the general level of the profit rate. For surplus labour time is a variable determined not only by labour productivity in the wage-goods sectors, but also by the commodity wage and therefore labour market conditions. But aggregate labour demand varies with the average capital composition (not only with the rate of capital accumulation) which, assuming differential labour-capital ratios between industries, will reflect the pattern of economic activity. There is, therefore, a mutual relation between distribution and allocation:

1 Given factor-ratio differentials, output patterns will be influenced by a wage change. The classics, Mill included, allowed conspicuously for industry contractions and expansions upon a wage variation; that is what the analysis of the price structure is all about.
2 There is also a *playback* of alterations in the commodity mix on the wage. This they failed to make explicit; but I can see no reason why any of them (except McCulloch) would have denied it on principle (see p. 227).

———◆———

De Marchi raises the question of what is intended by 'neo-classical economics'. I would be quite happy to leave the matter with his own excellent formulation which lists what, to my mind, are the primary constituents: the information-conveying and signalling role of prices, the notion of alternative costs, and the conception of market interactions. That is, more or less, what I intend by a neo-classical or marginalist or demand-supply perspective. At the same time, I have the impression that de Marchi takes too narrow a view of the role of competitive demand and supply in neo-classicism. Sir John Hicks' recent proposal to use the term 'catallactics' in place of 'marginalism' has the merit of emphasising the demand-supply dimension (Hicks 1983: 9–10). That for Jevons, 'demand was merely the superficial phenomenon that needed to be explained by something deeper' (quoted in de Marchi) is true; it is, however, far less true in the case of Walras, who diverged from Jevons by defining his *rareté* as 'l'intensité du dernier besoin satisfait par une quantité possédée', rather than a quantity *consumed* (cf. Jaffé 1983: 315). Even Jevons expressed his admiration for the 'wonderful analysis by Cournot of the laws of supply and demand, and of the relations of prices, production, consumption, expenses and profits' (1924: xxx–xxxi) and indicated in the 'ten remarkable pages' of his Preface – so described by Walras (1954: 45) – that the future of the subject considered as a whole lay along general equilibrium lines. As for the supposed contrast between Marshall and Walras, I find Lord Robbins' position convincing:

> The fundamental analytical techniques will be seen to be essentially the same in both systems. . . . In Walras they dominate all constructions to the virtual exclusion of other considerations. In Marshall their overt and rigorous statement is relegated to the celebrated Note XIV in the Mathematical Appendix . . . [but] the systems were to all intents and purposes the same. The differences were a matter of the shop-window.
>
> (Robbins 1970: 25)

And in fact de Marchi seems to allow this: 'These differences may not seem fundamental – just differences of focus'.

Let us now go a step further. What of the implications of marginal utility for the relationship of pre-1870 to post-1870? Even assuming that my textual evidence is accepted as a convincing reply to de Marchi's challenge, it might still be argued that since the classics envisaged no subjective underpinning to demand in consumer maximising behaviour, we are justified in regarding the 1870s as entailing a paradigmatic break.

I am unconvinced by such arguments. Much more is involved than Ricardo's recognition that 'if a commodity were in no way useful, – in other words, if it could in no way contribute to our gratification, – it would be destitute of exchangeable value' (1951, I: 11). Ricardo adopted the consumer's conception of wealth whereby

> a man is rich or poor, according to the abundance of necessaries and luxuries which he can command; and whether the exchangeable value of these for money, for corn, or for labour, be high or low, they will equally contribute to the enjoyment of their possessor.
>
> (275)

This led him to warn of a serious error by Lord Lauderdale, namely that of 'confounding the ideas of value and wealth, or riches' and asserting 'that by diminishing the quantity of commodities . . . – riches may be increased'. On the contrary:

> If value were the measure of riches, this could not be denied, because by scarcity the value of commodities is raised; but if Adam Smith be correct, if riches consist in necessaries and enjoyments, then they cannot be increased by a diminution of quantity.

In brief, value rises with increased scarcity, but wealth (that is, total utility) declines. Value is evidently determined at the margin, although of course Ricardo did not put the matter in these exact terms.

With this in mind we can appreciate Ricardo's reaction to a charge made by J. B. Say against Adam Smith. In an application of the principle of scarcity value, Ricardo comes very close to the distinction between total and marginal utility, the latter equalling zero in the case at hand:

> M. Say accuses Dr Smith of having overlooked the value which is given to commodities by natural agents, and by machinery, because he considered that the value of all things was derived from the labour of man; but it does not appear to me, that this charge is made out; for Adam Smith nowhere undervalues the services which these natural agents and machinery perform for us, but he very justly distinguishes the nature of the value which they add to commodities – they are serviceable to us, by increasing the abundance of productions, by making men richer, by adding to value in use; but as they perform their work gratuitously, as nothing is paid for the use of air, of heat, and of water, the assistance which they afford us, adds nothing to value in exchange.
>
> (Ricardo 1951, I: 286–7)

Wealth, therefore, for Ricardo, refers to real income. But it is typical classical practice to focus on wealth embodied in material goods. I touch now on the productive–unproductive classification, to which J. S. Mill devoted much attention.

The productive–unproductive distinction in no way implied a rejection of the role of utility in price formation. Mill admittedly did not accept the view of Say (and McCulloch) that all labour be regarded as productive, that is, 'useful', or engaged in producing 'a benefit or a pleasure worth the cost'; but he insisted, nonetheless, that 'what we produce, or desire to produce, is always, as M. Say rightly terms it, an utility. Labour is not creative of objects, but of utilities' (Mill 1965: 45–6). By 'productive labour' he intended labour productive of 'wealth', defined such that utility is a necessary (but insufficient) condition for the inclusion of material products within the national dividend:

> things which cannot, after being produced, be kept for some time before being used, are never . . . regarded as wealth, since however much of them may be produced and enjoyed, the person benefited by them is no richer, is nowise improved in circumstances.
>
> (Mill 1965: 48)

'For some time' is left undefined, and quite deliberately, for any degree of 'susceptib[ility] to accumulation', however small, suffices to distinguish wealth from 'a mere service . . . a pleasure given, an inconvenience or a pain averted, during a longer or a shorter time', that is, from the yield of 'unproductive' labour 'employed in producing a utility directly, not ... in fitting some other thing to afford a utility' (47).

Materiality as such was, for Mill, irrelevant. It is the flow of future utilities embodied in a (scarce) material product that renders it an item of 'wealth' – wealth constitutes a store of utilities. This fact governs the rationalisation given for an extension of the productive-labour category to include transport workers, merchants and dealers, namely that their activity

> adds the property of being in the place where they are wanted ... which is a very useful property, and the utility it confers is embodied in the things themselves, which now actually are in the place where they are required for use, and in consequence of that increased utility could be sold at an increased price, proportioned to the labour expended in conferring it.
>
> (Mill 1965: 47–8)

There is, thus, no conflict between a utility and a labour theory of value.

That materiality in and of itself is insufficient for a physical item to be counted as wealth and thus be included in the national dividend, is also apparent in the fact that

> productive labour may render a nation poorer, if the wealth it produces, that is, the increase it makes in the stock of useful and agreeable things, be of a kind not immediately wanted: as when a commodity is unsalable, because produced in a quantity beyond the present demand; or when speculators build docks and warehouses before there is any trade.
>
> (52)

Ricardo had also rejected the charge that political economists wished 'to heap up ... valuable commodities, without any regard to quantity' (1951, I: 248–9).

The major classical economists were evidently innocent of confusing the 'technical' and the 'economic' problem. It seems fair to conclude that while the post-1870 writers include a wider range of activities within 'national income' – the full range of *market* activities – there are no differences of principle separating their conception of value from that of the classicals, despite the latter's restricting the national product to material goods (produced by capitalist firms). A further conclusion is that the notion of marginal utility could easily have been fitted into the classical formulations. Marshall turns out to be perfectly justified in his rejection of Jevons' charge that Ricardo and Mill had rendered their account of value 'hopelessly wrong by omitting to lay stress on the law of satiable wants' (Marshall 1920: 101n); Jevons was 'only adding very important explanations'.

Whether the classicals would have welcomed the enormous attention subsequently given to the logic of consumer choice in cardinal-utility terms is another matter. We know at least that Mill regarded Jevons as engaging in unnecessarily complex exercises (Hollander 1985: 935). There is some reason to suspect that he would have preferred a more 'objective' choice-theoretic approach. Here we recall Ricardo's appreciation of the budget constraint, the income effect providing the key to his formal analysis of consumer response to changing prices. Thus, for example:

> An increase in the cost of production [and price] of a commodity, if it be an article of the first necessity, will not necessarily diminish its consumption; for although the general power of the purchasers to consume, is diminished by the rise of any one commodity, yet they may relinquish the consumption of some other commodity whose cost of production has not risen.
>
> (Ricardo 1951, I: 343–4)

Or again:

> The demand for corn, with a given population, is limited; no man can have a desire to consume more than a certain quantity of bread. . . . But the demand for commodities such as luxuries; or for services . . . is unlimited, or rather it is only limited by the means of the demanders.
>
> (1951, VIII: 272)

Mill carried this line of thought further, adding a splendid formulation of the 'Slutsky' substitution effect:

> You say [he wrote to J. E. Cairnes in 1865], if a tax is taken off beer and laid on tobacco in such a manner that the consumer can still, at the same total cost as before, purchase his usual quantity of both, his tastes being supposed unaltered, he will do so. Does not this assume that his taste for each is a fixed quantity? or at all events that his comparative desire for the two is not affected by their comparative prices? But I apprehend the case to be otherwise. Very often the consumer cannot afford to have as much as he would like of either: and if so, the ratio in which he will share his demand between the two may depend very much on their price. If beer grows cheaper and tobacco dearer, he will be able to increase his beer more, by a smaller sacrifice of his tobacco, than he could have done at the previous prices: and in such circumstances it is surely probable that some will do so. His apportionment of self-denial between his two tastes is likely to be modified, when the obstacle that confined them is in the one case brought nearer, in the other thrown farther off.
>
> (Mill 1965: 1089)

We are dealing with a matter Mill apparently took to be self-evident, so effortless is the formulation. There is no reason why this brilliant account of the impact of a relative price change on the range of choices available could not have been incorporated into the *Principles* in any of its earlier editions. The differences between Mill and Jevons take the extraordinary form of the former leaping ahead of the latter to reach a more advanced state of neo-classicism decades ahead of everyone else.

De Marchi raises against me recent contributions by Philip Mirowski. I shall limit my comments to Mirowski's 1984 article, not the unpublished manuscript referred to. There he argues that 'neoclassical economic theory is bowdlerised nineteenth century physics...the timing of its genesis is explained by the timing of the energetics revolution in physics' (1984: 377). In my view this position is unconvincing. But I shall take it on its own terms for the sake of argument:

> Neo-classical theorists, from the 1870s onwards, have surreptitiously assumed some form of conservation principle in their economic models. In the period of our present concern, the principle took two forms: (a) the income or endowments to be traded is assumed to be fully spent or traded; thus, for practical purposes, T (total expenditure on goods) is conserved; and/or (b) the transactors' estimation of the utility of the various goods is a datum not altered by the sequence of purchase, nor any other aspects of the trading or consuming process...so, in effect, the utility field is conserved.
>
> (Mirowski 1984: 367)

Now we have seen that Mill *accepted* the budget constraint and the ranking of alternatives in stable preference ordering. I therefore discern no differences between pre-1870 and post-1870 on these grounds. Mirowski (371–2) also refers to the 'law of one price' and 'the concept that traded goods in some sense are related as equivalents in equilibrium', as essential for neo-classicism and 'the introduction of a physics analogy into economic theory' after 1870. He is apparently unaware that both feature large in Mill's *Principles*.

Even if for some reason the foregoing arguments should be rejected, my 'continuity thesis', understood as a commonly held price analysis in terms of the allocation of scarce resources between competing uses, still holds good. I am satisfied to find de Marchi agreeing at least that classicism is 'compatible' with neo-classicism at the phenomenal level – indeed that the supply-and-demand framework 'was held in common'. After all, Ragnar Frisch in his Nobel Lecture denied this explicitly: 'The economic process is an *equilibrium affair* where both technological and subjective forces are at play. The subjective element was nearly left out by the classicists' (1981: 5). Arrow and Starrett similarly assert that the founders of the neo-classical school 'understood the glaring omission of demand from the classical model' (1973: 132–3); and we have the strong assertion by Sir John Hicks:

Ricardo was no Marshallian. He maintained, consistently, that prices are determined by cost; demand has nothing to do with them. It may indeed be objected that when he lets the [marginal] cost of food production rise, under pressure of population, he is admitting demand; it is the increased demand for food which forces the extension of cultivation. I do not believe that Ricardo looked at the matter like that.

(Hicks 1985: 317)

It is surely a sufficient achievement to have broken the back of this historiographical misconception.

References

Arrow, Kenneth J. and Starrett, D. A. (1973) 'Cost- and demand-theoretic approaches to the theory of price determination', in J. R. Hicks and W. Weber (eds) *Carl Menger and the Austrian School of Economics*, Oxford: Clarendon Press, 129–48.

Frisch, Ragnar (1981) 'From Utopian theory to practical applications: the case of econometrics', *American Economic Review*, 71 (December): 1–16.

Hicks, John (1983) '"Revolutions" in economics', in *Collected Essays in Economic Theory, III: Classics and Moderns*, Oxford/Cambridge MA: Blackwell/Harvard University Press, 3–16.

——(1985) 'Sraffa and Ricardo: a critical view', in G. A. Caravale (ed.) *The Legacy of Ricardo*, Oxford: Blackwell, 305–19.

Hollander, Samuel (1979) *The Economics of David Ricardo*, Toronto: University of Toronto Press.

——(1981) 'Marxian economics as general equilibrium theory', *History of Political Economy*, 13, 1: 121–55.

——(1984) 'The wage path in classical growth models: Ricardo, Malthus and Mill', *Oxford Economic Papers*, 36: 200–12.

——(1985) *The Economics of John Stuart Mill*, 2 vols, Toronto: University of Toronto Press.

Jaffé, William (1983) *William Jaffé's Essays on Walras*, ed. D. A. Walker, Cambridge: Cambridge University Press.

Jevons, William S. (1924) *The Theory of Political Economy*, 4th edn, London: Macmillan.

McCulloch, J. R. (1825) *Principles of Political Economy*, 1st edn, Edinburgh: William and Charles Tait.

de Marchi, N. (1987) 'John Stuart Mill interpretation since Schumpeter', in W. O. Thweatt (ed.) *Classical Political Economy: A Survey of Recent Literature*, Boston: Kluwer Academic Publishers.

Marshall, Alfred (1920) *Principles of Economics*, 8th edn, London: Macmillan.

Mill, J. S. (1965) *Principles of Political Economy, Collected Works of John Stuart Mill*, II, III, Toronto: University of Toronto Press.

——(1967) [1828] 'The nature, origin and progress of rent', in *Collected Works*, IV: 161–80.

Mirowski, Philip (1984) 'Physics and the "marginalist revolution"', *Cambridge Journal of Economics*, 8, 4: 361–79.

Ricardo, David (1951–73) *Works and Correspondence of David Ricardo*, 11 vols, ed. P. Sraffa; I: *Principles of Political Economy*; VIII: *Letters 1819–June 1821*; IX: *Letters July 1821–1823;*, Cambridge: Cambridge University Press.

Robbins, Lionel C. (1970) *The Evolution of Modern Economic Theory*, London: Macmillan.

Senior, Nassau (1821) 'Report on the State of Agriculture', *Quarterly Review*, 25 (July), 466–504.

Walras, Léon (1954) *Elements of Pure Economics*, 4th definitive edn (1926) translated and edited by W. Jaffé, London: George Allen & Unwin.

Chapter 12

John Stuart Mill's method in principle and practice

A review of the evidence with Sandra Peart[1]

Introduction: the state of play

Our concern is John Stuart Mill's methodological pronouncements, his actual practice and the relationship between them. We believe there to be strong evidence to refute a widespread and tenacious characterisation of Mill as championing and practising excessively *a priori* procedures. Our starting point is the celebrated declaration regarding verification in the essay 'On the definition of political economy; and on the method of investigation proper to it' (1836; hereafter *Essay*):

> By the method *à priori* we mean...reasoning from an assumed hypothesis; which...is the essence of all science which admits of general reasoning at all. To verify the hypothesis itself *à posteriori*, that is, to examine whether the facts of any actual case are in accordance with it, is no part of the business of science at all, but of the *application* of science.
>
> (Mill 1967 [1836]: 325)

The apparent position that the basic economic theory is impervious to predictive failure emerges also in a sharp criticism of the *à posteriori* method:

> Having now shown that the method *à priori* in Political Economy, and in all the other branches of moral science, is the only certain or scientific mode of investigation, and that the *à posteriori* method, or that of specific experience, as a means of arriving at truth, is inapplicable to these subjects, we shall be able to show that the latter method is notwithstanding of great value in the moral sciences; namely, not as a means of discovering truth, but of verifying it, and reducing to the lowest point that uncertainty before alluded to as arising from the complexity of every particular case, and from the difficulty (not to say impossibility) of being assured *à priori* that we have taken into account all the material circumstances.
>
> (Mill 1967 [1836]: 331)

The 'assumed hypothesis' of political economy includes a set of behavioural assumptions:

> Political economy does not treat of the whole of man's nature as modified by the social state, nor of the whole conduct of man in society. It is concerned with him solely as a being who desires to possess wealth, and who is capable of judging of the comparative efficacy of means for obtaining that end. It predicts only such of the phenomena of the social state as take place in consequence of the pursuit of wealth. It makes entire abstraction of every human passion or motive; except those which may be regarded as perpetually antagonizing principles to the desire of wealth, namely, aversion to labour, and desire of the present enjoyment of costly indulgences.
>
> (Mill 1967 [1836]: 321)[2]

The wealth-maximisation axiom is selected, more precisely, because it is 'the main and acknowledged end' in 'certain departments of human affairs' (323). Mill elaborates:

> It is only of these that Political Economy takes notice. The manner in which it necessarily proceeds is that of treating the main and acknowledged end as if it were the sole end; which, of all hypotheses equally simple, is the nearest to the truth. The political economist inquires, what are the actions which would be produced by this desire, if, within the departments in question, it were unimpeded by any other. In this way a nearer approximation is obtained than would otherwise be practical, to the real order of human affairs in those departments. This approximation is then to be corrected by making proper allowance for the effects of any impulses of a different description, which can be shown to interfere with the result in any particular case.
>
> (Mill 1967 [1836]: 323)[3]

In the *System of Logic* too, the 'immediately determining causes' are said to be 'principally those which act through the desire of wealth; and in which the psychological law mainly concerned is the familiar one, that a greater gain is preferred to a smaller' (1973–4 [1843]: 901).

The foregoing passage from the *Essay* alludes to 'impulses . . . which can be shown to interfere with the result in any particular case' – the 'result', that is, emerging as the outcome of ratiocination based on 'the main and acknowledged end'. Only in application – and in consequence of such 'disturbing causes' – does 'an element of uncertainty' enter the process:

> When the principles of Political Economy are to be applied to a particular case, then it is necessary to take into account all the individual circumstances of that case; not only examining to which of the sets of circumstances contemplated by the abstract science the circumstances of

the case in question correspond, but likewise what other circumstances may exist in that case, which not being common to it with any large and strongly-marked class of cases, have not fallen under the cognisance of the science. These circumstances have been called *disturbing causes*. And here only it is that an element of uncertainty enters into the process – an uncertainty inherent in the nature of these complex phenomena, and arising from the impossibility of being quite sure that all the circumstances of the particular case are known to us sufficiently in detail, and that our attention is not unduly diverted from any of them.

(Mill 1967 [1836]: 330)

Considering the apparent clarity of these passages, it is scarcely surprising to find it commonly alleged that Mill denied to verification the role of testing, and conceivably of modifying, theory:

in economics, as Mill had explained, we test the *applications* of theories to determine whether enough of the disturbing economic causes have been taken into account to explain what actually happens in the real world after allowing, in addition, for noneconomic causes. We never test the validity of theories, because the conclusions are true as one aspect of human behaviour, by virtue of the assumptions, which in turn are true by virtue of being based on self-evident facts of human experience.

(Blaug 1992: 68)

Similarly:

If a theory fails to predict accurately, Mill would have said, a search should be made for sufficient supplementary causes to close the gap between the facts and the causal antecedents laid down in the theory because the theory is true in any case *as far as it goes* by the nature of its true assumptions.

(67)

Professor Blaug is on record as stating that, for Mill, 'whether there is any way of showing a theory to be false is never even contemplated' (1980: 81).

In a careful review of Mill's method, Abraham Hirsch similarly understands Mill as denying to verification the task of 'test[ing] a theory by determining whether its implications accord with what actually happens' (1992: 847). For

if one *knows* that the implications of economic science will not generally accord very well with what happens because we have only reasoned on the basis of these three behavioural laws [above, p. 242], then what need is there to verify a theory of abstract or scientific economics that is based only on three causal laws? What is there to be learned from verifications that we know, because we have set things up this way, will only show the predictive limitations of the theory?

(862)

It is 'not ... merely that there is *more* uncertainty in applying theory than in deriving it; in Mill's view there is *certainty* in the business of science where the *a priori* [method] alone is used'. Again, 'when the *a priori* method is used no verification at all is needed and ... *certain* results are achieved' (863). As Hirsch reads Mill:

> Economic science is ... incomplete. When we apply it for practical purposes it needs to be supplemented in order to make better predictions than can be made with the science alone, but in application one tests the hypothesis used for making the prediction which postulates how the practical problem can best be dealt with. And while the abstract science is used in helping to formulate this hypothesis, it is primarily one's ability to identify the pertinent other causes in the particular situation that is being tested ... and not the abstract science. That is why verification for Mill in its very conception is part of the application and not of the science process.
>
> (Hirsch 1992: 848)

In line with this perspective Hirsch and de Marchi, in their joint study of Milton Friedman, observe regarding Millian verification:

> in the Millian system the evidence may be inconsistent with the implications of our theory, thus giving us little in the way of grounds of confidence, yet our belief in the scientific validity of the causal laws underlying the theory remains unaffected.
>
> (Hirsch and de Marchi 1990: 113)[4]

This position is represented as a 'radical' contrast with that attributed to Friedman:

1. Friedman does, but Mill does not, view extensive observation of specific experience as a necessary component in the process of deriving 'good' (meaning both scientifically sound as well as useful) theory in economics.

2. Friedman does, but Mill does not, view inquiry in economics as a continuous process where observation of specific experience and hypothesizing interact at every stage of the inquiry process.

3. Mill does, whereas Friedman does not, regard 'realistic' assumptions or premises – no matter how these terms are defined – as either necessary or sufficient to make theory provisionally acceptable as part of economic science.

4. Friedman does, but Mill does not, believe that the extent to which

a theory can predict (and retrodict) should have a bearing on how we judge its premises.

(Hirsch and de Marchi 1990: 124)

We believe an additional, and contrasting, interpretation of Mill's method is supported by the evidence. For in our view Mill insisted on the possibility of theory modification in the light of inadequacies revealed by empirical evidence, and also held that the central behavioural axiom is not of *universal* relevance but pertinent only to the *local* circumstances of contemporary Great Britain and America – and, even so, qualified as we shall see – that the axiom itself is empirically based. On our reading, there is more in common between his research strategy and that of Milton Friedman than is sometimes granted, at least when Friedman's position on theory appraisal is appreciated in the manner of Hirsch and de Marchi 1990. As Fels has paraphrased this position in a review:

> start with a thorough marshalling of facts, frame a hypothesis to explain them, make predictions from the hypothesis about facts not used in constructing it, compare the predictions with the actual facts, revise the hypothesis in response to the outcome of the tests, and continue in an iterative fashion.

(1991: 84)

Our study seeks, further, to shed light on just how seriously Mill took the role of verification in practice. For while the positions outlined above suggest that Mill made *no* allowance for theory modification in the light of the evidence, one study (Hirsch 1992) allows for the possibility of theory modification in Mill, but concludes that such modifications are rare: 'Mill does not say explicitly that the basic model is impervious to verification, but he leaves the strong impression that on his view the probability that it will be changed through verification is exceedingly small' (Hirsch 1992: 865).[5] Hirsch makes repeated qualifications of the same order.[6] But once we allow that there is at least the small likelihood of any such theory modification in consequence of verification or retrodiction, there is one obvious way of evaluating whether or not – in Mill's mind – verification, by revealing deficiencies, can generate corrections and improvements in theory, and if it can do so, the 'likelihood' of that occurring. This is by considering Mill's own practice. Though Mill's formal methodological pronouncements have been studied extensively, there is a general neglect of his actual procedures. Our intention is to redress this imbalance by assessing Mill's methodological practice. We find there to be compelling evidence in that practice to refute the view that for Mill verification serves only to point out the existence of disturbing causes.

In the second and third sections below, the formal pronouncements regarding science and the application of science, upon which so much weight has been placed, are examined. Here emerges Mill's case, in principle, for theory modification in the light of 'verification' and the justification of the wealth-maximising axiom in empirical terms. Thereafter we turn to a sampling of Mill's practice and illustrate theory improvement designed to account for new or newly realised circumstances. The fourth, fifth and sixth sections consider the central behavioural axiom in the context of pricing and market structure; the wage structure; and inventories and business cycles. A particular charge against Mill is taken up in the seventh section, namely that in consequence of his formally stated methodology he was unwilling – despite growing evidence – to admit the irrelevance, indeed the invalidity, of Ricardian growth theory, and proceeded by adopting various 'immunizing stratagems' (Blaug 1992: 65–8). In fact, it turns out that though Ricardian growth theory retained for Mill its validity especially with an eye to policy, he nonetheless engaged in major modifications of the land-based model by linking it with the phenomenon of regular business cycles, an intellectual feat of the first order conspicuously reflecting the need for model improvement in the light of new empirical findings. The Ricardian inverse wage-profit relation is addressed in the eighth section, where we take up Mill's concerns with its validity in the light of recent British and US data on the profit rate, and his proposed application of the basic model as solution to the apparent anomaly.

We make no claims for an exhaustive treatment of Mill's practice; our concern is illustrative. In each of our cases it is shown that Mill examined the empirical evidence relating to the state of business affairs in contemporary Britain relevant to his theoretical position and, in order better to explain observed phenomena, gave a prominent role to such experiential knowledge, either by respecifying the axiomatic framework, or by enriching the causal analysis. Much of our evidence has been set out in Hollander (1985) and Peart (1993, 1995). We have felt it necessary to restate the argument and again scrutinise some of the relevant texts, in order to reassess the role and significance of experiential evidence in Mill's economics. We hope in particular to use the case studies to shed light on the widely held view whereby in Mill's practice 'discrepancies between anticipation and actual facts do not show the original statement to be wrong, only "insufficient"'(de Marchi 1988: 152).[7] We are not seeking, in Mill, an 'ordered program of empirical inquiry' (152), since in our view this entails too stringent a condition. Nor do we deny that Mill combined the experiential techniques with 'logical demonstrations' or the 'inverse deductive method' (159). Our reading of the literature on Mill, however, suggests that he has been too often categorised as wholly or mostly an *à priori* theorist, and only infrequently has it been granted (see Hausman 1981, 1989) that Mill allowed for and relied on model improvement through verification. Consequently this paper seeks to redress the balance.

Mill on method: 'verification'[8]

The role of verification in Mill turns, in Hirsch's view, on the distinction between theory – which requires no verification – and application – which does. Certainly, for Mill verification is a key part of applied science. At one point in the *Essay*, as we have seen (above, pp. 242–3), Mill accords verification the apparently limited role of isolating the 'partial' or 'disturbing' causes at play in any particular case to assess their significance relative to the general causes – an exercise that is not itself a part of 'science' but of its application. But Mill in fact goes a step further. Those disturbing causes

> which operate through the same law of human nature out of which the general principles of the science arise ... might always be brought within the pale of the abstract science, if it were worth while; and when we make the necessary allowances for them in practice, if we are doing anything but guess, we are following out the method of the abstract science into minuter details; inserting among its hypotheses a fresh and still more complex combination of circumstances, and so adding *pro hâc vice* a supplementary chapter or appendix, or at least a supplementary theorem, to the abstract science.
>
> (Mill 1967 [1836]: 331)

Now, 'adding a supplementary chapter or appendix or a theorem *for this time only* (*'pro hâc vice'*), it has been said, 'hardly sounds like the process by which the revision of the basic model is carried out'; rather, the basic model remains unchanged 'since the disturbing causes remain in the disturbing ... category' (Hirsch 1992: 856). On our reading, however, since Mill chose to express the matter as bringing disturbing causes *'within the pale of the abstract science'*, the formulation suggests that the model itself *is* subject to modification, if only temporarily. It is the abstract science itself, Mill tells us explicitly, that is affected by the 'addition of a supplementary theorem'. Yet more important, two paragraphs earlier he had pointed out that some disturbing causes – like friction in mechanics –

> may at first have been considered merely as a non-assignable deduction to be made by guess from the result given by the general principles of science; but in time many of them are brought within the pale of the abstract science itself, and their effect is found to admit of as accurate an estimation as those more striking effects which they modify.
>
> (1967 [1836]: 330)

There is no reference here to *'pro hâc vice'*; and it is plausible to read this passage as alluding to cases of permanent revision of theory resulting from the cumulative effect of repeated 'failures' of prediction (or retrodiction). Additional support for this reading is Mill's observation that verification often discloses to us errors in thought, still more serious than the omission of what can with any propriety be termed a disturbing cause. It often reveals to us that the basis itself of our whole argument is insufficient; that the data, from which we had reasoned, comprise only a part, and not always the most important part, of the circumstances by which the result is really determined.

$$(332)^9$$

Two types of revisions of theory might thus result from the process of verification, though Mill never clarified how one is to distinguish between them. A set of general causes, A, B and C, is used to predict the outcome E. E^* is observed, leading the scientist to revise the causal framework by adding D – perhaps, though not necessarily, *pro hâc vice* – to the model. Alternatively, the procedure of verification might reveal that the axioms have been inferred from an incomplete set of circumstances – that the data are 'insufficient'. In this instance observation of E^* leads the scientist to revise A, B and C to A^*, B^* and C^* (see Peart 1993: 442).

It has been objected, however, that in fact Mill in the latter case is referring to particular circumstances rather than general causes (Hirsch 1992: 852). The discrepancy between this interpretation and ours turns on how widely applicable such cases are. Our reading suggests they may be general, though not universal. For Hirsch, since Mill defines 'disturbing causes' as 'circumstances . . . which not being common to it with any large and strongly-marked class of cases, have not fallen under the cognisance of the science' (see above, p. 243), it follows that no matter 'how great the effect of a cause in a specific instance', that cause remains in the disturbing-causes category if it is not a *general* cause (854). Yet Mill's passage is explicit that the concern is with 'errors in thought, still more serious than the omission of what can with any propriety be termed a disturbing cause', and follows directly upon a statement which is indeed concerned with the discovery of disturbing causes:

> We cannot, therefore, too carefully endeavour to verify our theory, by comparing, in the particular cases to which we have access, the results which it would had led us to predict, with the most trustworthy accounts we can obtain of those which have been actually realized. The discrepancy between our anticipations and the actual fact is often the only circumstance which would have *drawn our attention to some important disturbing cause which we had overlooked*. Nay, it often discloses to us errors in thought, still more serious than the omission of what can with any propriety be termed a disturbing cause.
>
> (Mill 1967 [1836]: 332, emphasis added)

It is in light of this contrast that one should read Mill's own comment on the passage now under discussion:

Such oversights are committed by very good reasoners, and even by a still rarer class, that of good observers. It is a kind of error to which those are peculiarly liable whose views are the largest and most philosophical: for exactly in that ratio are their minds more accustomed to dwell upon those laws, qualities, and tendencies, which are common to large classes of cases, *and which belong to all places and all time*; while it often happens that circumstances almost peculiar to the particular case or era have a far greater share in governing that one case.

(Mill 1967 [1836]: 332–3, emphasis added)

Tendencies 'common to large classes of cases', in the sense of belonging 'to all places and all time', can only mean universally applicable, in which case 'circumstances almost peculiar to [a] particular case or era', must relate to a *localised geographical and temporal reality* – to Britain or the United States, for example, under given conditions. When the term 'particular case' is read along with 'particular *era*', it becomes clear that verification might reveal a general – though not universally applicable – cause at play relating to the 'particular case' for which contemporary theory was designed to deal, namely to the advanced economies of Mill's day (we return to this issue in the third section below).[10]

We turn now to an explicit recognition by Mill that verification (in the sense of retrodiction) might reveal the economist's model to be 'imperfect even as an abstract system':

[The political economist's] knowledge must at least enable him to explain and account for what *is*, or he is an insufficient judge of what ought to be. If a political economist, for instance, finds himself puzzled by any recent or present commercial phenomena; if there is any mystery to him in the late or present state of the productive industry of the country, which his knowledge of principle does not enable him to unriddle; he may be sure that something is wanting to render his system of opinions a safe guide in existing circumstances. Either some of the facts which influence the situation of the country and the course of events are not known to him; or, knowing them, he knows not what ought to be their effects. *In the latter case his system is imperfect even as an abstract system; it does not enable him to trace correctly all the consequences even of assumed premises.*

(Mill 1967 [1836]: 335, emphasis added)

This would seem to constitute proof positive that for Mill economic theory is subject to 'correction' in consequence of verification. Yet Professor Hirsch suggests that Mill is concerned here not with an 'abstract system' in the sense of specialised 'economic science', but rather with 'speculative politics' more generally (Hirsch 1992: 858–9). Now, Hirsch rightly points out that sometimes 'Mill is not very clear about who does what in the process of verification' (857, n20). But in our present case Mill refers explicitly to the 'political economist' who 'finds himself puzzled' by the empirical evidence and becomes aware that 'his system is imperfect even as an abstract system', and whose task, in that case, 'is not yet completed'. It is true that in the next paragraph it is the 'speculative politician' who is said to be obliged to seek the explanation for any failure 'conscientiously, *not with the desire of finding his system complete, but of making it so*' (emphasis added); and who is duty bound to carry out a verification 'upon every new combination of facts as it arises'. He must allow for 'the disturbing influence of unforeseen causes', but he also

> must carefully watch the result of every experiment, in order that any residuum of facts which his principles do not lead him to expect, and do not enable him to explain, may become the subject of a fresh analysis, and furnish the occasion for a consequent enlargement or correction of his general views.
>
> (335–6)

To the extent that 'political economy' is represented as a branch of the science of 'speculative politics' (as at 321), this particular problem is eased. In any event, shortly thereafter, Mill writes more generally about the 'danger of falling into partial views' in which context he appears to have reverted to the 'theorist':

> All that we can do more, is to endeavour to be impartial critics of our own theories, and to free ourselves, as far as we are able, from that reluctance from which few inquirers are altogether exempt, to admit the reality or relevancy of any facts which they have not previously either taken into, or left a place open for in, their systems.
>
> (336)

And in the *Logic* it is further clarified that Mill is discussing the *economist's* 'knowledge of principle', and potential revelations of its inadequacy as a result of verification.[11] We have in mind two equivalent, but more detailed, statements to this very effect, entailing at key junctures almost identical terminology to the passage from the *Essay*.

The first extract appears in a section entitled 'Third stage; verification by specific experience', which addresses the problem that the 'direct observation and experiment' of *a posteriori* method are 'illusory when applied to the laws of complex phenomena':

> When in every single instance a multitude, often an unknown multitude, of agencies, are clashing and combining, what security have we that in our computation *à priori* we have taken all these into our reckoning? How many must we not generally be ignorant of? Among those which we know, how probable that some have been overlooked; and, even were all included, how vain the pretence of summing up the

effects of many causes, unless we know accurately the numerical law of each, – a condition in most cases not to be fulfilled; and even when it is fulfilled to make the calculation transcends, in any but very simple cases, the utmost power of mathematical science with all its most modern improvements.

(Mill 1973–4 [1843]: 460)

The remedy is provided by the 'test' of verification, 'the third essential component part of the Deductive Method; without which all the results it can give have little other value than that of conjecture'. As in the *Essay*, Mill is crystal clear that in the event of a failure of verification, the theory itself is 'imperfect, and not yet to be relied upon' in future application:

To warrant reliance on the general conclusions arrived at by deduction, these conclusions must be found, on careful comparison, to accord with the results of direct observation wherever it can be had. If, when we have experience to compare with them, this experience confirms them, we may safely trust to them in other cases of which our specific experience is yet to come. But if our deductions have led to the conclusion that from a particular combination of causes a given effect would result, then in all known cases where that combination can be shown to have existed, and where the effect has not followed, we must be able to show (or at least to make a probable surmise) what frustrated it: *if we cannot, the theory is imperfect, and not yet to be relied upon.*

(Mill 1973–4 [1843]: 460–1, emphasis added)[12]

All this is repeated later in the text, where social science is at issue. The deductive conclusions of social science were to be checked constantly against specific experience, the importance of combining '*à priori* reasoning' with verification increasing as the 'composition of causes' became more pronounced:

This remedy consists in the process which, under the name of Verification, we have characterized [460–3] as the third essential constituent part of the Deductive Method: that of collating the conclusions of the ratiocination either with the concrete phenomena themselves, or when such are obtainable, with their empirical laws. The ground of confidence in any concrete deductive science is not the *à priori* reasoning itself, but the accordance between its results and those of observation *à posteriori*.

(896–7)[13]

A typical problem pertaining to the 'more special inquiries which form the subject of the separate branches of the social science' – where 'the object is to determine the effect of any one social cause among a great number acting simultaneously' – is illustrated by the analysis of the effect of corn laws on 'industrial prosperity' (908–9). Now, Mill is evidently concerned here with the narrow realm of economics. He then elaborates on various problems of testing – that there are 'no previous empirical generalizations with which to collate the conclusions of theory', and that it is impossible to ascertain that 'the circumstances of [an] experiment [are] exactly the same with those contemplated in the theory'. Thus a 'trial of corn laws in another country or in a former generation, would go a very little way towards verifying a conclusion drawn respecting their effect in this generation and in this country'. The only solution 'towards verifying the general sufficiency of the theory' is that provided by retrodiction, which procedure Mill elaborates in a passage using several of the same terms and phrases as the *Essay*:

> The test of the degree in which the science affords safe grounds for predicting (and consequently for practically dealing with) what has not yet happened, is the degree in which it would have enabled us to predict what has actually occurred. Before our theory of the influence of a particular cause, in a given state of circumstances, can be entirely trusted, we must be able to explain and account for the existing state of all that portion of the social phenomena which that cause has a tendency to influence. If, for instance, we would apply our speculations in political economy to the prediction or guidance of the phenomena of any country, we must be able to explain all the mercantile or industrial facts of a general character, appertaining to the present state of that country: to point out causes sufficient to account for all of them, and prove, or show good ground for supposing, that these causes have really existed. *If we cannot do this, it is a proof either that the facts which ought to be taken into account are not yet completely known to us, or that although we know the facts, we are not masters of a sufficiently perfect theory to enable us to assign their consequences. In either case we are not, in the present state of our knowledge, fully competent to draw conclusions, speculative or practical, for that country.*
>
> (Mill 1973–4 [1843]: 909–10, emphasis added)

Even the 'speculative' model might thus be revealed to be inadequate. And in closing, Mill repeats that he is concerned with economic 'science' – not merely with the details of a 'particular case' – and that the presence of unexplained 'residuals', by generating further investigation, might lead to 'an extension and improvement of the theory itself':

> If there be anything which we could not have predicted, this constitutes a residual phenomenon, requiring further study for the purpose of explanation; and we must either search among the circumstances of the particular case until we find one which, on the principles of our existing theory, accounts for the unexplained phenomenon, or *we must turn back, and seek the explanation by an extension and improvement of the theory itself.*
>
> (Mill 1973–4 [1843]: 910, emphasis added)

There seems to be compelling evidence that Mill allowed formally and conspicuously for improvement of economic 'science', where the necessity for such improvement is revealed by a verification failure.

Mill on method: the behavioural axiom

Abstraction from the multitude of motivations that actually prompt action in a social context, and selection of the wealth maximisation axiom subject to the two 'perpetually antagonizing principles' (above, p. 242), is represented by Mill as a matter of practical necessity in the light of the 'complexity of causes':

> Not that any political economist was ever so absurd as to suppose that mankind are really thus constituted, but because this is the mode in which science must necessarily proceed. When an effect depends upon a concurrence of causes, those causes must be studied one at a time, and their laws separately investigated, if we wish, through the causes, to obtain the power of either predicting or controlling the effect; since the law of the effect is compounded of the laws of all the causes which determine it.
>
> (Mill 1967 [1836]: 322, cited 1973–4 [1843]: 902)

Here we focus on Mill's intention by his references to 'introspection' as the basis of the behavioural axiom (1967 [1836]: 329). Much more is involved than appears at first sight, since even within the 'complicated and manifold civilizations of the nations of Europe', there are discernible major behavioural differences. Consider the sharp contrast Mill made in the *System of Logic* between entrepreneurial motivation in Britain and the Continent:

> In political economy…empirical laws of human nature are tacitly assumed by English thinkers, which are calculated only for Great Britain and the United States. Among other things, an intensity of competition is constantly supposed, which, as a general mercantile fact, exists in no country in the world except those two. An English political economist, like his countrymen in general, has seldom learned that it is possible that men, in conducting the business of selling their goods over a counter, should care more about their ease or their vanity than about their pecuniary gain. Yet those who know the habits of the Continent of Europe are aware how apparently small a motive often outweighs the desire of money-getting, even in the operations which have money-getting as their direct object.
>
> (Mill 1973–4 [1843]: 907)

Given this sharp contrast, it is inconceivable that 'introspection' would yield the identical outcome in a British or American and (say) a French domain.[14] Yet Hirsch and de Marchi reject the conclusion that, for Mill, 'evidence drawn from introspection varies from time to time and place to place' (in Hollander 1985: 112–13), on the grounds that it 'run[s] together empirical and causal laws, on the one hand, and assumptions and implications on the other' (Hirsch and de Marchi 1990: 128, n3). This is spelled out in an earlier review by Hirsch, where Hollander's reading is said to go against 'both the letter and the spirit of Mill's position':

> Hollander argues (1985: 135) that for Mill 'the behavioral axioms of political economy... are "approximate generalizations",' which is counter to both the letter and the spirit of Mill's position. In Mill's philosophy science rests on causal laws which are invariant, exact, and universal and embedded in the premises of theory. One such causal law is the preference of mankind for a greater portion of wealth for a smaller. That is not to deny that Mill did admit that lower level generalizations or empirical laws could differ from place to place and time to time; he reconciled the exact and invariant causal law with the inexact empirical laws – or put somewhat differently, he explained the fact that the implications of the theory of political economy did not coincide with what actually happened in many places and many times – by bringing in 'disturbing causes' that accounted for the differences in empirical laws or generalizations. This made Mill far more open than the narrow thinkers, like Harriet Martineau, to whom even the implications of the theory of political economy, even without allowance for disturbing causes, were exact and universal. But it does not follow from this that for Mill 'the wealth-maximizing hypothesis... holds good only in the context of a specified nation and period' (Hollander, 136). Such a notion runs counter not only to Mill's views about the science of political economy but to his views of social science and science generally.
>
> (Hirsch 1986: 622)

Yet 'approximate generalization' happens to be *Mill's* term for the behavioural axioms:

> wherever it is sufficient to know how the great majority of the human race, or of some nation or class of persons, will think, feel, and act, these propositions are equivalent to universal ones. For the purposes of political and social science this *is* sufficient. As we formerly remarked [603], an approximate generalization is, in social inquiries, for most practical purposes equivalent to an exact one: that which is only probable when asserted of individual human beings indiscriminately selected, being certain when affirmed of the character and collective conduct of masses.
>
> (Mill 1973–4 [1843]: 847)

It is also Mill himself who, as we have seen, refers to 'the empirical laws of human nature' in describing the appropriateness of the wealth-maximisation axiom (and competition) for the analysis of Britain and the United States, but its inappropriateness in the analysis of Continental Europe.

So much for the letter of Mill's position. As for the spirit, both the terms 'approximate generalization' and 'empirical laws' are wholly appropriate as descriptions of the behavioural axioms, because Mill is attempting to convey their conditional nature in the context of the particular 'branches of social inquiry which have been cultivated as separate sciences' – conditional because of the primitive nature of the so-called 'science of ethology' and the weak understanding of 'the diversities of individual and national character' (905–6). For 'if we have not yet accounted for the empirical law – if it rests only on observation – there is no safety in applying it far beyond the limits of time, place and circumstance, in which the observations were made' (862); but the 'universal laws' – thus far uncovered – 'are those of the formation of character' (863), rather than a locally relevant behavioural axiom such as wealth maximisation.[15]

Hirsch, we have seen, also maintains that the (alleged) 'lower level generalisations or empirical laws' which do differ 'from place to place and time to time', are reconciled 'with the exact and invariant causal law' *by the device of disturbing causes*. Yet if the 'habits' of Continental Europe are such that 'the desire of money-getting, even in the operations which have money-getting as their direct object' is often outweighed by apparently small motives, it makes little sense to suppose that Mill would have adopted, for these locations, pecuniary maximisation as the main and acknowledged, or principal, objective to be embedded in the premises of theory, and have treated as 'disturbing causes' the predominating behaviour traits. As Mill distinctly expressed the matter: 'the generalizations [of political economy] must necessarily be relative to a given form of civilization and a given stage of social achievement' (1969 [1865]: 305).

The treatment in the *Essay* of the principle of population creates additional difficulties for the drawing of a sharply defined demarcation between theory and application in Mill. For Mill represented this principle as one of 'the most striking cases' – he specifies no other by name in this context – where the science of political economy 'interpolates into [its] expositions' behavioural patterns *not* dictated by wealth maximisation (and its two antagonising concomitants) rather than treat them as 'disturbing causes'. In such cases

> the strictness of purely scientific arrangement [is] thereby somewhat departed from for the sake of practical utility. So far as it is known, or may be presumed, that the conduct of mankind in their pursuit of wealth is under the collateral influence of any other of the properties of our nature than the desire of obtaining the greatest quantity of wealth with the least labour and self-denial, the conclusions of Political Economy will so far fail of being applicable to the explanation or

prediction of real events, until they are modified by a correct allowance for the degree of influence exercised by the other cause.

(Mill 1967 [1836]: 323)

Hirsch in fact sees here the 'one instance where the sharp separation between science and the application of science can be said to have given way', and attributes the 'breach' to Mill's wish to allow for 'purposes of instruction' (1992: 856n). Now it is true that in a paragraph that follows the remark regarding the population principle, Mill does refer to 'the didactic writer... [who] will naturally combine in his exposition, with the truths of the pure science, as many of the practical modifications as will, in his estimation, be most conducive to the usefulness of his work' (1967 [1836]: 323). But this paragraph – it closes the first section of the essay concerned with definition – does not relate specifically to the treatment of the population principle. Rather, Mill is reminding teachers of their obligation to deal with 'practical modifications' in the sense of 'disturbing causes' within their expositions. What he had to say of the population principle specifically related to its actual absorption by the science, albeit that it did not turn on the main psychological law of maximisation modified by the two perpetually antagonising forces. Does classical theory, for Mill, somehow partially exclude or place in a secondary class of importance the population mechanism because it is not based on the three psychological laws and is only allowed in for the sake of 'practical utility'? Needless to say, the single issue that most preoccupied Mill theoretically – because of the implications for welfare – is that of population growth in the presence of scarce land. It is 'practical utility' in the sense of policy implication (not merely instruction) that justified its incorporation into the theoretical structure.[16]

Price discrimination and 'monopolistic competition'

We proceed now to our second task, which is to lay out a series of theoretical modifications actually introduced by Mill in the light of empirical evidence. In some cases the evidence even undermines the basic assumption regarding maximising behaviour.

Mill declared famously that

> only through the principle of competition has political economy any pretension to the character of a science.... Assume competition to be their exclusive regulator, and principles of broad generality and scientific precision may be laid down, according to which they will be regulated. The political economist justly deems this his proper business: and as an abstract or hypothetical science, political economy cannot be required to do, and indeed cannot do, anything more.

(1965 [1848]: 239)

Similarly, the analysis of price formation in 'On exchange' sets out with the declaration that only in so far as prices are determined by competition, 'can they be reduced to any assignable law' (460). It is on these grounds that the analysis – turning on 'the axiom . . . that there cannot be for the same article, of the same quality, two prices in the same market' – is limited to the wholesale sector, since individual consumers *typically* fail to act in maximising fashion:

> The values and prices . . . to which our conclusions apply, are mercantile values and prices; such prices are as quoted in price-currents; prices in the wholesale markets, in which buying as well as selling is a matter of business; in which the buyers take pains to know, and generally do know, the lowest price at which an article of a given quality can be obtained. . . . Our propositions will be true in a much more qualified sense, of retail prices; the prices paid in shops for articles of personal consumption. For such things there often are not merely two, but many prices, in different shops, or even in the same shop; habit and accident having as much to do in the matter as general causes. Purchases for private use, even by people in business, are not always made on business principles: the feelings which come into play in the operation of getting, and in that of spending their income, are often extremely different. Either from indolence, or carelessness, or because people think it fine to pay and ask no questions, three-fourths of those who can afford it give much higher prices than necessary for the things they consume; while the poor often do the same from ignorance and defect of judgment, want of time for searching and making inquiry, and not unfrequently, from coercion, open or disguised.
>
> (Mill 1965 [1848]: 460)[17]

Now, notwithstanding his declaration regarding 'scientific' economics being limited to fully fledged competition, Mill does attempt to provide a theoretical account of observed retail-pricing practice in the presence of non-maximising consumer behaviour. For the very circumstance that pecuniary interest does not apply at the retail level, gives rise to price discrimination; the retailer acts in maximising fashion by resorting to price discrimination, but the consumer's *failure* to act 'on business principles' makes such discrimination possible:

> Not only are there in every large town, and in almost every trade, cheap shops and dear shops, but the same shop often sells the same article at different prices to different customers: and, as a general rule, each retailer adapts his scale of prices to the class of customers whom he expects. The wholesale trade, in the great articles of commerce, is really under the domination of competition. There, the buyers as well as the sellers are traders or manufacturers, and their purchases are not

influenced by indolence or vulgar finery [1865: 'nor depend on the smaller motives of personal convenience']: but are business transactions. (Mill 1965 [1848]: 242–3)[18]

Moreover, the retail trade is also characterised by Mill along lines of what today would be termed 'monopolistic competition', namely markets subject to freedom of entry, with competition 'instead of lowering prices, merely divid[ing] the gains of the high price among a greater number of dealers' (243). More specifically, 'custom' indicated a mark-up over the wholesale prices, and what competition there was avoided price cutting:

> even in countries of most active competition, custom also has a considerable share in determining the profits of trade. . . . There has been ['is', till 1862] in England a kind of notion, how widely prevailing I know not, that fifty per cent is a proper and suitable rate of profit in retail transactions. . . . If this custom were universal, and strictly adhered to, competition indeed would still operate, but the customer would not derive any benefit from it, at least as to price; the way in which it would diminish the advantages of those engaged in the retail trade, would be by a greater sub-division of the business.
>
> (Mill 1965 [1848]: 409–10)[19]

From 1852 on, Mill referred to the consequential losses in *efficiency* resulting when price competition had 'a limited dominion over retail prices':

> the share of the whole produce of land and labour which is absorbed in the remuneration of mere distributors, continues exorbitant; and there is no function in the economy of society which supports a number of persons so disproportioned to the amount of work to be performed.
>
> (410)

This formulation implies recognition of excess capacity.[20]

Mill remarked on the universality of the method, rather than the specific content, of economic theory (1967 [1834]: 225–6; 1969 [1865]: 305–6). His absorption into the theoretical model of features of reality reflecting 'custom' – notwithstanding his strong statements implying the contrary (see our Conclusion, below) – illustrates this theme. The entire analysis entails, in fact, an attempt to account theoretically for observations of contemporary market structures. It is of some interest that Mill found the ability to differentiate, by location if not by product, already weakened in the 'great emporia of trade' (1965 [1848]: 410) and likely to be further undermined by the transport revolution which breaks down the dependency of consumers on local dealers (243). It is thus a matter of circumstance how 'custom' is to be classified; in some instances its influence is so strong and pervasive that it must be treated as the *general* cause, relegating to competition the role of *disturbance*:

hitherto it is only in the great centres of business that retail transactions have been chiefly, or even much, determined, by competition. Elsewhere it rather acts, when it acts at all, as an occasional disturbing influence; the habitual regulator is custom, modified from time to time by notions existing in the minds of purchasers and sellers, of some kind of equity or justice.

Wage structure and non-competing groups

Mill's famous treatment of the wage structure similarly belies his strong declaration that analytical economics is constrained to purely competitive structures. Adam Smith (1937 [1776]: 100) had relied on the competitive market process to keep relative earnings in line, assuring equalising differentials and recognising only institutional constraints on geographic and occupational mobility. This analysis, initially accepted by Mill (1965 [1848]: 381–2n), was abandoned in the third edition, and on grounds of its empirical invalidity: 'it is altogether a false view of the state of facts, to present this as the relation which generally exists between agreeable and disagreeable employments' (383).[21] For the logic of the competitive structure presumed the global labour market to be in equilibrium; taking account of general unemployment and also allowing for 'natural and artificial monopolies', the differentials become distorted:

> {W}hen the supply of labour so far exceeds the demand that to find employment at all is an uncertainty, and to be offered it on any terms a favor, the case is totally the reverse. Desirable labourers, those whom every one is anxious to have, can still exercise a choice. The undesirable must take what they can get. . . . Partly from this cause and partly from the natural and artificial monopolies . . . the inequalities of wages are generally in an opposite direction to the equitable principle of compensation erroneously represented by Adam Smith as the general law of the remuneration of labour.
>
> (Mill 1965 [1848]: 383, emphasis added)

The reference to 'natural and artificial monopolies' involves a matter which 'Smith, and most other political economists, have taken into far too little account, and from inattention to which, he has given a most imperfect exposition of the wide difference between the remuneration of common labour and that of skilled employments' (385–6). We touch on the celebrated concept of 'non-competing industrial groups' – a term coined by Cairnes – reflecting social and financial obstacles to upward mobility. In his account, Mill makes some allowance for contemporary improvements due to broader educational opportunities; but there was still 'a much greater disparity than can be accounted for on the principle of competition' (387).

The 'non-competing groups' analysis has been described as 'the first major advance beyond [Smith's] theory in its recognition of the barriers to mobility created by the costs of education' (Stigler 1965: 7–8). This case is particularly interesting in the light of Hirsch's choice of wage differentials as an instance of an *excluded* disturbing cause:

> No matter how great the effect of a cause in a specific instance, if it is not common to a large class of cases it is in Mill's view a disturbing cause. For example, the argument based on economic theory that labor will move from company A to B because B pays higher wages, may have an insufficient basis because in this specific instance we have not taken account of the fact that working conditions in company A are better, with the result that the movement of labor may be in a direction opposite to what was expected. But this does not affect the fact that the level of wages paid is a general cause and working conditions a disturbing cause generally, as Mill conceives it.
>
> (Hirsch 1992: 854–5)

Excluded in this sense the matter of differentials may once have been, until the empirical evidence revealed the necessity to absorb the phenomenon into the formal model; what was once a 'disturbing' cause had been rendered by events 'general'. There is, we again find, no once-and-for-all distinction such as Hirsch and other Mill scholars envisage (847, 853).

The role of inventories and business cycles

In his famous essay 'On the influence of consumption on production', Mill refers to the importance, from a growth perspective, attached to the stimulation of consumption before political economy had achieved its 'comparatively scientific character' (1967 [1844]: 262). But now – unlike the case in earlier papers of 1823 and 1824 – Mill admitted to *'some strong appearance of evidence'* which had misled those who maintained the 'palpable absurdities' regarding consumption (263–4, emphasis added). For he was troubled by a theorem maintaining the impossibility of 'general gluts', considering firm evidence that the fortunes of the individual producer obviously depended 'in a great measure...upon the number of his customers', such that 'every additional purchase does really add to his profits' (266). More specifically, Mill points to 'three signal proofs' of this fact:

> Of the importance of the fact which has just been noticed there are three signal proofs. One is, the large sum often given for the goodwill of a particular business. Another is, the large rent which is paid for shops in certain situations, near a great thoroughfare for example, which have no advantage except that the occupier may expect a larger body of customers, and be enabled to turn over his capital more quickly. Another

is, that in many trades, there are some dealers who sell articles of an equal quality at a lower price than other dealers.

(Mill 1967 [1844]: 268)

This anomaly had to be explained, and the conclusion reached is that the fallacy of composition is not here relevant, for, even at the aggregate level, expanded consumption may indeed act as a stimulus. Mill, in brief, was absorbing into the theoretical structure features derived from observation of the business world.

The argument turns partly upon the observed circumstance that advanced economies cannot operate at full capacity in the literal sense, since inventories (and money funds) must be available at various stages of production to satisfy expected sales (and make necessary purchases). This is a 'technological' matter, for the 'perpetual non-employment of a large portion of capital, is the price we pay for the division of labour'. However, should the turnover period be somehow reduced, idle capital might be actively utilised in the expansion of physical plant, materials and wage goods (268–9). In brief, the sustainable growth rate of the system can be increased by 'technological' advances which, reducing the uncertainty and ignorance characterising even normal exchange relations, permit lower minimum inventory holdings. Yet the flexibility provided by inventories in a world of imperfect knowledge was essential to the smooth working of the system, and excess capacity of this nature could never safely be totally dispensed with (274–5). Mill warned therefore, against *unjustified* increases in turnover rates reflecting speculative purchases which encourage increased output and real capital construction but of an unsustainable order. 'The currency' is identified as a possible cause of 'general delusion', Mill conceding that 'an increase of production really takes place during the progress of depreciation', but only 'as long as the existence of depreciation is not suspected; and it is this which gives to the fallacies of the currency school, principally represented by Mr [Thomas] Attwood, all the little plausibility they possess' (275). When the 'delusion' dissipates these extended projects are proved unsustainable. It is noteworthy that Mill attributed Attwood's error to erroneous method – an appeal to 'practical experience' or an inductive logic, namely that because in 1825 general full employment had been achieved at a high level of prices, it was desirable to return to that situation on the presumption that the former had been caused by the latter. That full capacity was achieved in 1825, and in fact that capacity was then expanded, Mill attributed to a 'state of insane delusion, in its very nature temporary' – the excessive pressure on capacity usage and unjustifiable additions to capacity during the upswing constituting 'partly the cause of their lying idle now' (1967 [1833]: 191).

Mill's appreciation of destabilising speculation was the prologue, in the 'Influence of consumption in production', to an impressive discussion of regular cyclical variation in speculative mood characterising contemporary business activity:

> In the present state of the commercial world, mercantile transactions being carried on upon an immense scale, but the remote causes of fluctuations in prices being very little understood, so that unreasonable hopes and unreasonable fears alternatively rule with tyrannical sway over the minds of a majority of the mercantile public; general eagerness to buy and general reluctance to buy, succeed one another in a manner more or less marked, at brief intervals. Except during short periods of transition, there is almost always either great briskness of business or great stagnation; either the principal producers of almost all the leading articles of industry have as many orders as they can possibly execute, or the dealers in almost all commodities have their warehouses full of unsold goods.
>
> (Mill 1967 [1844]: 275)

The rejection of the Law of Markets in its extreme form, forced on Mill by the evidence,[22] turns on the contrast between a barter and a money system, allowing with eminent clarity for excess aggregate supply of goods with a counterpart in excess demand for money to hold:

> In order to render the argument for the impossibility of an excess of all commodities applicable to the case in which a circulating medium is employed, money must itself be considered as a commodity. It must, undoubtedly, be admitted that there cannot be an excess of all other commodities, and an excess of money at the same time.
>
> (277)

But not only does Mill provide a picture of temporary stagnation generated if people 'liked better to possess money than any other commodity', he suggests also a mechanism that assures recovery, such that the stagnation is only temporary, precluding unemployment equilibrium. Consider his observation at this juncture in the argument that real losses are suffered by those firms obliged to sell at low prices, in consequence of the fall in the purchasing power of the revenue on the recovery of prices, and the related notion that the expectation of recovery encourages firms to delay sales wherever possible:

> If it be said that when all commodities fall in price, the fall is of no consequence . . . we answer that this would be true if the low prices were to last for ever. But as it is certain that prices will rise again sooner or later, the person who is obliged by necessity to sell his commodity at a low money price is really a sufferer, the money he receives sinking shortly to its ordinary value. Every person, therefore, delays selling if he can, keeping his capital unproductive in the mean time, and sustaining

the consequent loss of interest. There is stagnation to those who are not obliged to sell, and distress to those who are.

Evidently at some stage during the crisis, the state of expectations has reversed itself, for the original feature under analysis had been the general attempt to *add* to money balances from sales proceeds – a 'general anxiety to sell'. The juxtaposition of this transition in mood with the emphasis upon the temporary nature of the crisis suggests that recovery sets in with expanded purchases in response to expected price increases.[23]

In the *Principles*, Mill distinguished his position from that of Malthus, Chalmers and de Sismondi, who, so he alleged, asserted that expansion of products in the aggregate is *necessarily* accompanied by a deficiency of purchasing power, thereby precluding sales at unchanged prices and profits (1965 [1848]: 571, cf. 66–8, 739–40). This 'over-production error' – like the error of Attwood – flowed from a misconceived appeal to experience, a reference to 'mercantile facts' which were better accounted for in terms of his own conception of commercial crisis:

> it is a great error to suppose . . . that a commercial crisis is the effect of a general excess of production. It is simply the consequence of an excess of speculative purchases. It is not a gradual advent of low prices, but a sudden recoil from prices extravagantly high; its immediate cause is a contraction of credit, and the remedy is, not a diminution of supply, but the restoration of confidence.
>
> (574)

The facts of the case pointed only to *temporary* price and profit movements, the problem of profitability residing precisely in their non-permanent character.[24]

We shall have more to say on the cycle in the next section. We would emphasise here that the methodological implication of the episode demonstrates how misleading is the common emphasis on Mill's formal statements regarding the behavioural laws (above, p. 242). For the formal essay on method makes no mention of that 'universal propensity of mankind to over-estimate the chances in their own favour' referred to in the early paper recognising a cyclical pattern (1967 [1826]: 77), and absorbed into the theoretical analysis of the cyclical phenomenon in that paper and in the 'Influence of consumption on production' and the *Principles*. Why Mill neglected to mention this alleged 'universal propensity' in the essay on method[25] is an interesting question (on which see de Marchi 1998: 23–4); but evidently the theoretical model cannot be said to be given once and for all, if a particular behavioural trait is treated not as a disturbing cause, but absorbed into the axiomatic base in order to account for observed cyclical phenomena.

Ricardian growth theory

Mill stood firmly by Ricardian orthodoxy as far as concerns secular trends. Yet the striking features of his account in the *Principles* of British conditions over several decades, are constancy of the profit rate despite rapid accumulation and rapid population growth, constancy of the real wage at a level above 'subsistence' (perhaps even an upward trend), and impressive evidence of productivity increase (1965 [1848]: 742, 159). The actual circumstances thus stood in sharp contrast with the theoretical, in that both capital and population were proceeding at a very rapid pace with the profit rate unchanged over time and the wage rate at worst unchanged and perhaps rising. As noted above (p. 243), one view has it that for Mill, the basic theory is inviolable, considering the character of the assumptions, and not subject to modification. Such methodological grounds would account for his refusal to concede the irrelevance of Ricardian theory with the passage of time. The evidence marshalled thus far points directly against this notion of the insulation of theory, suggesting that we must look elsewhere to account for Mill's continued reliance on a diminishing-returns-based model.

There is first the matter of Mill's use of theory in policy application. Specifically, as Mill read the evidence, prudential behaviour positively directed towards the achievement of higher wages characterised only skilled labourers in the British case (346), for the high earnings of the unskilled town workers had not encouraged a noticeable alteration in their conception of the minimum standard. Accordingly, future slackening in the growth rate of capital might lead to a fall in wages to the level of the common farm labourer. This was the ever-present shadow – for there was no guarantee the countervailing forces would continue at play – leading Mill to minimise labour scarcity. The same shadow was cast over the agricultural sector. There, wages had been kept up above subsistence by the attraction of labour into the towns, a movement that might decelerate, considering 'the present habits of the people' – again a reference to the unskilled (351). We must keep in mind also his evaluation that it was 'much more difficult to raise than to lower, the scale of living which the labourer will consider as more indispensable than marrying and having a family', leading him to question 'all propositions ascribing a self-repairing quality to the calamities which befal the labouring classes' (341–2). That Mill retained the Ricardian model can therefore be accounted for by a belief in its continued relevance from a policy perspective, rather than an alleged methodologically based insulation.

Some might denigrate this sort of position as 'Malthus mongering'. But we can see nothing unreasonable in a concern to assure behaviour modification on the part of the unskilled, considering the uncertain future of technology and industrial supremacy. For under adverse conditions in these respects, the model 'predicts' deceleration of the rate of accumulation and reduced real wages, and nothing that had occurred over the preceding decades could be said to have refuted this 'prediction', considering the countervailing forces which had been, and still were, at play. These Mill was most careful to spell out:

> To fulfil the conditions of the hypothesis, we must suppose an entire cessation of the exportation of capital for foreign investment. No more capital sent abroad for railways or loans; no more emigrants taking capital with them, to the colonies, or to other countries; no fresh advances made, or credits given, by bankers or merchants to their foreign correspondents. We must also assume that there are no fresh loans for unproductive expenditure, by the government, or on mortgage, or otherwise; and none of the waste of capital which now takes place by the failure of undertakings which people are tempted to engage in by the hope of a better income than can be obtained in safe paths at the present habitually low rate of profit. We must suppose the entire savings of the community to be annually invested in really productive employment within the country itself; and no new channels opened by industrial inventions, or by a more extensive substitution of the best known processes for inferior ones.
>
> (Mill 1965 [1848]: 739)

The charge that Mill 'insulated' the basic Ricardian growth model by 'empty[ing] the appropriate *ceteris paribus* clauses of whatever specific content they may once have had' (Blaug 1992: 65) is evidently baseless. To the contrary, he carefully investigated the record, *filling and extending* the *ceteris paribus* pound – the list extends far beyond the assumed state of technology, which is what commentators like to focus on – in line with his own recommendation to examine unexplained residuals (see above, second section).[26]

The foregoing is one line followed by Mill, in which the 'disturbing causes' – including technological change – are treated as exogenous phenomena unrelated to the land-scarcity-based tendencies.[27] A second line involves actual modification to the land-scarcity-based model in a very novel way better to account for the complete record. We have in mind the impressive integration of secular trend and cycle, and pick up the thread of the preceding section.

Of speculative periods Mill observed that 'all times are so, more or less' (1965 [1848]: 512), but he elaborated in detail on the 'quiescent' period and its place in the cycle.[28] The quiescent period entails expansion rather than stationariness: 'Each person transacts his ordinary amount of business, and no more; or increases it only in correspondence with the increase of his capital or connexion, or with the gradual growth of the demand for his commodity, occasioned by the public prosperity' (662). This expansion constitutes the necessary condition for the generation of regular cyclical fluctuations, considering the consequences flowing from the downward 'tendency' of the profit rate:

the gradual process of accumulation...in the great commercial countries is sufficiently rapid to account for the almost periodic recurrence of...fits of speculation; since when a few years have elapsed without a crisis, and no new and tempting channels for investment have been opened in the meantime, there is always found to have occurred in those few years so large an increase of capital seeking investment, as to have lowered considerably the rate of interest, whether indicated by the prices of securities or the rate of discount on bills; and this diminution tempts the possessor to incur hazards in hopes of a more considerable return.

(Mill 1965 [1848]: 651)

Again, that 'revulsions are almost periodical' is attributed – in the chapter on the 'Tendency of profits to a minimum' itself – to 'the very tendency of profits which we are considering'; for

the diminished scale of all safe gains, inclines people to give a ready ear to any projects which hold out, though at the risk of loss, the hope of a higher rate of profit; and speculations ensue, which, with the subsequent revulsions, destroy or transfer to foreigners, a considerable amount of capital, produce a temporary rise of interest and profit, make room for fresh accumulations, and the same round is recommenced.

(742)

Capital wastage in these contexts, be it noted, is not treated as a 'disturbing cause', to the extent that it is *induced* by the falling profit rate. There is, however, a further modification along similar lines – Mill's endogenisation of both invention and innovatory processes:

When the capital accumulated is so great and the rate of annual accumulation so rapid, that the country is only kept from attaining the stationary state by the emigration of capital, or by continual improvements in production; any circumstance [such as a profits tax] which virtually lowers the rate of profits cannot be without a decided influence on these phenomena. It may operate in different ways. The curtailment of profit, and the consequent increased difficulty in making a fortune or obtaining a subsistence by the employment of capital, may act as stimulus to inventions, and to the use of them when made. If improvements in production are much accelerated, and if these improvements cheapen, directly or indirectly, any of the things habitually consumed by the laborer, profits may rise, and rise sufficiently to make up for all that is taken from them by the tax.

(Mill 1965 [1848]: 827)[29]

Mill refers here specifically to the consequences of a tax on profits, rather than of the secular fall in the return on capital itself. Whether this was a deliberate omission is unclear. But the context involves a system operating at a 'low' range of profit such that any further reduction, as by a profits tax, would generate the results in question; at a higher range the artificial reduction might be less effective. The treatment of technical progress in the secular context purely as a 'disturbing cause' therefore becomes inappropriate. And in fact, Mill actually designates the profit-technology relation as a 'tendency' – 'the artificial abstraction of a portion of profits would have a real tendency to accelerate improvements in production' – according it formally the same status as pressure on profits of scarce land. As with 'capital wastage', the concept of a 'disturbing cause' is seen not to be given once and for all; all depends on context. It is true that Mill provided no hard and fast rule to determine when a disturbing cause should be incorporated into the analysis. Generality and quantitative effect were both considered; but beyond this the matter is left open-ended. Yet his appreciation of the enormous complexities of causation in social science led him to focus constantly on the adequacy of the causal structure involved.

The inverse wage-profit relationship

The Ricardian inverse wage-profit relation illustrates Mill's response to an 'anomaly' created by new quantitative evidence, in contrast to the foregoing instances involving qualitative evidence. We have in this episode a patently honest attempt to 'test' Ricardian theory against the evidence, Mill going to considerable lengths to acquire reliable data and seeking to strengthen the underpinnings of the basic explanatory model.

On Ricardian principles, the return on capital in the US should have been lower than in Britain, whereas the reverse was the case:

> Have you formed any opinion, or can you refer me to any good authority, respecting the ordinary rate of mercantile and manufacturing profit in the United States? I have hitherto been under the impression that it is much higher than in England, because the rate of interest is so. But I have lately been led to doubt the truth of this impression, because it seems inconsistent with known facts respecting wages in America. High profits are compatible with a high reward of the labourer through low prices of necessaries, but they are not compatible with a high cost of labour, and it seems to me that the very high *money* wages of labour in America, the precious metals not being of lower value there than in Europe, indicates a high cost as well as a high remuneration of labour.
>
> (Mill to Cairnes, 1 December 1864, in Mill 1965 [1848]: 1055)

The higher US interest rate, Mill himself went on to suggest, might be accounted for by the fact that investment was, by and large, of European origin, and this required an extra inducement (1056). Yet he remained uneasy, and appealed for more precise statistical data that might throw light on the issue (1088–9). 'I am much obliged to you', he wrote to Cairnes soon after, 'for the trouble you have taken to get information respecting the rate of profit in the United States, but ... [t]he scientific question remains as great a puzzle to me as ever' (1092); for the new data provided by Cairnes' US informants did not overcome the 'scientific puzzle' – the apparent refutation of Ricardian distribution theory:

> From their statements it is clear that the ordinary notion of the extravagantly high rate of profit in the United States is an exaggeration, and there seems some doubt whether the rate is at all higher than in England. But that does not resolve the puzzle, as even equality of profits, in the face of the higher cost of labour, indicated by higher money wages, is as paradoxical as superiority. This is the scientific difficulty I mentioned, and I cannot yet see my way through it.
>
> (1093)

Cairnes' proposed solution – the incomparability of the monetary units of the two centres in which wages were expressed – did not satisfy him:

> As far as it goes, I fully admit it; but my difficulty was, and still is, in believing that there can be *so great* a difference between the cost of obtaining the precious metals in America and in England, as to make the enormous difference which seems to exist in money wages, consistent with a difference the contrary way in the cost of labour.
>
> (1093–4)

Shortly thereafter, he cryptically suggested that he had hit on a satisfactory solution to the apparent anomaly: 'I am inclined to think that the real solution of the difficulty, and the only one it admits of, has been given by myself in a subsequent place' (1095). The proposed solution, not spelled out in detail, reverts to the cost of obtaining the precious metals – a line Mill had himself originally abandoned – as elaborated in the chapter 'Of money, considered as an imported commodity', which takes into account the broad implications of the general theory of international values, including transportation costs (619–20).

Concluding remarks: sources of interpretive differences

It remains to sort out the implications of the foregoing demonstrations, and to assess how our characterisation of Mill differs from the Mill commonly portrayed in the literature. The difference stems from the relative weights placed on the importance of *à priorism* and verification in Mill's method. For Hirsch, 'extensive feedback from the verification component of practical application to revision of the basic model of economic science' is 'not consistent with Mill's *à priori* approach to economic science' (1992: 860–1); and his 'disagreement' with Hollander, as he puts it, 'arises primarily because

I see Mill's a priorism as being far more important in his approach to science than Hollander does' (861). He even has Hollander attributing to Mill 'a kind of anti-*à priori* view' (865), insisting for his part that the *à priori* method for Mill is

> *the* method of economics... and its major characteristic is that the results it yields refer only to what happens *generally*.... This being the case it obviously makes little sense to test theory by observing how well its implications accord with what actually happens in specific instances. Even if retrodictive tests fail, the theory could still be true in general. That is why, of course, detailed investigation of specific experience is not considered by Mill to be part of the *a priori* and could not be considered part of the business of science.
>
> (Hirsch 1992: 861)

We do not intend in any way to play down the *a prioristic* dimension to Mill's scientific methodology; indeed, we maintain that Millian verification, since it is not part of *a priori* theorising as such, need not necessarily be carried out by specialist theorists. Rather, verification plays on theory indirectly, by suggesting to the theorist the need to improve his or her models in order to assure their practical relevance, especially for policy recommendation.[30] Furthermore, we fully agree with Hirsch and de Marchi that a failure of a retrodictive test – after allowance of course for 'disturbing causes' – will not *necessarily* affect the basic theory, only that it *might* do so. Our point is that Mill, realising this possibility, recommended continuous verification of theory and engaged in the constant reappraisal of theory in the light of evidence. Even the limited number of case studies considered above demonstrates that he engaged in major modifications of theory, better to allow for, and make sense of, new or newly recognised empirical evidence manifested in the 'actual commerce of human affairs' (1965 [1848]: 239) or the 'state of facts' (380, 383).[31]

Our conclusion is that Mill focused on observed phenomena that required to be accounted for analytically, frequently proceeding in line with his formal methodological account whereby, in the face of extreme causal multiplicity, the researcher might 'invert' the operation of deduction and induction, and commence with an observation requiring theoretical explanation; and that his attempt to account for anomalous facts yielded the novel imperfect-competition and wage-structure analyses and the abandonment of Say's Identity in general, and discernment of a linkage between secular trend and cycle in particular – all, in fact, major contributions to theory. On our reading, while Mill's notion of 'verification' is a far cry from a statistical test to which he would have objected strongly (see Peart 1995), his engagement with the real world is most impressive in its qualitative detail.[32]

How do we account for the widely divergent readings of Mill? There is, first, Mill's strongly worded statements – preeminently that verification 'is no part of the business of science' (above, p. 241). Professor Hirsch has focused in this context on who, professionally speaking, is to undertake the process of verification. This emerges in his reaction to a statement in the *Essay* regarding the function of the economic theorist:

> Although, therefore, a philosopher be convinced that no general truths can be attained in the affairs of nations by the *à posteriori* road, it does not the less behove him, according to the measure of his opportunities, to sift and scrutinize the details of every specific experiment. Without this, he may be an excellent professor of abstract science; for a person may be of great use who points out correctly what effects will follow from certain combinations of possible circumstances, in whatever tract of the extensive region of hypothetical cases those combinations may be found. He stands in the same relation to the legislator, as the mere geographer to the practical navigator; telling him the latitude and longitude of all sorts of places, but not how to find whereabouts he himself is sailing. If, however, he does no more than this, he must rest contented to take no share in practical politics; to have no opinion, or to hold it with extreme modesty, on the applications which should be made of his doctrines to existing circumstances.
>
> (Mill 1967 [1836]: 333)

Hirsch (1992: 856–7) finds here proof that Mill could not have believed 'that verification was the major route, or even *one* major route, through which revisions in the basic model were made'; for had this been his position, 'it would then have been vital for the professor of the abstract science to be concerned with verification; otherwise the professor would cut himself off from the basic source for the improvement of the basic model'. Rather, for Mill, 'the economic scientist, *as economic scientist*, need rely on introspection and casual observation' (original emphasis).

Such an interpretation, however, neglects Mill's insistence that the 'philosopher' is 'behove[n] ... according to the measure of his opportunities, to sift and scrutinize the details of every specific experiment'. Why should he put the matter this way if verification is not necessary to theory revision? The issue relates to the immediately preceding proposition in the *Essay* that verification

> often reveals to us that the basis itself of our whole argument is insufficient; that the data, from which we had reasoned, comprise only a part, and not always the most important part, of the circumstances by which the result is really determined.
>
> (cited above, p. 248)

'Such oversights', Mill believed, 'are committed by very good reasoners', and are 'a kind of error to which those are peculiarly liable whose views are the largest and most philosophical' (above, pp. 248–9). It seems plausible that when Mill referred to a neglect by the 'philosopher' of specific experience as an 'oversight' and 'a kind of error', he meant to be taken seriously. Most important, what would be the purpose of verification should it yield flaws in the body of theory (as Mill insists that it might) that may be ignored by theorists? A fundamental objective of theory, for Mill, is to serve in application, and the test of useful theory for that end is satisfactory retrodiction; yet on the reading of Mill we oppose there is no sort of verification failure that is to be allowed to affect the body of theory.

We do recognise that there is no necessity for the theorist himself to engage in verification; he need only be attentive to the outcome of verification, perhaps undertaken by others. Mill says just this when he expresses the yet-to-be-achieved ideal:

> But while the philosopher and the practical man bandy half-truths with one another, we may seek far without finding one who, placed on a higher eminence of thought, comprehends as a whole what they see only in separate parts; who can make the anticipations of the philosopher guide the observations of the practical man, and the specific experience of the practical man *warn the philosopher where something is to be added to his theory.*
>
> (Mill 1967 [1836]: 334–5, emphasis added)

But however the tasks are allocated,[33] theoretical demonstration amounted only to conditional demonstration – 'a demonstration nisi – a proof at all times liable to be set aside by the addition of a single new fact to the hypothesis' (334).

Our reading is reinforced by recalling that while verification may reveal the need for improvement in the axiomatic foundation or even in the logical process itself, it is not itself a device for the derivation of complex causal relations in the face of the problem of 'composition of causes'. That remains the function of *ratiocination*.[34]

As we have seen, Mill left himself open to misreading by some of his pithy formulations. Another striking instance occurs in his account of 'the creation of a distinct branch of [social] science' turning on 'one class of circumstances only', such that 'even when other circumstances interfere, the ascertainment of the effect due to the one class . . . is a sufficiently intimate and difficult business to make it expedient to perform it *once for all* and then allow for the effect of modifying circumstances' (1973–4 [1843]: 901, emphasis added). This and similar expressions would doubtless encourage the interpretation that we are challenging. But in the light of the evidence provided above, Mill must have intended not 'once for all' literally, but only a conditional, empirically based, first approximation. Mill himself, in this very context, justifies a specialist economics on the grounds that the relevant phenomena '*mainly* depend, at least in the first resort, on one class of circumstances only'. In brief, the behavioural axioms themselves are 'provisional'; and the specialist procedure only worked, 'even provisionally', when 'the diversities of character between different nations or different times enter as influencing causes only in a secondary degree' (906).[35] Accordingly, as he put the matter in a general account of hypothetical science, it is only 'if we find, and in proportion as we find, the assumptions to be true' that the process 'may be performed once for all, and the results held ready to be employed as the occasions turn up for use' (259).

Mill's forceful statements championing 'the method *a priori* in Political Economy' provide a further illustration. We suggest that they reflect his hostility towards the 'inductivists', and his condemnation of irresponsible and biased appeals to experience for substantiating causal relations.[36] As with all the classical economists, abstraction and deduction were held to be indispensable.[37] But this does not mean that he denied the essential role of 'experience' in verifying and possibly generating improvements to the theoretical formulation. His formal exclusion of 'verification' from the realm of deductive theory reflected not a belief that it can have no effect on theory, but the indirect nature of any effect it may have.

There is too the uncompromising assertion that the scientific basis for economics turned on the axiom of 'competition'. Yet we have seen that Mill himself proceeds on an 'unorthodox' behavioural basis, entailing non-maximising consumer behaviour – only some instances of retail pricing can be described in terms of high search costs – and pricing decisions by firms entailing 'customary' mark-ups, to achieve an analysis of price discrimination, and also one of monopolistic competition which recognised the efficiency losses of excess capacity with reduced market shares for each 'competitive' firm. Even custom is thus absorbed into the model to a degree, providing perhaps an instance of Mill's observation in the essay that 'disturbing causes ... which operate through the same law of human nature out of which the general principles of the science arise ... might always be brought within the pale of the abstract science, if it were worth while' (above, p. 247).

There are doubtless other explanations for the view that Mill excessively championed *a priorism*. Consider Mill's response to the apparent anomaly created for the Ricardian inverse wage–profit relation by the comparative US–UK data (above, eighth section). It is impossible to tell what steps he would have taken had he still remained unable to account for the empirical record. But until such time, he treated the Ricardian distribution model as 'robust', for there is in his approach a basic confidence in its validity, reflecting a belief that 1817 opened up a new era in theoretical economics, which would not in all likelihood be reversed. Here a suggestion by Schwartz comes into play – that Mill's philosophical perspective played down the likelihood of fundamental revisions (Schwartz 1972: 236–7); it is theory 'improvement' on the basis of the accumulation of factual knowledge rather than 'displacement' that is expected to flow from the testing process.[38] This orientation might lie behind the unfortunate pronouncements that the theory of competitive value neared perfection (1965 [1848]: 456); Mill allowed himself to be carried away, for we know that he applauded ongoing improvements such as those by W. T. Thornton, and, of course, himself made major contributions to the theory of equilibration. Such strong statements, however, do not negate Mill's clear allowances in principle and practice for the improvement of theory in the light of empirical evidence.

Notes

1 Sandra Peart, Department of Economics, Baldwin-Wallace College, Berea, Ohio, USA.

2 On Mill's intentions by 'the present enjoyment of costly indulgences', see below, note 18.

3 See also 326:

> The conclusions of Political Economy, consequently, like those of geometry, are only true as the common phrase is, *in the abstract*, that is, they are only true under certain suppositions, in which none but general causes – causes common to the *whole class* of cases under consideration – are taken into account.

4 See also de Marchi 1998: 22, 24–5. Coleman 1996 extends this sort of position to the whole body of 'English classical economics'.

5 Hirsch maintains that though Hollander (1985: 127) recognises 'that the basic model might indeed be impervious to verification', he 'considers it as only a remote possibility'. Hollander's original statement is actually neutral regarding the matter of likelihood:

> the basic model might indeed be impervious to verification . . . but [it] is conceivable that the testing procedure yields new information of general relevance – rather than of particular relevance in a specific case – and if that is so it must have an impact on the model.
>
> (Hollander 1985: 126)

This latter conclusion is stated too strongly; it *might* have an impact on the model is all that is intended.

6 Verification helps 'with the discovery of disturbing causes rather than the more general ones, and . . . would, except in very rare instances, therefore leave the basic model of an advanced science unaffected' (1992: 853); a failed test via retrodiction 'would not necessarily show up any shortcomings in the science but only that these causes are special and therefore are not included as part of science' (847–8); Mill 'gives the distinct impression that finding general causes not already known does not happen very often' (855); Mill

> did not seem to envisage that there would be much of a chance for verification to be a stimulus for revision of the basic model; rather, he leaves the impression that it is considerably more likely to lead to the discovery of disturbing causes which help only in the *application* of science.
>
> (859; 'application' italicised in original)

the evidence indicates that while Mill does not rule out the possibility that feedback from attempted verification is the channel from which the basic model of economic science is revised and improved, he seems to feel that the probability is very small.

(860)

when, in the course of application, retrodiction fails, Mill saw this as more likely to show that we do not know all of the pertinent causes than that we know the causes (both general and special), but cannot ascertain their effect.

(860)

7   De Marchi finds the evidence in Hollander 1985 to be 'less than compelling': 'In almost 1,000 pages [Hollander] can point to several examples of model-improvement, but only one convincing instance in which Mill actively subjected a theory to test against evidence'. De Marchi concludes, by contrast, that Mill 'did little in the way of active testing against evidence, and it is difficult to perceive in his efforts any *ordered program* of empirical inquiry (attempted verification)' (de Marchi 1988: 152). Elsewhere he finds more common ground:

> Hollander denies that simple (point) prediction is what Mill was about. I share this view. But Hollander also finds Mill to be very serious about the empirical basis of his axioms and about checking (and improving) his theory. On this I conclude, more circumspectly, that Mill was in principle an empiricist, but that he did not consistently do all that is required by this, sometimes falling back on logical demonstration (see the inconclusive discussion in Hollander 1985, vol. 1, 209–11; cf. 234–5, 236) and sometimes using the inverse deductive method in place of direct factual checking (140, 239; cf. 190).
>
> (159)

8   We draw here from both the earlier *Essay* and the *System of Logic*. Our general position is close to that of Hausman (1981, 1989) with this difference; that what Hausman finds only in the *Logic*, we find also in the *Essay*.

9   Mill goes on to say that this allowance '*even forms an indispensable supplement to {the} a priori method*' – indicating that, even in his formal statements, he did not regard the method of abstraction to be entirely separate from that of experience and verification.

10 Mill's reference (330) to 'the more striking effects' modified by disturbing causes might possibly suggest a quantitative criterion distinguishing the categories, as do the descriptions of the wealth-maximisation axiom (cited above, p. 242).

11 We shall have more to say regarding the matter of functional specialisation in our Conclusion.

12 The conditions are stringent: 'Nor is the verification complete, unless some of the cases in which the theory is borne out by the observed result, are of at least equal complexity with any cases in which its application could be called for' (461).

13 Mill adds:

> Either of these processes, apart from the other, diminishes in value as the subject increases in complication, and this is in so rapid a ratio as soon to become entirely worthless; but the reliance to be placed in the concurrence of the two sorts of evidence, not only does not diminish in any thing like the same proportion, but is not necessarily much diminished at all. Nothing more results than a disturbance in the order of precedency of the two

processes, sometimes amounting to its actual inversion, insomuch that instead of deducing our conclusions by reasoning, and verifying them by observation, we in some cases begin by obtaining them provisionally from specific experience, and afterward connect them with the principles of human nature by *à priori* reasoning, which reasoning are thus a real Verification.

(Mill 1973–4 [1843]: 897)

14 A role for 'observation and experiment' is, in fact, explicitly allowed in the establishment of the behavioural framework (454–5).

15 A science of ethology was still a matter for the future, so that there existed a continuous danger of claiming too much for empirical generalisations ('the common wisdom of common life'). For example,

when maxims . . . collected from Englishmen, come to be applied to Frenchmen, or when those collected from the present day are applied to past or future generations, they are apt to be very much at fault. Unless we have resolved the empirical law into the laws of the causes on which it depends, and ascertained that those causes extend to the case which we have in view, there can be no reliance placed in our inferences.

(Mill 1973–4 [1843]: 864)

On one occasion Mill maintains in a discussion of the *relative* strengths of various motives – 'the desire of wealth or of personal aggrandizement, the passion of philanthropy, and the love of active virtue' – that

[t]he only one of them which can be considered as anything like universal, is the desire of wealth; and wealth being, in the case of the majority, the most accessible means of gratifying all their other desires, nearly the whole of the energy of character which exists in highly civilized societies concentrates itself on the pursuit of that object.

(1977 [1836]: 129–30)

But the passage proceeds to exclude 'the most influential classes' and focus on the middle classes of Great Britain: 'Thus it happens that in highly civilized countries, and particularly among ourselves, the energies of the middle classes are almost confined to money-getting, and those of the higher classes are nearly extinct' (130).

16 Professor de Marchi's characterisation may place too little weight on the importance of the population principle:

It needs to be stressed that Mill's science was of very limited scope and potential. It dealt with one particular class of facts, the production and uses of wealth in so far as these are affected by the (psychological) drive to pursue material advantage. Also, it considered usually just one (composite) cause, the desire to maximise wealth with the least effort and subject to a certain degree of myopia. Occasionally it would incorporate in its laws the operation of 'environmental' principles, namely the urge to procreate and the limited powers of the soil [1967 (1836): 323]; but mostly the wealth motive was its sole concern.

(de Marchi 1986: 91)

Elsewhere the population mechanism is referred to as one of 'the underlying laws shaping economic investigations' which were 'both known and true' (98). In a recent manuscript, de Marchi writes of 'diminishing returns, and the law of population' that '[i]n practice Mill takes them as *exogenously* given' (1998: 23).

17 Interestingly, the focus on the array of possible behavioural motivations also pervades the economics of W. S. Jevons. See Peart (1996, 1998) for detailed discussions.

18 The reference to 'vulgar finery' recalls the term 'costly indulgences' in the statement of the basic behavioural axiom (1967 [1836]: 321, cited above, p. 242), suggesting that by the latter Mill intended conspicuous consumption, as well as time preference, which is the usual understanding (see de Marchi's term 'myopia', above, note 16; also de Marchi 1998: 23). But the expression 'the desire of obtaining the greatest quantity of wealth with the least labour and self-denial' (323) also suggests general time preference.

The edition of 1865 seems to distinguish 'rational' types of non-pecuniary interest from 'irrational' types, on which issue see Peart, forthcoming.

19 The qualification 'at least as to price', added in 1862, suggests product or quality differentiation.

20 The 'monopolistic competition' model emerges also in the discussion of professional remuneration where 'competition operates by diminishing each competitor's chance of fees, not by lowering the fees themselves' (243). Banking too is said to fall into the category, competition acting in part by reducing market shares to keep the return on capital on a par with opportunities elsewhere (1963: 306–8).

21 Mill cites Muggeridge's 'Report to the Handloom Weavers Inquiry Commission' (*Parliamentary Papers*, 1841, X: 38), and the 'Statistical account of Zurich', by Mr Escher, an appendix to the Poor Law Commission in 1840 (1965 [1848]: 381n).

22 Schwartz (1972: 35) refers also to Mill's *volte face* as early as 1826 reflecting his recognition 'of the realities of early capitalism':

> Very rarely, at any former period, have mercantile miscalculations been carried to so great a length. A vast majority of these enterprises failed; but not until, for the purpose of carrying them on, many persons had come under engagements, which nothing but the success of speculation could enable them to fulfil. The speculations proving unsuccessful, these persons became insolvent; and their ruin drew after it that of many others, who had not speculated, but who were dependent, for the means of fulfilling their engagements, upon the fulfilment of engagements towards themselves by persons who had.
>
> (Mill 1967 [1826]: 73)

Mill isolated four commercial 'revulsions', each preceded by speculation: 1810–11, 1814–15, 1819, and 1826.

23 Mill's presumption against 'unemployment equilibrium' will also be found in the *Principles* (1965 [1848]: 509). On the reversal of cyclical movements due to changes in the state of expectations, see Peart 1991.

24 Mill carried the analysis beyond the essay, allowing also for excess labour supply, and supplementing the inventory cycle by a cycle in fixed-capital formation. The allowance for unemployment and excess capacity is conspicuous in a discussion of various forms of 'capital wastage' during the cyclical process (741).

25 In the *Principles*, Mill designates the overestimate of the chance of outstanding success as 'another principle of human nature' (1965 [1848]: 383–4).

26 Needless to say, any test had to be fair, as is made very clear in a letter dated 10 October 1871, defending the Ricardian growth model on the grounds that criticism based on the reported circumstance that 'the high wages of the

United States cannot be caused by cheap land and sparse population, since land is cheaper and population sparser in Canada where wages are lower' was not definitive. Specifically:

> I should require to know, first, between what parts of Canada and what parts of the United States the comparison as to land and population and wages is made; secondly, whether the wages said to be lower in Canada are wages in gold, and, assuming that they are so, whether, when compared with the prices of articles of consumption, augmented as these prices are by your [US] tariff, they do not enable the Canadian laborer to be fully as well off as his neighbor on your side of the frontier. Finally, if those questions were all resolved in favor of Mr Greeley [the critic], the only inference that I should draw is, that the arts of production are less advanced and the labor of the community less efficient in Canada than in the United States; the natural effect of which would be to keep wages lower than the circumstances of the country with respect to land and population would otherwise make them. It should be remembered also that (as you observe) Mr Greeley's sovereign remedy, Protection, exists in Canada, though not to the same extravagant pitch as in the United States.
>
> (Mill 1972: 1840–1)

27 We recall here Mill's 'composition of causes' of the mechanical variety in his *Logic*, whereby each (separate) cause–effect relationship continues to operate even though disguised by the data: 'the separate effects of all the causes continue to be produced, but are compounded with one another, and disappear in one total' (1973–4 [1843]: 440–1). Mill applied the term 'tendency' to any *individual* causal relation.

28 On the reversal of cyclical movements, see note 23.

29 Elsewhere there is a notion that only under pressure do firms adopt or approach already known optima; see 739 regarding 'a more extensive substitution of the best known processes for inferior ones'.

We admit our inability to understand Mill's intentions by his remark that 'the abolition of the Corn Laws has given an additional stimulus to the spirit of improvement' (713–14).

30 See references above to the use of 'our speculations', or theoretical constructs, in 'guidance' or 'control' (pp. 252, 253)

31 Although Cairnes frequently reverts to the 'self-evident' nature of the basic axioms of theory, he yet also is on record as maintaining that 'the only test by which a theory is justified . . . [is that of] explaining facts, and if it be a new theory . . . explaining facts not explicable, or not so simply explicable, by received theories'; and Cairnes himself in his empirical work 'placed great weight on the systematic use of evidence to illustrate theory and to assess the predictions of theory' (Bordo 1975: 351–4). Bordo raises the question '[w]hether Cairnes would have been willing to discard a theory whose predictions were not consistent with the evidence'. At times he resorted to the search for disturbing causes; but he did use empirical evidence to reject Newmarch's theory (354).

32 Mill was preoccupied with the causal structure – assuring its adequacy by making revisions – in a way foreign to modern hypothesis testers who seek for a narrow H_O/H_A significance test and obtain a yes/no answer, but who desist from considering the entire set of causal relationships (see Peart 1995).

33 Mill even found a gender basis for specialisation in contemporary England:

> To discover general principles, belongs to the speculative faculty: to discern

and discriminate the particular cases in which they are and are not applicable, constitutes practical talent: and for this, women as they now are have a peculiar aptitude.

(1984 [1869]: 305).

34   Making allowance for the indirect nature of any effect that verification might have on theory reduced the contrast that Hirsch (1992) perceives between the second and third sections in Mill's *Essay*. In fact, Hirsch himself is bothered that 'the divisions are somewhat obscured by the fact that Mill sometimes uses the term "political economy" to refer only to abstract or scientific economics but at others to both abstract and applied economics together' (845), a practice generating a 'clumsiness' of outcome (846). This practice would be neither 'clumsy' nor 'obscure' were it Mill's actual position – as we believe it to be – that there is no fine distinction to be made between abstraction and application, in the sense that the two are part of an overall procedure entailing abstraction leading to verification which may reveal weaknesses in, and generate modifications to, the abstract structure.

Mill does indeed move back and forth between subject matter in the *Essay*. For example, in the second, not the third, part will be found both the allowance for the absorption of the population principle into an analytical structure, albeit supposedly based on the 'three behavioural laws', and also treatment of disturbing causes which interfere in 'particular cases', albeit the subject matter of application. Conversely, in the third part on application will be found the bulk of the texts recognising the possibilities of deficiencies to the theoretical structure revealed by verification, especially by retrodiction.

35   That Mill himself made no concerted effort to incorporate *knowledge creation*, we suggest, reflects the circumstance that the causal phenomena relevant for the generation of knowledge touched too closely upon the problem of social progress in the evolutionary sense (see Hollander 1985: 191f).

36   For the strength of his hostility in the *Essay* on method – it might account for its structure – see Mill 1967 [1836]: 334. Other samples spanning Mill's entire career will be found in Mill 1986 [1823]: 40; 1984 [1867]: 236–7.

37   Mill, however, gave himself a difficult task, for he was also – if perhaps not equally – concerned with over-confident theorists, all too ready to apply the *unqualified* results of the model, those, that is, who practised the (so-called) 'Ricardian Vice'.

38   Cf. Mill's early comment regarding the physical sciences as 'continually growing, but never changing: in every age they receive indeed mighty improvements, but for them the age of transition is past' (1986 [1831]: 240). Jevons objected strongly:

In the writings of some recent philosophers, especially of Auguste Comte, and in some degree John Stuart Mill, there is an enormous and hurtful tendency to represent our knowledge as assuming an approximately complete character. At least these and many other writers fail to impress upon their readers a truth which cannot be too constantly borne in mind, namely, that the utmost successes which our scientific method can accomplish will not enable us to comprehend more than an infinitesimal fraction of what there doubtless is to comprehend.

(1907 [1877]: 752–3)

References

Blaug, M. (1980) *The Methodology of Economics, or How Economists Explain*, Cambridge: Cambridge University Press.

——(1992) *The Methodology of Economics, or How Economists Explain*, 2nd edn, Cambridge: Cambridge University Press.

Bordo, M. D. (1975) 'John E. Cairnes on the effects of the Australian gold discoveries 1851–73: an early application of the methodology of political economics', *History of Political Economy*, 7 (autumn) 337–59.

Coleman, W. O. (1996) 'How theory came to English classical economics', *Scottish Journal of Political Economy*, 43 (May) 207–28.

Fels, R. (1991) Review of Hirsch and de Marchi 1990, *Journal of Economic Literature*, 29 (February) 84–5.

Hausman, D. M. (1981) 'J. S. Mill's philosophy of economics', *Philosophy of Science*, 48 (September) 363–85.

—— (1989) 'Economic methodology in a nutshell', *Journal of Economic Perspectives*, 48(2), 115–27.

Hirsch, A. (1986) Review of Hollander 1985, *Kyklos*, 39 (4) 621–3.

——(1992) 'John Stuart Mill on verification and the business of science', *History of Political Economy*, 24 (winter) 843–66.

Hirsch, A. and de Marchi, N. (1990) *Milton Friedman: Economics in Theory and Practice*, Ann Arbor: University of Michigan Press.

Hollander, S. (1985) *The Economics of John Stuart Mill*, Toronto: University of Toronto Press.

Jevons, W. S. (1907) [1877] *The Principles of Science: A Treatise on Logic and Scientific Method*, 2nd edn, London: Macmillan.

de Marchi, N. (1986) 'Mill's unrevised philosophy of economics: a comment on Hausman', *Philosophy of Science*, 53 (1) 89–100.

——(1988) 'John Stuart Mill Interpretation Since Schumpeter', in W. O. Thweatt (ed.) *Classical Political Economy: A Survey of Recent Literature*, Boston: Kluwer Academic Publishers, 137–62.

——(1998) 'Putting evidence in its place: John Mill's early struggles with history', paper presented at the Leverhulme Conference on Nineteenth-Century Historical Political Economy, King's College, Cambridge, 2–3 October 1998.

Mill, John Stuart. *CW* = *Collected Works of John Stuart Mill*, Toronto: University of Toronto Press.

——(1963) *The Earlier Letters, 1812 to 1848*, *CW*, XII–XIII.

——(1965) [1848] *Principles of Political Economy*, in *CW*, II–III. Last (7th) edn by Mill, 1871.

——(1967) [1826] 'Paper currency and commercial distress', in *CW*, IV, 71–123.

——(1967) [1833] 'The currency juggle', in *CW*, IV, 181–92.

——(1967) [1834] 'Miss Martineau's summary of political economy', in *CW*, IV, 223–8.

——(1967) [1836] 'On the definition of political economy; and on the method of philosophical investigation in that science', in *CW*, IV, 309–39.

——(1967) [1844] 'Of the influence of consumption of production', *Essays on some Unsettled Questions in Political Economy*, in *CW*, IV, 262–79.

——(1969) [1865] *Auguste Comte and positivism*, in *CW*, X: 261–368.

——(1972) *The Later Letters, 1849–1873*, in *CW*, XIV–XVII.

——(1973–4) [1843] *A System of Logic, Ratiocinative and Deductive*, in *CW*, VII–VIII.

——(1977) [1836] 'Civilization', in *CW*, XVIII, 117–47.

——(1984) [1867] *Inaugural address delivered to the University of St. Andrews*, in *CW*, XXI, 215–57.

——(1984) [1869] 'The subjection of women', in *CW*, XXI, 259–340.

——(1986) [1823] 'Errors of the Spanish government', *Newspaper Writings*, in *CW*, XXII, 39–42.

——(1986) [1831] 'The spirit of the age, II', *Newspaper Writings*, in *CW*, XXII, 238–45.

Peart, S. (1991) 'Sunspots and expectations: W. S. Jevons' theory of economic fluctuations', *Journal of the History of Economic Thought*, 13 (2) 243–65.

——(1993) 'W. S. Jevons' methodology of economics: some implications of the procedures for "Inductive Quantification"', *History of Political Economics*, 25 (3) 435–60.

——(1995) ' "Disturbing causes", "noxious errors", and the theory-practice distinction in the economics of J. S. Mill and W. S. Jevons', *Canadian Journal of Economics*, 28 (4b) 1194–1211.

——(1996) *The Economics of W. S. Jevons*, London: Routledge.

——(1998) 'Jevons and Menger re-homogenized? Jaffé after 20 years', *The American Journal of Economics and Sociology*, 57 (3) 307–26.

——(forthcoming) 'Foresight, self control and the irrationality of intertemporal choice in early neoclassical thought', *Canadian Journal of Economics*.

Schwartz, P. (1972) *The New Political Economy of J. S. Mill*, London: London School of Economics.

Smith, A. (1937) [1776] *The Wealth of Nations*, New York: Modern Library.

Stigler, G. J. (1965) *Essays in the History of Economics*, Chicago: University of Chicago Press.

Chapter 13

On J. S. Mill's defence of Ricardo's proportionality theorem

A Longfield connection?

In a paper on the reception of Ricardian economics (1995 [1977]: 293–6), I emphasised the influence of Mountifort Longfield on Robert Torrens, and the positive implications of that influence for the longevity of Ricardian theory. However, like other commentators, I failed to recognise that Longfield may have had a similar influence on J. S. Mill, or at the least, that Mill's justification of Ricardo's proportionality theorem in the *Principles* follows similar lines to that of Longfield. And while I do refer to Longfield's possible influence in my *Economics of John Stuart Mill* (Hollander 1985: 344), I now realise that it was not accurately stated, so that my account distorts the conclusions drawn from the evidence regarding both Mill's place in the history of classical (Ricardian) economic thought, and his consistency as analyst. This note is designed to correct these inaccuracies.

Torrens' challenge to Ricardian distribution theory

We set the stage by a brief review of a challenge thrown down by Torrens in 1826, following his reading of James Mill's version of Ricardian distribution theory. His point is that a technical improvement which reduces the capital (material) input will raise the profit rate, although the proportional shares of wages and profits in the *net* product may be unchanged. The profit rate varies without change in the proportional shares in the value of output, since the impact on profits operates independently of the value of labour (the real cost of producing wage goods):

> Let us suppose [wrote Torrens] that a capitalist advances to a labourer 20 quarters of corn as wages, and 20 quarters as seed; and let the produce returned to the capitalist at the end of the year be 60 quarters. In this case, if we deduct from the whole product, as Mr Hill [sic] contends we ought, what is necessary to replace the seed, 40 quarters will remain to be divided between wages and profit; and as, by the supposition, wages are 20, profits must be 20 also; that is, as the whole advances of the capitalist for wages and seed was 40 quarters, and as he has 20 quarters

remaining over and above the replacement of these advances, the rate of his profit will be 50 per cent.

Now, let us vary our supposition, and assume, that while the quantity of labour employed, and the quantity of product obtained, remain exactly as before, an improvement takes place in cultivation, which enables the farmer to crop his field with 10 quarters of seed, instead of with 20 quarters. In this case, when from the whole produce of 60 quarters, the 10 quarters required to replace capital, in Mr Hill's sense of the term, are deducted, 50 quarters will remain to be divided between wages and profit. Let these 50 be equally divided, as the 40 quarters formerly were, between the labourer and capitalist, each getting 25 quarters, and then the shares or proportions will remain exactly as before. But though the proportions, or proportional wages remain unchanged, yet profits will have risen from 50 to upwards of 70 per cent. The capitalist, after replacing his expenditure of 25 quarters for wages, and 10 quarters for seed, will have a surplus of 25 quarters remaining, while, in the former case, after replacing an expenditure of 20 quarters for wages, and 20 quarters for seed, he had a surplus of only 20 quarters remaining.

(Torrens 1826: xvi–xviii)

Essentially, Torrens insisted that the profit rate depends not only on the proportionate share of wages which governed the ratio of profits to wages, but also on the non-wage capital required. Thus a technological improvement in the wage goods sector permitting the relinquishing of fixed capital or materials – Marx's 'constant' capital – would imply a rise in the profit rate.[1]

So obvious, in retrospect, is the objection, that it is surprising that Ricardo managed to avoid the problem. In fact, a more serious objection may be raised – one which Ricardo neatly avoided – namely the probability that in the course of progress (and in the absence of new technology), the real cost of materials *rises* along with corn; in this case even if the 'money' wage is constant in the face of rising corn prices there will still be downward pressure on profits exerted by the upward movement in material prices.

Ricardo did mention the issue of higher materials' costs, but managed to avoid the dire implication by assuming that materials are required only in the manufacturing sector. In this case – as in any other where the disturbance impinges not universally but only partially – firms can pass on the burden to consumers:

There are few commodities which are not more or less affected in their price by the rise of raw produce, because some raw material from land enters into the composition of most commodities. Cotton goods, linen, and cloth, will all rise in price with the rise of wheat; but they rise on account of the greater quantity of labour expended on the raw material from which they are made, and not because more was paid by the manufacturer to the labourers whom he employed on those commodities.

(Ricardo 1951–73, I: 117–18)

Were materials required by production processes throughout the system, this argument would be inapplicable.[2] I have not seen the problem raised in the literature in this form; the complexity of savings in materials due to technical progress is first due, as explained, to Torrens in 1826.

Longfield's defence of Ricardo

Longfield came to Ricardo's defence, leading Torrens to a frank admission of error and a restatement of the Ricardian proportionality theorem (Torrens 1835: 22–35). Lord Robbins, who seems to have been the first to focus on Longfield's impact on Torrens, cites Longfield's argument that 'in the two cases which he [Torrens] supposes, I would not say that the proportional wages remained the same, because I should consider the sums spent in seed, as spent in wages' (Robbins 1958: 56, from Longfield 1971 [1834]: 173–4).[3]

Leaving the matter here, however, gives the impression that Longfield proposed the reduction of capital entirely to indirect or accumulated labour. This is how Robbins apparently understood the formulation (1958: 57). Torrens himself was later to write that Longfield had 'succeeded in removing the main objection to the reception of Ricardo's theory of profit', by 'showing . . . that the cost of production is to be measured by a single standard obtained by reducing previous and proximate labour to a common denominator' (1844: li–lii). And this is the position I take in *Oxford Economic Papers* (1995 [1977]) and later in *The Economics of John Stuart Mill* (1985: 344). But this reading is based on a truncated reading of Longfield's position. Although all advances are advances to labour, capital is not reducible to labour alone, since allowance must also be made for profit on those advances. Thus capital (materials) comprise *wages and profits* on those wages, and 'the term capitalist and labourer' is to be understood as 'a succession of capitalists and many labourers employed in production' – including those engaged 'from the very commencement' or the earlier stages of production:

> Now in all this I perfectly agree with Mr Torrens, with this slight verbal difference, that in the two cases which he supposes, I would not say that proportional wages remained the same, because I should consider the sums spent in seed as spent in wages. This supposition is necessary in order to take up production from the very commencement. The value of the corn consumed as seed may be measured in wages and profits; and so much as consists of profits, adds to the total profits of the capitalist, but

adds nothing to the rate of profit, since this addition is compensated by the greater length of time during which the capitalist is deprived of his advances. We use the term capitalist and labourer, although there has been a succession of capitalists and many labourers employed in production.

(Longfield 1971 [1834]: 174)

The upshot of the argument is that, *pace* Torrens, the Ricardian proportionality theorem still held good:

If all advances are made at the same interval, say a year before the sale of the article, and consist exclusively of the wages of labour, the rate of profits will depend upon, or will be the proportion between, the shares of the value of the complete article received by the labourer and the capitalist. But if some of the advances are made for other purposes than the payment of wages, the same proposition will be true, by considering such advances as if they were so much money then paid as wages; and if the advances were made at different intervals from the sale, the average of those intervals must be taken, and in proportion as that average is less or more than a year, the rate of profits must be considered as increased or diminished in the same proportion. Of those two qualifications, the second is clearly understood in every statement, and the first is only used in order to prevent the necessity of taking into consideration the succession of capitalists from the beginning to the complete work. The nature of those two corrections, and their effect, are the same, whatever the rate of profit is; and therefore, it is usual, still having those corrections in view, but not expressing them, to say, that *the rate of profit depends upon the proportion of the shares of the final value received by the labourer and the capitalist.*

(Longfield 1971 [1834]: 174–5, emphasis added)

J. S. Mill on capital and the proportionality theorem

In his essay 'On profits, and interest' (written in 1830 but first published in 1844), Mill argues that, 'in the ultimate analysis', Ricardo's inverse profit-wage principles required labour to be 'the only essential of production. To replace capital is to replace nothing but the wages of the labour employed' (1967 [1844]: 293). This he denied:

It is not correct . . . to state that all which the capitalist retains after replacing wages forms his profit. It is true that the whole return to capital is either wages or profits; but profits do not compose merely the surplus after replacing the outlay; they also enter the outlay itself. Capital is expended partly in paying or reimbursing wages, and partly in paying the profits of other capitalists, whose concurrence was necessary in order to bring together the means of production.

(Mill 1967 [1844]: 295)

From this it followed

that the rate of profit does *not* exclusively depend upon the value of wages, in [Ricardo's] sense, namely the quantity of labour of which the wages of a labourer are the produce; that it does *not* exclusively depend upon proportional wages.

(297)

A 'very slight modification', however, allowed Mill to reaffirm the Ricardian inverse wage-profit theorem, that 'profits cannot rise unless wages fall'. This entailed reinterpreting 'low wages' in terms of 'the *cost* of wages' rather than '*the value* of wages' or labour embodied in wages. Unfortunately, this adjustment entailed abandoning the proportionality property:

Mr Ricardo's principle, that profits cannot rise unless wages fall, is strictly true, if by low wages we mean not merely wages which are the produce of a smaller quantity of labour, but wages which are produced at less cost, reckoning labour and previous profits together. But the interpretation which some economists have put upon Mr Ricardo's doctrine, when they explain it to mean that profits depend upon the proportion which the labourers collectively receive of the aggregate produce, will not hold at all.

The only expression of the law of profits, which seems to be correct is that they depend upon the cost of production of wages. This must be received as the ultimate principle.

(Mill 1967 [1844]: 299)

Mill's criticism resembles that of Torrens, each maintaining that technical progress affecting the non-labour input impinges on the profit rate. But Torrens rejected the Ricardian theorem on distribution in both its forms – whether the profit rate is related to an inverse change in the value of wages or to a proportionate variation in wages. Mill for his part attempted to rescue the former version by his 'very slight modification', but in substance he too has diverged from the original.[4]

We come next to Mill's *Principles*. Here he withdraws his objections to Ricardo's proportionality theorem. The argument is identical with that of Longfield, who in his defence of that theorem considered the production process 'from the very commencement', using the terms 'capitalist' and 'labourer' to represent 'a succession of capitalists and many labourers employed in production' (above, p. 284). This precise point led Mill to conclude that '[w]hatever, of the ultimate product, is not profit, is repayment of wages':

A large portion of the expenditure of every capitalist consists in the direct payment of wages. What does not consist of this, is composed of materials and implements, including buildings. But materials and implements are produced by labour; and as our supposed capitalist is not meant to represent a single employment, but to be a type of the productive industry of the whole country, we may suppose that he makes his own tools, and raises his own materials. He does this by means of previous advances, which, again, consist wholly of wages. If we suppose him to buy the materials and tools instead of producing them, the case is not altered: he then repays to a previous producer the wages which that previous producer has paid. It is true, he repays it to him with a profit; and if he had produced the things himself, he himself must have had that profit, on this part of his outlay, as well as on every other part. *The fact, however, remains, that in the whole process of production, beginning with the materials and tools, and ending with the finished product, all the advances have consisted of nothing but wages; except that certain of the capitalists concerned have, for the sake of general convenience, had their share of profit paid to them before the operation was completed. Whatever, of the ultimate product, is not profit, is repayment of wages.*

(Mill 1965 [1848]: 412, emphasis added)

Mill does *not* assert here that capital goods can be reduced entirely to labour; he allows for past profits; and the statement of the Ricardian theorem in terms of the 'cost of labour' which follows (413) – *which is identified explicitly with labour's proportional share* – also does not relate to labour embodied in wages but to labour and past profits. In my study of Mill (1985: 343; see also above, p. 216) I asserted otherwise, on the grounds that Mill's earlier objections – which led him in the essay to include past profits in the cost of labour – had been withdrawn. It now appears to me more likely that Mill in 1848 stood by the position adopted in the essay, but recognised, by use of the 'Longfield gloss', that allowance for profit in capital did not damage the proportionality theorem. Mill, however, makes no explicit mention of Longfield in this context; the similarity might be a simple parallelism.[5]

There is much pointing to this view. Mill had his essay before him when composing the *Principles*. He raises the question (in his later chapter 'Of distribution, as affected by exchange') whether the inverse relation between profits and the cost of labour did not have to be 'slightly modified' – recall the almost identical phrase in the essay – because of 'that portion (though comparatively small) of the expenses of the capitalist which does not consist in wages paid by himself or reimbursed to previous capitalists, but in the profits of those previous capitalists' (1965 [1848]: 700); he illustrates the issue in terms of the standard problem – a technical change permitting the saving of materials supposed to affect all sectors of the economy – whereby the general profit rate appears to rise independently of the cost of labour; and for his reply, Mill sends the reader back to the essay:

> The question is too intricate in comparison with its importance, to be further entered into in a work like the present; and I will merely say, that it seems to result from the consideration adduced in the Essay, that there is nothing in the case in question to affect the integrity of the theory which affirms an exact correspondence, in an inverse direction, between the rate of profit and the Cost of Labour.
>
> (701)

In brief, the 'slight modification' is still needed.

At this specific point in Mill's argument, nothing is said of the proportionality version which had been rejected in the essay; Mill was concerned specifically with the relation between the profit rate and the 'cost of labour'. But as explained above, he had earlier in the *Principles* stated his renewed adherence to it, and this we have seen on grounds identical to Longfield's.

Some implications

Mill emerges on the foregoing account as more consistent than I once suggested (1985: 350). His referral of the reader of the *Principles* to the essay, which is difficult to understand if capital is reduced entirely to labour, now makes good sense.

More important than this are certain technical implications. Ricardo had argued that a wage increase has a lesser quantitative impact on cost price in the case of a capital-intensive than a labour-intensive good, his argument presuming that machinery should be envisaged as a produced commodity itself comprising a profit as well as a wage element, such that the wage increase leaves its price unchanged (1951–73, I: 61–2). If, as once appeared to me the case, Mill abandoned this notion of the capital input by reducing capital to labour entirely, there would be no apparent reason why upon a wage variation the Ricardian adjustment process – the response of supplies and therefore of prices to the new long-run cost levels – would be set in motion (1985: 350 n121, 359). Yet Mill *did* maintain the Ricardian position in this regard. This, it now turns out, is not a problem.

A second and related point involves the potential effect on distribution of a change in the pattern of final demand. As I show in my book (1985: 361–2), J. R. McCulloch maintained that such changes will have an impact, but only in the short run, 'for capital being itself the result of antecedent labour, whatever is expended upon it [a capital-intensive good] really goes to replace labour, and in the end is identical in its effects with a direct expenditure upon the latter' (1965 [1864]: 256). I proceed to argue that since Mill in the *Principles* came to take this view of the capital input, we have a possible reason for his formal neglect of the impact of changes in demand patterns on the wage. This rationale now breaks down, since Mill did *not* adopt the assumption that capital is wholly 'the result of antecedent labour'. There is then no *technical* reason why Mill, any more than Ricardo, would rule out on principle the link between demand patterns and distribution.

Notes

1　See on this Tucker (1960: 96).
2　Should materials be used universally (and uniformly), no price changes would result at all and the overall profit rate is necessarily reduced; if universally except for the money metals, then only the nominal prices of agricultural and manufacturing goods would rise (see Ricardo 1951–73, I: 123).
3　Longfield also refers to an earlier justification along these lines:

> And such reduction must be made, whenever we resort to labour as a common measure for comparing the values of commodities. Whatever advances are not made in labour, must be reduced to the measure of labour. If a capitalist expends £50 in raw materials, it must be considered as so much advanced on account of labour. In order to make use of labour as a measure of value, we, as it were, reduce every thing else of value to that denomination.
>
> (Longfield 1971 [1834]: 171)

4　Why Mill minimised the significance of the modification is discussed in Hollander 1985: 340.
5　Conceivably, Mill (and Longfield) might have found some help in Malthus' reduction of capital to dated quantities of labour (see Hollander 1997: 307).

References

Hollander, S. (1985) *The Economics of John Stuart Mill*, Toronto: University of Toronto Press.
——(1995) [1977] 'The reception of Ricardian economics', *Oxford Economic Papers*, 29 (July) 221–57; in *Ricardo – The New View: Collected Essays I*, London, Routledge: 283–322.
——(1997) *The Economics of Thomas Robert Malthus*, Toronto: University of Toronto Press.
Longfield, Mountifort (1971) [1834] *Lectures in Political Economy* (Dublin), in *The Economic Writings of Mountifort Longfield*, New York: Augustus M. Kelley.
McCulloch, J. R. (1965) [1864] *The Principles of Political Economy*, 5th edn, New York: Augustus M. Kelley.
Mill, John Stuart (1965) [1848] *Principles of Political Economy, Collected Works of John Stuart Mill*, II–III, Toronto: University of Toronto Press.
——(1967) [1844] 'On profits, and interest', *Essays on Some Unsettled Questions of Political Economics*, in *Collected Works*, IV: 291–308.
Ricardo, David (1951–73) *The Works and Correspondence of David Ricardo*, 11 vols, ed. P. Sraffa, I: *Principles of Political Economy*, Cambridge: Cambridge University Press.
Robbins, L. C. (1958) *Robert Torrens and the Evolution of Classical Economics*, London: Macmillan.

Torrens, Robert (1826) *An Essay on the External Corn Trade*, 3rd edn, London: Rees, Orme and Brown.

——(1835) *Colonization of Southern Australia*, London: Longman, Rees, Orme, Brown, Green and Longman.

——(1844) *The Budget: On Commercial and Colonial Policy*, London: Smith, Elder.

Tucker, G. S. L. (1960) *Progress and Profits in British Economic Thought*, Cambridge: Cambridge University Press.

Index